W9-CYT-198

THE
POLITICS
OF
POWER

THE
POLITICS
OF
POWER

A Critical Introduction to American Government

SIXTH EDITION . . . .

IRA KATZNELSON
Columbia University

MARK KESSELMAN
Columbia University

ALAN DRAPER
St. Lawrence University

 W. W. NORTON & COMPANY ▪ NEW YORK ▪ LONDON

W. W. Norton & Company has been independent since its founding in 1923, when William Warder Norton and Mary D. Herter Norton first published lectures delivered at the People's Institute, the adult education division of New York City's Cooper Union. The Nortons soon expanded their program beyond the Institute, publishing books by celebrated academics from America and abroad. By mid-century, the two major pillars of Norton's publishing program—trade books and college texts—were firmly established. In the 1950s, the Norton family transferred control of the company to its employees, and today—with a staff of four hundred and a comparable number of trade, college, and professional titles published each year—W. W. Norton & Company stands as the largest and oldest publishing house owned wholly by its employees.

Copyright © 2011 by W. W. Norton & Company, Inc.
All rights reserved
Printed in the United States of America

Editor: Aaron Javsicas
Project editor: Carla L. Talmadge
Assistant editor: Carly Fraser
Editorial assistant: Callinda Taylor
Senior production manager: Benjamin Reynolds
Managing editor, College: Marian Johnson
Marketing manager: Nicole Netherton
Book design: Jo Anne Metsch
Composition: Matrix Publishing Services
Manufacturing: Sheridan Books—Ann Arbor, MI
Cover design: Kimberly Glyder

Library of Congress Cataloging-in Publication Data

Katznelson, Ira.
    The politics of power : a critical introduction to American government / Ira Katznelson, Mark Kesselman, Alan Draper. — 6th ed.
      p. cm.
    Includes bibliographical references and index.
    ISBN 978-0-393-93325-3 (pbk.)
    1. United States—Politics and government—Textbooks.   I. Kesselman, Mark. II. Draper, Alan. III. Title.
    JK276.K37 2011
    973.92—dc22

                                                              2010017128

    W. W. Norton & Company, Inc., 500 Fifth Avenue, New York, N.Y. 10110
                              www.wwnorton.com
W. W. Norton & Company Ltd., Castle House, 75/76 Wells Street, London W1T3QT

                          2 3 4 5 6 7 8 9 0

To Robert and Clarice Draper, and in memory of Ephraim and Sylvia Katznelson, and Paul and Anne Kesselman.

BRIEF CONTENTS

. . . .

CONTENTS

WHAT DO YOU THINK? BOXES

. . . .

Our wish to provide a sixth edition of *The Politics of Power* has been shaped by three primary reasons. First is the dramatic change American politics has experienced, notably including the election of Barack Obama as president in 2008. His election as the country's first African American leader was made possible by a marked increase in votes from "the other America," to recall Michael Harrington's phrase, including low-income voters, African Americans, Hispanics, and young people. As a candidate, Obama excited people who do not normally participate in elections to go to the polls and cast a ballot.

Second is how the 2008 elections followed a prolonged period marked by an increase in economic inequality, political polarization, and the international isolation of the United States. As we revised this book, the United States was mired in two wars and devastated by the worst recession in more than half a century. These developments provide an opportunity for rethinking the politics of power. Rarely has it been more appropriate to invoke that overused Chinese proverb: May you live in interesting times!

The third reason is more personal. We are delighted to have a new publisher, W. W. Norton and Company, for *The Politics of Power*. We are indebted to their expertise and care in moving this edition to publication.

With the world and American politics having changed in important, fascinating, and sometimes troubling ways, *The Politics of Power* has changed as well. All its chapters have been thoroughly revised both to reflect new scholarship and to keep abreast of recent events. Further, partly thanks to excellent suggestions by reviewers, we have renovated the structure of the book. The section on political participation now includes a chapter integrating the study of political parties, elections, and public opinion, and another that is devoted to new material covering interest groups and social movements, including the women's movement, the environmental movement, and the conservative movement, more fully than in the past. Readers will also discover an in-depth analysis of the causes and consequences of the Obama presidency, including continuities and shifts in policy that flow from his election. Several chapters also highlight the severe recession that began in 2008, as well as relevant government economic policies and reforms.

This edition also includes pedagogical features that did not appear in previous editions. "What Do You Think?" boxes are sprinkled throughout the text. "Critical Thinking Questions" appear at the end of each chapter, prodding students to think for themselves about the material and arguments we have presented. A summary organized by subheadings also appears at the end of each chapter, and a glossary of key terms now appears at the close of the book.

Although *The Politics of Power* has been thoroughly recast, its aim remains the same: to introduce students to a critical perspective on American politics by highlighting how political conflicts, institutions, and processes are influenced by deep inequalities generated by the country's political economy. The text underscores the mutually supportive but uneasy relationship joining American democracy and American capitalism. We try to clarify this multifaceted association in the hope that our perspective and analytic framework will provoke thoughtful discussion. In so doing, we aim to assist students to develop their own approaches to the study of American politics, and to reflect on their role as citizens and participants.

Following the introduction, which provides a framework that analyzes key issues in democratic theory, the book is divided into four parts. Part I explores ties linking economics and politics. We show how economic power impacts political power by influencing who gets what, where, and how. Part II analyzes the political participation of citizens by looking at the diverse ways citizens organize to promote their views as well as how collective organization is affected by the mobilization of bias that results from economic inequality. Key topics include political parties, voting, and public opinion in Chapter 4 and interest groups and social movements in Chapter 5. Part III investigates the federal government's executive, legislative, and judicial institutions, focusing on the politics of power in operation. Part IV turns to how social, economic, and foreign policies have been shaped by the economy, by political participation, and by political institutions. It also reviews the impact these policies have had on American political and social life. The conclusion, in Chapter 12, reviews the main points developed in the text and points to future possibilities in American politics.

Throughout, we have tried to be direct without being simplistic, engaging without being flippant, critical without being cynical. We will be pleased if our writing animates students new to the study of American politics, engages more advanced students, and challenges professors who assign the book.

We are most grateful for the invaluable help we have received. Librarians at Columbia and St. Lawrence universities were enormously helpful in locating difficult sources and information. Reviewers of individual chapters were critical in offering advice that improved the book's argument and presentation. Our thanks to John Bokina, George Gonzalez, Marcus Pohlmann, John Pottenger, Chris Pyle, Wayne LeCheminant, Stephen Smith, and Nicholas González Yuen. Stephen Smith also lent his talents as the author of this edition's test bank, and Nicholas González Yuen served as an expert test bank reviewer. In addition, we were supported by friends and family who offered encouragement and diversion. Ira Katznelson and Mark Kesselman recognize the help they received from students and colleagues at Columbia University, especially Eldon Grant Porter, as well as from their families. Alan Draper would like to thank Pat Ellis and their extended family of children, including Sam, Rachel, Bryan, and Trevor. Collectively, we appreciate and acknowledge the gifted professionalism of Roby Harrington, Aaron Javsicas, Carly Fraser, and Callinda Taylor at W. W. Norton.

DEMOCRACY'S CHALLENGE

INTRODUCTION

It took three years to build at a cost of $7.5 million dollars—the equivalent of about $400 million today. It was almost 900 feet long—three football fields put end to end—weighed about 46,000 tons, and was 175 feet high from its keel to the top. Its owners said it was unsinkable. When it left the dock, the *Titanic* was the biggest, fastest, most luxurious ocean liner ever constructed.

The *Titanic* set sail on its maiden voyage from Liverpool bound for New York on April 10, 1912. On board were 2,228 people, as were 40,000 fresh eggs, 12,000 dinner plates, 6,000 tablecloths, and 1,000 finger bowls. As the boat cruised toward New York, first-class passengers spent their days swimming in a pool, exercising in a gymnasium, relaxing in a reading room, or exchanging pleasantries in a lounge reserved for them. In the evening they enjoyed elegant parties, drank fine wine, and ate sumptuous meals before retiring to their spacious staterooms. Many of the first-class passengers on board were familiar names from high society, such as John Jacob Astor IV, whose grandfather struck it rich in lumber and real estate; George Widener, whose family made its fortune in streetcars; as well as members of British nobility, such as the Countess of Rothes and Sir Cosmo Duff Gordon.

Passengers in third class did not have it as good. Families in third class were crowded into small rooms, which could barely accommodate two bunk beds and a toilet. Single men and women were housed in separate, congested, unpleasant holds below on opposite ends of the ship. There were only two bathtubs for use by the seven hundred passengers in third class. In addition, they were restricted from moving about the ship and from using the amenities reserved for first-class passengers. Many brought food for the duration of the trip across the ocean because they could not afford to dine on board. The price of the ticket had exhausted their savings. Unlike the Anglo-American aristocracy in first class, many third-class passengers were non-British immigrants from such distant places as Poland, Italy, and Russia. They were fleeing persecution and poverty in the countries they had left behind in hopes of finding freedom and prosperity in America.

As the ship crossed the Atlantic, everything first appeared calm. Anxious to gain a competitive edge in the ruthlessly competitive steamship business—then the only means of transatlantic travel—the owners of the *Titanic* instructed the captain to increase the ship's speed. Dismissing the risks involved, the owners hoped to break the record for transatlantic travel and arrive in New York a day early. This would attract even more publicity for the ship's arrival and humble the competition. With its engines at full throttle, the *Titanic* entered treacherous waters off Newfoundland. Then disaster struck. An iceberg tore a 200-foot hole along the ship's hull. The *Titanic* began to sink. Bedlam broke out on board. The *Titanic* was equipped with all sorts of luxurious facilities, but the owners had outfitted the ship with only enough lifeboats to evacuate half the passengers. When the *Titanic* began to sink, the ship's owners ordered that first-class passengers be evacuated first. Meanwhile, third-class passengers trying to reach the lifeboats sometimes found the doors to the deck locked or blocked. Those fortunate enough to reach the deck found that first-class passengers were given priority on the lifeboats. Two-thirds of the first-class passengers were saved. The results of that tragic night were quite different, however, for the passengers in steerage: two-thirds froze to death in the icy waters of the Atlantic. Just as wealth, income, and social standing influenced how people lived on board ship, so it influenced who would die.

In many ways, the tale of the *Titanic* offers a powerful metaphor for key features of American society and politics even today. The United States remains the richest and strongest nation in the world. It is the biggest, fastest, most luxurious ocean liner around. Like the *Titanic*, it is also characterized by massive disparities in wealth and income that separate first- and third-class passengers. The richest 20 percent of American households earn more than half the country's income; the poorest quintile earn just 3 percent. Since 1980, increases in earnings have been concentrated at the top. During the past thirty years, the average income of the top 5 percent of households grew at a rate more than four times as fast as the average income of the bottom 80 percent, the vast majority of the population. The U.S. Census recently reported that the top 5 percent of households earned just under $300,000; the next 15 percent earned about $120,000, and the remaining 80 percent averaged approximately $40,000. Disparities in wealth are far greater. Wealth—including housing, stocks, and bonds—is remarkably uneven. The best recent measures date to the start of this

The *Titanic* sailing from Southampton, England, April 10, 1912.

decade, when the top 1 percent of households owned just over $13,000,000 in assets; the next 9 percent $1,645,000; the next 40 percent $272,000; and the bottom 50 percent just $22,000. The combined salary, perks, and bonuses for those at the highest rungs of large firms are astonishing. In 2008, the CEO of Motorola earned $104 million; of Citigroup, $38 million; of J.P. Morgan, $36 million; of American Express, $43 million; of Philip Morris, $37 million. These packages were further improved by attractive stock options, generous retirement benefits, and other benefits. Just before the steep economic downturn of that year, the top one-tenth of 1 percent earned 976 times more income than the bottom 90 percent. This degree of inequality is even greater than the situation that prevailed on the eve of the Great Depression that started in 1929, when the top hundredth of 1 percent of American families earned 892 times more than the bottom 90 percent.[1]

These gaps are greater in the United States than in any other economically developed country. High-income people have more purchasing power than the rich anywhere else, while the poor, the bottom 10 percent, can buy less than the equivalent group in Canada and Western Europe. Differences in wealth are also noteworthy. The top 20 percent of households own about 65 percent of the wealth in Canada, and 70 percent in Germany. That figure tops 80 percent in the United States. At the bottom of the social order, the number of poor Americans increased by more than 5 million between 2000 and 2008, and nearly

WHAT DO YOU THINK?

Capitalism and Equality

As an economic system based on private enterprise and markets, capitalism has been widely interpreted both as creative and productive for the way it produces wealth and well-being, and as a supporter of economic and political freedom. Others have argued that capitalism is a system of exploitation for the way it generates significant benefits for some at the expense of others, and thus curtails individual freedom for those at the bottom of the distribution of wealth and income. Are these alternative positions equally convincing?

one in five children under the age of eighteen fall below the government's standard for poverty.[2]

Americans may all be passengers on the same ship, but they have very different experiences of the journey based upon their class position. Citizens who are at the top of the income and wealth distributions can afford first-class tickets. They have bigger homes, drive nicer cars, live in finer neighborhoods, and send their children to better schools than do citizens who can afford only third-class tickets. As on the *Titanic*, deep inequality also influences who lives at all. Membership in a higher social class reduces the risk of heart attack, diabetes, infectious disease, arthritis, and some cancers, and it is a more powerful predictor of health and mortality than genetics, exposure to carcinogens, and smoking.[3]

Another system of inequality overlaps that of class. Even after the election of Barack Obama, the country's first African American president, and even after the longer-term growth of the black middle class of which he is a member, first- and third-class passengers often continue to be distinguished by the color of their skin. Whites earn more, are more fully employed, are more educated, are less victimized by crime, and live longer than racial minorities. A 2008 study reported the median, or midpoint, of white earnings to be $30,485 per person. For African Americans the equivalent figure was $23,025, and for Latinos it was $20,255. The median net worth for whites was just over $140,000; for African Americans and Latinos, just under $25,000. Only 1 in 10 whites has less than a high school diploma, compared to 2 in 10 for African Americans and 4 in 10 for Latinos. Further, there is a persistent gender gap.

The median income for a man was a little less than $33,000; for a woman, just $22,000.[4]

The example of the *Titanic* even extends beyond how class, racial, and gender inequalities shape and distort the quality of life. The opulence on board while the ship's owners skimped on lifeboats is all too reminiscent of the immense resources society devotes to satisfying extravagant consumer desires while investments in the public sector, such as schools, the environment, and the safety net—especially in difficult economic times—are stressed and underfunded. Historically, the American **welfare state** has not provided enough lifeboats to those who need medical care, child care, or income support. More than 16 percent of American households would live below the poverty standard without the help of existing government programs that reduce that number to some 12 percent. Elsewhere, governments do much more to counter inequality. Although their poverty rates are equivalent, or even higher, before public policies kick in, welfare state programs in other rich industrialized nations have a bigger impact on poverty. In Great Britain, the welfare state reduces the poverty rate to about 6 percent, in the Netherlands to just over 3 percent, and in Sweden to merely 2 percent of the population.

Further, the degree to which businesses put profits above other values is eerily similar to the way the owners of the *Titanic* recklessly endangered the lives of their passengers. The tragedy off the Newfoundland coast occurred in part because the *Titanic*'s owners were intent on arriving early to gain favorable publicity and overshadow the competition. Regrettably, there are all too many examples of corporations seeking profits at the expense of their customers' welfare. Recent examples include Medtronic implanted heart devices that malfunctioned in hundreds of patients and contributed to at least five deaths, Peanut Corporation of America (PCA) products infected by salmonella, and Phillip Morris cigarettes that cause cancer. Manufacturers who knew of the dangers they were causing decided it was cheaper not to make changes that were needed to enhance safety. Sometimes the price of greed can be more widespread and more systematic. Financial firms sought to take advantage of the housing frenzy of the early years of this century by creating new forms of debt instruments based on pools of mortgages. As a result, they became vastly overextended. When many borrowers could not afford the loans they had been encouraged to take, the whole financial system was put at risk and saved only by a massive bailout by the federal government.

CONSTITUTIONAL DEMOCRACY AND CAPITALISM

Although powerful, the *Titanic* as a metaphor breaks down at a crucial point. The United States is a constitutional democracy. The *Titanic* was not. The captain of the *Titanic* was accountable to the owners who employed him; the passengers did not elect him. By contrast, Americans can choose the people who govern. All adult American citizens today (except for prisoners and ex-felons in some states) have the right to vote, and each citizen gets the same single vote. Democrats and Republicans, as well as a host of minor political parties, compete actively to win the support of the electorate. Few countries allow as much freedom to engage in political debate. Citizens can mobilize to criticize the government and make demands for change. Newspapers and television provide regular reports of government activities, debate the wisdom of public policies, and expose wrongdoing by high government officials, including presidents.

These **rights** developed over time, often as the result of conflict and struggle. American constitutional government was first fashioned at a time when other countries were ruled by kings and emperors, not by elected officials whose actions were constrained by citizen rights. This revolutionary development came eleven years after the Second Continental Congress adopted the Declaration of Independence in 1776, rejecting British rule of the thirteen colonies and declaring that all human beings are owed the "unalienable rights" of life, liberty, and the pursuit of happiness. The government it first fashioned under the Articles of Confederation was relatively weak because each state retained its sovereignty and independence. There was no president; Congress was placed at the center of government and had the power to make war, sign treaties, borrow or coin money, and manage relations with Native American Indians.

It soon became clear that this limited national government was insufficient. The Constitutional Convention that met in May 1787 was called to invent a better, more practical, and more effective government. It found a solution to the problem that some states were more heavily populated than others by arranging for seats in the House of Representatives to be allocated by population so that bigger states had more representation; it also arranged for each state, regardless of its number of inhabitants, to have two members of the Senate. It adapted to the existence of slavery by deciding to count every five slaves as three persons for the purposes of apportioning seats in the House of Representatives, even though slaves were not citizens and could not vote. In this way, and by prohibiting Congress from abolishing the importation of slaves until 1808, and by including a fugitive slave clause that provided for the return of escaped slaves to their owners, the **Constitution** recognized slavery as legitimate within the country's constitutional democracy.

Most of us are familiar with the basic features of the Constitution. All House members are chosen by direct election every two years. Senators have been elected directly since 1913 (until then, they were selected by state legislatures), and have six-year terms that are staggered, so that one-third of the Senate is up for election every two years. Congress has specific powers. These include regulating commerce, borrowing money, collecting taxes, maintaining the armed forces, and declaring war. The president heads the executive branch of government. Elected by the electoral college every four years after the people vote, the holder of this office manages foreign affairs, serves as commander in chief, oversees the federal bureaucracy, and can veto congressional legislation. The judicial branch is topped by a Supreme Court whose members, appointed by the president and approved by the Senate, serve for lifetime terms. Their main task is to resolve constitutional controversies, including determining when federal and when state law applies and ruling on how citizen rights should be understood and carried out. The Constitution became the supreme law of the land once it was ratified by the states in 1789.

American citizens possess rights that are designed to prevent public authorities from acting in arbitrary ways. In 1791, four years after the Constitution was written, the ten amendments called the **Bill of Rights** were added. These amendments place limits on what government can do. Congress is not free to designate any single religion as having an official or established capacity, and it may not limit religious freedom, freedom of speech, assembly, and petition. The executive branch is not free to infringe on the right to keep arms, cannot arbitrarily take homes for use by the military, and cannot search for or seize

WHAT DO YOU THINK?

Poverty and a Minimum Standard

The Constitution is silent about economic inequality. Yet in setting out to enhance "life, liberty, and the pursuit of happiness," it seems to imply that good government should not tolerate too much inequality and should be concerned about poverty because too few resources make it difficult, and sometimes impossible, for citizens to work to achieve these goals. Should the Constitution have done more to mandate equality, such as setting a minimum level of income and wealth for each citizen?

evidence without getting a court order on the basis of the probable existence of a crime. The judiciary is also constrained. Citizens cannot be indicted for serious crimes without a grand jury. Courts must offer speedy justice, provide trials by jury, and offer the right of the accused to know the charges and evidence and confront witnesses. Courts also cannot compel people to testify against themselves, nor can they try people more than once for the same offense. Punishment cannot be excessive, bail must be reasonably set, and property cannot be taken without proper compensation. An imprisoned person has the right of habeas corpus, the capacity to file a petition demanding that the courts determine whether the imprisonment is lawful. Moreover, the last amendment of the Bill of Rights, the Tenth, reserves to the states or the people any powers not explicitly assigned to the federal government.

Compared to those in other countries, most public authorities in the United States are accessible and responsive. Because it is limited by the country's constitutional system, their rule is not arbitrary or unaccountable. Powers are divided—not, as in most political regimes in human history, concentrated in specific offices or persons. The national government is characterized by a **separation of powers**, and the capacity to govern is shared by the executive branch (led by the president), by the legislative branch (Congress), and by the judicial branch (the Supreme Court). These branches are in a relationship of **checks and balances** with each other. The president can veto congressional legislation; the Senate must approve key presidential appointments; the Supreme Court can review laws passed by Congress and signed by the president. The political system is characterized by **federalism**, a system that limits national power by reserving many powers and functions to the governments of the country's fifty states. The country also has thousands of county, municipal, and township governments, as well as special-purpose units like school districts, in all of which residents have voting rights and decisions are made by majority rule. Government, in short, is accountable to the people, who are invited into the political process as participants. In the last resort, the people are sovereign.

Democracy cannot be judged, however, only by these cherished rights and formal procedures. It must be evaluated based on how they actually work; that is, by substantive as well as procedural democracy. Trials, for example, are often not speedy, and evidence is sometimes withheld from defendants who are not adequately represented by defense lawyers. Governmental power is at times arbitrary. Checks and balances do not always constrain the abuse of power. The substance of democracy, moreover, is also deeply affected when the democratic features of American government are combined with deep inequalities, and when the unequal distribution of wealth and prospects between first-class passengers and those in steerage affects their ability to influence public policy. To what extent is **popular sovereignty** possible in a society characterized by large inequalities of resources?

We explore these issues in the pages that follow. We ask whether and how American democracy is distorted by large inequalities. When do political institutions function to permit, even promote, inequalities, and when do they make it possible for ordinary citizens to shape public policies and effect social, economic, and political change? We have two starting points—the country's democratic institutions that are grounded in the Constitution that has governed the United States since it was ratified in 1789, and the character of the capitalist economic system, including the special informal status possessed by the country's major business firms.

The country's capitalist **market** economy—an economy that has produced great prosperity and economic development as well as significant inequality, insecurity, and cycles of boom and bust, some greater than others—is inherently not democratic. It is based on the capacity of some persons and firms, especially the largest, to invest capital in order to gain the largest returns. They take risks to maximize profits. When things go well, markets operate to generate productive investments, create jobs, and correct economic imbalances. When things go poorly, the sum of business decisions helps produce circumstances that put the whole economy in crisis. But in good times and bad, the basic economic decisions are made by those who own the means to produce goods and services, well outside the sphere of popular sovereignty.

Leaders in the marketplace have disproportionate power not only because they have more money and the ability to secure access and influence through lobbying and campaign donations but also because governments must act in ways that promote the prosperity of the private economy, the country's great engine of wealth and employment. The well-being of everyone as measured by jobs and income depends on the investment decisions and the profits of private firms, and on corporate executives who decide about technology and the organization of work, where firms and factories will be located, how resources should be allocated, and how much executives and workers are paid. In observing this status and such developments, the political economist Charles Lindblom shrewdly observed how "business leaders thus become a kind of public official and exercise what, on a broad view of their role, are public functions."[5] Because leaders of the private economy cannot be ordered to invest or perform effectively for the greater good, they sometimes have to be prompted and persuaded to do so. Public policies concerned with taxation, trade, and regulation, among other matters, are the instruments the government utilizes to achieve this goal.

Business thus commands a privileged position in public life. "In the eyes of government officials," Lindblom notes, "businessmen do not appear simply as the representatives of a special interest, as representatives of interest groups do. They appear as functionaries performing functions that government officials regard as indispensable."[6] Business leaders in general, but especially the leaders of major corporate firms, have a double advantage in the country's democracy. With more money, they can afford to hire lobbyists, contribute to campaigns, create organizations, gain access to decision makers, and thereby influence debates about public policy. Even more important, they hold a key structural position—the jobs and income of many Americans depend upon corporate investment strategies and decisions. Consequently, they informally become key partners of government in what might be called a **corporate complex**. When key sectors of the private economy fail spectacularly, as the automobile industry recently has, government has little choice but to step in to shepherd them back to self-sustaining health. Thus when Chrysler and General Motors collapsed into bankruptcy in May and June 2009, the government spent over $60 billion, and temporarily took control of GM, in order to restore the companies to profitability while also overseeing a process that reduced the wages of automobile workers, laid off a third of the auto industry workforce, and cut the health benefits of retirees as well as current employees.

One consequence of the close relationship between business and government is that political views are unevenly represented in public debate. Key issues of manifest public significance—such as what to produce, where and how to produce it, and what to do with the resources generated by production—are decided by CEOs, managers, and governing boards with little public discussion, at least until a crisis occurs. The result is a public sphere more limited than the cacophony of debate between liberals and conservatives might suggest. The principle of majority rule, the very centerpiece of representative democracy, often applies to a confined range of questions. Some of the most important issues affecting the welfare of citizens are decided in corporate boardrooms that are well outside the reach of majority rule.

It is impossible to understand the politics of power in the United States without paying attention to the many ways democracy and inequality intertwine to affect virtually every aspect of American life, including economic opportunities across lines of race and gender, the quality of city neighborhoods, the provision of services, the health of the environment, and the scope and character of political choices made by government officials and citizens. These are the issues we place front and center in this critical introduction to American government that highlights both the remarkable aspects of American political democracy and the recurring problems that distort it to make the country's political system less democratic than it might be.

STANDARDS OF DEMOCRACY

When we judge American democracy, we have to start with the rights, institutions, and procedures that enable individuals and groups to make their views known and fairly select their leaders and public officials. These include civil liberties and civil rights, including freedom of speech, freedom of assembly, freedom of the press, and the absence of discriminatory barriers to participation. Without such procedural guarantees, it is extraordinarily difficult for people to formulate and express their interests. We have to consider the structure of government, the character of its institutions, and the mechanisms by which public policy is made. But we also must direct attention to the impact of deep and persistent patterns of inequality and investigate how, and with what consequences, valued features of democracy are affected by disparities in income, wealth, and life chances.

Efforts to assess American democracy by examining how popular influence and control are affected by the uneven distribution of income, wealth, and other assets have produced some of the best work by political scientists on American politics. In 1961, the political scientist Robert Dahl published a brilliant and influential study of politics in New Haven, Connecticut; his book *Who Governs?* has become a classic in political science. By commonly accepted standards, he argued, the city was a democracy. Virtually all of its adult citizens were legally entitled to vote, they had a choice of candidates, and their votes were honestly counted in free elections. In New Haven, Dahl found that "two political parties contest elections, offer rival slates of candidates, and thus present the voters with at least some outward show of choice." Yet, he observed, although the city's residents were legally equal at the ballot box, they were unequal in other ways that contrasted sharply with their formal political equality. Less than one-sixteenth of the taxpayers owned one-third of the city's property. In the wealthiest ward, one family out of four had an income three times the city average; most of the families in the poorest ward earned under $2,000 per year. Only one out of thirty adults in the poorest ward had attended college, in contrast to nearly half of those in the richest ward.[7]

Can this combination of legal equality and class inequality be designated as democratic? Dahl put the question this way: "In a system where nearly every adult may vote but where knowledge, wealth, social position, access to offi-

cials, and other resources are unequally distributed, who actually governs? . . .
How does a 'democratic' system work amid inequality of resources?"[8] He
placed quotation marks around the term *democratic* because its meaning in
this situation is unclear. Should a democratic system be measured only by such
matters as fair and open elections, or should it be measured by the control
and distribution of resources? What, in short, is the relationship of **capitalism** and democracy?

In New Haven, Dahl was heartened to find that no single elite group made
the city's key political decisions. Rather, different groups determined policy in
matters of urban renewal, public education, and the nomination of candidates
for office. However, there was one feature that ran across different aspects of
New Haven's life. In each area, there was a wide disparity between the ability
to make decisions by politically and economically powerful people, on the one
hand, and average citizens, on the other. As a result of such disparities, Dahl
noted, New Haven was "a long way from achieving the goal of political equality advocated by the philosophers of democracy and incorporated into the creed
of democracy and equality practically every American professes to uphold."
Nevertheless, he concluded that "New Haven is an example of a democratic system, warts and all."[9]

Like New Haven a half-century ago, the United States can be considered a
democracy, warts and all. But our understanding of American politics would be
incomplete and inaccurate if we treated its limitations and flaws as minor or
unfortunate exceptions. This book invites us to think about American democracy not only in terms of formal rules and rights, but by asking whether and
when citizens have relatively equal chances to influence and control the making
of decisions that affect them. Democratic procedures and institutions are essential to democracy. However, they do not guarantee it. What matters as well is the
substance of democracy. The right to free speech is precious. But even in an age
when the Internet and its blogs have opened up new means of communication,
information can become distorted when those who own the media use it to
express their views to millions while most Americans lack the equivalent means
to disseminate their opinions to even a few. Political rights, such as the right to
vote, are an essential part of any democracy. But these rights are undermined
when candidates shape policies favorable to the wealthy, who can provide them
with campaign contributions that ordinary citizens cannot afford. Civil liberties
are to be cherished. But these are perverted when, for example, some people can
afford to hire expensive lawyers to take advantage of the right to a fair trial when
others must rely on overworked and underpaid court-appointed attorneys to
defend them. The point of these examples is that procedural rights are impor-

tant, but they are also not enough. A successful working democracy requires (1) widespread participation in decision making, (2) an absence of restrictions on who gets to participate and on the fair terms of their participation, and (3) inclusive representation of the interests, values, and beliefs of citizens.

Democracy implies rule by the many, not the privileged few. Effective and extensive citizen involvement in decision making long has been regarded as a centerpiece of democracy. In the famous view of eighteenth-century French political theorist Jean Jacques Rousseau, persons develop political skills as active citizens when they can exercise real control over how political life is conducted and when they help shape the content of public policy. As political theorist Carole Pateman put it in her interpretation of Rousseau's *The Social Contract*, "the more the individual citizen participates, the better he is able to do so. . . . He learns to be a public as well as a private citizen."[10]

When the country was founded, American democracy was limited and constrained because the majority were not permitted to participate in political life. Initially, many states and localities imposed property restrictions on voting. These limitations were eliminated by the early 1830s. Women lacked the right to vote before the Nineteenth Amendment, in 1920, which brought them into the electorate. African Americans, including ex-slaves, were formally guaranteed the franchise by the earlier Fifteenth Amendment in 1870, five years after the end of the Civil War. But in practice they were largely kept out by a host of devices—including literacy tests, poll taxes, discrimination by electoral registrars, and a good deal of violence—until the Voting Rights Act of 1965.

Over the course of the history of the Republic, American constitutional government became more and more democratic, in the sense of including more and more citizens inside the political system as participants and voters, as a result of struggles to widen the franchise. With the passage of the Twenty-Sixth Amendment in 1971, nearly all adults over the age of eighteen became formally eligible to participate in American politics. As the country became more democratic, it also became a global beacon. Tens of millions fleeing oppressive conditions and seeking economic opportunity flocked to the United States, producing an increasingly varied population. At first, the population was divided between a majority of whites, mainly Protestants from northern Europe, especially Great Britain, and minorities of African slaves and Native Americans. Over time, immigrant streams from Ireland and Germany, then from southern and Eastern Europe, and most recently from Mexico, the Caribbean, Asia, Africa, and Latin America have fashioned a population that is heterogeneous in race and ethnicity in the world's most diverse democracy in terms of religion, culture, and place of origin.

Direct political participation is much easier to achieve in small groups and settings like juries, town meetings, or face-to-face community organizations than it is in societies as a whole, especially in a society as large and complex as the United States. For this reason, when we gauge whether the interests, values, and beliefs of citizens are present in an inclusive manner, we have to think not only about their ability and propensity to vote in elections, join campaigns, belong to political parties, take part in interest groups, or mobilize as activists in social movements, but how the country's system of political representation actually works.

It is impossible for all citizens to participate simultaneously in making political and policy decisions. As a result, they depend on having their preferences literally "re-presented" by others inside the political process. This is what happens in legislatures—in Congress, in state legislatures, and in city councils—that are democracy's core institutions. We elect persons who represent our views, who seek to make laws that serve both particular and general interests, and who are periodically judged by their constituents.

In assessing how well representative democracy is working, some key questions come to the fore. First, do the country's representatives—the persons who make the laws and decide the policies—reflect the characteristics of the persons they formally represent, or is there a systematic bias that limits the presence of representatives based on class, race, ethnicity, sex, or religion? Having a diverse body of representatives is important because the more they reflect the range of the population, the more likely it is that the interests of different types of citizens will be adequately represented. Group members are much more likely than others to vigorously represent their own interests.[11]

Second, are representatives aware of, and responsive to, their constituents' concerns? In practice, ordinary citizens often find it much more difficult than do the most privileged to achieve a representation of their interests, since those with more resources tend to perceive and promote their particular interests more accurately and effectively than other citizens. Thus, a key issue in a representative democracy is not who rules, but how those who rule use their power. How well do representatives perceive the preferences of their constituents, and how do they act on their behalf? Further, do they do so effectively?

Third, and broadest, is the question posed by Robert Dahl: "How does a 'democratic' system work amid inequality of resources?" As capitalism and democracy coexist in varied and changing ways, their character and content now, as in the past, are contested. High degrees of inequality stand as a barrier to the achievement of the fullest degree of democracy; that is, a democracy in which all citizens have relatively equal chances to influence the making of deci-

WHAT DO YOU THINK?

Patterns of Political Representation

Before the ratification of the Nineteenth Amendment to the Constitution in 1920, most women could not vote. Before the Voting Rights Act of 1965, most African Americans were excluded from the franchise. These landmark legal changes widened democracy. How important is office holding, in proportion to their numbers, by women, African Americans, and other historically marginalized groups for the democratic potential of voting to be realized?

sions that affect them. In turn, the openness of democratic political life invites and even promotes persistent challenges to the various dimensions of inequality that limit the meaningful scope of political life. By coming to understand the politics of power, we can better grasp the current limits of and opportunities for American democracy.

POLITICAL CHANGE

These issues are not new. They date to the earliest days of the Republic and have taken different form at different moments in American history. Within the ambit of the country's representative democracy, Americans have weighed up the proper role for government in the economy, the extent to which inequalities of wealth and income are acceptable, and what, if anything, government should do to manage and limit these differences. The political system has been the focus of great debates about how foreign affairs dovetail with domestic concerns and about who should qualify to be a citizen and who should not. The meaning of federalism (how much power the federal government should have as compared to the states) and the character of the separation of powers (what balance should be struck between the president, Congress, and the Supreme Court) also have been been contested. So too have the ways capitalism should be managed and regulated by the government, and how the operation of the economy affects the daily lives and opportunities of Americans.

The particular situations and conditions within which such matters have been debated and resolved have never been constant or static. Each generation confronts these matters in a particular way. Each generation thus must reassess

American politics anew as it grapples with large-scale patterns of change that affect the character and contours of the country's democracy. In the current era, three matters have come to the fore that have dramatically reshaped the character and agenda of American politics. As we explore the politics of power, we need to bear in mind these issues of great significance.

As the Lone Superpower, the United States Confronts a More Interconnected and More Unpredictable World

After the Cold War ended in 1989 and the Soviet Union collapsed in 1991, the United States was left as as the only **superpower** in the world. Its military power is unrivaled. Hundreds of thousands of American troops equipped with the most advanced weaponry are stationed in over 61 military bases in 19 countries, and American military personnel are deployed in another 800 smaller installations across the globe. Spending more on defense than the next fifteen highest-spending nations combined, the United States has the most technologically sophisticated, best-equipped military in the world, bar none. The United States launched the Iraq War on March 20, 2003, and subdued the military forces of Saddam Hussein within weeks.

The biggest and most powerful military helps serve and protect the biggest and most powerful economy in the world. The United States is the largest national market, home to more leading corporations than any other country. Although it contains only about 5 percent of the world's population, the American economy accounts for about a third of the world's gross domestic product (GDP). Even in difficult economic times, the dollar continues to be the principal international medium of exchange, the currency in which the rest of the world does business.

This combined military and economic power underpins the country's extraordinary influence in international affairs. There are few significant places or issues around the world where the United States does not project its power, from sending humanitarian aid to fight against the AIDS epidemic in Africa to negotiating trade agreements with China, from mediating the Arab-Israeli conflict to sending troops to fight the Taliban in Afghanistan, from confining people designated as enemy combatants to confronting drug smugglers in South America. Yet the more the United States has outdistanced all other rivals, the more it has become clear that world security after the Cold War is difficult to guarantee, that military power alone does not assure the United States will be unchallenged, and that a proper balance between liberty and security is not easy to find. The most visible instances of this uncertainty and vulnerability remain the shockingly successful terrorist attack on the World Trade Center and Pentagon in September 2001, and the failure of the American occupation of Iraq to bring peace or order to the country over the course of many years. Key perpetrators of 9/11 remain at large, the closing phase of the Iraq War has brought uncertain prospects, and the region centered on Iran, Afghanistan, and Pakistan remains persistently—even increasingly—dangerous.

In all, the world has become a more complicated stage. There are now more countries with more weapons of mass destruction, including growing nuclear arsenals, that can cause vast damage. Small conflicts now have a greater chance of escalating into larger ones that draw surrounding countries into the turmoil. The threat of terrorism remains and continues to haunt American society. And with the nation's economy more integrated with the rest of the world, it is subject not only to deep challenges at home but also to market changes that occur beyond its borders and that it has little control over. As the world has become more interdependent, domestic politics has become less insulated than ever before. Throughout American history, the country has been shaped by war and trade; but the scope and velocity of today's movements of people, ideas, money, goods, and weapons across national boundaries are unprecedented. Greater global interdependence increases American power and vulnerability at one and the same time. As a result, the politics of power is not crisply divided between domestic and international affairs. Issues that concern the interplay of democracy and capitalism cannot be confined to domestic politics.

Politics Has Become More Polarized

It used to be a truism of American political life that ideology was muted, that party differences were relatively small. Over the past thirty years, these patterns have been upset, even reversed. The Democratic and Republican parties have increasingly moved apart, both in their mass appeal and in their behavior in Washington. During this period, more and more Americans have recognized ever starker differences between the conservatism of Republicans and the liberalism of Democrats. More and more voters have become fixed in their partisan positions and ideological preferences, and elections are determined by relatively small shifts in the middle of the spectrum. Many Americans remain disengaged from politics, but those who participate tend to reliably line up on opposing sides.

From the 1910s to the early 1960s, the Democratic Party housed liberal and progressive politicians who supported unions, civil rights, and social equality. It also sheltered the country's leading segregationist politicians from the South, where Jim Crow defined the law of the land. The Republican Party likewise was quite heterogeneous; it included internationally minded, relatively liberal members and isolationist, more conservative party leaders. But conservative Democrats and moderate Republicans have become endangered political species. The most significant cause of these developments has been the partisan realignment of the South. Although the South was once solidly Democratic in its voting patterns, today it usually votes Republican in national elections and, increasingly, in local contests as well. The result is more partisan combat, less civility, more party unity, and less willingness to compromise.

This gulf has been shaped by divisions of class, race, and culture. In 1956 and 1960, those in the top income quintile were only slightly more likely than those in the bottom quintile to identify themselves as Republicans; but today they are more than twice as likely to do so. American politics is even more sharply divided by race. With the mass departure of southern whites from the Democratic Party after Congress passed civil rights legislation in the 1960s, the majority of the country's white voters became reliably Republican. By contrast, African Americans and Latinos support Democratic candidates by significant margins. Black voters in particular rarely give less than 80 or 90 percent of their votes to Democrats. There also has been a growing religious division in the electorate. Evangelical Protestants heavily tilt Republican. Mainline Protestants and Catholics are rather closely divided. Jews and secular persons heavily lean Democratic.[12]

Both as a cause and as a reflection of these developments, differences *within* the parties have gotten smaller at the same time as differences *between* the parties have become larger. The Republican triumph in 1994, led by Newt Gingrich, brought into the fold committed conservatives who sought to govern on the basis of a common platform they called Contract with America. The return of Democratic Party congressional control in 2006 was part of a strong liberal tilt that was reinforced in 2008.[13] Roll call votes in Congress today are more divided between the two parties than at any time in the past half-century; liberals are grouped almost exclusively in the Democratic Party and conservatives in the Republican Party.

Economic Crises Returned, Calling into Question Both the Virtues of Markets and the Promise of Government

During the Great Depression of the 1930s, the New Deal program dealt with the collapse of many industries and widespread unemployment by transforming the role of government and extending its reach into the economy. As mar-

---

WHAT DO YOU THINK?

Is Political Conflict Damaging to the Public Interest?

In 1950, a committee of the American Political Science Association criticized American political parties for being too alike and insufficiently committed to distinctive ideologies. Today, politics has become more polarized between Democrats and Republicans, liberals and conservatives. This polarization has become a source of concern for placing politics ahead of a search for the public interest. Who has the better argument—the advocates of more or less polarization?

---

kets failed, they were resurrected by bold legislation and public programs. For the four decades that followed, democracy and capitalism learned to coexist on terms that extended the scope of governmental responsibility.

The election of Ronald Reagan as president in 1980, after a decade of economic difficulties culminating in high inflation rates, signaled the triumph of a more conservative ideology that called the role of big government into question. Four years before the election, Robert Bartley, then in charge of the editorial page of the politically conservative *Wall Street Journal*, observed that liberalism as an "establishment . . . has ordered our political and intellectual lives for the past two generations." He predicted that "over the next few years we will see an increasing challenge to the very heart of liberal . . . thinking."[14] The new ideology Bartley and other conservative intellectuals advocated, as a distinctly minority position, at the time was thought to be well outside the political mainstream. It held that government should do less, not more; that government should be smaller, not bigger; that more decisions should be left to the marketplace, not elected officials; and that society should provide more opportunity, not more equality. Just four years later, President Reagan drew on the ideas of a new generation of conservative intellectuals to implement this design for a more modest government and more reliance on the marketplace. As a result of the Reagan revolution, conservatives came to set the main terms of public debate. The political center shifted to the right. Democrats, including President Bill Clinton, also invoked the virtues of smaller government, balanced budgets, and the marketplace. President George W. Bush and the Republican Party invoked these ideas and successfully appealed to a strong belief in the virtues of markets as they gained control over all three branches of government following the 2002 and 2004 elections.

The huge global crisis of 2008 and the deep recession's slump in economic performance that followed called into question the ideology and practice of a less regulated capitalism. Even some of the most notable advocates of free-market capitalism had second thoughts. Alan Greenspan, who served as chairman of the Federal Reserve from 1987 to 1996, and who had been one of the country's most articulate and important advocates of a smaller role for government and reduced regulation, found himself "in a state of shocked disbelief" that caused him to rethink his free-market ideology. Asked during congressional testimony in October 2008 whether "your view of the world, your ideology, was not right, it was not working," he replied, "absolutely, precisely. . . . I have found a flaw [in that view]. . . . I have been very distressed by that fact."[15] Late in the Bush administration, and especially in the early period of the Obama presidency, government was called on to save the banking system, restore faith in Wall Street, stimulate the economy by massive public works spending, and initiate new ways to regulate reckless and speculative economic behavior.

Big government—as an idea and as a set of public policies—had returned. If the pro-market ideology of the past three decades had been a response to what were seen as failures of heavy-handed policies and bloated bureaucracies, the financial collapse and steep recession that began in 2008 undercut the idea that markets on their own can effectively correct themselves. But the return of a strong role for government comes with doubts and uncertainties about its capacities, programs, and choices. Will policymakers advance far-reaching structural changes, or shore up an older system? Will they cushion big business against risk or regulate how risk is apportioned? How will democratic pressures change or even transform the character of capitalism? Will attitudes and policies toward an ever greater degree of inequality alter? How will social policies seek to reduce insecurity and deal with those left most vulnerable to economic change? How will the globe's increasingly integrated economy compete for attention with national imperatives and the wish to protect American citizens? How will global challenges and political **polarization** advance or impede a balancing role for government in managing risk and providing economic security? What new patterns linking capitalism and democracy will emerge?

CONCLUSION

The tension between democracy and capitalism, the manner in which formal, legal equality and real, substantive inequality interact, is the principal subject of this book. Capturing how the interplay of democracy and capitalism shape the politics of the United States is its task.

In Part I, "American Political Economy," we consider the close relationship in Chapters 2 and 3 between the national government and the country's market economy at a time of growing economic globalization by examining the changing role of government in advancing, regulating, and counteracting market forces.

Part II, "Political Participation," analyzes how citizens interact with their government. Chapter 4, treating parties and elections, studies polarization and new patterns of electoral mobilization, as well as the strategies used to affect outcomes. Interest groups and social movements are the subjects of Chapter 5, which analyzes how associations and patterns of activity in civil society shape American politics and open possibilities for change.

Having described how political preferences are transmitted to policymakers, Part III, "Political Institutions," turns in Chapters 6, 7, and 8 to the interplay of political economy, political culture, and political participation in the institutional settings of the presidency, Congress, and courts.

Part IV, "Public Policy," treats the public policy outcomes that these processes produce. Chapters 9, 10, and 11 reflect, respectively, on economic, social, and foreign policy. Finally, our conclusion, Chapter 12, reviews the main points of the text and discusses possible futures for American politics and society.

CHAPTER SUMMARY

Introduction
Like the *Titanic,* the United States has different social classes. The capitalist market economy has produced economic progress and much prosperity, but also a significant degree of poverty and disparities in wealth and income that are wider than those found in other economically developed countries.

Constitutional Democracy and Capitalism
The United States is a constitutional democracy, a form of government that prevents public authorities from acting in arbitrary ways, and is based on formal procedures for electing officials, making laws, and implementing policies. American democracy guarantees citizens the right to vote, to participate in political debate, to criticize leaders, to mobilize and organize for desired ends. Key questions are how American government

and politics either reinforce or modify the country's patterns of inequality in wealth and income, and which citizens have more power to influence these outcomes.

Standards of Democracy

American democracy can be judged by a number of criteria. First is the extent to which all citizens can participate in selecting leaders and making decisions. Second is whether elected officials reflect the characteristics of the people who select them. Third is whether these leaders are responsive to the concerns of their constituents. Fourth is how democracy operates to reduce those inequalities that make it difficult for citizens to have relatively equal chances to influence in three dimensions.

Political Change

The character of American democracy is not static; it is vitally affected by large-scale change. Three recent changes have reshaped the content of American politics. As the lone superpower, the United States confronts a more interconnected and more unpredictable world. Politics has become more polarized. With the return of economic crises, both the virtues of markets and the promise of government have been called into question. In these circumstances, the book probes these main questions about the politics of power: How do deep inequalities affect the operation of American democracy? When does democracy heighten these disparities, and when does it become a tool to moderate these differences among its citizens?

Critical Thinking Questions

1. How much inequality based on class, or race, or gender is consistent with democracy?

2. Does citizenship exclusively include civil and political rights, or does it also contain social rights? If so, what are they?

3. Should we think about power as the capacity of some to get others to do what they want, or as the ability of the whole society to achieve goals citizens have in common?

Suggested Readings

Larry M. Bartels, *Unequal Democracy: The Political Economy of the New Gilded Age*. Princeton, NJ: Princeton University Press, 2008.

Robert A. Dahl, *Democracy and Its Critics*. New Haven, CT: Yale University Press, 1989.

Robert A. Dahl, *On Democracy*. New Haven, CT: Yale University Press, 1998.

Charles E. Lindblom, *Politics and Markets*. New York: Basic Books, 1977.

Nolan McCarty, Keith T. Poole, and Howard Rosenthal, *Polarized America: The Dance of Ideology and Unequal Riches*. Cambridge, MA: MIT Press, 2006.

Carole Pateman, *Participation and Democratic Theory*. New York: Cambridge University Press, 1970.

PART I

AMERICAN POLITICAL ECONOMY

In the 1960s, Flint, Michigan, was a prosperous city. The town was built around automaker General Motors (GM), the world's largest corporation. GM employed over 40,000 workers in Flint, and the roads in town bore such names as Chevrolet Highway and Buick Freeway—an indication of Flint's connection to two of GM's automotive divisions. Working in the auto plants throughout the city was hard, but the union, the United Automobile Workers (UAW), helped to ensure that workers were rewarded for their efforts.[1] In 1969, average earnings in Genesee County, where Flint is located, were roughly $2,000 above those in the rest of Michigan and $7,000 higher than average income throughout the United States.[2] Unemployment was low and poverty was negligible. In one of the first quality-of-urban-life surveys ever conducted, Flint ranked 18th out of 66 medium-sized cities.

Fast forward to 1980. In that year, Flint led the nation's cities in joblessness with an unemployment rate of 20.7 percent. Unemployment in Flint remained twice as high as in the rest of Michigan in the decade that followed. By the turn of the century, Flint was among the ten worst metropolitan areas in terms of jobs lost.

As jobs disappeared, so did people. Flint's population fell from 190,000 in 1970 to 125,000 in 2000. Depopulation left its mark on Flint as once proud, stable neighborhoods were defaced by abandoned buildings and dilapidated housing. Public services declined. Aggregate real earnings slumped 9 percent between 1969 and 1993. All of these indignities—poverty, unemployment, bankruptcies, crime, and urban decay—combined to earn Flint last place in *Money Magazine*'s quality-of-life survey of three hundred cities.[3]

What explains why Flint was transformed from one of the most attractive to one of the least attractive cities in the country? The answer can be summed up in two words: General Motors. Beginning in the 1980s, GM decided to disinvest, closing factories and moving product lines out of the city. GM closed plants in Flint not out of malevolence, but because its share of the U.S. auto

A shuttered GM plant in Flint, Michigan.

market tumbled—from 46 percent in 1980 to just 28 percent by 2002. GM lost market share because it responded too late to the challenge of more efficient cars imported from Japan, experienced turmoil within the ranks of its board of directors, had the worst labor relations of the Big Three car companies, had greater administrative overhead than any of its competitors, and pursued an expensive and failed strategy of replacing workers with robots.

Michael Moore, who grew up in Flint, left home in the 1970s to pursue a career in journalism and filmmaking. When he returned to Flint years later, he found a city on its knees and decided to make a film explaining why. Moore went looking for the person whose decisions were crucial in producing the tragedy afflicting his beloved hometown. He did not go looking for the mayor of Flint or the city council. Nor did he go looking for the governor of Michigan or any other public official. Instead, he went looking for Roger Smith, the chairman and chief executive officer of General Motors. Moore believed that decisions made by General Motors had more consequences for the city than any action taken by any public official. Moore's film, *Roger & Me* (1990), provides a graphic and tragicomic description of how Flint's dependence on its corporate sponsor led to the city's ruin and describes Moore's futile attempt to impress on Roger Smith the tragic consequences that GM's plant closures had on Flint and its citizens.[4]

But Roger Smith's decision to close plants in Flint was not the result of venality or callousness on his part. GM's decisions were dictated more by the imperatives of profit seeking in a capitalist economy than by the moral character of management. The costs that GM's decisions imposed on Flint and its citizens were invisible from the perspective of GM's balance sheet. They were an unfortunate, unintended by-product of management's attempt to maximize earnings. The movie ends with Roger Smith presiding at a lavish Christmas celebration in Detroit while Moore is back in Flint filming the sheriff evicting another family from its home during the holiday season.

The story of GM, and its relationship with Flint and GM autoworkers, continued long after Michael Moore produced *Roger & Me*. GM continued to decline throughout the new century; its market share has now dipped below 20 percent, and its deterioration continues to have devastating effects on Flint. By 2009, this once prosperous city of 200,000 had only 110,000 citizens, a third of them living in poverty. When budget constraints forced police officers to be laid off and the city jail to be closed, Flint was rated the third most dangerous city in America. Foreclosures and abandoned homes were so numerous that the city sponsored a process of planned shrinkage that involved demolishing whole neighborhoods. People would be congregated in the areas that remained viable so that city services could be concentrated among them, and the rest was left to return to nature.[5] From a peak of 80,000 GM workers employed in Flint in 1970, only 5,000 were left by 2008. As plants shut down, Flint collapsed along with them. One union leader summed up what happened: "People talk about closing a plant. We closed a city here."[6]

Analyzing how GM controlled the fate of Flint illuminates basic features of the way that power is exercised in the United States. Part I of *The Politics of Power* examines the **political economy** of the United States, that is, the interaction between the economy and government. Chapter 2 highlights the impact that corporations, such as General Motors, have on politics. Chapter 3 provides a history of the American political economy, analyzes government's role in sustaining capitalism, and describes the sometimes tense, sometimes smooth relationship between political and economic power.

CAPITALISM AND DEMOCRACY

INTRODUCTION

This chapter explores the relationship between America's democratic political system and its capitalist economic system. It highlights the contrast between the rules of the game that govern the two spheres. Whereas democratic procedures govern the political sphere, they are largely absent from the economic sphere.

Capitalism is usually defined as a system in which capital—what can be defined as the capacity to produce goods and services—is privately owned and controlled. Capital is typically organized within business firms and corporations that hire employees to produce goods and services for sale. Business decisions are primarily driven by the goal of achieving the greatest return on the firm's investments, that is, profits. To do so, firms must outcompete their rivals in the market by offering comparable goods for sale at lower prices.

Markets are arenas in which producers of commodities—goods and services—offer what they produce for sale at a given price. The arena may have a physical location: a farmers market, store, or the trading floor of the New York Stock Exchange on Wall Street (where corporate stocks are bought and sold). Markets may also have a virtual existence—increasingly so in the age of eBay and Amazon. A production system based on markets is decentralized and largely self-regulating. No central institution directs the process; the exchange between buyers and sellers is voluntary. If consumers judge that the price is right—that is, sufficiently low—for a commodity they want, they purchase the commodity. Even so, markets are never wholly free or self-regulating. They always require a framework of rules specifying what kinds of behavior are and are not permissible. (For example, a government agency verifies that a processed food contains the ingredients specified on the label.) In brief, markets require regulation by an outside source. The foremost such agency has been government. Without regulation, capitalism could not survive for a day.

Capitalism, the system based on market production, has proved remarkably able to satisfy people's needs relatively cheaply and efficiently—so much so that it is the only viable economic game in the modern world. The major recent rival was communism, which involved centralized and authoritarian control of the economy as opposed to the decentralized, market-based system of capitalism. Communism crumbled in part because it was unable to match the productive achievements of capitalism. Capitalism has unleashed energies and initiative in regions throughout the world, including North America, Europe, and, more recently, China and India. (China continues to call itself Communist but is an amalgam of a one-party political system and a market-based economy.)

THE DILEMMAS OF MARKETS

Market-based production is a superb mechanism for encouraging innovation and risk taking, unleashing energy, and promoting efficiency. These are desirable by-products of competition among business firms to reduce their costs of production, thereby enabling them to lower prices, increase profits, and capture greater market share. However, the same factor that accounts for the dynamism of capitalism—the search for profits—also produces collisions with public interests. Here are several examples.

- Unless business firms are required to pay the costs of doing business, they will avoid doing so. When they succeed, a firm's products appear cheaper to produce than they actually are. Economists designate as **externalities** those costs that a firm can successfully avoid paying that do not affect its balance sheet. Consider mining for coal and other minerals. For generations, mining companies had a free hand to deface the natural environment, employ dangerous methods of extraction, and pollute streams and soil by discarding immense, often toxic, piles of slag. Although these actions were highly costly for miners, their communities, and the entire society, they were external to the company's balance sheet and therefore cost-free. This situation partially improved following passage of the Federal Mine Safety and Health Act of 1977 and the Clean Water Act of 1972 that require companies to use safer and greener methods of mining. One lesson is that unless government obligates companies to internalize socially harmful costs, the community will be forced to pay for them. Another lesson (actually, the other side of the same coin) is that well-crafted government regulation can promote public interests.

- More generally, what is good for individual companies, or for capitalism as a whole, may not be good for the society. Two examples: First, pharmaceutical companies have an interest in developing products for consumers who can afford to purchase their commodities; they have no interest in meeting public needs for which they cannot obtain adequate profits. Pharmaceutical companies' priorities are shaped by what is most profitable, not what is most needed. Second, during the housing crisis of 2008–09, the government allocated $75 billion in assistance to help homeowners who faced foreclosure to renegotiate their mortgages, thereby enabling them to remain in their homes. However, according to a report in the *New York Times*, "many mortgage companies are reluctant to give strapped homeowners a break because the companies collect lucrative fees from delinquent loans. Even when borrowers stop paying, mortgage companies that service the loans collect fees out of the proceeds when homes are ultimately sold in foreclosure. So the longer the borrowers remain delinquent, the greater the oportunities for these mortgage companies to extract revenues."[1] Like GM's actions at Flint, the behavior of these companies makes perfect sense from the point of view of their balance sheet. However, it makes no sense from the point of view of the wider community.

- To thrive, capitalism requires a constant expansion of commodity production and consumption. This imperative collides with the realities that the world has finite resources and that ecosystems are fragile. This is another illustration of an inherent conflict between what promotes the well-being of capitalism (i.e., in this case, the production and sale of ever more commodities) and what promotes the well-being of the community and the planet (conservation, frugality, and environmental protection). In a perverse twist, there is a near consensus among economists that economic growth is the best measure of a society's well-being. Yet economic growth is a composite measure that includes elements genuinely promoting well-being, such as the purchase of labor-saving devices, along with expenditures that do nothing to improve the quality of life on an individual or social level. In a report prepared for the French government, Nobel Prize–winning economists Joseph E. Stiglitz and Amartya Sen cite "increased driving, which weighs in as a positive within the framework of economic growth, as it requires greater production of gasoline and cars, yet fails to acount for the hours of leisure and work time squandered in traffic jams, and the environmental costs of pollution unleashed on the atmosphere."[2]

- The dynamism of capitalism, its revolutionary thrust, is also the source of its instability. Supply and demand are not coordinated. Investment, production, and consumption fail to balance, resulting in social dislocations such as inflation, recession, and unemployment. Business cycles occur in which periods of economic growth, measured by output, employment, and profits, are followed by periods of economic contraction in which production declines, unemployment increases, and bankruptcies rise. When a downturn is fairly mild, involving negative economic growth for at least two quarters, it is designated as a **recession**. (Some accounts broaden the definition to include a decline in other indicators, such as employment and investment.) A prolonged period of sustained economic stagnation, such as occurred in the United States in the 1930s, is designated as a **depression**. A depression involves severe unemployment, idle productive equipment, declining living standards, and extensive social dislocation.

- The alternation of boom and bust is a universal characteristic of capitalism, exemplified most recently by recessions in the late 1990s, with the bursting of a bubble involving dot-com startups, and 2008–09, produced by the bursting of bubbles in the housing and financial sectors. Thus, contrary to classical economic theory, markets are not always self-correcting. Left to themselves, they exhibit self-reinforcing tendencies toward extremes of boom and bust.[3]

- Capitalism is an inherently undemocratic form of production. Employers have the right to hire and fire, set wages and salaries, determine what tasks employees do, and direct them how to do them. Although within broad limits these decisions are limited by government regulation, the key word is *broad*. Those who own and manage businesses have considerable freedom to direct employees. Consider the simple case of using the restroom. No federal law requires supervisors to allow workers to take a restroom break. Management can restrict the number of restroom trips employees make, regulate their duration, specify when they will occur, and penalize workers for violating these rules.[4] Although this example refers to management's power to govern the workplace, the example of GM's impact on Flint demonstrates that management decisions have an impact that ripples far beyond the firm.

A key dilemma that cannot be easily resolved is that at the same time that capitalism promotes these troubling tendencies, it has proved uniquely qualified to promote efficiency and productivity. The politics of power often involves conflicts about how to reconcile capitalist production and democratic politics. Many chapters of this book provide empirical illustrations of these challenges.

Making Sense of Capitalism

The major question involving economic systems these days is not whether or not to adopt capitalism, but what is the most attractive variety to adopt. That is, capitalism is organized in quite distinctive ways in countries with roughly similar political systems and levels of economic development. A key difference in their political economy is the extent of government regulation of markets and provision of social programs. In the United States, markets are more free and less regulated than in most other democratic capitalist countries. This produces greater economic inequalities and, as discussed in Chapter 10, imposes harsh social costs.

Capitalism nowadays is a far cry from the world of early capitalism. A key difference, with important political implications, is the emergence of corporations commanding massive amounts of capital and consequently enormous concentrations of power. As the introduction to Part I describes, corporate decisions deeply affect local communities and the entire nation. For this reason, we suggest that our economic system—that is, capitalism—can be considered a form of **private government**, a system that resembles **public government** in that its policies have a fundamental impact on people's lives and their communities.

The government's welfare is heavily dependent on corporate prosperity. Government benefits when business flourishes. Conversely, when economic conditions turn sour, the government is blamed for the resulting job layoffs, wage reductions, and so on. Because the government is so dependent on favorable economic conditions, it is in effect held hostage by business, and one of its first priorities is to promote business-friendly conditions.

Corporations are far from all-powerful. First, they are engaged in competition with domestic and foreign producers. Second, they must contend with other groups that may have differing interests. In a democratic political setting, even one tilted in favor of corporate interests, the results of political struggles are often uncertain. Yet this does not mean that all interests have equal power to shape outcomes. In the next section we describe how business enjoys a structural political advantage because of its dominant economic position. We also review the global character of American corporate capitalism, changes in the occupational order, and sources of cohesion and conflict among capitalists. This chapter describes how, compared to other countries with capitalist economies and democratic governments, business interests have exceptionally great power in the United States. The chapter concludes by analyzing the unstable character of American capitalism that was especially evident in the deep recession of 2008–09.

THE SYSTEM OF CORPORATE CAPITALISM

Suppose it was learned that a small group controlled vast economic resources and political power in the United States. Imagine that, in a country with a population over 300 million people, several thousand Americans—unrepresentative, not democratically chosen, not even known to most people—dominated the economy. This small group determined the level of investment, where investment would occur, what would be produced, and how production would be organized. It owned and controlled the offices and factories in which production occurs, as well as the media that help shape our values and attitudes. Yet members of the group were not democratically chosen, and they based their decisions not on what the country needed but on what would be most profitable for themselves and the companies they directed. While they were buying islands in the Caribbean, 17,000-square-foot mansions, Jetstream planes, and Lamborghini Gallardo sports cars, millions of their fellow citizens had difficulty purchasing medical care, paying the rent, providing adequate care for their kids, or putting food on the table.

The small group at the top of the economic pyramid also had enormous political influence. They provided a substantial proportion of campaign contributions to political candidates and parties. They hired high-priced lobbyists and lawyers to represent their interests. They controlled the media. It would hardly be surprising if a government gave high priority to protecting this group's interests.

A troubling question is whether a government, political system, and society could be described as democratic if it tolerated, indeed promoted, the existence of a small group with immense wealth along with a far larger group with meager income. And yet everything that has been described is fact, not fiction. A convenient shorthand label for the system in which a small group controls the U.S. economy and, consequently, possesses immense political power, is **corporate capitalism**. What consequences flow from the fact that capitalists own and control capital?

Whether to Invest

Investment decisions by industrial corporations and financial institutions— investment banks, stockbrokers, private equity firms, and hedge funds— determine the level of goods and services produced in the United States. What drives investment decisions is what promises to fetch the highest profit. The well-being of entire communities can be affected by the result, as Flint discovered to its dismay. When investment lags, production lags, wages stagnate, and unemployment rises. When investment booms, then production booms, jobs are plentiful, and wages rise as employers compete for workers.

One consequence of this process, with important implications for politics, is that citizens tend to identify their personal welfare with the welfare of business. This tendency helps explain the widespread support for capitalism in the United States, and it is further fueled by pro-business propaganda created by schools, businesses, political parties, and the media.

There is a rational basis for pro-capitalist beliefs. The fact that the entire society depends on business firms to generate jobs and prosperity is consistent with claims by business leaders that their interests are aligned with the interests of the wider society and that profitable businesses are necessary to provide the investment, jobs, wages, and tax revenues on which we all depend. Capitalism is the goose that lays the golden eggs. This situation creates a terrible paradox for workers. Their jobs depend on the profits of their firm, which, perversely, increases its profits by squeezing these very same workers. As one autoworker observed with obvious irony: "Believe me—we know how hard it is to make a profit—we spend 50 to 60 hours a week at the company, working to make a profit for our employers."[5] Workers in Flint recognized the awful horns of this dilemma when, in the midst of GM's crisis, they joked, "The only thing worse than working for General Motors is not working for General Motors."

Citizens certainly perceive the complexities of this situation. Workers in Flint hardly needed reminding that GM sacrificed their jobs because of its declining competitive position. Yet they also recognized that their fate was closely bound up with that of GM, which translated into a desire for GM to flourish. More generally, there coexists both widespread support for capitalism in the United States and a readiness for workers and other citizens to challenge many features of capitalist control. Workers resist their employers' demands for wage concessions. Environmental activists protest industrial pollution and demand stricter environmental controls on business. Voters elect candidates who question corporate power. Tenants organize rent strikes demanding that landlords maintain their buildings. Women oppose sexual discrimination inside and outside the workplace, and unions fight for better working conditions.

One way that Americans resolve the paradox is that they tend to support capitalist values, such as individualism and minimum state interference, mostly in the abstract. However, when asked about specific government programs to assist the poor, Americans tend to express broad approval for such activities. Political scientist Elizabeth Sanders writes that "whatever their reservations about government power," nonelite Americans "have shared a powerful belief in community, collective action, and the government's responsibility to remedy market 'defects.'"[6] Even during the heyday of conservatism in the 1980s, when Republican presidents Ronald Reagan and George H.W. Bush were regularly denouncing the sins of big government, large majorities of the public continued to support social programs like Social Security.[7]

Where to Invest

In a capitalist system, corporate leaders are free to decide where to locate their facilities, subject to government regulations such as zoning laws. The decision is made on the basis of which location will minimize production costs and maximize sales and profits. Such factors as proximity to suppliers, raw materials, and markets are taken into account. Corporations also consider whether the local community is sympathetic to their needs. States and local governments compete with each other by offering tax incentives, loans, anti-union laws, and weak environmental regulations.[8] These factors explain why, for decades beginning in the 1920s, there was a massive movement of textile firms and other industries from New England and the Midwest to the South. A particular attraction was that, thanks to their passage of what are known as right-to-work laws, southern states discouraged union organizing.

Since the 1960s, firms began leaving the South to invest in less developed countries like Bangladesh, China, Mexico, and the Dominican Republic that offer still lower wages, higher subsidies, and a more anti-union climate. The shift of capital beyond U.S. borders, that is, offshoring, outsourcing, and foreign direct investment, are important elements of **globalization.**

What to Invest In

Investment decisions also determine the kinds of goods available in society. As with other business decisions, companies decide to invest in what they judge will be most profitable. For example, pharmaceutical companies devote more resources to devising medications for relatively harmless ailments for consumers in affluent countries than to devising medications to treat or prevent tropical diseases found among low-income groups in the global South. One example: elephantiasis, a painful disease producing serious swelling of the lower body, is caused by a parasite spread by mosquito bites and afflicts 120 million people in the world. From the viewpoint of pharmaceutical companies, it is rational to place priority on commercially profitable drugs; what might be needed from a medical point of view is secondary.

How Production Is Organized

New recruits at a Springfield, Arkansas, poultry plant receive orientation in a classroom with a prominently displayed sign: "Democracies depend on the political participation of its [sic] citizens, but not in the workplace."[9] Unlike the democratic rules that govern the political arena, workplace rules in a capitalist society are undemocratic. Private managers decide who will be hired, fired, and promoted; what tasks employees will perform; and what kind of technology will be utilized. The British historian R. H. Tawney put it this way: "[T]he man who employs, governs. . . . He occupies what is really a public office. He has power, not of pit and gallows . . . but of overtime and short-time, full bellies and empty bellies, health and sickness."[10]

Management seeks to fully control the process of production because profits depend on how efficiently labor can be managed. While company executives view the content of tasks and pace of work through the lens of productivity and production costs, their employees perceive these as issues of personal health and quality of life. There is thus a constant tug-of-war. On the one side, capitalists attempt to exert greater control. On the other, workers attempt to maximize their autonomy. Although the battle is one sided, workers have scored significant gains through the years. One way is by forming labor unions. Collective bargaining agreements between employers and unions often include

WHAT DO YOU THINK?

The Tense Relationship of Capitalism and Democracy

At the heart of the American political economy is a tension between the undemocratic organization of capitalism and the democratic procedures that regulate the elected branches of the national government. Try to think of two examples of how undemocratic capitalism and democratic politics conflict. When such conflicts occur, how are they resolved? Could this tension be resolved so that the spheres are organized along the same lines? Would such a pattern be preferable to the present pattern? Why or why not?

work rules that restrict management's power on the shop floor and in offices.[11] Workers have also exercised their power as citizens to pressure government to enact legislation mandating improved labor standards. Examples include minimum-wage laws, requirements for overtime pay, and occupational health and safety regulations.

THE MOBILIZATION OF BIAS

The decisions made by business firms are usually regarded as nonpolitical or private. Yet, because they deeply affect the entire society, we consider them as preeminently political. Similarly, political economist Charles Lindblom observed, "Because public functions in the market [that is, capitalist] system rest in the hands of businessmen, it follows that jobs, prices, production, growth, the standard of living, and the economic security of everyone all rest in their hands."[12] The *New York Times* provided a vivid illustration of Lindblom's point when it reported, in the midst of an economic slump, "Any chance that the United States economy will revive rests largely on the shoulders of corporate managers. It is their choices about fresh investment that will go a long way toward determining whether the nation limps along with modest growth or returns to robust economic health."[13] Similarly, during the 2008 economic recession, economists, business executives, talk-show hosts, and citizens eagerly scrutinized reports of business investment, hiring, and sales for clues about where the country was heading.

Because society depends on what only capitalists can deliver, and capitalists will deliver only if they find it profitable, they enjoy a unique advantage in the political arena. Elected officials are under enormous pressure to offer inducements to business. In the nineteenth century, the federal government gave railroad companies more land than the entire area of France to encourage the construction of the transcontinental railroad. Typically, the government offers business more prosaic inducements, such as patent protection, tariffs, tax breaks, research and development subsidies, vocational training, and military protection. Government generosity is especially great during crises. In the recession of 2008–09, despite widespread popular opposition to bailing out banks and other firms, the government provided hundreds of billions of dollars to stabilize the system of "private" production and finance.

Politicians often offer incentives to inspire that intangible but vital phenomenon of business confidence. Unless corporations judge that investments will be profitable, unless banks have confidence that loans will be repaid, they refuse to invest and make loans. The resulting recession or depression can wreak havoc with politicians' electoral prospects. Conversely, when business leaders are confident that good times lie ahead, they are likely to invest, hire, and increase wages. It is therefore in politicians' self-interest to provide business with incentives in order "to motivate them to provide jobs and perform their other functions," according to Lindblom.[14]

The distinctive political advantage that business enjoys by virtue of its economic power has been described as the **mobilization of bias**, a term coined by political scientist E. E. Schattschneider. Political scientists Peter Bachrach and Morton S. Baratz suggest that a mobilization of bias occurs when "the rules of the game" tend to favor one group over another; that is, when the playing field is tilted in one group's favor. How the game is set up may have as much to do with the outcome as it does with the relative strengths of the players on the field.[15]

The U.S. economic and political system is fundamentally biased in favor of business. This bias is deeply embedded in the political framework. Even before the first vote is cast, the first campaign contribution is made, and the first lobbyist contacts a member of Congress, business possesses a political advantage stemming from its ownership and control of the productive system.

Although business begins with a special political advantage, that does not guarantee success. Enjoying a head start in a race does not dictate reaching the finish line first. As the political scientist Neil J. Mitchell explains, business must engage in policy struggles that involve "a shifting set of adversaries, and volatile public preferences."[16] Despite the advantages that business enjoys, it is not assured of winning.

There are several reasons why business interests may be thwarted.[17] Companies often compete with each other and have conflicting interests depending on their region and industry, whether they produce for local or international markets, whether they are capital or labor intensive, and so on. Business groupings have had conflicting positions on public policies from the time slaveholders and manufacturers fought over the tariff in the 1800s to more contemporary struggles over trade policy between domestic producers and export-oriented firms.

Second, democratic procedures require policymakers to respond to many pressures and interests beyond those of business. The political burden of proof is much greater for popular movements than it is for business interests, but public opinon cannot be wholly ignored. Popular movements have periodically achieved significant political victories over business, especially during economic crises like the Great Depression of the 1930s.

A significant victory over business occurred during President George W. Bush's presidential tenure following corporate scandals involving the issuance of fraudulent financial statements, insider trading, and stock analysts' misleading recommendations. Two large companies, Enron and WorldCom, went bank-rupt after their fraudulent accounting was exposed, and Arthur Andersen, a major accounting firm, went down when it was convicted of cooking Enron's books. Public outrage forced Congress to pass legislation providing for tougher regulation of accounting and securities trading despite stiff lobbying by busi-ness against the bill. On the other hand, public outrage may not be sufficient to overcome business pressure. When public anger churned during the 2008–09 recession, the Obama administration proposed increasing government regula-tion of business, including creation of a consumer financial protection agency. However, reform proposals were considerably weakened in the face of fierce opposition by the financial sector as well as deep divisions in Congress.

This book examines the complex relationship between democratic politics and the undemocratic private government of capitalism. The politics of power is affected by the capitalist organization of the economy, and the capitalist organ-ization of the economy is affected, in turn, by the democratic political system. Although the mobilization of bias favors business, democratic pressure is capa-ble of partially mitigating the pro-business bias. *The Politics of Power* describes both sides of this complicated coin. In the following sections, we review the structure of corporate capitalism, who owns America's private government, the occupational structure of the American economy, the extreme form of market capitalism that prevails in the United States, and capitalist instability.

THE CHANGING LANDSCAPE OF AMERICAN CAPITALISM

Corporate capitalism includes the country's largest mining and manufacturing companies, investment banks, financial services firms, retail chains, utilities, high-tech companies, media companies, and corporate law firms. The giant companies listed in the Fortune 500 (a list of the 500 largest corporations, com-piled annually by *Fortune Magazine*) are the core of corporate capitalism. Fig-ure 2.1 lists the top twenty U.S. companies.

Giant companies and several hundred midsize firms tend to be capital inten-sive, highly productive, diversified, and global in their reach. They can be dis-tinguished from the other 22 million businesses in the United States, which range from convenience stores to car repair shops to locally owned restaurants. These firms are not only much smaller in terms of profits, sales, assets, and workforce, but they sell in local markets and are more labor intensive.[18] Small firms do not exist independently of the corporate sector. They often are sup-pliers to large corporations, are dependent on them for orders, provide retail sales outlets for corporate products, and repair what large firms produce. Small

FIGURE 2.1

TOP 20 FORTUNE 500 COMPANIES

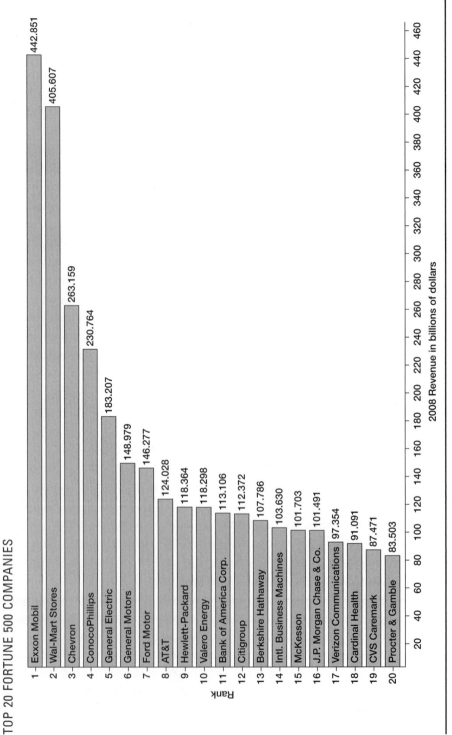

2008 Revenue in billions of dollars

SOURCE: CNN Money.com, "Fortune 1000," <http://money.cnn.com/magazines/fortune/fortune500/2009/full_list/index.html> (accessed Sept. 16, 2009).

businesses also act as shock absorbers for the corporate sector: they are usually the first firms to fail when recessions occur, because they lack the resources to ride out hard times.

In the past few decades, the structure of the American economy has undergone an important change involving a double movement. On the one hand, competition has intensified; on the other, a wave of corporate mergers has resulted in the creation of some corporate behemoths.

Greater competition has occurred because of two intertwined factors: globalization and technological innovation. In the postwar era, when national economies were relatively closed, giant corporations enjoyed large and stable market shares. For example, GM, Ford, and Chrysler produced virtually all cars bought in the United States. Globalization has broken open U.S. markets to competition from abroad. Nowadays the big three U.S. automakers must compete with Toyota, Honda, Hyundai, Mercedes, Nissan, Volkswagen, and others.

Globalization is intertwined with a technological revolution in transportation and communication that further promotes economic competition. Containerized shipping and a new generation of giant tankers have greatly compressed distance. So too has a great leap forward in information technology (IT), based on the miniaturization and plummeting cost of semiconductors (the hardware that drives computers and other electronic devices). Top management at transnational corporations—that is, firms with operations in several countries—can quickly and cheaply communicate within the firm and with suppliers and distributors around the world. This enables headquarters to integrate and direct operations in a way that was previously unimaginable. As a result, corporations can decentralize the production process to far-flung regions in order to maximize cost-savings and other advantages and integrate these global production chains in a seamless web. Globalization is a two-way street: at the same time that U.S.-based corporations now routinely outsource their operations, locate suppliers, and sell to customers across borders, foreign corporations can more easily reach American consumers, including by locating production facilities in the United States.

Advances in transportation and IT have lowered barriers to entry in many fields, thereby making it possible for more firms to compete in a given market. Formerly, large corporations mostly controlled the design, production, and marketing of products. Nowadays, ingenious entrepreneurs with a laptop computer can develop new products and capture (or create) niche markets. Examples include the meteoric rise of Google, eBay, and Facebook. As a result, the stable, highly bureaucratized, even ossified giant corporations characteristic of the post–World War II period have been forced to adapt or perish. Markets churn far more quickly than in the past and, as the example of GM testifies, woe to the corporation that believes success lies in repeating past practices.

At the same time that formerly closed markets are now open to new competitors, a wave of corporate mergers and acquisitions has increased corporate concentration in some sectors. Oil giants Mobil and Exxon merged to become the world's largest industrial corporation, and telephone companies merged to produce nationwide empires. The increased revenues of the largest corporations far outpace the increase in the gross domestic product (GDP).

Because the media provide the information on which an informed citizenry depends, they warrant special attention. A number of mergers in the twenty-first century significantly reduced independent media providers. Some important examples include Disney's purchase of Capital Cities/ABC, resulting in a $16 billion communications empire; Time Warner's merger with CNN, which produced a $20 billion conglomerate; and Westinghouse's purchase of CBS for $5.4 billion, followed by the merger of CBS and Viacom. These deals were puny compared to the sale of Time Warner to America Online (AOL) for $165 billion in 2001. (Such mergers are not always profitable: Time Warner and AOL decided to part ways in 2009.)

The purchase of many locally owned newspapers by large chains like Gannett has further contributed to the decline of independent media. At the same time, there has been a sharp falloff in newspaper readership recently, in some cases by 30 to 40 percent.[19] An explosion of cable news programs, bloggers, tweeters, and social networking has partially offset the decline in newspaper readership. However, these outlets often feed on rumors, highlight the sensational, and reach small, specialized audiences. Although nowadays motivated news junkies can obtain high-quality, specialized news 24/7, most citizens are less politically informed than in the past.

Throughout the economy, when production becomes concentrated, control becomes centralized in fewer hands. Democracy is threatened because this concentration of economic power tends to promote the concentration of political power. Business professor Jeffrey E. Garton has warned that corporate concentration has produced a "growing imbalance between public and private power in our society."[20] Corporate giants, especially in the financial sector, have begun to be regarded as "too big to fail" and as "systemically important"—phrases often used during the recent recession. Because their failure would have endangered the entire economic system, they were able to call on government to come to the rescue and subsidize their mistakes. This privileged position gives them extraordinary clout and enables them to take greater risks than is the case for small businesses or ordinary citizens.

WHO OWNS AMERICA'S PRIVATE GOVERNMENT?

Given the enormous power of America's private government, the question is of vital importance. One way to answer it is by identifying who owns the giant corporations that collectively comprise America's private government. Individual investors or firms such as pension funds can purchase a share of corporate assets by purchasing the corporation's stock. Stockholders are entitled to a share of the corporation's profits and can vote for the board of directors of the corporation. The corporate board selects top management and reviews its performance and decisions. The number of votes that investors cast depends on the amount of stock they own in the corporation. The question of who owns America's private government can thus be rephrased as, how is corporate stock ownership distributed?

Some argue that anyone can purchase stock in publicly owned corporations, that a shareholder democracy exists in the United States. As one Wall Street executive explained, "In our system of free enterprise, the capitalist system, industry is owned by the American public."[21] However, the notion of shareholder democracy is highly misleading. Fully half of all American households do not own stock in any form at all, either directly or indirectly through mutual funds or retirement plans. Moreover, shareholding is highly skewed among the remaining half of households. In 2004, the wealthiest 1 percent of all American households held 37 percent of the value of all U.S. stocks, and the next wealthiest 9 percent of households owned 42 percent of stocks. Thus, this small group—one household in ten—owned four-fifths of the value of all stocks in the United States. This left the remaining fifth of stocks to be shared among 90 percent of Americans.[22] The answer to the question of who owns America's private government is thus quite simple: one-tenth of the population. So much for the notion of shareholder democracy.

In addition to the enormous power they wield, those at the top of the corporate hierarchy provide themselves with handsome rewards. In 2008, the average compensation package of CEOs in the country's largest corporations was $10.4 million. Moreover, although top executives in the United States have always earned far more than their employees, the gap has dramatically increased in recent decades. Whereas in 1980, CEOs of major U.S. corporations received 42 times the compensation of an average factory worker, in 2007 CEO compensation was 344 times that of the typical factory worker.[23] Top corporate executives are paid in one day what the average worker earns in a year.

In Chapter 1, we suggested that one way to evaluate the quality of democracy is by the extent to which political representatives reflect the social diversity of a society. When we apply this standard to the corporate elite, the results are dismaying. Those who run corporate capitalism are with few exceptions white and male. In 2008, there were fifteen female CEOs leading the companies on the Fortune 500 list. Fortune did not bother compiling figures on African American or Hispanic CEOs of the top companies, because their numbers are so small. Moreover, far more significant than the relatively small number of women and racial minorities who have broken into the corporate elite is the inequality that is so pervasive in the general population. We further explore the issue of income inequality later in the chapter.

The Capitalist Class

Capitalist economies are in constant motion. The engine of change is competition among firms for markets and profits. But corporate capitalism is also characterized by cooperation and coordination among firms. In 1935, Schattschneider noted, "Businessmen collectively constitute the most class-conscious group in American society. As a class they are the most highly organized, more easily mobilized, have more facilities for communication, are more like-minded, and are more accustomed to stand together in defense of their privileges than any other group."[24] Since Schattschneider's time, the Internet and travel by corporate jet have increased the facilities for business communication and cooperation.

Capital is linked through a dense organizational network. One mechanism is exclusive social clubs, such as the Links and Century clubs in New York, the California Club in Los Angeles, and the Pacific Union Club in San Francisco. Social clubs promote **capitalist class** cohesion by creating information and friendship networks among the elite. The exclusive social club is the culmination of a process of elite socialization that begins in prep school, is reinforced at prestigious private colleges, is strengthened at selective law and business schools, and is polished at corporate headquarters.[25]

Along with elite social clubs, networking occurs in organizations such as the World Economic Forum, a group that hosts an annual forum at the posh Alpine resort of Davos, Switzerland. The Forum provides an opportunity for not only American but world business and political leaders to socialize and exchange opinions.

Peak business associations are another source of capitalist class cohesion. At the very top is the Business Roundtable, which seeks to develop common positions on public issues among CEOs of the largest corporations in the United States. In 2009, the Roundtable consisted of 159 corporations. These firms employ nearly 10 million people and have combined revenues of $5 trillion. The Roundtable has a small support staff of lobbyists. Instead, chief executives convey the Roundtable's position on key public issues to legislators and policymakers directly in one-on-one exchanges.

At a broader, less elite level, thousands of large and small firms belong to the U.S. Chamber of Commerce and the National Association of Manufacturers. These peak associations seek to represent the collective interests of business across industries. At the level of specific industries, countless trade associations represent the interests of firms in the sector, from the relatively inconsequential Fresh Garlic Association to the powerful American Banking Association. Chapter 5 analyzes the role of business and other interest groups.

A third source of capitalist class cohesion is corporate interlocks, in which the member of one corporate board of directors also serves on the board of another corporation. Interlocks facilitate communication between firms. According to sociologist Michael Useem, interlocks promote "the flow of information throughout the [corporate] network about the practices and concerns of most large companies."[26] Directors who sit on multiple corporate boards comprise what Useem characterizes as the "inner circle" of capital. Their perspective goes beyond the interests of any particular firm or industry to encompass the interests of corporate capitalism as a whole.

No single organization enforces discipline and unity among the firms that comprise corporate capitalism, especially when globalization has jostled the formerly closed world of U.S.-based firms. In the absence of threats to the framework of capitalism, competition among different firms and economic sectors is more prevalent than unity. Yet on issues affecting the interests of private property and capitalism as a whole, the social clubs, peak business associations, and corporate interlocks reviewed earlier help promote a class-wide response. For example, in 2009 business mounted a massive campaign to oppose congressional passage of the Employee Free Choice Act, a proposal promoted by organized labor to ease legal restrictions on the formation of labor unions.

THE CHANGING STRUCTURE OF EMPLOYMENT

Below the top level of corporate executives that comprise the capitalist class is a workforce that is shaped by the changing needs of capital. An industrial occupational order based on manual, blue-collar factory workers has been largely replaced by a postindustrial order in which professionals, service employees, and white-collar office workers predominate.

Industry first began to overtake agriculture as the basis of employment after the Civil War. Workers employed in manufacturing increased from just 2.5 million in 1870 to over 11 million by 1920. Hand tools were replaced by machines, workshops were replaced by factories, artisans were replaced by unskilled manual workers, and crafted items were replaced by standardized products. Foreign immigrants and native farmers took jobs as industrial work-ers in factories, transforming villages into towns and towns into cities. Pitts-burgh grew up around steel, Akron around rubber, and Detroit around cars. Flint was transformed from a sleepy town of 13,000 in 1900 into a bustling city of 150,000 that by 1929 employed over 60,000 industrial workers, many of them in GM factories.[27]

As the industrial workforce grew, it created the need for an occupational order based on the growth of white-collar occupations. As productivity in industry increased, firms hired salespeople and market researchers to find and create new outlets for their prodigious output. As capitalists discovered the ben-efits of applying science to production (i.e., using technology to improve pro-ductivity), firms hired technical experts to develop new products and improve existing methods. As companies took the skill out of many jobs on the shop floor and in the office, firms hired engineers to design the labor process and supervisors to manage it. As companies increased in size and became more bureaucratic, the number of office workers, lawyers, and managers increased to coordinate the flow of work within the firm and manage conflicts with other firms. As increasing numbers of women entered the labor force, business firms hired fast-food workers, cleaning-service workers, child-care workers, and nursing-home workers to sell services that women previously provided within the family. An increase also occurred in public sector service workers and pro-fessionals, such as teachers and social workers. In brief, the growth of a postin-dustrial workforce did not occur separately or independently from the grimy world of industrial production but developed in tandem with the demands of industry and the social changes it provoked. What has been dubbed the New Economy that emerged in the 1990s, based on the explosion of activity on the Internet, is a further development of the postindustrial order.

The shift from an industrial to a postindustrial workforce is reflected in Fig-ure 2.2, which reports government statistics on the occupational distribution of the workforce. In 1960, the number of factory and operative jobs (i.e., employment in manufacturing) outnumbered jobs in the service sector (includ-ing sales, service, and clerical). In 2008, there were more than triple the num-ber of service sector jobs compared to manufacturing jobs. Further, the proportion of manufacturing jobs within total employment declined from 42.4 percent in 1960 to 14.2 percent in 2008.

As the postindustrial occupational order emerged several decades ago, the occupational structure began to bifurcate; both good and bad jobs grew at the expense of the middle. According to Figure 2.2, managerial and professional jobs—ones that are well compensated and require a college or postgraduate education—have increased in number.

FIGURE 2.2

OCCUPATIONAL DISTRIBUTION, 1960 AND 2008, SELECTED OCCUPATIONS

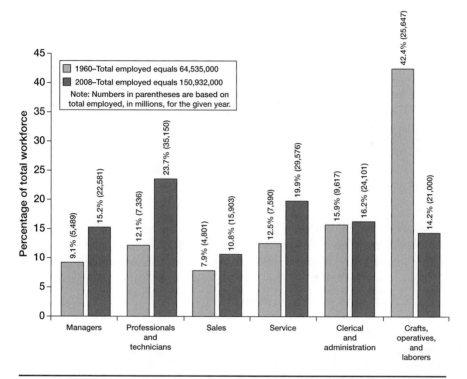

SOURCE: For 1960 figures, see *Historical Statistics of the United States: Colonial Times to 1970* (Part 1) (Washington, DC: U.S. Government Printing Office, 1971), 139. For 2008 figures, see Bureau of Labor Statistics, "Table 1.6: Occupational Employment and Job Openings Data, 2008–18, and Worker Characteristics, 2008," at www.bls.gov/emp/ep_table_106.pdf (accessed April 12, 2010).

Among well-paying jobs, those in the financial sector merit special attention. Although a complex economy requires specialists to assess risk and manage credit, the U.S. financial sector, whose firms often pay high salaries and bonuses, recently has ballooned in size. Although the recent recession slowed the process, many talented college graduates now head to law school or business school in hopes of landing lucrative jobs with hedge funds, venture capital firms, investment banks, and law firms. Once there, they are paid to lobby government officials, locate tax loopholes, and devise exotic financial products—the kind that helped produce the economic crisis. As described by Paul Krugman, Nobel Prize winner in economics and *New York Times* commentator, "Over the past generation—ever since the banking deregulation of the Reagan years—the U.S.

economy has been 'financialized.' The business of moving money around, of slicing, dicing, and packaging financial claims, has soared in importance compared with the actual production of useful stuff."[28] The financial sector's share of the GDP has doubled since 1960, thereby draining talent and resources from productive and socially useful sectors of the economy.[29]

Well-paying jobs have increased in the United States, but bad jobs have increased even faster. They are concentrated in the service and sales occupational categories; the proportion of sales jobs has doubled since 1960. These jobs tend to be poorly paid, offer few fringe benefits, require menial and routine labor, and rarely enjoy labor union protection. According to the U.S. Bureau of Labor Statistics, seven of the ten occupations with the greatest job growth are low-wage jobs requiring little education; they include janitor, cashier, nurse's aide, and salesperson. The trend is illustrated by comparing GM, formerly the country's largest private employer, with Wal-Mart, which has become the largest employer. Meanwhile, Wal-Mart offers part-time, low-wage work with few fringe benefits. Thus far, the company has been successful in preventing its employees from obtaining union representation. The result is that nowadays, according to *New York Times* economics reporter David Leonhardt, "the modern American economy distributes the fruits of its growth to a relatively narrow slice of the population."[30]

WHAT DO YOU THINK?

What Criteria Should Determine How Much People Should Be Paid?

It is often claimed that economic inequalities within capitalism are justified. Inequality is a great way to motivate people, because those who work harder and are better at competing in the market receive greater rewards. Inequality reflects people's unequal contributions to social welfare. According to this line of reasoning, those who contribute more deserve to be given greater rewards. Critics of this view counter that the way capitalism distributes rewards cannot be justified on the basis of merit. For example, poets, firefighters—and professors!—have far lower incomes than do stockbrokers. But poets, firefighters, and professors—as well as office workers, engineers, and nurses' aides—do not necessarily work less or contribute less to society than stockbrokers. Where do you stand in this debate? How do patterns of economic inequality in the United States strengthen or weaken your argument?

One way economists measure trends in income distribution is to compare the income of different quintiles (fifths) of the population. This comparison reveals the striking extent of income inequality in the United States. Whereas the top quintile of households captured half of all income in 2007, the bottom quintile received 3.4 percent. And income is further stratified at the top end. The richest 5 percent obtained 21.2 percent of all income in 2007.[31]

Is this situation inevitable? A cross-national comparison suggests that it is not. Consider the data in Figure 2.3, which compares the share of national income of the top 0.1 percent of the population in the United States and other rich capitalist democracies. These are the most recent data available. Income inequality has become even further skewed since 2000.

A country's political choices thus play a key role in shaping the extent of inequality. To provide a concrete example, what are considered junk jobs here are compensated better elsewhere due to the greater power of unions and government regulations. Whereas the federally mandated minimum hourly wage in the United States is $7.25, it is $12.30 in France, a country with a combat-

FIGURE 2.3

INCOME SHARE OF TOP 0.1 PERCENT IN RICH COUNTRIES, 2000

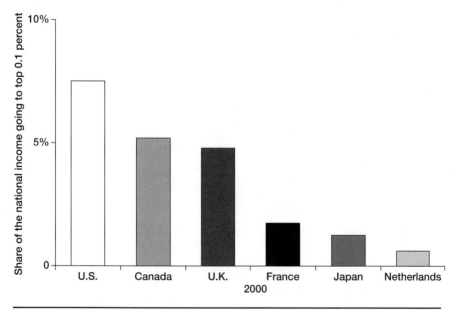

SOURCE: A. Gelman, D. Park, B. Shor, J. Bafumi, and J. Cortina, *Red State, Blue State: Why Americans Vote the Way They Do* (Princeton, NJ: Princeton University Press, 2008), 58. Derived from data of Thomas Piketty and Emmanuel Saez.

ive labor movement and strong leftist parties. Markets tend to generate inequality and to compensate unskilled labor with poverty-level wages unless these tendencies are checked by a strong countervailing force. Such forces are weak in the United States. The U.S. labor movement is tiny compared to labor movements in comparable countries, the party system is skewed toward the right of the political spectrum, and government is relatively unresponsive to the interests of lower-income groups. The result is what we describe next as the extreme market capitalism that prevails in the United States.

The increasing concentration of income at the top is a result of politics, as we explore further in Chapters 3 and 9, as well as a cause of political change, as we discuss in Chapter 4. The tiny group of Americans with vast income and wealth that owns America's private government is immensely better situated than the vast majority of citizens to shape the political system to serve their interests.

AMERICA'S EXTREME MARKET CAPITALISM

Capitalism comes in many flavors; the American variant, which we refer to as **extreme market capitalism**, is one of them.[32] Countries with capitalist economies can be arrayed along a continuum with relatively free and unregulated markets at one end and highly regulated markets at the other. At the first pole are countries where most goods and services are produced and distributed by the market mechanism, and business firms are regulated lightly. At the other end are countries where many goods and services are publicly provided and where government regulations limit what business firms can do. The United States is close to the first pole. So too are Japan and Australia. Compared to most affluent capitalist countries, the sphere of market-provided goods and services is larger in the United States, the extent of publicly provided good and services smaller. This tendency has increased since the 1980s. Though markets have always been regulated with a relatively light touch in the United States, the wave of deregulation beginning in the 1980s has increased business autonomy. As Chapter 3 describes, this trend has been partially reversed by the Obama administration. Many West European countries, including Germany, France, and Sweden, are at the other pole. Governments in these countries regulate business more closely and levy higher taxes than in the United States. In return, they provide their citizens with more extensive social services. (Other contrasts will be described below.)

America's extreme market capitalism has three distinctive features. First, compared to most industrialized democracies, the public sector in the United States is quite small. State, local, and federal employment account for just 15 percent of the nation's workforce; this proportion is far less than the quarter to third that the public sector typically comprises in other rich democracies. In addition, no advanced industrialized country collects a lower proportion of its GDP in the form of taxes than the United States does; and U.S. government spending as a share of GDP is at the low end. As a result, the federal and state governments in the United States provide relatively few public services. In most other countries, citizens are entitled as a matter of right to low-cost health care, just as they have a right to unemployment insurance or assistance from the fire department if their home is on fire. In the United States, until the passage of comprehensive health insurance legislation in 2010, health care was considered a private commodity. Like other commodities, medical treatment was available only to those able to afford to purchase it through health-care insurance. (An exception was those who were enrolled in government-sponsored Medicare and Medicaid programs.)

Second, and related to the first point, there are fewer constraints on business firms in the American model of extreme capitalism. In the United States, as we saw earlier, corporate management mostly decides who gets what, where, and how.[33] Government regulation of the workplace is unusually thin in the United States. "By most international standards," one study concluded, "American employers are . . . confronted with fewer direct regulations of employment conditions than employers in other countries."[34] According to two labor experts, private employers in the United States "have more authority in deciding how to treat their workers than do employers in other advanced countries."[35]

In many European countries, labor laws require the creation of elected workers' councils that possess significant power, stipulate that workers are entitled to representation on the company's board of directors, and require employers to provide severance pay when they lay off workers or close plants.

Another reason that business firms are more autonomous than their counterparts elsewhere is that labor unions—organizations representing workers that typically represent a countervailing force to management—are smaller and weaker here than in virtually any other rich democracy. As Table 2.1 reveals, with union density at 12.4 percent of the work force, the United States has among the lowest proportion of unionized employees of any industrialized democracy. In the absence of unions, employers can unilaterally set wages and working conditions, and workers can take them or leave.

Union weakness helps account for the exceptionally high income inequality in the United States. Union members in the United States enjoy 30 percent higher wages than employees doing the same kind of work who do not belong to unions.

The decline of American unions is due to many factors. First was the failure of unions to organize in the South in response to the move there by northern firms during much of the twentieth century. The South was a refuge for nonunion

TABLE 2.1

PERCENT OF LABOR FORCE IN LABOR UNIONS, 2003

Country	Union Density Rate
Australia	22.9%
Austria (2002)	35.4%
Belgium (2002)	55.4%
Canada	28.4%
Denmark	70.4%
France	8.3%
Germany	22.6%
Ireland	35.3%
Italy	33.7%
Japan	19.7%
Netherlands	22.3%
New Zealand	22.1%
Norway	53.3%
Spain	16.3%
Sweden	78.0%
United Kingdom	29.3%
United States	12.4%

NOTE: This is an abbreviated list.
SOURCE: Jelle Visser, "Union Membership Statistics in 24 Countries," *Monthly Labor Review*, January 2006, table 3, p. 45.

firms that would later become the vanguard, setting the nonunion standard for the rest of their industry.[36] The South also harbored conservative, anti-union politicians. Their handiwork provides the second reason why unions have declined: restrictive labor legislation. Laws such as the Taft-Hartley Act of 1947 placed obstacles in the way of union-organizing campaigns and restricted strike activity. Third, beginning in the 1980s, employer strategy toward unions changed from one of reluctant acceptance to uncompromising opposition. Management increased its efforts to oppose union-organizing drives by illegally discharging union activists and threatening to close plants whose workers voted to organize a union. Employers stepped up their demands for concessions in bargaining and often provoked strikes to permanently replace workers and rid themselves of unions entirely. Unions often failed to respond adequately to these threats. They did not inspire their members, vigorously contest the new offensive by employers, or invest in organizing new regions, sectors, or groups not traditionally part of the labor movement. We review this issue further in Chapter 5.

Fourth, as a result of the previous factors, extreme market capitalism dominates our lives to an extent not found elsewhere. Business not only controls

Americans' work lives more closely; it is also a more intrusive presence in our leisure time. Americans are constantly bombarded with advertising, for example, by corporate branding of sports stadiums and sports contests and by the enormous time devoted to advertising in television programs. Indeed, product placement in films and television programs has eroded the distinction between straight programming and advertising.

Recent advances in information technology have provided corporations with new ways of invading our personal space. Cookies and spyware provide details about our Internet use. Corporate advertisers mine mountains of data on our credit card purchases, mortgage payments, and financial history so they can tailor advertising to individual consumers' profiles. Cablevision Systems has developed "technology to route [cable TV] ads to specific households based on data about income, ethnicity, gender or whether the homeowner has children or pets. . . . During the same show, a 50-something may see an ad for, say, high-end speakers from Best Buy, while his neighbor with children may see one for a Best Buy video game."[37] Another recent innovation enables advertisers to provide consumers with "different versions of Web sites than other consumers and even receive different discount offers while shopping—all based on information from their offline history. Two women in adjoining offices could go to the same cosmetic site, but one might see a $300 Missoni perfume, the other the on-sale house-brand lipstick for $2."[38]

Former Labor Secretary Robert Reich entitled his survey of the evolving American political economy *Supercapitalism*. He analyzes the ways that commodity production and consumption, and our roles as consumers and investors, have increased at the expense of the importance of the public sphere and our role as citizens.[39]

For many years, U.S. political leaders trumpeted extreme market capitalism as a model for the rest of the world, the hands-down winner in global competition among varieties of capitalism. But even before the economic crisis of 2008–09, the American model claimed more credit than it deserved. Although economic growth was often higher in the United States than in Western Europe, the lion's share of growth was captured by those at the top of the income pyramid. Further, lax business regulation and pinched social programs meant that life was more insecure for most Americans compared to citizens in comparable countries elsewhere. Further, part of the reason for America's prosperity has been that Americans spend more time working. For example, the average American works about one-fourth more hours per year than a German worker: 1,817 versus 1,446 hours.[40] Governments in most European countries require employers to provide workers with 3–6 weeks of paid vacations every year. Employers in the United States are not legally obligated to provide paid vacations. Nor are free markets and extensive inequality necessary to obtain the relatively high level of employment found in the United States. Denmark, the Netherlands, and Austria have less inequality and more public services than in the United States, yet they have higher levels of employment.

Whatever the merits of the claim that extreme market capitalism led the pack for generations after World War II, the severe economic recession beginning in 2008 that originated in the United States and quickly spread throughout the globe extensively tarnished the U.S. model. It is now widely agreed that the U.S. model of extreme market capitalism is especially prone to exhibit tendencies toward instability and crisis.

CAPITALIST INSTABILITY AND CRISIS

Instability is a systematic, inherent, and centrally important feature of a capitalist economy. The reason is that, under capitalism, production and exchange (sales) are decentralized. Economic activity consists of countless producers and consumers of goods and services engaging in voluntary sales agreements within the market. The state plays a key role, as we shall see in Chapters 3 and 9, but neither the state nor any other agency directs economic activity. Given the lack of central coordination of economic activity under capitalism, the tendency toward instability—that is, periodic boom and bust, and, at the extreme, recession or even depression—is ever present.

When a recession turns vicious, meaning that the economic collapse is greater and more durable than a recession, it is designated as a depression. Depressions are economic tsunamis that destroy countless businesses, throw large numbers of people out of work, significantly reduce living standards, and destabilize the entire society. The most recent depressions occurred in 1873 and during the 1930s; both lasted over a decade.

In 2008, a severe recession erupted that soon threatened to develop into a full-fledged depression. Each month, another half a million Americans lost their jobs. With over 6 million unemployed, the rate of unemployment climbed above 10 percent, and an additional 6 percent of Americans were forced to work part-time or were not included in unemployment statistics because they gave up job hunting.

Unemployment did not affect all groups equally. Few affluent, educated Americans experienced job loss. For those in the highest tenth of the income pyramid, unemployment was just over 3 percent in 2009. For the next-highest income tenth, it was a slightly higher 4 percent. The unemployment rate for those in the middle third of the class structure (with household incomes of $40,000 to $75,000) was significantly higher—just under 8 percent. However, those at the bottom of the class structure bore the heaviest costs of unemployment. Among the lowest tenth of income earners, unemployment was a staggering 30.8 percent; for the second-lowest tenth, it was 19.1 percent.[41]

While losing a job was among the most damaging effects of the recession, a more than 30 percent decline in the stock market meant that the retirement funds owned by millions of Americans plummeted. Another key element of the recession was the bursting of a housing bubble. Many homeowners (especially those out of work) defaulted on their mortgage payments and lost their homes by foreclosure. Several corporate giants declared bankruptcy; others came close. Even stable financial institutions stopped granting loans to individuals, businesses, and each other because they feared they would not be repaid. Once the credit system became paralyzed, it dragged down the entire economy. In 2008, profits of the Fortune 500 corporations were one-sixth as great as in 2007.

Until September 2008, the recession appeared severe but limited. The economy was kept afloat in part because the government provided substantial funds to prop up some large financial institutions. For example, it took over mortgage giants Fannie Mae and Freddie Mac. However, on September 15, 2008, Treasury Secretary Henry Paulson drew a line in the sand by refusing to bail out faltering investment bank Lehman Brothers. Paulson's decision immediately produced a financial deluge. Wall Street insiders refer to the date as 9/15, a financial counterpart to 9/11. Thomas Priore, chief executive of the hedge fund Institutional Credit Partners, declared, "This is an earth-shattering event, this is a tectonic plate shifting event."[42] Following Paulson's announcement, the stock market plunged 500 points in one day, the largest decline since 9/11. Within days, giant industrial corporations (GM and Chrysler) and financial institutions (Bank of America and Citigroup) came close to following Lehman Brothers to bankruptcy court. (Despite receiving $50 billion in government subsidies, GM eventually was forced to reorganize under the bankruptcy laws.)

The principal cause of the housing crisis was that mortgage lenders—banks, mortgage brokers, and other financial institutions—peddled risky mortgages that fueled a sharp rise in housing prices in the first years of the century and created the illusion that the boom would rise forever. During this period, financial wizards devised three time bombs that exploded beginning in 2007, a year before the crisis spread to other sectors and produced the recession. The first was **subprime mortgages**, that is, high-risk, adjustable rate mortgages sold to people whose income, according to prudent rules of risk management, was inadequate. The result enabled the roller coaster to speed merrily along—until it crashed.

An assistant to a floor trader watches the stock market decline at the New York Stock Exchange, September 15, 2008.

Why should traditionally conservative bankers have hawked incredibly risky subprime mortgages? Because of the second innovation in housing, the practice of **leverage**; that is, borrowing funds at low interest rates and using the loan to purchase securities that appreciated rapidly in value. This made it possible to repay the initial loan, garner a tidy profit, and purchase more securities. Leveraging funds can be highly lucrative—on condition that the newly purchased asset rises in value. If its value falls, leveraging multiplies not profits but losses. And the greater the amount of leveraged funds, the exponentially greater the losses. For decades New Deal banking regulations had limited the extent of bank leverage. However, in Bill Clinton's last days in office, deregulation reforms greatly eased restrictions on leveraging.

The danger posed by leveraging was compounded by the third innovation: **securitization**—the practice of slicing and dicing mortgages, bundling the slices into the mortgage-backed securities just described, and selling these questionable assets to other financial institutions. Even though bundling risky—often worthless—mortgages and selling the toxic asset for a high price only multiplied the risk, the bank could protect itself if it sold the bundled asset quickly.

Mortgage-backed securities were often so complex that it was impossible to calculate their underlying value. But when they are sold like hot potatoes, the incentive to exercise prudence disappears. On the contrary, the more that mortgages can be securitized the better, because profits are linked to the volume of toxic assets that can be sold.

When the bubble eventually burst, the impact reverberated around the world and quickly spread to many other sectors, including investment banking, stock markets, and industrial production. Because in retrospect the causes of the crisis appear shockingly clear, an obvious question is why the crisis was allowed to happen in the first place.

One way to appreciate the logic underpinning what seems so irrational is by describing a gigantic **Ponzi scheme** that made headlines in 2009. In a Ponzi scheme, a con artist hoodwinks victims into investing with the promise of obtaining high returns. Until the bubble bursts, investors are rewarded with returns that seem too good to be true. In fact they *are* too good to be true. To maintain the illusion of success, high "returns" are generated by skimming funds from one investor's account to pay another's. In 2009, Bernard L. Madoff's decades-long scam unraveled, after he had bilked investors of $65 billion. In retrospect, it is clear that Madoff's talent lay not in making shrewd investments but in deceiving wealthy clients into believing that he knew how to make shrewd investments. Rather than investing the funds that he collected, Madoff concocted a shell game to divert colossal funds for his personal enrichment. He and his assistants "generated bogus account statements . . . and created false paper trails for [stock] trades that never occurred."[43] When the economy tanked in 2008 and Madoff could no longer obtain new sources of funds, he confessed, pleaded guilty at his trial, and was sentenced to 150 years in prison.

Although the comparison is imperfect, the complex financial innovations involving subprime mortgages and their securitization resemble a form of Ponzi scheme many times larger than Madoff's, and one that was for the most part entirely legal. A stellar array of financial institutions participated in creating, guaranteeing, and certifying the toxic housing assets, including the nation's largest banks, Citigroup and Bank of America; investment firms Morgan Stanley, Goldman Sachs, and Lehman Brothers; insurance giant American International Group (AIG); mortgage providers Freddie Mac and Fanny Mae; and credit rating agencies Moody's and Standard & Poor. When the bubbles in real estate and finance burst, the amount of assets that evaporated into thin air made Madoff's venture seem puny.

Right after Paulson decided to deny further government assistance to the financial sector, the unthinkable—another depression—became more thinkable by the day. The Bush administration reluctantly reversed course. In late 2008, with the economy in free fall, banks teetering on the brink of ruin, and financial activity screeching to a halt, the Bush administration sponsored a $700 billion financial bailout package and the Federal Reserve Board granted banks virtually interest-free loans, hoping to entice them to use the funds to make loans to revive the stagnant economy. Barack Obama went even further when he took office in 2009. We describe the government's economic crisis management in Chapters 3 and 9. The costliest government handout in U.S. history helped prevent the worst recession for over half a century from morphing into a depression.

The government's bailout poses a puzzle. A central feature of America's extreme market capitalism is that government protects the functioning of markets at a general level by developing and enforcing rules of the economic game, but it does not become a player in the game by intervening in its day-to-day operations. Yet how then to explain that Republican and Democratic administrations alike sponsored government interventions of this kind by providing immense sums to private firms?

From the perspective of the Oval Office, the choice came down to which alternative was the lesser of two evils: to maintain ideological convictions at the cost of the collapse of capitalism, or to violate ideological convictions in order to rescue capitalism from its own mistakes. When forced to choose—and both presidents Bush and Obama decided they could not avoid choosing—the decision was a no-brainer. A lesson to take away from this crisis is that government's hands-off relationship to the capitalist economy is shelved when capitalism is in jeopardy. The government's action also clearly demonstrated that, despite the claims by cheerleaders for capitalism that the economic system is self-regulating, markets can self-destruct when left to their own devices.

At the same time, the bailout package had its critics. Joseph Stiglitz described it as "America's Socialism for the Rich" and a "new form of ersatz capitalism, in which losses are socialized and profits privatized. . . . The too-big-to-be-restructured banks know that they can gamble with impunity."[44] According to Stiglitz, "America has expanded its corporate safety net in unprecedented ways, from commercial banks to investment banks, then to insurance, and now to automobiles, with no end in sight. In truth, this is not socialism, but an extension of long standing corporate welfarism." He attributed the lack of aggressive financial reform to the fact that banks "are too politically powerful. Their lobbying efforts worked well, first to deregulate, and then to have taxpayers pay for the cleanup." In a similar vein, Paul Krugman described government assistance to banks as "Bailouts for Bunglers."[45] In his view, the government "seems to believe that once investors calm down, securitization—and the business of finance—can resume where they left off a year or two ago. . . . But the underlying vision remains that of a financial system, more or less the same."[46]

Those who defended the government's actions countered that, disasteful as it might be, the government had no choice but to provide emergency assistance to the financial sector, given that the alternative was financial collapse. In this view, the government was correct in tamping down the fire first and taking time next to craft appropriate measures aimed at preventing future fires. Which side is proved correct largely depends on whether the enormous sums that government provided to shore up the financial system are followed by substantial regulatory reforms that minimize the chance of a similar crisis occurring again. This key issue is analyzed in Chapters 3 and 9.

CONCLUSION

Capitalism does not simply distribute money and wealth unequally. It also distributes economic power unequally. Although globalization and technological change have increased competition and the pace of change, a small elite of corporate executives and large shareholders own and control the means of production, have power over the working lives of their employees, and make decisions that have far-reaching consequences for the entire society. Capitalists decide whether to invest, where to invest, and what to invest in based on what will yield the greatest profit, not the greatest good. Moreover, their economic wealth and power enable them to wield great political influence that produces a mobilization of bias in their favor. Business enjoys a structural advantage based on the fact that the welfare of the community depends on business prosperity.

At the same time, the short-term interests of business may collide with the interests of groups in the community. There is thus both harmony and conflict between business firms and other groups. When conflicts occur, the results depend on a host of factors, including how unified capitalists are and the extent of popular opposition that they encounter. Mobilization from below can mitigate and counteract the power of business.

Below the group at the top of the economic pyramid is a workforce divided between professional, technical, and educated employees who are relatively well compensated, and poorly paid service sector and manufacturing workers. The chapter argues that the American form of capitalism, that we describe as extreme market capitalism, is characterized by managerial autonomy, weak unions, small government, and relatively unregulated markets. The result has been increased economic instability. An extreme instance was the severe recession of 2008–09. The government's actions during the recession amply demonstrate that the relationship of government to the economy is not simply one of hands off. Chapter 3 describes the paradox of how extreme market capitalism developed in the United States at the same time that government has often intervened extensively to assist capitalist development.

CHAPTER SUMMARY

Introduction

There is a fundamental tension between the democratic organization of the political sphere and the undemocratic character of a market-based or capitalist system of production. Historical experience in the United States and elsewhere demonstrates that capitalism has a unique capacity to efficiently produce goods and services that are desired by consumers. It has also displayed an extraordinary ability to promote technological innovation, material well-being, and economic growth. Markets encourage dynamism, initiative, productivity, and efficiency.

The Dilemmas of Markets

Markets also exhibit a variety of questionable features. These include a tendency to impose socially harmful costs on the society (that is, externalities) and the need to constantly expand in order to obtain a return on invested capital, thus straining the ecosystem. Other harmful features include the periodic recurrence of cycles of boom and bust, and an inherently authoritarian organization of the workplace.

The System of Corporate Capitalism

Capitalism can be considered a system of private government. A small and undemocratically chosen group exercises substantial ownership and control over the American economy. It controls a range of vitally important economic decisions that affect the fundamental welfare of the society, including whether to invest productive resources (capital), where to invest, what to invest in, and how production is organized.

The Mobilization of Bias

There is a structural bias, what we term the mobilization of bias, inherent in a system of corporate capitalism. Business firms enjoy a unique political advantage because the entire society is dependent on companies to provide jobs, products, and services. By virtue of controlling the economy, business firms possess immense power to affect the well-being of all members of the society. This provides them with unique political leverage. The result is that the political playing field is tilted to give special consideration to the needs and demands of business.

The Changing Landscape of American Capitalism

The system of corporate capitalism involves an immense concentration of wealth and power. In the current period, one can identify two opposite tendencies. On the one hand, corporate growth and mergers among giant corporations have produced increased economic concentration. On the other hand, globalization and technological changes have opened markets, promoted greater competition among firms in many industries, and increased the opportunity for small startup firms to achieve breakthroughs.

Who Owns America's Private Government?

The ownership of corporate stock and the distribution of income and wealth in the United States are highly concentrated. As a result, a small minority of Americans, most of whom are in the corporate and financial sector, own and control a vastly disproportionate share of economic resources in the United States. Members of this small group are predominantly white, they are united by informal social ties, and their interests are further promoted by formal organizations such as trade associations and interest groups.

The Changing Structure of Employment

There have been vast changes in the structure of employment in the last two centuries. Many Americans were initially employed on farms. Industrial development involved the recruitment of large numbers of native-born and immigrant Americans for unskilled or semi-skilled jobs. A shift to a service economy has produced a reduction in manufacturing jobs and economic hardship for those with meager skills and education. The growth sectors in service employment involve low-paid sales and clerical jobs. A far smaller number of highly paid jobs are found in the financial and corporate management sector. These changes in the structure of employment have been accompanied by a sharp increase in economic inequality in the twenty-first century as the corporate and financial elite have reaped the lion's share of national income and gains from economic growth.

America's Extreme Market Capitalism

The American variant of capitalism is unusual compared to most wealthy capitalist economies and is characterized by three interrelated features. First, the public sector is smaller in the United States and the sphere of markets is larger. This is a result of weak labor unions and a lack of political parties promoting expansive social services. Second, government has historically regulated capitalism less than is the case elsewhere. One result is that financial firms and corporations have been free to devise exceptionally risky ventures to amass wealth. The most recent scheme, involving the creation and securitization of subprime mortgages, fueled the severe recession of 2008–09. Third, capitalism is especially pervasive in American social life.

Capitalist Instability and Crisis

Because the capitalist system of production is decentralized (that is, there is no single agency to coordinate the production of goods and services with demand), there is a built-in tendency toward boom-and-bust, or instability. This tendency is intensified when government regulation is lax, which partially explains the severe economic recession that occurred in the United States in 2008–09. The recession began with the bursting of "bubbles" (excessive expansion) in the housing and financial sectors, a natural result of using questionable methods to artificially maximize profits. The crisis soon spread to the entire economic system as large banks and corporations teetered on the edge of collapse and unemployment soared. What stabilized the economy was the federal government's decision to abandon its limited role and to spend massive amounts of cash to rescue the financial sector and stimulate the economy.

Critical Thinking Questions

1. Do you agree that capitalism is a "system of private government?" In what ways does it differ from public government?

2. Should government have provided large public funds to bail out the banks in the 2008–09 financial crisis? What are the pros and cons of its decision to do so?

3. Identify two ways that the American economic system can be characterized as an extreme form of capitalism. What are some advantages and disadvantages of this form?

Suggested Readings

Peter Bachrach and Morton S. Baratz, *Power and Poverty: Theory and Practice.* New York: Oxford University Press, 1970.

Peter A. Hall and David Soskice, eds., *Varieties of Capitalism: The Institutional Foundations of Comparative Advantage.* New York: Oxford University Press, 2001.

Lawrence R. Jacobs and Theda Skocpol, eds., *Inequality and American Democracy: What We Know and What We Need to Learn.* New York: Russell Sage, 2005.

David Cay Johnston, *Free Lunch: How the Wealthiest Americans Enrich Themselves at Government Expense (And Stick You with the Bill).* New York: Portfolio/Penguin, 2007.

Paul Krugman, *The Conscience of a Liberal.* New York: Norton, 2007.

Paul Krugman, *The Return of Depression Economics and the Crisis of 2008.* New York: Norton, 2009.

Charles E. Lindblom, *Politics and Markets: The World's Political-Economic Systems.* New York: Basic Books, 1977.

Robert Pollin, *Contours of Descent: U.S. Economic Fractures and the Landscape of Global Austerity.* London: Verso, 2005.

Robert B. Reich, *Supercapitalism: The Transformation of Business, Democracy, and Everyday Life.* New York: Knopf, 2007.

Andrew Ross Sorkin, *Too Big to Fail: The Inside Story of How Wall Street and Washington Fought to Save the Financial System—and Themselves.* New York: Viking, 2009.

Joseph E. Stiglitz, *Freefall: America, Free Markets, and the Sinking of the World Economy.* New York: Norton, 2010.

3

THE HISTORY OF AMERICAN POLITICAL ECONOMY

INTRODUCTION

In Chapter 2 we described how capitalism creates a mobilization of bias that gives the corporate elite a decisive advantage. Ownership and control of the means of production give it the power to manage the workforce, organize production, make investment decisions, and retain profits. These decisions, made in corporate boardrooms and not by elected public officials, are beyond the reach of democratic decision making. Yet politicians have a stake in such decisions; their reelection depends on them because corporate control over investment, employment, production, and plant location affect whether incomes grow, jobs are available, and standards of living increase. If voters' economic conditions deteriorate, politicians risk being repudiated at the polls. Consequently, politicians try to promote their own career goals by encouraging investment through offering inducements and incentives to corporations.

This chapter examines the development of the relationship between the American state and corporate capitalism. By *state*, we mean the totality of public institutions that form the government of a country. The core of the state is the executive—in the United States, the president, the office of the president, and the executive branch or bureaucracy along with the military. But the state also includes Congress, the courts, and, in a federal system such as ours, state and local governments.[1]

Capitalism is often described as a system in which production for private profit is organized and coordinated through markets that are free of political direction. But the free market has always been a fiction. Markets cannot exist without a government to maintain order, enforce contracts, create currency, and provide a host of other public goods. To function, markets require a protective, facilitating political order.

Even in the United States, where the government's role within the economy has been less extensive than elsewhere, the government has been deeply implicated in the economy from the very start. Soon after the founding of the United States, following ratification of the Constitution in the late eighteenth century, state and local governments developed a commercial code and legal framework to bring order and stability to economic activity, created a common currency to facilitate trade and exchange, employed a military and police to secure property and markets, financed the building of roads and bridges to facilitate production and trade, and provided rudimentary social services. As capitalism matured, the different forms of government assistance increased. The invisible hand of the market has always been supplemented and supported by the visible hand of the state.

The relationship between the state and market-based production for private profit (or capitalism) is especially complicated in those countries, such as the United States, where capitalist production exists alongside democratic political institutions. A tension may exist between capitalism, an economic system based on profits for the few, and democracy, a political system based on democratic rights for the many.[2]

The way in which this tension between capitalism and democracy is managed at any given time depends on the outcome of political struggles. Farmers and industrialists, workers and employers, men and women, whites and minorities, the South and the North, have each tried to impose their vision of the proper balance between capitalism and democracy. Nor have members of these groups always defined their interests similarly or been unified politically. Some corporate managers support regulation of their industries; others oppose it. Some whites support affirmative action; others oppose it. And the politics of power extends beyond the issue of whether the government should intervene to also include struggles over what institutions of government should be responsible, what policies they should follow, and who should benefit. The politics of power includes struggles not only over "how much" government is needed but also over what it should do, which branches and agencies should do it, and which interests they should serve.

Although the result of these political conflicts is uncertain, some groups have had more power to prevail than others. Over the course of American history, business has been unusually successful in these struggles. It has limited the government's ability to influence the behavior of private firms, shaped the institutions through which intervention would occur, and influenced the policies those institutions would implement.

But under popular pressure, state policy has sometimes diverged from business interests. At different junctures, farmers, workers, and environmentalists and other groups have risen up to challenge business successfully and required the government to adopt policies that regulate markets for the public interest and promote more equitable results. Indeed, one can discern periodic swings throughout American history in which the power of business has ebbed and flowed, and the government has supported and limited the play of free markets. Since the 1930s, as we describe in more detail later, there have been three major swings of the pendulum, the latest of which began in 2008 in response to the deepest and fastest economic decline since the 1930s.

The pendulum first swung in favor of a more expansive role for government during the 1930s in response to the Great Depression. Under Democratic Party control, the government's size and scope increased enormously from the 1930s through the 1970s. The initial enthusiasm and justification for this expansion of government occurred in response to the Great Depression of the 1930s. President Franklin Delano Roosevelt's **New Deal** created the outlines of the modern welfare state to cope with the distress. This was followed by the government's enormous success in managing and coordinating the transition to a wartime economy during World War II. Prosperity followed in the 1950s and 1960s as the standard of living increased for many Americans. But the formula for success that the government followed was exhausted by the 1970s, which saw unemployment and **inflation** take their toll on living standards.

Economic decline created an opening for Republican Party political success that began with Ronald Reagan's presidency in the 1980s. Under Republican Party rule, the pendulum swung in the opposite direction. Government was condemned as the problem, not the solution. Markets needed to be freed from unnecessary government regulations and taxes needed to be cut. Corporate managers needed to be given more autonomy to respond to a fast-changing and global marketplace. Groups seeking to restrict market forces in order to defend the environment, help the less affluent, protect consumers, and safeguard the interests of workers were thrown on the defensive. But faith in the self-correcting and beneficent nature of the market dissipated in the first decade of the twenty-first century when the worst economic crisis since the Great Depression hit, leaving a tidal wave of home foreclosures, massive unemployment, and innumerable bank failures in its wake.

The deep recession that began in 2008 initiated another swing of the pendulum and another switch in political power. The Democratic Party captured control of the presidency and expanded majorities in both the House of Representatives and the Senate in the 2008 elections. Moreover, the government responded aggressively to the economic crisis. Government was no longer regarded as the problem, but the solution. It guaranteed loans to assure panicked creditors, bought bad debts from banks to repair their balance sheets, arranged marriages between sick and healthy banks to stabilize the banking system, and made loans available when firms could not get credit from normal sources. The federal government now owns stakes in the biggest banks, guarantees half the mortgages in the country, controls one of the biggest insurance companies in the world, and is the major stockholder in General Motors.

In this chapter, we study the state's changing relationship to the economy. In each instance, economic crisis and political change initiated a new policy paradigm that realigned the relationship between government and the economy and created different winners and losers. We detail this relationship from the early days of the Republic, in which government prepared the ground for capitalist production, to the present, in which government collects the debris after capitalism fails.

COMPETITIVE CAPITALISM

The first expansionary phase in American history, starting in the 1840s, was based on a revolution in transportation.[3] New roadways, canals, and railroads allowed farmers in the Ohio and Mississippi valleys to ship their products more quickly to seaboard cities like New York, Baltimore, and Philadelphia. Shipping midwestern grain to New York by wagon took almost two months; by canal, it took three weeks; by rail, it took just seven days.[4] Regional and even national markets in labor and commodities soon developed as a result of these efficiencies in transportation. In addition, railroad construction required massive inputs of labor and material, which also propelled the entire economy forward.

But the revolution in transportation would not have had the impact it did without a powerful helping hand from government. Almost a century ago one historian wrote that, despite popular images of the United States as "the land of private enterprise *par excellence;* the place where 'State interference' has played the smallest part, and individual enterprise has been given the largest scope, it is a fact that this country was one of the first to exhibit the modern tendency to extend the activity of the State into industry."[5] The mistaken impression of minimal state interference in the economy persists because people often look for the state in the wrong place. *State governments*, far more than the federal government, were involved in shaping the contours of the pre–Civil War political economy.[6]

Nowhere was the influence of state governments more apparent than in their contribution to railroad development. For example, a number of state governments built and operated railroads themselves or invested heavily in privately owned railroads. State and local governments financed almost 30 percent of the more than $1 billion invested in railroads before the Civil War. In addition, state governments regulated railroads through charters they issued to private railroad companies, appointments to railroad commissions, and the railroad rates they set.[7]

During this classic era of **competitive capitalism**, when small firms competed in local markets, the federal government's role was quite limited. Political scientist Stephen Skowronek found that "[t]he national government throughout the nineteenth century routinely provided promotional and support services for the state governments and left the substantive tasks of governing to these regional units."[8] The national government's jurisdiction in economic matters was limited basically to establishing tariff policy and banking and monetary policy, managing public lands, collecting taxes, and maintaining order.

The activities pursued by state and national government in the early nineteenth century were essential to creating a framework within which business could grow. They challenge the common belief that, before the twentieth century, government did little to influence the economy. But the economic role governments played in the early nineteenth century paled in comparison to the range and level of activity that governments pursued later in that century, as they tried to respond to the challenges posed by industrialization, the rise of corporate capitalism, and economic instability.

The first wave of economic expansion, which was initiated by the transportation revolution, ended in 1873. Prices fell 25 percent throughout the last quarter of the nineteenth century as fierce competition drove entrepreneurs to introduce new, efficient production methods in an attempt to cut costs and prices. The downturn initiated a wave of business consolidations and acquisitions, creating large corporations that could dominate their markets. Citizens were at the mercy of these corporations, forced to accept the wages they offered and the prices they charged. Labor historian Melvin Dubofsky quotes a Pennsylvania coal miner who lamented: "The working people of this country . . . find monopolies as strong as government itself. They find capital as rigid as absolute monarchy. They find their so-called independence a myth."[9]

These grievances soon found expression in organized political movements. In the 1870s, farmers mobilized through the Farmers Alliance and the Grange to put pressure on state legislatures and on Congress to demand fairer rates from the railroads. Workers also mobilized in what became known as the Great Uprising of 1877. Railway workers from Baltimore to San Francisco struck to protest wage cuts. Local governments were either sympathetic to the workers' demands or overwhelmed by their protests, which led the federal government to dispatch troops to crush the first national strike in U.S. history. At the same time that workers manned picket lines, farmers in the South and the West joined the Populist Party. The Populists challenged both major political parties and criticized their ties to banks and large corporations.

All of these disparate movements opposed the growth of large corporations able to dominate their markets at the expense of farmers, workers, and consumers. They shared a belief in equality; a sense that labor, not capital, created wealth; a fear that big business and their Wall Street financiers had captured political power; and an optimism that the majority could tame the corrupting influence of capital.

Although these broad-based social movements failed to capture government from the capitalists they believed had usurped it, they did leave a legacy. First, these movements left a local heritage of radicalism, which later generations could draw on. For example, in the 1900s, the Socialist Party garnered remarkable support from farmers in the Southwest because it could draw on an earlier tradition of populism in the region.[10] Second, the political program of these groups became the basis for later reforms of the Progressive period, which sought to restrain corporate capitalism.[11] Finally, these movements created an alternative to the dominant culture of competitive individualism—one based on the dignity of labor, the benefits of a rough equality, the value of solidarity, as well as the the virtues of self-sufficiency.[12]

THE RISE OF CORPORATE CAPITALISM

By 1900, small firms that existed in competitive markets were steadily being driven out of business or were capitulating by combining with larger firms. "American industry is not free," Princeton professor and later president Woodrow Wilson wrote, because "the man with only a little capital is finding it harder to get into the field, more and more impossible to compete with the big fellow. Why? Because the laws of this country do not prevent the strong from crushing the weak."[13] The result was a wave of corporate mergers and greater industrial concentration. By 1904, a total of 318 corporations held 40 percent of all U.S. manufacturing assets. The House of Morgan alone held 341 directorships in 112 corporations with a net worth totaling

$22 billion, more than twice the assessed value of all property in the states of the Old Confederacy.

What is called the Progressive era, from 1900 to 1916, marked a profound change in the American political economy. The rise of trusts—large corporations that had the raw power to dominate their markets and exploit consumers, farmers, and employees—generated popular demands for government action. In the past, state governments had intervened in the economy to *promote* business. Now citizens demanded that the federal government intervene to *regulate* it. President Theodore Roosevelt articulated the view of many citizens when he argued that if "this irresponsible outside power is to be controlled in the interest of the general public, it can be controlled in only one way—by giving adequate power of control . . . to the National Government."[14] Under popular pressure, the federal government assumed increased responsibility for regulating business activity, but in a distinctively American way that avoided big government and retained a great deal of freedom for corporations.[15] Rather than closely scrutinizing corporate behavior as many demanded, the federal government would simply prohibit corporations from engaging in what was described as "unreasonable restraint of trade," such as price fixing. Hence, firms would continue to enjoy a free hand, and government's role would be limited to preventing unfair business practices.[16]

Government intervention in the economy substantially increased during World War I (1917–19) because of the pressing need to mobilize all available resources. The federal government formed tripartite committees, composed of representatives from business, labor, and the government, to develop policy that would coordinate production for the war effort. Although highly successful, the tripartite committees were disbanded at business's insistence when the war ended. In the ensuing prosperity of the 1920s, national income rose throughout the decade. But it rose faster for those at the top of the income scale than it did for those at the bottom. Despite the boom, a majority of families did not have sufficient income to reach "the American standard," a modestly defined measure of minimum comfort, and almost one-quarter of all families lived in severe poverty.[17]

The Roaring Twenties ended on October 21, 1929, when the stock market crashed. The Dow Jones Industrial Average, a barometer of the entire market, lost half its value in just two weeks. The "era of good feelings" was replaced first by gloom and then by despair. Unemployment rose steadily, from 4 million in January 1930 to 6 million by November and then to 8 million by the following January. Employers increased the distress by cutting wages. Each line of defense against poverty—first, family savings; next, private charities; and then state and local government relief programs—was overwhelmed by the demands for help placed upon it. Meanwhile, Republican President Herbert Hoover stubbornly remained faithful to the prevailing economic orthodoxy, which claimed that the government should not engage in spending and active policies to lift the economy out of depression.

The depth and persistence of the Depression undermined people's faith in capitalism, in capitalists, and in the government. Bread lines, soup kitchens, and millions of unemployed led people to demand large-scale change. Farmers struck, refusing to bring their crops to market because

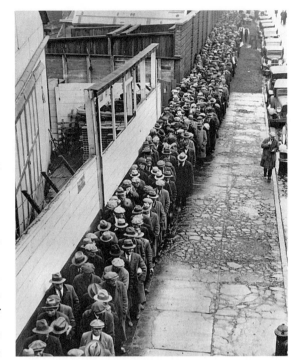

A long line of jobless men in New York City waiting for a free dinner during the Great Depression.

prices had dropped below production costs. Workers in the great manufacturing centers began to organize into unions. General strikes closed down San Francisco and Minneapolis. Rubber workers in Akron, Ohio, and autoworkers in Flint, Michigan, held sit-down strikes and occupied factories until their demands for union recognition were met. A group of unions broke away from the conservative American Federation of Labor (AFL) to organize unskilled workers in mass production industries into a new, more militant labor federation called the Congress of Industrial Organizations (CIO). By the end of the thirties, unions affiliated with the CIO boasted over 3.6 million members.

A NEW DEAL

From one end of the country to the other, from farms to factories, people demanded change. In 1932, a new electoral coalition of working people, Catholics, Jews, and southerners elected Democratic candidate Franklin Delano Roosevelt as president. In dramatic contrast to President Hoover's dithering,

Roosevelt boldly promised a New Deal. He proposed that the government devise measures to end the Depression, provide relief, and manage the economy to restore growth. Roosevelt was not hostile to capitalism but believed that greater management by the federal government was required to save it. But as the Depression was superseded by a new emergency—World War II—a subtle but significant shift in prevailing economic ideas occurred. The Roosevelt administration's priorities shifted from promoting growth through greater state intervention to promoting growth through increasing consumption.

This new economic paradigm, in which consumption drove the economy, was based on ideas first developed by the British economist John Maynard Keynes. Keynes claimed that the major cause of the Depression was inadequate consumer demand. The economy was caught in a vicious circle in which mass unemployment reduced the demand for goods. As inventories piled up for lack of consumers to purchase them, firms laid off even more workers. To break the destructive cycle, government would have to step into the breach. By running a deficit in the federal budget—spending more than it collected in taxes— government would increase the amount of money in circulation and thereby increase demand. Once people had money to spend again, business would react to the new consumer demand by rehiring workers and stepping up production. With workers back on the job earning and spending wages, demand would grow and the economic recovery would become self-sustaining. Thus, Keynes argued, deficit spending by the government in times of slack demand was the key to transforming vicious circles of stagnation into virtuous circles of growth.

Corporations frightened by the potential radicalism of the New Deal found Roosevelt's new emphasis on increasing consumption preferable to earlier, more ambitious New Deal proposals. Budget deficits required no change in the distribution of economic power between government and business, whereas the initial proposals had involved more sweeping structural reforms such as government planning. According to historian Alan Brinkley, New Dealers now spoke less about redistributing economic power and more about increasing mass purchasing power.[18]

In many ways, the Depression and World War II emergencies represented a missed opportunity to regulate private economic power.[19] More structural changes were considered but eventually lost out in favor of the less threatening solution to use government to stimulate demand. That these more radical proposals were discarded in no way minimizes the substantial changes that took place. For example, the outlines of the welfare state were forged during the New Deal, offering citizens some protection against the swings of the business cycle. Unemployment insurance and Social Security created at least a minimal safety net where none existed previously. The labor market also came in for a degree of regulation as child labor was outlawed and a minimum wage law was passed. Labor unions grew from 3 million members in 1929 to 14 million by 1945, offering workers some protection against the unilateral power of management. The federal government also grew. Federal expenditures that were just 3 percent of the gross domestic product (GDP) in 1929 were 10 percent of GDP a decade later. The number of federal employees almost doubled in the same ten-year period. The growth of the welfare state, unions, and the federal government were consolidated after World War II and were accepted as legitimate by most Democrats and Republicans until the 1970s.

Significant as these changes were, when set against comparable developments that occurred in Europe, we see how they might have gone even further. Although the federal government emerged from World War II owning 40 percent of all capital assets in the United States, there was no vigorous push to nationalize such basic industries as telecommunications, airlines, utilities, railways, and steel as occurred in many European countries. In addition, the government applied the most conservative form of **Keynesianism** possible. For example, Keynes believed that full employment was essential to increasing aggregate—total—demand. Consistent with this belief, President Truman (who replaced President Roosevelt when the latter died in office) submitted the Full Employment Act to Congress in 1945, just two weeks after the end of World War II. However, conservatives in Congress proceeded to dilute the bill beyond recognition, even removing the term *Full* from what was now simply called the Employment Act.[20] Keynes also believed that some kind of redistribution of income from the top to the bottom was required. He identified as one of the "outstanding faults of the [capitalist] economic society in which we live . . . its arbitrary and inequitable distribution of wealth."[21] But Keynes's prescription to redistribute wealth was rejected in America. Welfare state spending was lower and less redistributive in the United States than in Europe. Finally, the conservative form Keynesianism took in the United States was evident in the way it ran deficits. Both Democratic and Republican administrations chose to pursue deficit spending through cutting taxes rather than increasing expenditures.[22] Demand would be stimulated through increasing private consumption as opposed to promoting public goods. And even when the government did prop up demand through spending, it did so disproportionately through increasing military as opposed to welfare state outlays.

In brief, a conservative form of Keynesianism became the new economic orthodoxy following the war, accepted not only by Democrats but eventually by Republicans as well. The American version of Keynesianism included only a symbolic commitment to full employment; economic stimulation through military spending, not redistribution; and deficit spending through tax cuts, not public investment. When recast in this form, even business, which was initially hostile to Keynesianism, came to appreciate its benefits. Although the Democratic Party was the first to embrace Keynesianism, by the 1970s even Republican President Richard Nixon could declare, "We are all Keynesians now."[23]

THE RISE AND FALL OF THE GOLDEN AGE

Many feared that the economy would slide back into recession once the artificial stimulus of World War II was removed. Instead, the United States experienced the most prosperous twenty-five years in its history, often dubbed the **golden age** of capitalism. Median family income almost doubled between 1950 and 1970. As historian Jack Metzgar recalls in his memoir of the period, the affluence of the postwar years was "new, and surprising—like a first kiss."[24] Urban working families moved out of tenements and acquired new homes in the suburbs. Televisions, cars, washing machines, and telephones—beyond the reach of most families in 1940—were now owned by a majority of families just twenty years later.

The success of the U.S. economy can be attributed to an unusual coincidence of national and international factors that distinguish this period from what came before—and after. First, pent-up consumer demand fueled the postwar economy. Production for the war effort restricted the supply of consumer goods at the same time that it put people to work and money in their pockets. The combination of disposable income and pent-up demand led Americans to spend freely once wartime controls were lifted.

Second, the huge demand for consumer goods led businesses to expand capacity and invest in new plants and equipment. Third, labor relations simmered down following the 1946 strike wave, the largest in American history. Employers did not fully accept the legitimacy of unions but now resentfully acknowledged them as a fact of life they could not avoid. Fourth, big government contributed to the new affluence. Government spending climbed steadily from $47.1 billion in 1950, or 21 percent of GDP, to $236.1 billion by 1970, or almost 27 percent of GDP. Big government was not a drag on economic growth during the golden age of capitalism but, rather, was essential to it.

Finally, the postwar economy profited from the emergence of U.S. global dominance. American firms were busy not only satisfying the voracious appetite of American consumers but also supplying war-torn Europe with food and clothes as well as equipment and other supplies to rebuild its devastated economies. Moreover, American firms had the world market to themselves. The only potential competitors, in Europe and Japan, were heavily damaged from World War II and needed to devote their resources to wartime recovery.

By mid-century, the terms of the informal national bargain that had been struck between business and government were clear. Strategic decisions governing the American economy—how much to invest, where to invest, what to invest in, how to organize the work—would be made by corporate capital. Government would not intrude on corporate decision making or engage in economic planning that might interfere with business's right to manage. Instead, by smoothing out the business cycle, educating workers, stimulating consumption, funding research, and protecting corporate markets and investments abroad, government would create a political and economic environment that would encourage corporate investment and job creation.[25]

Over the course of the 1970s, however, prosperity waned as the economy began to experience **stagflation**, an unprecedented situation in which unemployment and inflation occurred simultaneously. In the past, unemployment and inflation moved in opposite directions. Now they both rose together. The average rate of unemployment was 6.2 percent in the 1970s, compared to just 4.8 percent in the 1960s. The inflation record was even worse. The exceptional conditions that so clearly favored American firms in the golden age crumbled. For example, European and Japanese industry, which were in ruins following World War II, had been rebuilt and could now compete with American manufacturers in world markets.

Symptomatic of America's economic decline was slower productivity growth, which squeezed profits. Managers tried to restore productivity growth and relieve the profit squeeze by coercing employees to work harder for less money. Business threatened to close plants if unions did not agree to wage and work rule concessions in collective bargaining. Meanwhile, business engaged in old-fashioned union busting to reassert managerial control and speed up work. In 1978, Auto Workers President Douglas Fraser bitterly charged, "I believe leaders of the business community, with few exceptions, have chosen to wage a one-sided class war in this country—a war against working people, the unemployed, the poor, the minorities, the very young and the very old, even many in the middle class of our society. The leaders of industry, commerce, and finance in the U.S. have broken and discarded the fragile, unwritten contract previously existing during a period of growth and progress."[26]

Conservative Keynesianism collapsed in the 1970s, defeated by unemployment, inflation, lower productivity growth, and rising trade deficits. The end of growth undermined confidence in the Democratic Party and discredited its formula of conservative Keynesianism. A new economic paradigm articulated by a resurgent Republican Party would soon replace Keynesian orthodoxy.

THE RISE OF EXTREME MARKET CAPITALISM, 1980–2008

In 1980, American voters, battered by stagflation and polarized by race, turned to the Republican Party and elected Ronald Reagan as president. Reagan was at the forefront of a new majority coalition that articulated a new economic philosophy—what we call extreme market capitalism. In the previous era, government intervention was regarded as useful in reducing inequality, policing corporate behavior, and stabilizing the business cycle; but the burden of proof had shifted. Now free markets were regarded as appropriate and beneficial, and government oversight of them was perceived as inefficient and illegitimate. Even Bill Clinton, the only Democrat elected president during the period of extreme market capitalism, declared approvingly in his 1996 State of the Union address to the country, "The era of big government is over."

The Republican Party practiced extreme market capitalism, which is premised on the faith that markets are rational, self-correcting, and beneficial. That is, that prices set by markets reflect the actual value of what goods and assets are worth (rational); that the business cycle has been tamed and government regulation is unnecessary (self-correcting); and that the results of leaving markets alone to work their magic are good for society (beneficial).

The shift from conservative Keynesianism to extreme market capitalism required two policy changes. First, prosperity would no longer depend on the welfare of workers whose wages propelled aggregate demand, as was the case with conservative Keynesianism. Now, according to the new theory of supply-side economics, prosperity would depend on the welfare of the affluent, whose savings supplied the capital for investment.

Supply-side economics argued that the economy suffered from insufficient investment capital, not insufficient demand. To boost the supply of investment capital, Republicans proposed to cut taxes—most of all for the rich. Those who needed tax relief the least received the most, on the premise that they were more likely to save and contribute to the stock of capital needed for investment.

Supply-side economists forecast that the powerful growth resulting from tax cuts would increase tax revenue despite the cut in tax rates. Campaigning against Reagan in the Republican primaries in 1980, George H. W. Bush dismissed this as "voodoo economics." But he joined Reagan's administration as his vice president to pass one of the largest tax cuts in American history. His son, George

W. Bush, became president in 2000 and soon passed a tax cut that even surpassed that of President Reagan. George W. Bush's 2001 tax cut reduced revenue by $1.4 trillion through 2010 and reserved the lion's share of the savings for the rich, thanks to lower tax rates on high incomes and elimination of the estate tax. Then, in 2005, millionaires received 44 percent of the tax relief from President Bush's next round of tax cuts, while 6.5 million taxpayers earning less than $20,000 received no tax breaks at all.

Tax cuts were supposed to have political, as well as economic, advantages. First, they rewarded the wealthy, a base of the Republican Party. But the political consequences of tax cuts go beyond a crass payoff to loyalists. Tax cuts were also intended to impose fiscal restraint on the government, to starve the government of the funds it needed to pursue policies that offered an alternative to the marketplace. With less money coming in, the government would have less to spend. If government did not reduce spending, deficits would result, which would also discourage spending. Increased outlays for programs that have more demands placed on them (such as medical care for the aged) or new programs to address new challenges (such as homeland security) appear fiscally irresponsible when the budget is in deficit. Either way, whether lower taxes led to lower spending or to deficits, the goal was the same as one supply-sider revealed: to reduce "the size and scale of government by draining its lifeblood," by starving government of the funds it needed.[27]

Finally, tax cuts were politically valuable because the Republicans could use them to reward voters and bind them to the party, just as Democrats before them had used spending programs to pay off its supporters. Republicans had previously posed as defenders of fiscal responsibility, criticizing reckless Democratic spending programs that produced deficits and created liabilities that future generations would have to pay. But Republicans were now determined to beat Democrats at their own game. Balanced budgets, they now believed, "were for chumps."[28] Democratic Party bidding for votes based on which party could spend more would be replaced by the new Republican standard of bidding for votes based on which party could offer voters more tax breaks.

Alongside tax cuts, Republicans adopted a policy of **deregulation** that was also intended to shift the paradigm. They argued that regulations such as environmental standards and consumer protections needed to be rolled back if business was going to compete in a fast, global marketplace. Deregulation would restore business's right to manage without being hampered by expensive, burdensome rules. Republicans pursued deregulaton by cutting agency budgets to reduce their effectiveness. For example, from 2000 to 2007, when the Republicans controlled Congress and the presidency, funding for the Environmental Protection Agency (EPA) declined by $1.3 billion, or 15 percent of its budget.

As a result, the EPA could not do enough inspections to ensure that environmental standards were followed or develop new rules to keep pace with new pollutants.

Deregulation also proceeded by greater White House oversight of new rules that agencies proposed. Rules had to pass cost-benefit analysis stress tests administered by the White House before being approved. The White House also developed procedures designed to frustrate new regulations by permitting industry at any point along the rulemaking process to question the data agencies used in support of them. Finally, deregulation proceeded through appointment in which the foxes were invited to guard the chickens; that is, people who were opposed to the mission of regulatory agencies were appointed to direct them. In 1981 President Reagan appointed James Watt to direct the EPA. Watt's previous post was founder of the Mountain States Legal Foundation, which frequently sued the EPA on behalf of industry. More recently, under President George W. Bush, Gib Mullan was appointed head of the Office of Compliance for the Consumer Product Safety Commission. Mullan previously served as a lawyer in private practice and had defended General Motors against claims that fuel tanks on its pickup trucks exploded.

WHAT DO YOU THINK?

Which Poses the Greater Danger: Market Failure or Political Failure?

Some people believe that society benefits when governments intervene in the economy, as occurred under the Democrats and their policies of conservative Keynesianism; others believe that society suffers when the government intervenes and we are better off following the Republican model of extreme market capitalism. Those in the former group believe that government intervention is necessary to protect society from market failure. Left alone, the market leads to too much inequality and too much neglect of the public good. The latter group believes that government intervention leads to political failure. Left alone, politicans will spend recklessly to attract voters and invest in projects with the biggest political, not economic, payoffs. Does government intervention yield better results for citizens than free markets? What criteria should be used to evaluate whether more government is preferable to more markets?

Extreme market capitalism pursued through tax cuts and deregulation had three significant outcomes. First, it created large budget deficits in which the government spent more than it received in taxes. During the period of conservative Keynesianism, the national debt as a percentage of the GDP had declined steadily, from about 90 percent of GDP in 1950 to about 33 percent when President Jimmy Carter left office in 1980. Since then, the federal deficit as a proportion of GDP has almost doubled to about 63 percent when President George W. Bush left office in 2009. Much of this deficit is not due to increased federal outlays, which have remained fairly steady as a percentage of GDP since 1980, but to declining revenues as a result of tax cuts. In 2000, before Bush's tax cuts, federal tax receipts were 21 percent of GDP. Four years later, after numerous tax cuts were implemented, federal revenue had fallen to just 16.3 percent of GDP. Actual government receipts declined from $2.03 trillion in 2000 to just $1.8 trillion in 2004.[29]

Second, extreme market capitalism also contributed to growing inequality, as revealed in Table 3.1.

From 1950 to 1980, during the Golden Age, the middle quintiles (each quintile equals one-fifth) fared better than either those at the top or at the bottom. The bottom two quintiles, composed of the poorest households, lost some ground; they received 15.7 percent of all income in 1950 and 14.6 percent thirty years later by 1980. The next two quintiles, however, fared better as both saw their share of household income rise. The middle quintile and those whose earnings put them in the top four-fifths of all households saw their share of income rise by 0.8 percent and 2.8 percent, respectively. The biggest losers were the highest income earners, those in the top fifth of households. Their share of

TABLE 3.1

HOUSEHOLD SHARES OF AGGREGATE INCOME, 1950–2006

Year	Bottom Quintile	Second Quintile	Third Quintile	Fourth Quintile	Top Quintile	Top 5%
1950	4.8	10.9	16.1	22.1	46.1	21.4
1980	4.3	10.3	16.9	24.9	43.7	15.8
2006	3.4	8.6	14.5	22.9	50.5	22.3

SOURCE: For 1980 and 2006 figures, see U.S. Census Bureau, Current Population Survey, "Annual Social and Economic Supplements," table H-2, at www.census.gov/hhes/www/income/histinc/h02AR.html (accessed April 16, 2010). For 1950 figures see Paul Ryscarage, *Income Inventory in America: An Analysis of Trends* (New York: Sharpe, 1998), table 6.6, 154.

income declined from 46.1 of all income in 1950 to 43.7 percent in 1980. The steepest losses within this group were among the top 5 percent of households, whose share of income declined dramatically from 21.4 to 15.8 percent.

But then a stunningly different pattern emerges as one moves into the period of Republican control, characterized by their program of extreme market capitalism from 1980 to 2008. The share of income received by the bottom 40 percent of households dropped from 14.6 percent to 12 percent—more than twice the decline that this group experienced from 1950 to 1980. The middle quintile also saw its share of income fall from 16.9 percent to 14 percent, as did households in the top four-fifths of income, whose share fell from 24.9 to 22.9 percent. The only group whose share of income grew was the top 20 percent, which by itself now accounted for more than half of all household income—more than the combined income of four-fifths of all American households—and even within this select group, income had become more concentrated among the richest 5 percent of all American households. The biggest losers under the Democratic Party program of conservative Keynesianism had become the biggest winners under the Republican program of extreme market capitalism.

Greater inequality over the course of extreme market capitalism had many sources. Accompanying tax cuts for the rich were spending cuts for the poor, who lacked the political power to prevent them. Income assistance for the poor failed to keep pace with inflation, reducing its value; and new legislation pared the welfare roles, increased eligibility requirements, and limited the amount of time people could receive welfare benefits.

But as we saw, it wasn't only the poor who fell further and further behind. So did households in what we would call the middle class, those in the middle and second-highest quintiles. President Bill Clinton expressed frustration with his own failed efforts to restore the middle class's fair share of the national income when he acknowledged, "I came to this job committed to restoring the middle class and I did everything I knew how to do. We lowered the deficit. . . . We expanded trade frontiers. . . . We have an all-time high in the stock market. We have more new businesses then ever before. . . . And most people are still working harder for lower pay than they were making the day I was sworn in as president."[30]

President Clinton's disappointment was due to the way income was now divided between labor and capital, which contributed to inequality. Unions were in retreat and could no longer serve as pacesetters for wages. In 1981, President Reagan fired 14,000 air traffic controllers who were on strike and proceeded to hire replacement workers for them. Employers took the signal and engaged in similar tactics to impose concessions on their workforce or to drive unions out entirely. Consequently, even though economic growth was fairly robust and unemployment relatively low for much of this period, wages and living standards for working-class people stagnated. This situation marked a significant shift from what had happened before. Following World War II under conservative Keynesianism, wages managed to keep pace with productivity growth. Workers were able to share in the wealth they produced. But during the period of extreme market capitalism, the wealth created by increasing productivity was captured by corporations in the form of rising profits, not rising wages. Profits were then distributed to large shareholders in the form of dividends and to corporate executives in the form of exorbitant compensation packages. A 1997 study by the investment company Goldman Sachs concluded that "[t]he share of gross value added going to wages and salaries has declined on trend in the U.S. since the 1980s. . . . We believe that the pressures of competition . . . have forced the U.S. industry to produce higher returns on equity capital and that their response to this has been to reserve an increasingly large share of output for the owners of capital."[31]

Finally, extreme market capitalism coincided with and helped produce a profound shift in the basis of the economy, from industry to finance. Deindustrialization and the contraction of core industries, such as autos, steel, machine tools, and electrical goods, accelerated dramatically. **Industrial capital** that produced something was eclipsed by financial capital that produced nothing. In 1980, at the beginning of the shift to extreme market capitalism, not one bank or company active in financial services was included in the top 100 firms of the Fortune 500. Instead, it was populated by auto (GM), oil (Mobil), steel (US Steel), paper (Weyerhauser), and chemical companies (DuPont) that produced real assets and material wealth. In contrast, in 2007, financial services companies that produced intangible assets and paper wealth comprised one-fifth of all the firms in the top 20 of the Fortune 500, and another 5 were among the largest 50 firms in the United States. The financial sector's share of total U.S. corporate profits was 10 percent on average from the 1950s to the 1980s. It then doubled to 22 percent in the 1990s and then rose by half again to 34 percent on average during 2000–05—more than twice the share of profits as energy, the next largest sector. Pay in the financial sector also rose dramatically. From 1948 to 1982, average compensation in the financial sector ranged between 99 and 108 percent of the average for workers in all domestic private industries. But beginning in 1983, pay per worker in the financial sector shot upward to 181 percent of the average compensation per worker in the United States by 2007. Whereas the finance industry once accounted for just 3 percent of all wages and salaries in the 1950s, its take had doubled to 7 percent by 2007.[32] As if to announce the financial sector's new economic dominance, eight major league baseball stadiums currently are named for banks and insurance companies.

The impact of the shift from industrial to **finance capitalism** has been corrosive in many ways. Banks that are considered too big to fail are considered so indispensible that politicians are reluctant to challenge their policy preferences. Consequently, the financial sector has been able to wield extraordinary influence over the government, affecting policies that create new sources of profits for banks but also increase risk, debt, and instability throughout the economy.

The financial dominance of banks has also had a disproportionate effect on the way people behave economically. Debt is valued over savings, and the virtues of consumerism have replaced those of thrift. Under Democratic rule, the ratio of debt to household disposable income increased only modestly from 55 percent in 1960 to 65 percent by the 1980s. But in the ensuing period of extreme market capitalism, debt more than doubled to 133 percent of household disposable income by 2007. Low interest rates and easy access to borrowed money that banks offered through credit cards and home loans enticed families to live beyond their means. Consumption as a share of GDP rose from 62 percent in the 1960s to 73 percent by 2008. As consumption increased, the savings rate dropped from 12 percent of household income to less than zero by 2005. All of this debt-feuled consumption then contributed to rising balance of trade deficits as Americans used their borrowed money from banks to buy goods produced in China.[33]

THE CRISIS OF EXTREME MARKET CAPITALISM

The recession struck with a ferocity and quickness that few had anticipated. Since 2007 about $12 trillion of wealth has evaporated as housing prices collapsed and the stock market tumbled. The precipitating factor for this calamity was the collapse of the housing market in 2007. Housing prices had been escalating, driven by low interest rates set by the Federal Reserve Board (the Fed) and easy lending practiced by banks. The Fed kept the interest rate it charged banks so low that for 31 consecutive months, from 2001–03, it was negative after adjusting for inflation. Money was essentially free to the banks who were anxious to give out loans that generated fees and interest. Consequently, the banks loosened their lending standards in order to make more loans. Lenders required little documentation and provided NINJA loans (no income, no job, no assets) to people who would not ordinarily qualify for them. Subprime lending to less creditworthy customers jumped from $145 billion in 2001 to $625 billion in 2005, more than 20 percent of total home loans.[34]

As discussed in Chapter 2, banks then bundled these loans together and sold them as securities, or negotiable assets, to get new money and make even more loans. Other banks and investors bought these securities because they had been given AAA ratings by companies that vouched for them as safe investments. And bank regulators were unconcerned about the amount of debt banks took on to provide more loans because they trusted banks to assess their own sense of risk. Everyone made money: people who bought homes would flip them six months later for a profit; banks received interest and fees on mortgage loans to homeowners; and investment firms made fees by selling securities of mortgages that had been bundled together.

As the housing market boomed, however, it became a speculative bubble, driven by new waves of investors hoping to cash in on rising housing prices, creating more demand and ever higher prices. But then the music stopped. Investors who provided the seed money for housing loans to banks became skeptical of the housing values underlying the mortgage securities they bought. When the money dried up to keep this confidence scheme afloat, housing prices began to fall. In Fort Myers, Florida, the median price of a home that had been as high as $322,000 in December 2005 fell to an astonishing $106,900 by January 2008. Subprime homeowners who had borrowed on easy lending terms offered by banks could not pay their debt, which was now greater than their homes were worth. Others who had bought homes in hopes of flipping them at a profit were now stuck with property that would not sell; and they, too, could not afford their loans. As more homes were put up for sale, prices fell. New homes that had been constructed in anticipation of the boom stood empty and were now joined by an inventory of foreclosed homes, which depressed prices even more. Just as rising demand for houses had pushed home prices higher, which attracted more investors who drove prices even higher, so did the increasing supply of unsold homes now drive prices lower, creating its own momentum in the other direction.

Housing defaults cascaded all the way through the system. Banks that had become highly leveraged with debt in order to provide mortgages now found themselves with loans they could not recover. Nor did they have enough assets to cover their losses. The investment bank Lehman Brothers, for example, had $700 billion in various investments at the time of its bankrupcy in 2007, but its shareholder equity was only $23 billion. All the rest of its investments were supported with borrowed money. Other banks also sustained heavy losses; they had borrowed money to buy mortgage securities for themselves that had lost much of their value, and could not find investors for the securities they held and intended to sell.

With banks collapsing, the wheels of commerce ground to a halt. As quick as they were to lend money in good times, banks were reluctant to lend it in bad times. Banks hoarded capital and would not extend credit. Without access to credit, firms could not pay suppliers, meet payrolls, or purchase goods. The crisis in housing now threatened to take down the entire economy. To restore confidence and credit, the government stepped in to bail out the banks. It took stock in failing banks, such as Citigroup and Bank of America, that were deemed too big to fail; this step injected them with the money they needed to keep operating. The government also passed a $787 billion stimulus bill to ward off recession, guaranteed loans to restore confidence, and oversaw the reorganization and partial nationalization of the auto industry. The era of extreme market capitalism had led to an embarrassing and inglorious crisis that forced the government to rescue the ailing economy from its effects.

A NEW FOUNDATION

The return of the Democrats to power in 2008 and the recent recession have opened the way to a new economic formula to replace the discredited model of extreme market capitalism. It is clear that the premises on which the model was based were flawed. Markets do not behave rationally but are subject to what Keynes referred to as "animal spirits." Markets are subject to emotion and unwarranted outbreaks of confidence that lead to speculative bubbles, just as they are subject to crises of confidence that build on themselves and lead to credit crunches. People behave economically more like Homer Simpson than the rational, calculating *homo economicus* that market fundamentalists presume.

Nor are markets self-correcting. In the midst of the housing bubble, former Chair of the Federal Reserve Bank Alan Greenspan informed Congress there was nothing to worry about: "Market pricing and counterparty surveillance can be expected to do most of the job of sustaining safety and soundness."[35] But Greenspan, as he later admitted, was wrong. The temptation for banks to take outsize risks was too great to resist, especially because compensation for bank executives was tied to profits. It became apparent that government regulation was necessary to prevent firms from acting badly and ensure that they act in ways that are safe for them and the public.

Finally, leaving decisions to the market does not always lead to the best results for society. It contributes to instability and inequality. Economic volatility creates insecurity and demoralizes people's ability to plan for the future. Inequality undermines social cohesion and corrupts democracy.

In the 1980s, advocates of tax cuts and deregulation silenced critics by asserting, "There Is No Alternative" (what came to be known as TINA) if the mistakes of the previous period under Democratic rule were to be avoided. TINA was a powerful bludgeon that Republicans used to intimidate liberals, and it limited the range of legitimate policy options to those who took the virtue of markets for granted.

But TINA is now invoked by President Obama and Democrats who want to expand government's role in the economy, not reduce it; by those who want to regulate markets, not extend them. Advocates of government claim there is no alternative if the costly blunders of extreme market capitalism under the Republicans are to be avoided. TINA—the true sorcerer's stone in politics, giving power to whoever can wield it—has switched sides.

President Obama has tried to restore the legitimacy of government. But it is still unclear to whose benefit government will be used. To restore lending, the Obama administration rescued failing banks by injecting money into them on very favorable terms. The government took stock, becoming a majority shareholder in many banks, but has been at pains to minimize government influence over the strategy and operations of banks it has invested in. Taxpayers have taken on the risks of ownership without enjoying any of the privileges. The banks that received the most bailout money have been the most aggressive in jacking up checking account charges and credit card fees on consumers. Nor has government ownership prevented banks from lavishly compensating their executives. The investment bank Goldman Sachs paid its employees more compensation in 2009 than it did in pre-crash 2007.[36] When accused of playing favorites and bailing out the banks and their shareholders, Fed officers reply: "Nobody here is trying to do anything but support the economy and support market functioning. We are worried about the stability of the system, not any individual institution."[37] But so far there does not appear to be any daylight between the Fed's efforts to stabilize the financial system and promoting the interests of the banks that comprise it.

President Obama's regulatory proposals are also marked by timidity. He has proposed a new regulatory regime to supplement the one already in place. But the regulatory holes that the bank failures revealed are bigger than Obama's proposals to fill them. Instead of breaking up banks that are too big to fail, President Obama's administration proposes to subject them to more regulation by the very regulators whose oversight failed because they were too cozy with banks in the first place. And instead of getting smaller, these banks have actually become bigger. JPMorgan Chase holds $1 of every $10 on deposit in the United States, as do Bank of America and Wells Fargo. These three banks and Citigroup now issue one of every two mortgages and about two out of every three credit cards. Moreover, President Obama's proposals did little to rein in financial innovations, called derivatives, that proved so risky in the current downturn. Finally, though the government has given implicit and explicit guarantees to almost all major financial institutions, it still has not found a way to protect taxpayers from excessive risk taking that might result. With government guarantees in place, financial institutions may bet big and collect handsomely if they are right and leave taxpayers with the bill if they are wrong. If the banks were too big to fail before, now that they are even bigger they may assume the government will cover their risky bets if they fail again.

But the Obama administration has been very aggressive when it comes to fiscal policy; it is using the federal budget to stimulate the economy. The gov-

President Obama and Democratic National Committee chairman and Virginia governor Tim Kaine visit a construction site in Springfield, Virginia financed by the Obama administration's economic stimulus bill.

WHAT DO YOU THINK?

Should the Government Bail Out Banks?

With banks failing due to insufficient reserves to pay their debts, what should the government do? Should Presidents Obama and Bush have let the banks fail, or should the government have given them bailouts and rescued them? On the one hand, the banks were victims of their own greed and appetite for risk. If the government rescues them with taxpayer money, what will prevent the banks from being reckless again? And why should the banks be given a reprieve by the government when other businesses that can't pay their debts are not? On the other hand, banks are essential to the economy. They provide the credit that businesses and consumers depend upon. One might argue it is not a matter of ethics whether banks deserve to be rescued, but a matter of necessity given the role banks play in the economy. What alternatives do you think would have been preferable to bailing out the banks? What should the government do now to prevent bank bailouts in the future?

ernment intends to run large deficits in order to promote production and commerce. Moreover, the deficits the Obama administration has called for are of a different order than those that occurred under his predecessor, President George W. Bush. The deficits that accumulated under Bush were the result of repeated tax cuts, which reduced federal revenue. The Obama administration anticipates lower tax revenue as a result of less economic activity, but the greatest contribution to the deficit under Obama will be on the spending side. Federal outlays have increased dramatically from 20.7 in 2008 to 25.4 percent of GDP in 2010. Most of the additional spending was devoted to economic recovery, such as the 2009 $787 billion stimulus bill and 2010 $17 billion jobs bill, as well as increased outlays on social welfare programs and defense.

President Obama came to power with a commitment to push back the frontiers of the market in favor of more government intervention. But it is not yet clear whether government will be used merely to restore and stabilize the economy or whether policy will push beyond that necessary minimum to include a "social democratic surplus" that redistributes power and rewards to those at the bottom, not the top.[38] The answer depends upon political struggle, as different factions within and outside the Obama administration seek to define the extent and direction of political change. The politics of power, as it always has, will determine who benefits regardless of where the new frontier separating the public power of government and the private power of capital is set.

CONCLUSION

The American political economy, the balance struck between state and markets, between public and private power, has been the result of unremitting conflict. Conflict has occurred over not only how much the government should intervene in the market, but which government institutions should be responsible, what policies they should adopt, and who should benefit. Promotion of industry by state governments in the nineteenth century was replaced by regulation of industry by the federal government at the beginning of the twentieth century.

The Great Depression of the 1930s not only initiated a shift in political power but in the balance between states and markets. Democrats replaced Republicans as the ruling party and more actively tried to manage capitalism in response to its failure. They created the modern welfare state to establish a safety net for citizens who fell out of the market, used government budgets to stabilize production, and engaged in more regulation to protect the public interest. But the Democratic formula was exhausted by the 1970s, leading to both inflation and unemployment. The Democratic Party lost power and its economic model was replaced with a new paradigm calling for less government intervention. Republicans took office determined to redraw the boundary between states and markets. They initiated tax cuts in order to limit government by starving it of the funds it needs, and removed regulations on business in order to restore managerial authority.

Just as the Democrats lost power when their economic model failed, so did the Republicans lose power as their economic paradigm failed in the financial meltdown and recession that began in 2008. Democrats proceeded to use the instruments of government to restore and stabilize capitalism, and to push it back from the brink. They proposed new regulations to rein in Wall Street, ran budget deficits to stimulate production, and brought more government control to the health-care market.

Shifts in the balance between states and markets have always been preceded by shifts in the political balance of power. New ruling coalitions take power that propose new economic models. But whether each new model creates a new set of winners and losers depends on political struggle. The Obama administration has changed the paradigm. Whether new winners and losers emerge from this epochal shift is stilll up for grabs.

CHAPTER SUMMARY

Introduction

American history has been replete with conflict over how much government should intervene in markets and private firms, what parts of the government should be responsible for economic policy, and what policies they should follow. Business often has been successful in these struggles, but their outcomes are always open and contingent, dependent on the political capacity of contending groups.

Competitive Capitalism

State governments, more than the federal government, were extraordinarily active in promoting capitalist development in the early days of the Republic. But small firms producing for competitive markets soon gave way to large firms able to dictate prices and wages. Workers and consumers increasingly looked to the federal government for protection from the market power of large corporations.

The Rise of Corporate Capitalism

By the 1880s, large corporations dominated industrial production. Their economic power precipitated protests that forced their allies in the Republican Party to accept some regulation of corporate practices. But the public lost faith in both the Republican Party and large corporations when those organizations failed to respond adequately to the Great Depression.

A New Deal

President Roosevelt and the Democratic Party took power in 1932 amidst the Great Depression and introduced a new model of economic policy based on more government intervention. Roosevelt's New Deal included the welfare state, more regulation of business, and a plan to stimulate the economy through increasing demand by putting people to work, supporting unions, and promoting deficit spending.

The Rise and Fall of the Golden Age

The Democrats retained power following World War II and continued using the state to support capitalist production by smoothing out the business cycle, expanding the welfare state, educating workers, funding research, and protecting markets abroad. But the policies Democrats followed were conservative to the extent they did not redistribute income to those who needed it most, government outlays increased more for the military than for the welfare state, and there was little effort to change the balance of public and private power through either nationalization or planning as occurred in Europe. Democrats and their formula of conservative Keynesianism were discredited in the downturn of the 1970s.

The Rise of Extreme Market Capitalism, 1980–2008

Republicans came to power beginning in the 1980s and proposed a new economic model, based on tax cuts and deregulation, that was designed to roll back the frontier of government. Extreme market capitalism led to economic growth but also contributed to larger deficits, more inequality, and a shift in the balance between industrial and finance capital. Both the Republicans and their model of extreme market capitalism lost credibility when the housing market collapsed in 2007, leading to bank failures and the deepest recession since the 1930s.

The Crisis of Extreme Market Capitalism

The drop in the housing market precitated a financial crisis because banks were awash in bad debts. Lending ceased as bankers tried to conserve capital, choking off credit that the economy needed. Government rallied to rescue the banks to revive credit. Belief in the recuperative power of the market gave way to faith in the restorative power of the government.

A New Foundation

Democrats returned to power and used government aggressively to rescue the banks and restore economic growth. It intervened in the economy—investing in banks and auto companies as well as setting executive pay—in ways that would have been unimaginable under the previous regime. But it is still unclear whether this new government activism will simply repair a broken financial system without disturbing which groups it has served, or whether more government intervention will redirect the economy to meet the needs of different, more lower-class groups than it has in the past.

Critical Thinking Questions

1. Why weren't Populist and Progressive critiques of corporate capitalism more successful?

2. Was the New Deal a success?

3. Have Republicans been better economic managers than Democrats?

4. Can anything be done to tame the business cycle and prevent bubbles from arising and bursting with such calamitous force as occurred during the recent recession?

Suggested Readings

American Social History Project, *Who Built America?* Vols. I and II, 3rd ed. New York: St. Martin's, 2008.

Harry Braverman, *Labor and Monopoly Capitalism.* New York: Monthly Review Press, 1975.

Alan Brinkley, *The End of Reform: New Deal Liberalism in Recession and War.* New York: Knopf, 1995.

Paul Krugman, *The Great Unraveling: Losing Our Way in the New Century.* New York: Norton, 2003.

Robert B. Reich, *Supercapitalism: The Transformation of Business, Democracy and Everyday Life.* New York: Knopf, 2007.

Elizabeth Sanders, *The Roots of Reform: Farmers, Workers and the American State, 1896–1917.* Chicago: University of Chicago Press, 1999.

Mark Zandi, *Financial Shock: Global Panic and Government Bailouts—How We Got There and What Must Be Done to Fix It.* Saddle River, NJ: FT Press, 2009.

PART II

POLITICAL PARTICIPATION

I t is easy to imagine how democracy would work in small-scale societies. Citizens would gather in a public space, such as a town hall, to decide issues among themselves. Direct democracy, in which people engage in face-to-face discussion and decision making, would occur. Under these circumstances, democracy is vibrant. But what happens when one moves from a small-scale society to a large one of over 300 million citizens, such as the United States in the twenty-first century? A pulsating direct democracy in which all citizens participate directly in decision making is simply not possible.

Moreover, the United States is not only a large society but a diverse one. It includes people with many different lifestyles, preferences, situations, and interests. It is not easy to identify a single group that represents "the people" who can make decisions representing the common good when society is driven by deep racial, economic, and gender inequalities. "The people" are divided into groups that have unequal access to resources and power.

Some democratic theorists have retreated in the face of these dilemmas to propose that the best we can do is some sort of procedural democracy, some rules for choosing, by election, among competing political leaders. And it is better we do so, according to the economist Joseph Schumpeter. In his influential account, he criticized what he called the classical conception of democracy, in which citizens participate in politics by reflecting on which policies are most desirable and choosing representatives to implement those policies. He proposed a new way to think about democracy, based on the fundamental claim that political elites are more competent than ordinary citizens to make decisions. Given this situation, he contended, democracy should be thought of as a market, parallel in the political sphere to economic markets where goods and services are bought and sold. Just as consumers choose among competing products, Schumpeter suggests that voters should be considered political consumers who choose among competing elites.[1]

We share the view of critics who reject Schumpeter's emasculated version of democracy and stress the importance of active citizenship and robust political participation. In our view, democracy should not be reserved simply for election day, when citizens choose among the candidates offered to them. Democracy should be broader and fuller. Part II takes up the challenge to make democracy broader and fuller, to extend it beyond the limits of procedural democracy that Schumpeter argued was the best we could do in a large, diverse society.

Chapter 4 focuses on political parties and elections, the major—although far from only—arena in which citizens participate in politics. The chapter highlights the importance of the two-party system in the United States and analyzes reasons for low turnout, changes in the social and ideological composition of the two major parties' support base, the issue of political polarization, the outcome of the 2008 elections, and the importance of the new media in American politics.

Chapter 5 looks at other mechanisms of political participation, such as interest groups and social movements. Both require a higher level of political engagement and commitment by citizens than voting. They also tend to be more pointed and targeted forms of political action in comparison to voting. When change through the ballot box appears closed, groups look for other alternatives. But at the same time that these different forms of political participation are alternatives to one another, they also supplement each other. Voting, interest group activity, and social movement participation are not mutually exclusive forms of political participation but can overlap.

These chapters make clear that the most privileged in society tend to be the most politically active. They have more time, money, and organization to devote to political participation than do other groups. Consequently, politicians tend to be more responsive to their demands. But political inequality is not a foregone conclusion. Citizens in the United States enjoy political rights that permit them to organize and develop their political voice to influence policymakers. This is especially true when large numbers of them are mobilized at the polls, in interest groups, and through social movements to make their demands heard: when they go beyond the bounds of procedural democracy to the richer and fuller terms of direct democracy.

4

POLITICAL PARTIES, ELECTIONS, AND PUBLIC OPINION

INTRODUCTION

What a difference a few years—even a few months—can make. In 2004, President George W. Bush was reelected president and the Republican Party retained comfortable majorities in both house of Congress. In 2008, the elections produced a Democratic president, comfortable Democratic majorities in both houses of Congress, and a dispirited Republican Party. Yet within a few months of the Democratic landslide, a resurgent Republican Party was confidently anticipating that the 2010 congressional elections would erase the bitter memory of its dismal performance in 2008. This chapter analyzes the reversals in fortunes of the two parties and situates these changes within the larger context of American political parties, elections, and public opinion.

The 2008 elections were an exception to some enduring patterns in American politics. For starters, a Democratic candidate broke the Republican Party's firm grip on the presidency: Republicans won seven of the ten presidential elections held between 1968 and 2004. Barack Obama's election marked a rupture with a far older and more deeply embedded pattern in American politics. Until 2008, every one of America's forty-three presidents was white. Obama, an African American who is the offspring of a Kenyan father and a white mother, alluded to this fact in his victory speech on election night, "If there is anyone out there who still doubts that America is a place where all things are possible, who still wonders if the dream of our Founders is alive in our time, who still questions the power of our democracy, tonight is your answer." Obama's rival, John McCain, highlighted the same point in his concession speech that night, "This is a historic election, and I recognize the significance it has for African Americans and the special pride that must be theirs tonight. We both realize that we have come a long way from the injustices that once stained our nation's reputation."[1]

This chapter examines the history of the American party system and the Democrats' rise to power in 2008, along with the party's difficulty in the following years to capitalize on its 2008 victory. The chapter analyzes several interrelated changes: more polarization in American politics, more ideology, more money spent on elections and campaigns, and the impact of the new media.

THE ORIGINS OF THE TWO-PARTY SYSTEM

According to political scientist E. E. Schattschneider, "The political parties created modern democracy and modern democracy is unthinkable save in terms of the parties."[2] Political parties are the agencies that organize and transmit the will of the majority to the government. They are the heart of any democracy because they pump the blood of electoral consent that informs and flows through political institutions. Political parties are above all organizations committed to winning elections, but they also educate and mobilize voters, and recruit and nominate candidates for office. In addition, they advocate policies that link voters to candidates and connect elected officials from the same party to each other.

Given their importance to the functioning of democracy, it might seem strange that the Constitution made no provision for political parties; they have no official status in our political system. One reason is that the authors of the Constitution viewed political parties with contempt and believed they were a threat to liberty. The Founders, according to historian Richard Hofstadter, "hoped to create not a system of party government under a constitution, but rather a constitutional government that would check and control parties."[3] Indeed, Hofstadter notes that "the creators of the first American party system on both sides, Federalists and Republicans, were men who looked upon parties as sores on the body politic."[4]

So, even while condemning parties in theory, the Founders helped create them in practice. Parties emerged quickly in Congress as legislators formed opposing stable alliances in response to pressing issues. Legislators then appealed to the people to settle party divisions brewing in Congress. A partisan press emerged, officials began to campaign for office, and July Fourth celebrations turned into partisan rallies. Party in government gave birth to party in the electorate.[5]

From the start, parties proved to be a democratizing force in the United States. They expanded political participation, mobilized eligible voters, and broke down a deferential system of politics in which only the socially privileged and wealthy could participate.[6] By the time of Andrew Jackson's presidency

(1828–36), historian Michael Schudson writes, "the rule of gentlemen was replaced by the rule of majorities."[7] In 1824, turnout of eligible voters for president was under 30 percent; by the time parties were fully established in 1840, turnout increased to 78 percent.

As the nineteenth century proceeded, parties developed solid organizational bases and a mass following.[8] With its voters mobilized through parties, the United States can be considered the first popular government in the modern world. This point, however, must be strongly qualified because women, Native Americans, and blacks were excluded from the electorate. The United States did not attain universal suffrage until the 1960s, when the passage of voting rights legislation finally enabled southern blacks to exercise the franchise.

AMERICAN PARTIES IN COMPARATIVE PERSPECTIVE

Americans tend to think of the two-party system as natural and inevitable. Yet in most democracies, three or four political parties each garner a significant share of the vote. The distinctive American two-party system can be attributed to many factors. First is the **plurality system** of voting. Election procedures stipulate that whoever gets the most votes wins. Under these winner-take-all rules, there are no rewards for parties and candidates that lose. Consequently, most voters fear wasting their votes on candidates from small parties, since these parties stand little chance of gaining a plurality. Instead, voters tend to choose a candidate from the two major parties. Further, this pattern tends to get locked in through time by socialization: young people often adopt their parents' party identification.

The major alternative to the winner-take-all or plurality system is **proportional representation (PR)**, where legislative seats are allotted to parties based on the percentages of the vote they receive in multimember districts. This system is used to elect the legislature in most democracies around the world. Because even parties receiving less than a plurality receive some representation in the legislature, voters can vote their conscience without fear of wasting their vote. Thus, PR tends to promote multiparty systems.

Second, the winner-take-all procedure used to elect the U.S. president further strengthens the two-party system. Parties have a strong incentive to form broad **coalitions** in order to improve their chances of winning the ultimate prize, the most powerful office in the entire government. The Republican Party's failure to be sufficiently inclusive partially explains its 2008 electoral setback (Figure 4.1). (We explore this issue later in the chapter.) Further, third parties in the United States must contend with a strong media bias. The media devote

FIGURE 4.1

DISTRIBUTION OF ELECTORAL VOTES IN THE 2008 ELECTION

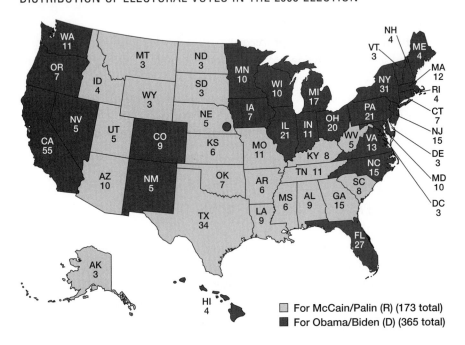

☐ For McCain/Palin (R) (173 total)
■ For Obama/Biden (D) (365 total)

most coverage to the two major parties and ignore third-party candidates. Consequently, voters do not perceive third-party candidates as viable alternatives. The result is a self-confirming prophecy: Since only candidates from the two major parties are considered serious contenders, voters come to view them as such, polls reflect this opinion, and the media follow the polls by confining coverage to the two parties' candidates.

Finally, the Democratic and Republican parties form a tacit cartel to marginalize America's many splinter parties. Two examples: The system of public finance created by legislation passed by the two major parties makes it difficult for third parties to obtain public funds. And the highly important televised presidential debates are usually limited to Democratic and Republican candidates.

Although third parties find it hard to break the two-party mold, it has been done. The Republican Party emerged in the 1850s as a third party and successfully replaced the Whigs. In addition, third parties can take advantage of American federalism and establish themselves at state and local levels. There are many examples of third parties electing mayors and other local officials. Although countless "third parties"—actually, third, fourth, and fifth parties—

are on the ballot in virtually every election, the two major parties tend to monopolize voter choice. However, third-party candidates do still sometimes affect electoral outcomes. In 1992, maverick conservative Ross Perot won 19 percent of the popular vote, which probably enabled Democrat Bill Clinton to defeat incumbent President George H.W. Bush. In 2000, if several hundred of the 97,000 votes cast for Green Party candidate Ralph Nader in Florida had gone to Democratic candidate Albert Gore, Gore would have won Florida and the presidency. (Nader countered in self-defense that if Gore had won his home state of Tennessee, he would have been elected despite his loss in Florida.)

The structural logic of multiparty systems encourages parties to highlight their separate identities and appeal to distinctive segments of the electorate. The result is that parties often tend to adopt more ideologically sharp-edged positions compared to the centrist parties of two-party systems. By contrast, in two-party systems the usual tendency is for each party to seek to assemble a plurality by melding the votes of centrist elements with those of its core supporters, who are located toward the ideological extreme. Thus, two-party systems generally foster moderation, stability, and predictability. At the same time, their centrist tendencies usually limit innovation. When an exception to this pattern occurs—for example, when the Republican Party veered off center in recent decades—it requires particular explanation. We explore how this occurred later in the chapter.

CRITICAL ELECTIONS AND PARTY DECAY

As a general matter, the two-party system limits the choices available to voters and tends to encourage the major parties to be broad coalitions of diverse and sometimes conflicting groups. For example, for many years the Democratic Party included both blacks who supported integration and southerners who opposed it. Similarly, for years the Republican Party included a group that was moderately conservative on economic issues and socially liberal, along with a group further to the right on both dimensions. In general, parties that do not offer a big tent to welcome diverse groups are doomed to defeat. Most of the time, American political parties try to contain conflicts by being evasive on issues. American political parties blur issues, ignore new demands, and fail to adapt to new conditions. The result is that demands build up, pressure in the system increases, and dissatisfaction with the lack of alternatives offered by the parties grows as the party system increasingly fails to reflect changes occurring in the broader society.

At first, citizens seek answers outside the existing party system, in the form of protests and social movements. Eventually, however, one party (usually the minority party) capitalizes on this dissatisfaction by seeking to recruit those whose concerns are not adequately represented within the existing party system and by championing the issues they favor. The minority party may be rewarded by winning, in which case political scientists refer to the tidal shift as a **critical or realigning election**. Such elections are relatively rare, for they shake up the established order and usher in a new era of stability.[9] Critical or realigning elections are characterized by unusually high turnout and more intense ideological conflict between the parties. The winning party reshapes the ideological agenda for years to come, as party conflict becomes organized around the new set of issues. Voters are realigned and party coalitions shift. Some groups defect, shifting their loyalty from one party to another. Other groups that were previously unattached may join the coalition of one of the parties.

Ronald Reagan's election in 1980 helped realign American politics. It ushered in a period of conservative rule that challenged the New Deal orientation of increased government economic regulation and social provision. When Barack Obama was elected in 2008, political scientists questoned whether it might mark another realignment in American politics. The answer depends both on the Democratic Party's success in consolidating its hold in office and on whether the Democratic coalition can legislate a reform agenda that reshapes the orientation of government. The party's mixed record on both counts after 2008 suggest that the present period is one of flux and uncertainty rather than realignment.

The American party system has undergone considerable changes since its formation two centuries ago. A period that is often considered the high point of American political party development was in the late nineteenth century, when parties were powerful organizations that, according to Stephen Skowronek, lent "order, predictability and continuity to governmental activity."[10] They were complex, well-staffed organizational structures that reached down into the grass roots, communicated to voters through a partisan popular press, and controlled the nomination of candidates and the platform on which they ran.[11] Turnout was high, and there was little of the class bias so evident in turnout patterns today. Perhaps their greatest achievement was to integrate within American politics and society the millions of immigrants who poured into the United States in the late nineteeenth and early twentieth centuries. Still, one should avoid idealizing the political parties of this period. Parties mostly depended on patronage and spoils to motivate activists and voters. Urban **political machines** integrated workers and immigrants as voters in a way that insulated business from democratic challenge.[12] High voter turnout, especially by members of the working class, did not guarantee that economic elites would be challenged. And yet it is hard to imagine class issues emerging or business being challenged politically in the absence of high levels of turnout by low-income voters.[13]

Party decline set in following the critical election of 1896, when the pro-business Republican Party took over. Turnout in presidential elections declined from 79 percent in 1896 to 49 percent in 1924; nonvoters were concentrated among the working class and the ethnic and racial minorities. This demobilization was due to many factors. First, party competition declined dramatically following the 1896 election. Both the South and the North became one-party regions. The Democrats enjoyed a political monopoly in the South, where the party became the vehicle for the defense of white racism, while the Republicans dominated elsewhere. Without meaningful competition, voters lost interest and turnout fell.

Second, following the 1896 critical election, business groups and middle-class reformers made a vigorous and effective effort to weaken parties. They disliked the expense and corruption of urban political machines. Moreover, they feared that incorporating in the party system the influx of working-class immigrants might produce a radical turn. Under the banner of ending political corruption, business progressives sponsored measures to weaken political parties by cutting off the flow of incentives they could offer voters. Civil service positions would now be awarded according to merit based on competitive exams, and not by party control of patronage. Local elections were held on a nonpartisan basis, weakening the parties' grip on urban governments.

Finally, turnout was depressed by erecting legal barriers to voting. In particular, Southern states, which traditionally relied on fraud and violence to keep blacks from the polls, now institutionalized racial—as well as class—repression through such devices as poll taxes (which required paying a hefty fee to vote), literacy tests, and tests of "good character." Three-quarters of all citizens in the South—especially blacks and poor, uneducated whites—lost the right to vote through these stratagems. Turnout in the South in presidential elections declined from 57 percent in 1896 to a mere 19 percent of eligible voters by 1924.[14]

Northern elites pursued a goal similar to that of their southern counterparts, although by less violent and racist methods. Complicated voter registration systems discouraged voting by imposing residency requirements, setting early closing deadlines to register to vote, and opening voter registration offices only for short and inconvenient periods. Although the formal right to vote remained, introducing these procedural obstacles prevented millions of citizens from actually exercising that right.[15]

The process of party decline beginning after 1896 lasted for decades. Party organizations decayed as their major functions were hived off. Political scientist Andrea Louise Campbell points out: "A series of technological, institutional, legal, and cultural shifts diminished [parties'] once central function as the organizers and inclusive mobilizers of American elections. They ceded control over nominations and were pushed aside by new candidate-centered campaigns. Technological advances allowed candidates to speak directly to the people, and the parties lost their monopoly on electoral contestation in the United States."[16] Campbell suggests that in the recent period "parties [have] reconfigured themselves as fund raisers and providers of services to candidates."[17]

The rise of candidate-centered campaigning warrants special emphasis. Candidates nowadays raise their own money through computer-generated direct mail and fund-raisers with affluent supporters. They hire polling organizations and political consultants to conduct focus groups and do market research to advise them how to fine-tune their message. They reach voters through television advertising and, in Obama's case in 2008, the Internet; and they rely less on the party's campaign workers.

Some political scientists suggest that American parties are experiencing a revival in the past few years. Local party organizations may be hollow, but state party organizations now have full-time staffs, ample budgets, and services they can offer to candidates and supporters.[18] Party organization is even more robust at the level of each party's **national committee**. The Republican National Committee (RNC) was the first to modernize its operations in the 1980s. The RNC's success compelled the Democratic National Committee (DNC) to follow suit. According to political scientist Paul S. Herrnson, "[N]ational parties are now stronger, more stable and more influential in their relations with state and local party committees and candidates than ever before."[19]

However, increased levels of activity by party organizations and their increased ability (thanks to campaign finance laws) to funnel funds to candidates is not the same as increased party strength. Party organizations have, in essence, become political consulting firms at the service of candidates. Although parties still control one unique and indispensable feature—nominating candidates for office—they are mere shadows compared to the past. Primaries have undermined party control of nominations, candidates raise their own money, and personal ties count more than party loyalty when elected officials make appointments to key administrative positions. The parties may be more active, provide more services, and raise more money than in the past, but *they do so in a context in which they play a more subordinate* role to candidates.[20]

American political parties have not always been weak. But they have always been decentralized and fragmented. At the national level, the separation of powers between Congress and the president promotes a tendency toward parties being divided into a congressional and presidential wing. Further, party organizations reflect the federal structure of government; parties are located at the national, state, and local levels. Relationships among the different levels of the party are not hierarchical. The DNC or RNC cannot issue instructions to the party's lower levels because the different levels are relatively independent of each other: state and local parties decide on their own slate of candidates and programs without direction from above. Candidates and state and local parties are free to define for themselves what it means to be a Democrat or Republican.

Primaries are apparently a more democratic way for parties to nominate candidates than through **party conventions** controlled by party leaders. But the matter is not so simple. Turnout in primaries is very low. The primary electorate is even more unrepresentative of the country than the general electorate. It is more ideological, more educated, and more affluent than voters who turn out in regular elections. Given the small size of the primary electorate, the playing field is highly uneven. Wealthy candidates who are free to spend unlimited amounts of their own funds, as well as candidates who can raise substantial funds and candidates with close ties to interest groups and dedicated supporters, have a clear advantage.

WHAT DO YOU THINK?

Are Political Parties Weapons of the Weak against the Strong?

Robert Michels, an Italian sociologist, famously declared that political parties are weapons of the weak against the strong. By this he meant that, because parties enable the weak (who are numerous) to act collectively, they are able to check the power of the strong (who are few in number). In what ways have American political parties enabled the weaker members of American society to check the power of the strong and privileged? What factors have limited the way that parties have redistributed political power? What reforms might make parties more effective weapons of the weak against the strong?

By determining who will be the party's candidates, primaries shape the character of the party. An important reason for the Republican Party's right turn since the 1980s (a story discussed later in this chapter) involved the ability of highly conservative activists, allied with well-financed pro-business lobbies and think tanks, to successfully contest Republican primaries and place hard-right candidates on the ballot. On the other side of the spectrum, the skills that Barack Obama honed as a community organizer in Chicago enabled him to out-organize Hillary Clinton and score a surprising upset in the nation's first nominating contest, the Iowa presidential caucus (a modified form of primary) in early 2008.

TURNOUT AND AMERICAN VOTERS

If Schattschneider's claim (quoted earlier) that political parties are the measure of democracy's health is accurate, then American democracy urgently needs medical care. American political parties are suffering from a case of severe political anemia. Although turnout did increase in the last three presidential contests, compared to other countries the American party system still lacks vitality. One study found that the United States ranked fourth lowest in turnout among over thirty-four democratic countries![21]

Many factors contribute to low turnout in the United States. First, low turnout reflects widespread popular cynicism. Citizens are sullen and suspicious of political elites from both parties, who are perceived as simply out for themselves. Conversely, Barack Obama's message in 2008—"Yes we can"—inspired millions of Americans who had never voted to come to the polls.

Second, political scientist Robert Putnam argues that low turnout is due to generational replacement. The elderly, who vote regularly, are dying off and being replaced by new generations of younger citizens who are not in the habit of casting a ballot. To put the point in personal terms: the students who read this book (and their parents) are much less likely to vote than their grandparents. Putnam argues that older generations developed the habit of voting and confidence in the electoral process because parties responded effectively to the Depression and World War II. As parties became less effective, later generations became skeptical and cynical.[22]

Third, casting a ballot in the United States is especially difficult. In most states, one must register long in advance. (For those who do register, turnout is in fact very high: 80 percent in the 2004 election.[23]) Citizens unable to vote at their local polling booth often cannot obtain an absentee ballot. An analysis of the 2008 elections—when, recall, there was record turnout—reported, "Four million to five million voters did not cast a ballot in the 2008 presidential elections because they encountered registration problems or failed to receive absentee ballots."[24] The report noted that an additional 2–4 million registered voters were discouraged from voting by long lines or voter identification requirements. Turnout is further reduced because thirteen states permanently deprive convicted felons of voting rights; many other states deprive felons of voting rights not only while in prison, but until they have completed parole and probation. These measures reduce the electorate by more than 5 million Americans. Finally, because elections in the United States are held on Tuesday, citizens must carve time out of the working day to vote. In most countries, elections are either held on Sunday or Election Day is declared a national holiday. According to political scientist Walter Dean Burnham, there is a hole in the American electorate where working-class, less educated, and low-income Americans should be.[25] Nonvoting is not distributed randomly but tends to be concentrated among these groups. The greatest difference between the rich and the poor (and the highly and less educated) is not whom they vote for but whether they vote at all. Lower-class citizens in the United States vote at roughly 60 percent the rate of upper-class citizens, a far greater difference than one finds in other Western nations.[26]

Does this matter? It surely does. As political scientist Stephen Wayne observes, "Those who are most disadvantaged, who have the least education, and who need a change in conditions the most actually participate the least. Those who are the most advantaged, who benefit from existing conditions and presumably from public policy as it stands, vote more often."[27]

Because parties are in the business of electing their candidates to office, one would expect them to promote increased turnout. But parties are reluctant to raise issues that appeal to nonvoters because doing so might weaken elites' dominance within the party. According to political scientists Matthew Crenson and Benjamin Ginsberg, party leaders view nonvoters as unreliable and are thus apprehensive "about expanding the universe of participants."[28] On those relatively rare occasions when an innovative or audacious candidate or movement mobilizes previously disconnected citizens, the resulting surge in turnout often produces an electoral shift. Barack Obama's election in 2008 was an example of this pattern.

We conclude this discussion by quoting a report by the Task Force on Inequality and American Democracy of the American Political Science Association (APSA). It described the typical pattern as follows:

> Today, however, the voices of American citizens are raised and heard unequally. The privileged participate more than others and are increasingly well organized to press their demands on government. Public officials, in

turn, are much more responsive to the privileged than to average citizens and the less affluent. The voices of citizens with lower or moderate incomes are lost on the ears of inattentive government officials, while the advantaged roar with a clarity and consistency that policymakers readily hear and routinely follow. [The result is a] growing concentration of the country's wealth, income, and political influence in the hands of the few. . . . We find that our governing institutions are much more responsive to the privileged and well-organized narrow interests than to other Americans.[29]

One other issue should be mentioned regarding the conduct of elections and the tabulation of votes: the ominous possibility of fraud and corruption in the conduct of elections. Although dishonest methods were common a century ago—bribing voters, stuffing ballot boxes, and so on—it is usually assumed that such practices are a thing of the past. Not so. There is extensive evidence that both parties—but primarily the Republican Party—have engaged in dishonest means of rigging elections. For example, following the 2004 presidential elections, journalist David Corn enumerated some of the fraudulent practices that contributed to George W. Bush's victory in the key state of Ohio: "odd voting patterns, suspicious election day activity, voter suppression, 'spoiled' ballots and the susceptibility of e-voting machines to errors or, worse, hacking. . . . Was there an organized GOP effort to tamp down the vote in Kerry strongholds? Probably."[30] A particularly unsettling issue is that many of the frequently used electronic voting machines these days are produced by Diebold, a firm that Corn points out is "headed by a GOP fundraiser." Nor was Ohio the only state where there were suspicions of rigged voting machines. In Florida, many Kerry voters reported that their touch-screen voting machines indicated they had voted for Bush.

MONEY AND ELECTIONS

We have already noted that candidates need more than votes to succeed; they also need money—and lots of it. The comment by Mark Hanna, a key Republican strategist in the early 1900s, remains as relevant today as it did a century ago: "There are two things that are important in politics. The first is money, and I can't remember the second."[31] Money pays for political ads and media time, pollsters and political consultants, research and advance work, as well as travel costs and overhead expenses. As discussed in Chapter 1, the increase in the importance of political money is one of the major trends in current American politics. For example, the amount spent in each presidential electoral cycle makes previous outlays seem puny.

In 2004, President Bush raised a record $365 million in his reelection campaign, and John Kerry was close behind with $334 million. Obama's performance in the 2008 presidential elections put these figures to shame. His war chest of $742 million—contributed by 4 million contributors—exceeded the *combined* amounts raised by Bush and Kerry in 2004.[32] This figure represented about $10 million in new donations each week. Obama's achievement was especially noteworthy because he was the first candidate ever to opt out of the public finance system. By forgoing the $84 million in public money that he would have received, he was free to raise unlimited amounts of private donations. Although much of his funds came from small contributions—the median donation was under $200—he also relied heavily on large contributions.[33] (Indeed, according to the Center for Responsive Politics, Obama raised $89 million from Wall Street, that is, the securities and investment industry.[34]) By brilliantly using the new media, such as Facebook and online fund-raising (one-third of his contributions came from the Internet), the Obama campaign revolutionized the way political campaigns are financed and conducted. By raising nearly triple McCain's $261 million, Obama was far better able to fund state and local campaign organizations and purchase TV and radio time.

Although Obama's performance in 2008 was exceptional, it was part of a larger pattern: political campaign spending has skyrocketed in recent years. In 2000, interest groups, parties, and candidates in congressional and presidential races spent about $3 billion. In 2004, total expenditures on federal elections approached $4 billion. In 2008, $4.9 billion was spent on the presidential contest alone, and another $1.5 billion on congressional elections.[35]

These colossal expenditures occurred despite campaign spending laws, dating from the early twentieth century, that have limited corporate and labor union spending. However, a landmark case narrowly decided by a 5–4 decision of the Supreme Court in 2010—*Citizens United v. Federal Elections Commission*—overturned an important limit on corporate and labor spending. The Supreme Court ruled that government could not prevent corporations (and, probably, labor unions) from spending their own funds to endorse and promote their preferred political candidates. (Before this decision, corporations and unions could run issue ads and contribute to political parties and political action groups, but they were prohibited from directly endorsing candidates and spending funds directly to help elect them.) One commentator observed that the "ruling may make the hundreds of millions spent in past presidential and congressional elections look like a pittance."[36]

With the partial exception of the 2008 presidential election, business firms and wealthy individuals provide most political contributions, and this situation became even more common after the *Citizens United* decision. Candidates appeal to well-heeled groups for contributions for the same reason that famed bank robber Willie Sutton said he robbed banks: because that's where the money is. One study found that families with incomes over $75,000 were ten times more likely to contribute money to political campaigns than families that earned less than $15,000; the affluent were significantly overrepresented in comparison to middle-income citizens as well.[37]

To understand why wealthy donors and corporations contribute to political campaigns, it is useful to think of contributions as investments rather than donations. Jerome Kohlberg, a founding partner of the Kohlberg, Kravis Roberts & Co. investment firm, commented, "[C]ontributions are a small price for big corporations to pay to gain political influence. . . . [C]orporations give for one reason: self interest. They can easily justify their expenditures because they get an outstanding return on their investment."[38] Enron Corporation, for example, which committed one of the largest corporate frauds in American history, gave money to no fewer than 71 senators and 188 members of Congress. Justin Dart, corporate leader, large political contributor, and fund-raiser, expressed the impact of political contributions beautifully when he observed that dialogue with politicians "is a fine thing, but with a little money they hear you better."[39] To illustrate, consider Robert Wolf, a big Wall Street fund-raiser for the Democrats and head of the American division of the Swiss bank UBS. Wolf was appointed to the Presidential Economic Recovery Advisory Board, a high-level consultative body created to advise President Obama. Wolf is a frequent visitor to the White House and has "played golf, had lunch and watched July 4 fireworks with the president."[40] Wolf is in an excellent position to be heard loud and clear.

American political campaigns last longer, cost more, are less regulated, and are financed by a higher proportion of private (as opposed to public) funds than in any other Western democracy. Scandals and public outcry over the purchase of political influence by large contributors has periodically resulted in the passage of reform legislation. But the power of money has time after time proven stronger than efforts to control it. In 1971, Congress passed the Federal Election Campaign Act (FECA) and amended it in 1974 to limit political contributions, control spending, and require public disclosure of all receipts and disbursements. However, donors exploited loopholes in the law to engage in even more abusive activities. For example, FECA prohibited businesses, unions, and other groups from contributing money directly to federal election campaigns. This restriction was evaded when groups formed **political action committees (PACs)** that solicit money from individuals and then funnel it to candidates. It was altogether eliminated by the Supreme Court's 2010 decision in *Citizens United*. Most PACs are corporate sponsored. Their number grew from 433 in 1976 to 2,480 only twenty years later—they represented more than half of all registered PACs in 1996 and spent twice as much as unions, the second-largest group of contributors.[41] A decade of reform efforts have failed to restrict PAC spending. But even as the issue of PAC money remained unresolved, it was superseded by a more urgent problem—a deluge of so-called soft money. *Soft money* refers to funds that may be used for so-called educational and party-building purposes. This might include meeting a party's overhead and administrative costs, funding voter registration and get-out-the-vote drives, or paying for issue advocacy ads whose barely disguised message is that voters should support a particular candidate. **Soft money**, which is unregulated and unlimited, is distinguished from **hard money**, which is contributed directly to a candidate's campaign. There are ceilings on how much hard money donors can give directly to candidates, and such contributions must be reported. However, donors are allowed to contribute unlimited and unregulated amounts of soft money to parties.[42]

Public disgust with the amount of money being spent to influence elections fueled further demands for reform. In 2002, Congress passed the Bipartisan Campaign Reform Act (BCRA), also known as McCain-Finegold after its two senatorial sponsors. The purpose of BCRA was to restore contribution limits by closing the soft money loophole in FECA. It restricted certain political advertisements and prohibited political parties from raising and spending soft money. The price for closing the soft money loophole was increasing the hard money limit that donors could give. Moreover, in 2007, the Supreme Court weakened BCRA restrictions on political advertising on grounds that they violated the First Amendment right to freedom of speech. And they were virtually eliminated by the *Citizens United* decision.

One major effect of political money is to vastly increase the chances that the race goes not necessarily to the best but to the wealthiest. In 2004, for example, 96 percent of the House races and 91 percent of the Senate races were won by the better-financed candidates.[43] Money does not guarantee victory in politics or happiness in life, but financial security sure helps.

Another baneful effect of money is to feed public cynicism about politics. Because politicians are forced to begin fund-raising for the next election cycle the morning after their election, this conveys the impression that they are for sale to the highest bidder. Politicians are probably no less ethical than corporate executives, salespeople, carpenters, or college professors. However, the system of private campaign finance—above all, politicians' need to raise ever larger campaign chests and the disparity in resources between affluent corporate and individual donors versus others—taints the entire political sphere.

Those at the top of the income pyramid provide the bulk of political contributions, which means that political finance marches in lockstep with increasing economic inequalities. The causal arrows probably point in both directions. As the APSA Task Force on Inequality and American Democracy pointed out, "The direct impact of rising economic inequality may be most directly apparent in campaign contributions. As wealth and income have become more concentrated and the flow of money into elections has grown, wealthy individuals and families have opportunities for political clout not open to those of more modest means."[44] In brief, increases in economic inequality and political spending go hand in hand; the increase in one contributes to the increase in the other. Rather than the party system acting as an engine of democracy, the way that parties are financed skews the political system toward the interests and preferences of affluent Americans and business interests.

We have focused until now on the institutional mechanisms that organize citizens' electoral choices. We next analyze the changing social bases of the two parties, a factor that affects the kinds of policies that governments will enact.

THE RISE AND FALL OF THE NEW DEAL AND REAGAN COALITIONS

Two durable political coalitions have dominated American politics and policy for much of the past century. The first was the New Deal coalition led by the Democratic Party that held office from 1932 until roughly 1968. The second, following a period of transition from 1968 to 1980, was the Republican-led coalition that reached power with Ronald Reagan's election in 1980 and governed until 2008. In both cases, the dominant party of the era won most presidential elections and shaped the American political agenda. It defined the most pressing issues, and it proposed—and often succeeded in implementing—policies to address the issues. Not coincidentally, the policies were also crafted to reward the dominant party's social base, cement its power, and help ensure its reelection. Barack Obama's election in 2008 at least temporarily ended Republican dominance. It is uncertain, however, whether the Democratic Party's victory in 2008 will produce a durable realignment comparable to the two previous periods of party dominance because of the institutional gridlock that occurred following Obama's election.

The New Deal Coalition

The critical election of 1932, conducted during the Great Depression, voted Franklin Delano Roosevelt into office and ushered in decades of Democratic

Party control. The New Deal coalition that Roosevelt forged over four consecutive presidential terms (1933–45) included blacks, who received some (albeit an unequal share) of the benefits from New Deal programs targeted for the poor and unemployed; southerners, whose Democratic sympathies dated back to the Civil War; immigrant Jewish and Catholic workers from southern and eastern Europe, who appreciated Roosevelt's efforts to end the Depression; Irish supporters of big city machines; and a handful of financiers and corporate executives, who believed that the New Deal could help end the Depression. Above all, the party involved an uneasy partnership between its southern, white, segregationist wing that was passionately hostile to federal policies that would benefit blacks and undermine the South's feudal structure, and a Northern, liberal wing based in large urban areas with millions of first- and second-generation working-class immigrants. The groups forming the New Deal coalition supported the Democratic Party for the benefits they could derive from the federal government. But that was where the consensus ended. The coalition was a marriage of convenience in which the partners were content to lead separate lives and use their union to enlarge the federal government in order to extract benefits from it. FDR and his successors designed programs in such a way as to distribute benefits to broad segments of the population—but, thanks to the power of southern white Democrats in Congress, programs were designed to withhold benefits from millions of southern blacks, who lived and worked in a state of semi-bondage.[45]

The Democratic Party leadership became less successful in holding together the southern and northern wings of the party as the civil rights movement of the 1960s gained momentum. When President Lyndon Johnson relied on northern Democrats and moderate Republicans to pass legislation that outlawed racial discrimination, furious white southerners retaliated by deserting the Democratic Party. Native white southern identification with the Democratic Party dropped from 74 percent in 1956 to half that level by 1984.[46] At first, white southerners supported only Republican presidential candidates. Beginning in 1968, the South became a Republican bastion in presidential elections. But southerners gradually began voting for Republican candidates for state and local offices.[47] By 1994, for the first time in the twentieth century, Republicans comprised a majority of the southern delegation to both the Senate and the House, and they occupied a majority of Dixie's gubernatorial offices. Southern realignment has been the single most important factor behind the Republican Party's success in recent decades.[48]

The New Deal coalition was further weakened by the emergence of issues that created political and cultural conflict within the Democratic Party. The

Vietnam War divided the Democratic Party as students and liberal Democrats challenged party leaders who prosecuted the war. Issues involving feminism, gay rights, abortion, and crime further fragmented the New Deal coalition. One faction of the party was comprised of traditional working-class voters who were economically liberal but socially conservative. They supported federal regulation of markets and welfare state programs but opposed policies defending gay and abortion rights. The other wing was composed of wealthier, more educated, and more recent supporters. They were economically conservative but socially liberal. These Democrats saw the party as a vehicle for challenging gender hierarchies and sexual stereotypes but opposed programs that sought to redistribute wealth. Reconciling the two wings of the party was a difficult balancing act.

The New Deal coalition was further wounded by the decline of labor unions because union members are more reliable Democratic Party voters than their nonunion counterparts. Union membership as a proportion of the workforce has declined steadily from its peak of 33 percent in 1953 to less than 13 percent today.

Finally, the New Deal coalition was a victim of policy failure. The New Deal policy of conservative Keynesianism offered economic growth with relatively little redistribution, and fiscal fine-tuning as a substitute for structural economic change (see Chapter 3 for a description of conservative Keynesianism). The inadequacy of this formula first became apparent in the 1970s, when economic growth faltered and both inflation and unemployment accelerated. Conservative Keynesianism could no longer deliver the economic growth that the New Deal coalition needed to satisfy the demands of its various constituents. Nor did the Democrats develop a new economic formula around which to revive their faltering coalition.

The Reagan Coalition

As the Democratic majority lost ground, the Republican Party gathered momentum and changed direction ideologically. A party's platform is a complex mix of proposals that party leaders calculate will be the most electorally profitable, proposals that party activists pressure to include, and proposals sought by affluent donors and powerful forces in the party's coalition. Because there may be divergences among the three, a party's orientation is often a diverse and even contradictory patchwork. At the same time, successful parties are regarded as championing some core values.

When the Democratic-led New Deal coalition faltered, the Republican Party seized the opportunity. From having been the party that grudgingly supported the basic philosophy of the New Deal, partly because it had little new to offer, the Republican Party became the spearhead of a conservative revolution. The point of departure for the party's transformation was its nomination of highly conservative Senator Barry Goldwater from Arizona for president in 1964. The choice signaled that power had shifted from the Eastern Establishment of moderate conservatives to ultra-right conservatives from the South and the West who were militantly anti-government, anti-taxes, anti-union, and anti-Communist. The Sun Belt nourished a new brand of conservative Republicanism because it was the home of many defense industries and military bases; the federal government owned large tracts of western land and was perceived as intrusive; and new, homogenous, mostly white suburbs made it easier to find consensus and build institutions among a basically conservative group of middle-class migrants to the area.[49]

Although Goldwater lost the 1964 election by the largest margin in American history, the Sun Belt forces that engineered his nomination eventually triumphed. After years of patiently funding PACs, conservative think tanks, and grassroots groups, these forces were victorious in 1980 when their standard-bearer, Ronald Reagan, was elected president. As one historian noted, "If there had been no Barry Goldwater, there would have been no Ronald Reagan."[50] One might add that if there had been no Ronald Reagan, there would have been no George W. Bush; Bush greatly extended policies initiated by Reagan, including deregulation of the economy and environment, tax cuts skewed toward the rich, conservative social policies, and the attempt to partially privatize Social Security. However, Bush pursued harder-right policies than Reagan ever dreamed of trying, largely because in the intervening years the Republican Party became increasingly united around the conservative banner.

After freeing itself from the influence of the New Deal and developing a distinctive—in most respects opposite—policy orientation from the New Deal, the Republican Party became the center of political action for several decades. Five factors help explain the Republican Party's rise to power. First, white males became more Republican in their voting patterns as Republican candidates successfully played to their fears about dismantling racial and gender hierarchies. Second, the party developed an enthusiastic base among religious fundamentalists. The Christian Right mobilized through the Republican Party to challenge what members regarded as the moral decay around them. Previously, Protestant evangelicals were fairly evenly divided in their political loyalties. Third, the business community became much more united in supporting the Republican Party following the election of the strongly pro-business Ronald Reagan in 1980. It showered the party with money and funded think tanks that developed conservative proposals challenging New Deal economic policies and liberal social positions. The party added to its traditional business base among northeastern financiers and midwestern industrialists with a new breed of maverick multimillionaire entrepreneurs from the Sun Belt who were fiercely opposed to government regulation. Fourth, the party benefited from population growth in the suburbs and the Sun Belt, areas that had little labor union presence and were deeply "sympathetic to Republican appeals of self-reliance and less government."[51]

Fifth, the Republican Party was rebranded by a network of highly conservative organizations that worked with leading Republican strategists. Political scientists Jacob Hacker and Paul Pierson observe, "The past few decades have witnessed the gradual replacement of an older generation of political moderates and fiscal conservatives with a new generation of hard-line conservatives and radical tax cutters."[52] In brief, the Republican revival was the product of brilliant strategy and patient organizational effort by "ideological extremists" who successfully moved the party to the right. The term *ideological extremists* comes from an authoritative source: moderate Republican Christine Todd Whitman, former governor of New Jersey, whom George W. Bush appointed to be Environmental Protection Agency administrator and who chaired Bush's 2004 reelection campaign in New Jersey.[53]

The decades-long changes re-centered the Republican Party ideologically and geographically.[54] During its glory days from the 1980s until 2008, the Republican Party was electorally dominant, intellectually vibrant, and financially prosperous. With a secure base in the South and Rocky Mountain states, it simply needed to win several **swing states** in the Midwest to maintain dominance. The party also had a sufficiently large social base to assure repeated victory. The Republican Party traditionally attracted wealthier voters.[55] Its conservative turn enabled it to secure the loyalty of white Protestants, especially evangelicals. Catholics, who once identified with the Democratic Party, became evenly split. Still, the most important religious division among voters is not what religion they belong to but how frequently they practice it. Citizens who attend religious services regularly are more likely to vote Republican. The Republican Party also polled well among white men, married couples, and rural voters.

The Democratic Party's support base, which we analyze next in the context of the 2008 elections, was the mirror image of the Republican Party's. The Democratic Party was more popular among voters in the Northeast and Pacific Coast states. Its socioeconomic support derived from low-income voters, especially those belonging to labor unions, African Americans and ethnic minorities, unmarried people, Jews, youth, and the less religiously observant. It has also polled well among liberal and well-educated voters.

Although throughout the period of Republican dominance the party's candidates won more often than did Democrats, they frequently did so by small margins and sometimes because of quite unpredictable developments. If Ralph Nader had not been on the Florida ballot in 2000, Al Gore might have won the state and been elected president. If Osama Bin Laden had not released a video just before the 2004 election theatening another attack—thereby stoking widespread anxiety and enabling George W. Bush to claim that he was better qualified to keep the country safe—John Kerry might well have been elected.

THE 2008 PRESIDENTIAL ELECTION AND THE CHALLENGE TO REPUBLICAN DOMINANCE

In 2008 a perfect storm of developments produced a dramatic break with the political alignments of the Reagan coalition. Some changes had been gestating for years—notably, when the Democratic Party gained control of both houses of Congress in the 2006 midterm elections. Others occurred during the 2008 presidential campaign. Analyzing the 2008 presidential election helps explain the flip-flop in fortunes that brought the Democrats to power and highlights the character of the Democrats' enlarged support base.

Table 4.1, based on a nationwide exit poll of voters, highlights the contrast between the coalitions supporting the two major parties' presidential candidates in 2008.[56] Barack Obama benefited from a significant shift in his favor among several large groups, including women (who are 53 percent of the electorate), youth (18 percent of the electorate), and unmarried voters (34 percent). An important demographic trend that contributed to his victory might portend future Democratic successes: whereas pro-Democratic groups are growing in size, pro-Republican groups are a shrinking proportion of the electorate. To illustrate, Hispanics are the nation's largest ethnic minority group and one of the fastest growing. The number of Hispanics eligible to vote increased by about a fifth from 2004 to 2008.[57] In the past, Hispanics divided their support fairly evenly between the two parties. For example, Kerry won 53 percent of Hispanic voters in 2004. However, 66 percent of Hispanic voters chose Obama in 2008. Although the Republican Party's harsh policy toward immigrants was popular among its core conservative base, it repelled most Hispanics.

The most pro–Democratic Party group of voters in the country are African Americans. Long before Barack Obama was on the ballot, black voting has been

TABLE 4.1

2008 VOTING PREFERENCES OF SELECTED GROUPS

Category	Obama	McCain	% of Total Electorate
Male	49	48	47
Female	56	43	53
Sex by Race			
White men	41	57	36
White women	46	53	39
Race/Ethnicity			
White	43	55	74
Black	95	4	13
Hispanic/Latino	67	31	9
Asian	62	35	2
Age			
18–29	66	32	18
30–44	52	46	29
45–64	50	49	37
65+	45	53	16
Education—Last Grade of School Completed			
Did not complete high school	63	35	4
High school graduate	52	46	20
Some college	57	41	31
College graduate	50	48	28
Postgraduate study	58	40	17
Family Income			
Under $50,000	60	38	38
$50,000–$99,999	49	49	36
$100,000 or more	49	49	26
Religious Observance—Attend Religious Services			
Weekly	43	55	40
Occasionally	57	42	42
Never	67	30	16
Religion			
Protestant	45	54	54
Catholic	54	45	27
Jewish	78	21	2
Something else	73	22	6
None	75	23	12
Currently Married			
Yes	47	52	66
No	65	33	34
Population of Area			
Over 500,000	70	28	11
50,000–500,000	59	39	19
Suburbs	50	48	49
10,000–50,000	45	53	7
Rural	45	53	14

SOURCE: Msnbc, "Politics/2008 Election Results/Exit Polls: United States—President," at http://www.msnbc.msn.com/id/26843704 (accessed Nov. 7, 2009).

bloc voting. For example, 88 percent of the African Americans who turned out in 2004 voted for John Kerry. From Washington, D.C., to Washington State, from professors to postal clerks, blacks have voted as one to reward the Democratic Party for its support of liberal social programs and civil rights legislation. Obama's 95 percent support among African Americans therefore involved a difference of degree but not of kind. More generally, Obama and the Democratic party have strong support from racial and ethnic minorities, who comprise an increasingly significant proportion of the American electorate. Whereas black, Hispanic, and Asian voters were 12 percent of the electorate in 1988, they were 22 percent in 2008.[58]

Women were another important group in the winning coalition of Obama and the Democratic Party in 2008. Women, who are over half the electorate, have supported Democratic candidates for many years; but when 56 percent of them supported Obama, they assured his victory. At the same time, there was a deep racial and ethnic split among women, in that white women favored McCain by 53 to 46 percent. (White men were even more likely to support McCain: 57 percent of them supported McCain.) There also was a marriage gap: two-thirds of singles supported Obama, compared to less than half of married voters. Young voters have been pro-Democratic since 1992, but they stampeded to Obama in 2008, when two-thirds voted for him. (By contrast, 53 percent of elderly voters suported McCain.) Moreover, young voters surged to the polls in much higher numbers than in the past, both because of a massive voter registration drive by the Obama campaign and because of the affinity that young voters felt for the youthful and "cool" Obama.

A religious cleavage played an important role in the 2008 presidential election. Whereas only 43 percent of those who attend religious services weekly voted for Obama, 67 percent of those who never attend services voted for Obama. The split was especially great between white Protestant evangelicals, 26 percent of whom voted for Obama, non-evangelical white Protestants (44 percent for Obama), and all other voters: 67 percent were pro-Obama.

There was a strong rural-urban split in voting preferences in 2008. Whereas 45 percent of residents from rural areas and towns smaller than 50,000 voted for Obama, 70 percent of voters in cities over 500,000 supported Obama.

Union members are traditionally reliable Democratic voters. For decades, they have supported Democratic candidates in national elections at a 17 percent higher level than is the case for nonunion members.[59] In 2008, the gap narrowed but remained substantial: 59 percent of voters in union households supported Obama, compared to 51 percent of voters in households without a union member.

The 2008 voting preferences of groups of varying educational attainments and income reveals an unusual pattern. Obama received strong support from both the least and the most educated voters, and from those wth the lowest and highest incomes. Regarding education, 63 percent of voters who did not complete high school, and 58 percent of those with postgraduate education, supported Obama. A slim majority of those with high school diplomas or college education were also pro-Obama. The pattern is similar for income. The most pro-Obama voters were those with family income under $50,000, voters with somewhat higher incomes favored McCain by small margins, while the richest voters—with family income exceeding $200,000—supported Obama by 52 to 46 percent.

The electorate has always been split along social lines. But it is increasingly divided along ideological lines as well. Liberal voters are now far more likely to support the Democratic Party, conservatives to support the Republican Party. The 2008 exit poll asked voters which of the following two statements comes closer to their view: "Government should do more to solve problems" or "Government is doing too many things better left to businesses or individuals." Seventy-six percent of Obama voters chose the first (liberal) response, compared to 27 percent of McCain supporters. A process of ideological self-sorting has occurred in which voters' policy and party preferences are now closely aligned. We further explore the question of ideological polarization later in this chapter.

Overall, the two candidates' electorates reflected different Americas. McCain supporters were likely to be white, male, Protestant, religiously observant, married, from rural areas and small towns, and fairly affluent. Obama supporters were likely to be ethnically and racially diverse, young, female, single, low or high on the income scale, and less religiously observant.

Our analysis has thus far ignored some significant factors in the 2008 presidential election. For a starter, consider the fact that Barack Obama is African American. Contrary to what was often predicted, the racial factor did not have a real impact on the outcome of the 2008 presidential election. More surprising, perhaps, is that to the extent it mattered, it helped Obama. When, for the first time in American history, one of the two major parties nominated a black candidate, the usually low turnout among African Americans was nearly the same as the rest of the electorate.[60] On the other hand, except for some counties in the deep South, where whites voted 80 percent for McCain, it does not appear that many white voters oppposed Obama on racial grounds. His overall level of support among white voters was 44 percent, which exceeded the 39 percent average level that Democratic candidates received from white voters from 1968 to 2004.[61]

Another factor in the 2008 presidential election was outgoing president George W. Bush. When the election campaign began, Bush's disapproval rating of 66 percent—the highest level in over half a century of public opinion polling—constituted a severe liability for John McCain. (Disapproval rose to 70 percent by the time of the election.) Two key reasons for Bush's unfavorable rating were the enormously unpopular Iraq War and the gathering economic storm.

In 2004, Americans' support for the war had contributed to Bush's reelection. By 2008, however, most Americans opposed the war and held the Bush administration and Republican Party responsible for having initiated it. John McCain's support for the war probably cost him votes. The recession that exploded in fall 2008 was an even greater burden for McCain. During the summer of 2008, before the stock market crash that followed the collapse of Lehman Brothers investment bank in September, Obama and McCain were neck and neck in the polls. However, when the stock market plummeted in mid-September, Obama surged ahead. More generally, although he tried, McCain was unable to distance himself from Bush and the Republican administration's record. (McCain and Bush met in public only once during the entire campaign.) Obama relentlessly challenged McCain's claim of being a maverick and criticized McCain's support for the Bush administration's economic policies, including its pro-business tax cuts and deregulation reforms.

Obama's immensely successful fund-raising efforts and pioneering use of new media to fund-raise and mobilize voters, discussed elsewhere in this chapter, also contributed to his victory. Last but not least, McCain's choice of Sarah Palin as running mate was a strategic blunder. Palin's profound ignorance of public affairs was revealed in a TV interview with CBS' Katie Couric that, when posted on YouTube, was visited by millions. Palin became a favorite target of *Saturday Night Live* and late-night comedians, and it was not long before 60 percent of voters judged her unqualified to be president.[62] Worse yet for McCain was that many voters questioned his judgment in selecting Palin, especially given that he was the second-oldest major party presidential candidate in history. (The oldest, by a year, was Robert Dole, the unsucccessful Republican candidate in 1996.)

The factors reviewed here help explain Obama's **popular vote** margin of 53–47 percent, the best performance by a Democratic candidate since Lyndon Johnson trounced Barry Goldwater in 1964. By gaining majorities in 28 states, Obama won two-thirds of **Electoral College** delegates (the actual count was 365–173). The reason for the much greater disparity between the Electoral College outcome and the popular vote is the **unit rule** practiced by most American states.

The unit rule specifies that the candidate who wins a plurality of the state's popular vote is awarded 100 percent of the state's delegates to the Electoral College. We discuss the unit rule further in Chapter 6.

The 2008 election produced a dramatic change in regional voting patterns. Obama increased his share of the vote in all the states won by recent Democratic presidential candidates. Further, he edged out McCain in six traditionally Republican states: three in the Republican Party's southern turf (North Carolina, Virginia, and Florida) and three in the formerly Republican preserve of the Rocky Mountain/Plains states: Colorado, New Mexico, and Nevada. Obama also won three midwestern swing states that had voted Republican in 2004: Iowa, Indiana, and Ohio. He also came close to winning several other red states.

Democratic victories in 2008 were not confined to the White House. The Democrats substantially expanded their majorities in both houses of Congress. They came close to reaching the sixty-vote threshhold in the Senate that would ensure a filibuster-proof majority and later did secure sixty senatorial votes for several months. However, when a Republican won an election held in Massachusetts to fill the seat held by deceased Senator Edward Kennedy, the Democratic majority again dipped below sixty. (The importance of this threshhold is discussed in Chapter 7.)

By expanding their reach, the congressional Democratic delegation also became more ideologically diverse. Many of the newly elected Democrats were from rural areas or small towns in southern and western states with moderate or conservative constituencies. With an eye on their reelection prospects, these representatives opposed many liberal features of the Obama reform agenda.

The mirror image of Democratic Party advances in 2008 was the Republican Party's retreat to its core bases of regional, social, and ideological support. This explains the party's full-throttle opposition to President Obama's proposals. Not one Republican member of the House of Representatives voted for Obama's economic recovery plan. Only three Republican senators broke ranks to support it, and all three were harshly criticized by Republican Party leaders and activists. One of the three, Arlen Specter from Pennsylvania, faced reelection in 2010. When a hard-right conservative supported by the Club for Growth announced that he would challenge Specter in the primary, Specter bolted the Republican Party and became a Democrat. In announcing his decision, he lamented, "Since my election in 1980 . . . the Republican Party has moved far to the right. . . . I now find my political philosophy more in line with Democrats than Republicans."

Specter's decision highlighted a cleavage in the Republican Party about the party's future course that pitted hard-edged conservatives against moderate, pragmatic conservatives. The first group claimed that the party lost because it was not sufficiently conservative. For example, South Carolina Senator Jim DeMint declared, "The best way to [win] is to have a core group of Republicans who really do what they say and stand for their principles." On the other side of the divide, Republican moderates countered that the party needed to broaden its appeal. Lindsay Graham, South Carolina's other senator, warned, "We are not losing blue states and shrinking as a party because we are not conservative enough."[63]

Republican members of Congress papered over their differences in the years following Obama's election by nearly unanimous opposition to most Democratic Party initiatives. Because congressional Democrats were less successful in maintaining unity, the Republican strategy hindered passage of the Obama administration's reform proposals. Yet Republican unity did not extend outside Congress. A fierce battle raged between the party's moderate and hard-right factions. Many conservative Republicans supported the Tea Party movement and were loyal participants in CPAC (the Conservative Political Action Conference). This cleavage was evident in many Republican primaries for state and local offices, where incumbent Republicans faced challenges by those claiming incumbents were not sufficiently conservative.

POLARIZATION AND AMERICAN POLITICS

A favorite topic of TV and radio talk shows in recent years, as well as the subject of extensive scholarly research, is the polarization of the American body politic. Politicians, pundits, and citizens alike lament the bitter partisan atmosphere, the decline of civility among politicians, and the intensity of conflicts on political, social, and economic issues. Indeed, Barack Obama first captured national attention in 2004 when, as a young state senator from Illinois running for the U.S. Senate, he delivered the keynote address at the Democratic nominating convention that year. Obama's electrifying speech stressed the need to reduce polarization and partisanship, a theme that he repeated time and again in his 2008 presidential campaign and after becoming president. The most memorable passage in the speech, one he often repeated in his quest for the presidency, was: "There is not a liberal America and a conservative America. There is the United States of America." Obama went on to challenge "pundits who like to slice-and-dice our country into Red and Blue states."

And yet there is considerable merit to the "red states/blue states" distinction to describe political polarization in the United States, as well as the importance of polarization at the level of political institutions. In presidential elections in most American states, a majority of voters consistently support the same party's candidate time after time. Only a handful of states change majorities from one election to the next—the swing states whose voting shifts determine the outcome of presidential elections. As we have seen, Obama's victory represents an exception to this pattern because of the large number of states with shifting majorities.

As we described when reviewing the 2008 elections, political polarization these days is closely tied to ideological polarization. (Recall the gap between Republican and Democratic voters concerning the appropriate role of government.) Political scientists Earl and Merle Black claim that "For American voters who call themselves Democrats or Republicans, the social and cultural differences between the two national parties are infinitely greater in the first decade of the twenty-first century than they were in the past."[64] Further, because voters sort themselves geographically, the two parties' social bases reinforce their distinctive regional bases of support. Figure 4.2 (constructed by Black and Black) describes this situation.

FIGURE 4.2

CHANGES IN PARTIES' SOCIAL BASE

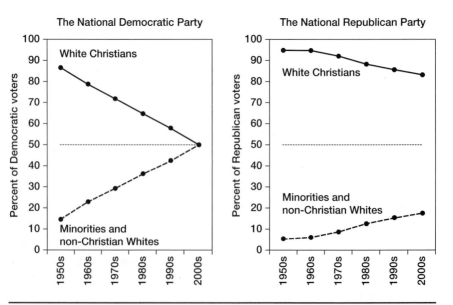

SOURCE: Earl Black and Merle Black, *Divided America: The Ferocious Power Struggle in American Politics* (New York: Simon & Schuster, 2007), 257.

Detailed historical analysis is needed to explain why different regions have developed relatively stable partisan loyalties as well as to explain how the Obama campaign destabilized this picture in 2008. Consider the South, a key to explaining Republican dominance in the 1980s through 2008. The South switched from being a one-party region securely under Democratic Party control, for three reasons. The first is race. The divorce between the South and the Democratic Party began in 1964 when President Lyndon Johnson (LBJ) sponsored the Civil Rights Act, followed by the Voting Rights Act of 1965. Most white southerners, the vast majority of southern voters in this era of racial repression, fiercely opposed racial integration and voting rights for African Americans. During the bitter congressional fight to pass the Civil Rights Act, LBJ accurately predicted what would follow: "We may win this legislation, but we're going to lose the South for a generation."[65] Second, the South is the most religiously observant region, the home of a large number of Protestant evangelicals. Ever since Ronald Reagan, the Republican Party has been highly successful in courting this group. Third, southern voters were quite conservative on economic issues. When Ronald Reagan moved the Republican Party further right, southerners had an additional incentive to switch party preference.

Not all political scientists accept the importance of the red state/blue state cleavage. Political scientist Morris Fiorina questions its importance, as well as the claim that there is intense partisan polarization nowadays among the electorate.[66] He claims that the source of political polarization in the United States is not the general electorate. Indeed, he cites public opinion data documenting a recent *decline* in polarization among rank-and-file citizens. For example, he finds an increase in public acceptance of a woman's right to choose abortion and of gays having the right to teach in public schools and to marry.

According to Fiorina, what has changed is that ideological positions are more closely aligned with partisan preferences. One can more accurately predict nowadays what people's stands will be on issues by knowing which party they favor. Thus, what is new is that political parties are more ideologically homogeneous and more distinct from each other than in the past. According to Fiorina, parties have become more ideologically distinct because party elites have made them that way. That is, elites have sponsored an ideological sorting process resulting in partisan polarization. The result is that the broad middle swath of voters is marginalized. In the 1950s and 1960s, both parties were broad tents in which a moderate (that is, centrist) and more extreme faction coexisted—a more liberal faction for the Democratic Party, a more conservative faction for the Republican Party. The defection of the South to the Republican Party tipped the balance in the party toward the conservative side of the spectrum and left the Democratic Party more liberal, especially when formerly

Republican voters in the Northeast bolted to the Democratic Party in reaction to the Republican Party's right turn.

Is the process of partisan and ideological self-sorting symmetrical—that is, have both parties moved equally far from the ideological center? Political scientists Jacob Hacker and Paul Pierson claim that the Republican Party has moved much further right than the Democratic Party has moved left.[67] They highlight, as we described earlier in the chapter, that the Republican Party was taken over by a coalition of hard-right conservative groups, including the Christian Right and free-market economic conservatives, organized in churches, interest groups, voluntary associations, and think tanks.

Yet a puzzle remains: why did a party so far out of line with majority opinion score so many electoral and policy successes for nearly three decades? Hacker and Pierson emphasize a point made earlier in this chapter; that is, those who are politically active are not representative of the entire citizenry. Wealthy citizens are more likely to vote in primaries and general elections, and they usually support more conservative policies than does the general electorate.[68]

Finally, voters *did* eventually punish the Republican Party for having strayed off center. In the 2006 midterm elections, Democrats won control of the House of Representatives and Senate; and in 2008 they enlarged their

WHAT DO YOU THINK?

Is America Polarized?

There has been a lively debate among political scientists regarding the extent and character of polarization in American politics. Some political scientists claim that rank-and-file Americans have moved from centrist or moderate political views and adopted more sharply edged positions on economic and social issues. Other political scientists suggest that polarization has occurred not because Americans are more ideologically extremist but because party coalitions are becoming more homogeneous; that is, like-minded voters are gravitating to the same party. As a result, although the distribution of opinions in the electorate has not changed, party coalitions have become more polarized. How can we assess which view—or yet another one— best helps us understand the character of polarization in American politics?

majority in the House, briefly gained a sixty-vote majority in the Senate, and won the supreme prize of the presidency.

We have analyzed here polarization among party leaders as well as in public opinion and voting behavior. Polarization also exists within political institutions. Chapter 7 describes partisan polarization in Congress, which reached a peak in the years following the 2008 elections.

THE NEW MEDIA AND PUBLIC OPINION

The most noteworthy milestone of the 2008 presidential election was probably the election of an African American president. Another milestone was identified in a front-page article, published on Election Day in the *New York Times* and entitled: "The '08 Campaign: A Sea Change for Politics As We Know It."[69] According to *Times* reporter Adam Nagourney, "The 2008 race for the White House . . . fundamentally upended the way presidential campaigns are fought in this country. . . . It has rewritten the rules on how to reach voters, raise money, organize supporters, manage the news media, track and mold public opinion, and wage—and withstand—political attacks, including many carried by blogs that did not exist four years ago." An adviser to George W. Bush's 2000 and 2004 presidential campaigns agreed: "I think we'll be analyzing this election for years as a seminal transformative race. The year campaigns leveraged the Internet in ways never imagined. The year we went to warp speed."

The media have always influenced voters' perceptions of political campaigns. Citizens see and hear candidates through the medium of news reports. And the character of the medium has an influence all its own. A classic example was the first televised presidential debate ever held—between John F. Kennedy and Richard M. Nixon in 1960. Whereas those who heard the debate on radio rated Nixon the winner, those who watched the debate on television rated Kennedy's performance as superior. The reason is that television highlighted Nixon's perspiring face and five o'clock shadow and revealed that he appeared nervous and ill at ease; Kennedy, on the other hand, appeared fresh, relaxed, and radiant. More recently, Barack Obama's presidential prospects received a significant boost in his first televised debate with John McCain. While McCain paced the stage, fidgeted, and appeared visibly irritated, Obama remained calmly in place and exuded an air of confidence and authority.

Newspapers, radio, and television continue to play an important role in political campaigns these days. But, as mentioned earlier, they must now compete for voters' attention with a new kid on the block—the Internet. Although the new media first appeared on the political scene early in this century, they came into their own in the 2008 presidential election. According to constitutional scholar and technology analyst Cass Sunstein, whom President Obama appointed to direct the White House Office of Information and Regulatory Affairs, there were 55 million blogs in 2007, and 40,000 new ones are created every day! Although impressive, this number pales in comparison with the more than 19 billion websites in existence.[70] Political analyst Greg Mitchell observes that the 2008 election was "the first national campaign profoundly shaped—even, at times, dominated—by the new media, from viral videos and blog rumors that went 'mainstream' to startling online fundraising techniques."[71] In 2008, social websites like Facebook and YouTube connected voters to candidates—especially Obama, whose mastery of the new media gave him a substantial boost. To some extent, the Internet promotes interactive communication as opposed to the previous top-down pattern of one-way communication. At the same time, many politicians have ruefully learned that an ill-considered remark delivered to a small, private gathering quickly becomes public when it is recorded and posted for the whole world to see.

Politicians have recently made use of e-mail, blogs, instant messaging, and websites to persuade, attack, and defend; and to fund-raise, promote voter registration, and mobilize supporters on Election Day. Obama's superior ability to embrace the new media—and a huge war chest that enabled him to exploit the media to the hilt—significantly contributed to his victory. During the campaign, 2 million people signed onto MyBO, a website that combined social networking and volunteer work. Five million people connected to the Obama campaign on Facebook and other social websites. As discussed earlier in the chapter, much of Obama's extraordinary fund-raising success derived from online contributions. The generation gap separating the two presidential candidates was reinforced by a technology gap. Whereas Obama displayed easy familiarity with the new media, McCain confessed that he didn't know how to use the Internet.

Once in office, Obama continued to make extensive use of the new media. He is the first president whose Oval Office desk sports a laptop computer. One of his noteworthy postelection successes was to persuade the Secret Service to allow him continued use of his BlackBerry. Moreover, many pro-Obama campaign networks remained in place after the election. The 13 million supporters who signed up for e-mail messages during the campaign continued to receive messages from Obama on a reconfigured website.[72] The Obama team redesigned and upgraded the White House website to enable the president to reach citizens directly rather than rely on the traditional news media

President Obama sends an e-mail message to supporters.

to get out his message. Obama's campaign manager created Organizing for America, an Internet-based effort within the Democratic Party designed to maintain contact with Obama's supporters. Soon after assuming office, Obama held the first-ever virtual town meeting, in which he invited citizens to submit questions electronically. More than 100,000 questions were posted, and 3.6 million people voted to select the ones that Obama would answer. The result was surely not what the president expected: the most popular question asked whether Obama supported legalizing marijuana. (He replied that he did not.)

Media analysts disagree about the political significance of the new media. Some claim that 24/7 cable news channels and the avalanche of blogs, tweets, texting, and websites like Politico, FiveThirtyEight, the Drudge Report, and Huffington Post—many of which have a sharp-edged ideological perspective—produce a more involved and informed public. Other analysts believe that the mountain of information provided by the new media increases the gap between the politically connected and the uninterested.[73] Moreover, the blizzard of messages transmitted without careful editing and fact-checking makes it difficult to separate fact from fiction. Eric Schmidt, chief executive of Google, warned that the Internet can potentially be "a cesspool" of false information.[74] The blogosphere contributes to fragmenting the electorate into self-sorted, ideologically isolated groups. More generally, the new media (and the traditional print and broadcast media) contribute to two of the recent trends discussed earlier involving parties and elections: greater ideological intensity and greater polarization. However, the new media may partially offset the increased importance of money in American politics.

CONCLUSION

The fundamental idea of democracy is that the preferences of citizens deserve equal consideration and that citizens should have equal ability to influence political outcomes. This chapter has focused on political parties, finance, and elections, the core mechanisms of political participation. We have highlighted the increase since the 1980s of ideology, polarization, and political money. These changes, along with the impact of new media, have produced more starkly divided parties. Though the parties offer voters more clear-cut choices, the result has been to poison the political air. Barack Obama ran on a platform advocating greater civility and partisan cooperation. However, there has been little change in the political climate since he took office.

The chapter has demonstrated that political participation in the United States is slanted toward the rich in terms of voting turnout, campaign contributions, and political activism. Every recent major study confirms a pattern reported in a classic study of participation by political scientists Sidney Verba, Kay Lehman Schlozman, and Henry E. Brady: "Over and over, our data showed that participatory input is tilted in the direction of the more advantaged groups in society—especially in terms of economic and education position, but in terms of race and ethnicity as well."[75]

Republican dominance for several decades was a product of this situation. Barack Obama was elected because he weakened the link between wealth and a pro-Republican vote and because his campaign energized millions of voters who are typically less connected. His election demonstrated that, despite unequal resources, all adult citizens can potentially raise their political voice. Unlike dictatorial regimes, where political participation is actively repressed, citizens in democratic regimes can participate in the choice of leaders and can influence the laws that govern them. The majority is not voiceless, especially when large numbers are mobilized. When citizens do so, political participation, which so often reinforces privilege and inequality, can also counteract advantages of class, race, and gender.

After the convention that drafted the Constitution concluded its work in 1787, the revered elder statesman Benjamin Franklin was asked to evaluate the result. He is famously recorded as replying, "It's a republic if you can keep it." Political parties and elections potentially enable citizens to keep—and deepen— the United States' republican and democratic forms of government. However, for this to occur, citizens must mobilize to challenge the power of money and the tendency for inequalities in political participation to parallel economic inequalities. The politics of power turns on these central issues.

CHAPTER SUMMARY

Introduction

Although the balance between the two major parties may be stable through time, it can also change dramatically from one election to the next. The 2008 presidential election provides an illustration of a rapid shift. After twenty-eight years when Republicans occupied the White House (interrupted only by eight years when Democrat Bill Clinton was president), Barack Obama—the nation's first African American candidate—was elected president by a solid majority in 2008.

The Origins of the Two-Party System

Political parties are key elements in a democracy. They structure electoral and policy choices, nominate candidates for office, and connect citizens to government. Although they play a fundamental role in the American political system, parties are not identified in the Constitution, and the Founders thought parties were divisive and undesirable. Yet parties developed relatively early in the country's history and, by the 1830s, became a permanent fixture in American politics. One of their key roles was to transform politics from an elite to a popular activity by mobilizing citizens to turn out to vote. (At the same time, the electorate remained restricted to white males for many years.)

American Parties in Comparative Perspective

America's two-party system is quite unusual. The party system in most democratic countries includes three, four, or more major parties. A key reason for the two-party system in the United States is that elections for president and congressional representatives are held according to a winner-take-all plurality system based on single-member districts. Given these electoral procedures, citizens tend to vote for a large party, one that stands a good chance of winning, rather than for smaller parties with little prospect of being elected. Another reason for the U.S. system is that the two major parties use their position to sponsor measures, such as public financing of large parties, that strengthen the two-party system. A third reason for the persistence of the two-party system is socialization. Once the two-party system is established, it tends to reproduce itself because children follow their parents' lead in identifying with one party or the other.

Critical Elections and Party Decay

A relatively constant feature of America's party system is that parties have rarely presented sharply differing programs. Periodically, however, when a critical election occurs, there has been a shift from one broad partisan coalition to another. For much of the nineteenth century, parties were highly influential in integrating newly arrived immigrants and mobilizing citizens to turn out in elections. Progressive reforms in the early twentieth century considerably weakened parties, and there was a corresponding decline in voting turnout. Parties were further weakened by the advent of radio, television, public opinion polling, and professional consultants. These developments weakened parties in favor of candidate-centered campaign organizations. The rise of presidential primaries in many states since the 1970s further weakened party organizations. Parties may have experienced a renewal in the current period by strengthening their capacity to provide services to candidates.

Turnout and American Voters

Turnout in the United States is unusually low compared to other industrialized democracies. Several factors explain this situation. First, there is widespread popular cynicism and suspicion of political elites. This is especially true among younger voters, who turn out to vote in smaller proportions. Further, barriers to voting are caused by difficulties in registering and voting on Tuesdays, which are workdays for most Americans. Although these factors depress voting levels throughout the electorate, they are especially likely to affect lower-income, less educated, and working-class Americans—whose turnout rates are particularly low. One result of unequal rates of turnout is to promote policies that favor the interest of affluent Americans and business interests.

Money and Elections

Political parties and candidates require large sums of money to wage nomination campaigns and compete in the general election. Campaign contributions reflect the mobilization of bias in that the bulk of political money is provided by affluent citizens, business firms, and organized interests. However, small donors can have an impact, as illustrated by Barack Obama's ability to raise much of his record $742 million from small contributions, often made online. Although campaign finance laws somewhat limit the influence of large donors, wealthy individuals and business interests continue to have an enormous influence on elections by providing the bulk of campaign contributions. This tendency has been increased by the 2010 Supreme Court decision, *Citizens United v. Federal Elections Commission,* that eliminated a prohibition on corporate endorsements of candidates and direct contributions to their campaigns.

The Rise and Fall of the New Deal and Reagan Coalitions

Within the past century, there have been two critical electoral realignments. The first occurred in the 1930s, when a conservative Republican coalition was replaced by FDR's progressive Democratic coalition based in the South and in the working class of the industrial North and Midwest. In the 1980s, the faltering New Deal coalition was ousted by a resurgent conservative Republican coalition of white voters, men, and the religiously observant, led by Ronald Reagan and his successors.

The 2008 Presidential Election and the Challenge to Republican Dominance

Barack Obama's election in 2008 upset traditional voting patterns in a number of ways. For the first time, an African American was elected president, and by a comfortable margin. His support coalition was the mirror image of the Republican alliance that had generally ruled since 1980. Obama's victory resulted from retaining the loyalty of traditional Democratic states in the Northeast and West and winning some states in traditionally Republican regions, including the South, the Southwest, and the Rocky Mountains and Plains. Obama also benefited from a surge in voting turnout among young voters and increased support by racial and ethnic minorities. However, his inability to make a substantial dent in unemployment, as well as the Democratic Party's difficulties in passing notable legislative reforms in the years following Democratic victories in 2008 resulted in political uncertainty rather than secure Democratic dominance.

Polarization and American Politics

Obama's victory partially altered patterns of polarization in American politics. For example, by gaining majorities in traditionally Republican states and regions, he challenged the red state/blue state cleavage. Political scientists debate whether polarization is primarily a product of a chasm between citizens of different outlooks or a result of party leaders who have moved both parties, and particularly the Republican Party, toward the ideological extremes.

The New Media and Public Opinion

The political landscape has been significantly altered by the new electronic media. Barack Obama's skillful use of the new media gave him a powerful advantage in raising funds, communicating with voters, and mobilizing them to turn out in elections. The impact of the new media are not clear. They enable citizens to become far better informed—on condition that citizens are motivated to seek out specialized sources of information. The new media also tends to fragment publics by encouraging citizens to confine their consumption of political news to outlets reflecting their own ideological orientation.

Critical Thinking Questions

1. What are the advantages and drawbacks of electing representatives by the single-member-district plurality system as opposed to proportional representation (PR)? Which system is preferable, and why?

2. The Supreme Court has held that the usual limits on campaign contributions do not apply to candidates, who are authorized to spend unlimited amounts of their own funds on their political campaigns. The Court held that limiting the amount that candidates were authorized to spend on their candidacy would violate their First Amendment right to free expression. Do you agree? Why or why not?

3. What is the political impact of the new media? In particular, which of these two effects is more important, and why: the new media have increased the amount of political information available to those interested in obtaining it; and the new media have reduced the average level of public knowledge and increased the amount of unsubstantiated rumors presented as accurate news.

4. What are two factors that explain why Barack Obama was elected president? Which of the two factors you cited is most important, and why?

Suggested Readings

Earl Black and Merle Black, *Divided America: The Ferocious Power Struggle in American Politics.* New York: Simon & Schuster, 2007.

Walter Dean Burnham, *Critical Elections and the Mainsprings of American Politics.* New York: Norton, 1970.

Morris Fiorina, with Samuel J. Abrams and Jeremy C. Pope, *Culture War? The Myth of Polarized America.* New York: Pearson Longman, 2006.

Andrew Gelman, David Park, Boris Shor, Joseph Bafumi, and Jeronimo Cortina, *Red States, Blue States, Rich States, Poor States.* Princeton, NJ: Princeton University Press, 2008.

Jacob S. Hacker and Paul Pierson, *Off Center: The Republican Revolution and the Erosion of American Democracy.* New Haven, CT: Yale University Press, 2006.

Paul Pierson and Theda Skocpol, eds., *The Transformation of American Politics: Activist Government and the Rise of Conservatism.* Princeton, NJ: Princeton University Press, 2007.

Frances Fox Piven and Richard Cloward, *Why Americans Don't Vote.* New York: Pantheon, 1988.

Robert D. Putnam, *Bowling Alone: The Collapse and Revival of American Community.* New York: Simon & Schuster, 2000.

Sidney Verba, Kay Lehman Schlozman, and Henry E. Brady, *Voice and Equality: Civic Voluntarism in American Politics* (Cambridge, MA: Harvard University Press, 1995)

INTEREST GROUPS AND
SOCIAL MOVEMENTS

INTRODUCTION

First, glacial ice sheared off rock, exposing steep granite cliffs. Above those cliffs, water cut deep canyons into the mountains and then plunged over exquisite falls to form glistening pools in the valley floor below. When the naturalist John Muir visited Hetch Hetchy Valley in Yosemite National Park, he marveled at its beauty, describing it "as a great landscape garden, one of Nature's rarest and most precious mountain mansions." He saw waterfalls that thundered over stark 1,700-foot cliffs and mountain brows that "reached to the sky" while their feet were "set in emerald meadows" below.[1]

If visitors want to see the majesty of Hetch Hetchy today, they need to go to Hartford, Connecticut, where paintings of the valley by Albert Bierstadt hang in the Wadsworth Atheneum Gallery. The problem is not that the valley is off-limits or inaccessible but that it is submerged in 300 feet of water. In 1923, the City of San Francisco built a dam across the valley, using its steep granite cliffs that had so enthralled John Muir to catch and store water for a reservoir. The gray granite walls of the valley that were once regarded as one of the wonders of the national park system are now encircled with bathtub ring when San Francisco draws down its water supply.

The unsuccessful fight to save Hetch Hetchy is now regarded as "the first environmental cause that attracted national attention."[2] Opponents of the dam organized and inundated Congress with letters beseeching it to save the valley; they testified at congressional hearings, arguing that there were cheaper alternatives for water outside the national park boundary; and they tried to shape public opinion by writing editorials and distributing literature. But they were outspent, outlobbied, and outmaneuvered by proponents of development.

Although the environmental movement may still be outgunned in many situations, it is, at least, better armed today. The "Big Ten" environmental groups raised over $1.2 billion in donations in 2008.[3] In addition, they are adept at using Internet technologies to recruit and mobilize supporters, employing focus groups to craft and develop their message, navigating the halls of Congress to lobby representatives and senators, and participating in coalitions to increase and broaden their support. The environmental movement includes long-established interest groups, such as the Sierra Club and Wilderness Society, that are organizationally coherent (collecting dues, electing officers, and holding meetings) and that engage in traditional forms of political pressure (**lobbying**, contributing money to candidates, educating the public, and testifying before Congress). But it also includes social movement groups, such as Earth First! and the Earth Liberation Front, that are less formal and hierarchical and that engage in more disruptive and unconventional forms of political activity. An example of such social movement activism occurred at Hetch Hetchy in 1987 when an environmental guerilla rappelled down the side of the dam, drew a crack across it, and wrote "Free the Rivers" before escaping into the night.

We discuss interest groups and social movements together in this chapter because they are forms of political participation that are complementary to voting and elections, covered in the previous chapter. Citizens join interest groups

The O'Shaughnessy Dam across the Tuolumne River floods Hetch Hetchy Valley to create a reservoir.

and participate in social movements in order to express their demands to decision makers. These different forms of political participation—voting, interest group, or social movement activity—are not mutually exclusive or neatly sealed off from one another. Rather, political actors devise strategies that they judge are appropriate given the resources they have and the opportunities available to them. Depending upon the circumstances, activists may mobilize voters, lobby officials, and organize demonstrations simultaneously, anticipating that each form of political participation will supplement and support the others. For example, every year on Earth Day, environmental groups stage rallies, remind supporters to register to vote, and encourage them to contact members of Congress. Political actors not only engage in different forms of political participation simultaneously but also sometimes pursue different forms of participation sequentially. For example, the civil rights movement shifted strategies from marches and protests to voter registration and mobilization as the rewards of the former declined and opportunities for the latter increased. One form of political participation paved the way to another. And finally, activists sometimes pursue one form of political participation at the expense of others. For example, as voter turnout declined through the last half of the twentieth century, interest group formation and activity increased. In other words, as citizens lost confidence in the electoral process, they pursued their political interests through other means.

Like water trying to escape through the weakest part of a dam, political actors are always looking for the weakest point in the wall of power. They may engage in different forms of political participation simultaneously, or they may concentrate exclusively on mobilizing voters, lobbying officials, or organizing protests. But the appropriate mix of strategies depends upon the circumstances that political actors confront. Consider the difference between the mass demonstrations that marked opposition to the Vietnam War in the 1960s and the relative absence of such protests by opponents of the Iraq War forty years later. Antiwar activists participated in mass demonstrations against the Vietnam War because electoral politics was a dead end for them. There was no alternative to direct action because both the Democratic and Republican parties supported the war. Forty years later, peace activists faced different circumstances. By 2004, Democrats had come out against the Iraq War. Opponents of the Iraq War now eschewed direct action because, unlike the situation with Vietnam, electoral alternatives were available to them.[4] The sequence in which different forms of political participation appear, and whether they supplement or substitute for one another, depends upon the resources political actors can mobilize and the opportunities they have to deploy them.

Interest groups are organizations that citizens form to influence policy-makers. Groups seek to influence what bills are proposed, what provisions they contain, and how legislators vote on them. They also try to affect such matters as administrative rulings by federal agencies, executive and judicial appointments, and the awarding of government contracts. Examples of interest groups include such well-known organizations as the National Rifle Association (NRA) and Mothers Against Drunk Driving (MADD) as well as more obscure ones such as the Rocky Mountain Llama and Alpaca Association and the Bass Anglers Sportsmen Society. Interest groups such as these connect individuals with government. They are a means for citizens to express their demands and preferences to public officials. Indeed, a variety of interest groups are found in every contemporary democracy, and it is difficult to imagine any democracy without them.[5]

Although interest groups share many properties with political parties and social movements, they can be distinguished from both. Like political parties, they raise money, mobilize voters, and campaign for candidates; but they do not nominate candidates to run for office. Like social movements, interest groups draw together people who share common interests with the intent of influencing policymakers; but they tend to be more formally structured, more durable, and less disruptive in their tactics.

Social movements, such as the antiwar movement of the 1960s or the antiabortion movement of today, engage in unconventional and confrontational forms of political activism. Social movements are also distinguished from interest groups in that they are less formally organized, less hierarchical, and less bureaucratic. Finally, social movements are a more demanding form of political participation than joining an interest group or voting because the risks of social movement activism are so much greater. Consequently, social movements tend to attract people with intense feelings about an issue who are more committed and willing to assume the greater risks that social movement participation entails. Social movements are often identified with groups that have liberal, progressive agendas. But conservatives have also formed social movements to influence public policy. The ideological commitment to participate in social movements is not the monopoly of any one tendency but can be found across the political spectrum.

This chapter first reviews how the interest group universe has changed to include a greater number and variety of groups than in the past. Today, there are interest groups to cover all the policy bases. But that does not mean all interest groups are equally powerful or successful. Groups that represent corporate interests—such as policy offices representing individual firms, trade associations representing specific industries, and peak associations representing businesses across industries—remain the most influential, largely due to the extensive resources at their command. We then proceed to show that interest group formation cannot be taken for granted. Activists have to offer incentives in order to recruit members. The section on interest groups ends with a comparative discussion of **"pluralist" interest group systems** that are found in the United States as opposed to **"corporatist" interest group systems** that are found in Western Europe.

The second half of the chapter is devoted to social movements. Social movements, as we alluded to earlier, are not as hierarchical or formally organized as political parties or interest groups, tend to be more ideological and contentious, and move participation up to a more active and demanding level than other forms of political participation. We then provide an extended case study of the American labor movement as an example of a social movement. But new social movements have emerged recently that are not based on economic issues or occupation, such as those among workers or farmers. Social movements today are frequently based on shared racial, sexual, or ethnic identities; shared values; or quality-of-life issues. Consequently, we provide smaller, capsule accounts of the women's movement, the Religious Right, and the environmental movement to capture the emergence of these new forms of social movements alongside their older, more work-based counterparts.

INTEREST GROUPS

In Chapter 4 we saw that voters and political parties have changed much since the 1960s. So, too, have citizens and interest groups. Membership is more passive at the same time interest groups are more active. Since 1970, the number of interest groups has proliferated, and more groups are raising more demands than ever before. But as new interest groups emerged, it became evident that they were operating in very different ways from those groups that preceded them. They were more centralized and less participatory, more professional and less voluntary, more specialized and less inclusive. Their professionalization means that interest groups now make fewer demands of their members, but their proliferation means they now make greater demands of government.

Before the interest group explosion in the 1970s, the vast majority of interest groups seeking to influence policy represented business: either individual firms like General Motors and General Electric, trade associations like the Association of American Railroads or the Electronic Industries Alliance, or peak organizations like the National Association of Manufacturers or the U.S. Chamber of Commerce. These organizations exerted influence through "subgovernments" that dominated policy in specific issue arenas. Subgovernments, or iron triangles, were composed of three actors whose interests overlapped and were mutually supportive of one another: interest groups that had a stake in an issue, congressional subcommittees that had jurisdiction over the issue, and federal agencies that had responsibility for that issue. All three types of actors benefited from the relationship and consequently cooperated and compromised with one another. For example, one of the most formidable subgovernments was in the realm of defense contracting, where all participants sought to increase defense expenditures. For defense contractors, more defense spending meant more contracts and profits; for members of the House Armed Services Committee, more defense spending meant more military bases in their districts; and for the Pentagon, more defense spending meant more sophisticated weaponry and more career opportunities. Subgovernments were exclusive, discouraging intervention from outsiders; stable, encouraging familiarity and agreement among participants; and insular, protecting their shared interests at the expense of the public interest.[6]

While subgovernments can still be found in issues that involve "low visibility, noncontroversial routine policy making," they are not as prominent or widespread as they once were.[7] New participants have forced their way into the game, and their goals often conflict with those of the established players. Beginning in the 1960s, interest groups that were previously underrepresented, such as environmental and consumer activists as well as civil rights advocates and women's groups, emerged to alter the geometry of iron triangles. Their presence shattered the insular and collusive world of subgovernments. Issues that had been the concern of a few were now the concern of many. As the policy community grew and included more players, it also now included more dissident views, thus breaking up the closed, incestuous relationships that had defined policymaking in the past.

The emergence of these new interest groups was an outgrowth of the civil rights, environmental, consumer, and feminist social movements of the 1960s. As these social movements matured, they experienced a shift that civil rights leader Bayard Rustin called "protest to politics." Their focus changed from marching on Washington to lobbying it, from condemning politicians to endorsing them, and from engaging in spontaneous actions to building permanent organizations.

The shift from protest to politics that saw the energy of the 1960 social movements expressed in the interest group explosion of the 1970s and 1980s was a

WHAT DO YOU THINK?

Is the Shift from Protest to Politics a Sign of Failure or Success for Social Movements?

As groups make the transition from outsiders to insiders, some argue they are selling out, losing their radical edge in exchange for approval and respect by the very groups they once ridiculed. They are giving up the threatening pose from which they drew their power. It is precisely their noncompliance that gives them power, requiring policymakers to grant them concessions to maintain order. Others argue that the transition from protest to politics is part of the maturation process for social movements. Social movements burn out if they can't make this transition to finally achieve the concessions they want through conventional political bargaining. Far from capitulation, political bargaining is necessary to achieve the payoffs groups seek. Otherwise, supporters become discouraged and exhausted by the risks and demands of mobilization. Which of these views do you find more persuasive?

sign of their success as much as their exhaustion. Groups that previously had been excluded because they were either dismissed or unorganized, such as feminists, minorities, consumers, and environmentalists, were now testifying before deferential members of Congress and offering their expert judgment to appreciative federal agencies. Outsiders had finally achieved their goal of becoming insiders.

But the interest group explosion was not only the result of movements from below that successfully elbowed their way in. Government expanded the range of its activities, and new interest groups emerged around the affected policy areas. Each new policy initiative by government created a new group of stakeholders anxious to influence it. New policies create interest groups as much as they are created by them.

Finally, institutional changes in Congress that made it more accessible and inviting to outside influence also contributed to increased levels of interest group formation and activity. As the realms of federal policy expanded, congressional procedures became more democratic, providing interest groups with more opportunities to press their demands. Congressional hearings were opened to the public, and subcommittees became more numerous and assertive.

The new accessibility of Congress encouraged groups to organize and take advantage of the opportunities that were now available.

DAVID AND GOLIATH

Despite the addition of new groups articulating voices that were previously unorganized and unheard, business remains the largest, most organized, best-funded interest group of all. The emergence and success of the new kids on the block generated a counter-mobilization from business to defend its turf. It was like the awakening of a sleeping giant; business began responding to the challenge these new groups posed to them in the form of new environmental, consumer protection, and fair employment legislation. Businesses and industries that previously did not have a presence in Washington now created corporate government affairs offices to represent their interests. Those that were already established now invested more in their existing political operations. Although the interest group universe may now be more crowded and diverse, business interests still predominate within it.[8] Businesses can put more players on the field, and they also enjoy a size advantage. Business groups have more resources—more money, staff members, and social connections—to devote to influencing policymakers. In their research, Frank Baumgartner and Beth L. Leech found that businesses and trade associations comprised more than half of their sample of lobbying groups, and were "by far the best endowed and the most active." They accounted for 85 percent of the total lobbying expenditures that organizations reported, more than all the other types of organizations combined, and they were active across a greater range of issues than other types of groups.[9]

Take the case of Google. Before 2005, after Google's public stock offering transformed the little search engine that could into a market behemoth, the company still did not have a Washington office. But as Google grew, it became a political target. It found itself locked in political combat with telephone companies over net neutrality—that is, whether the phone companies could control what went over their network—and the target of antitrust investigations by the Department of Justice. In response, Google opened a Washington office in 2005 and hired a lobbyist, Alan Davidson, who acknowledged, "It's been the growth of Google as a company and a presence in the industry that has prompted our engagement in Washington."[10] From humble beginnings, Google's Washington presence has grown dramatically. Lobbying expenses increased 160 percent from 2007 to 2009, and now total more than $4 million. In addition to retaining four outside public relations companies and such entrenched Washington lobbying firms as the Podesta Group and the Franklin Square Group, Google's political operation now includes nine registered lobbyists, a dozen or so policy experts, and four people devoted to public relations. Google's political staff has grown so large that it had to move out of its original Washington office to make room for all of them.

Google is a relatively new player in Washington, but its lobbying efforts are fast approaching those of other corporations its size. Even so, these expenditures by an individual company pale in comparison to what industry trade groups spend to influence policy. No group spends more on lobbying the government than the pharmaceutical industry. The drug lobby has more registered lobbyists than there are members of Congress. In addition, many of its lobbyists are either former members of Congress or former congressional staff members, so that when they go to work they are often lobbying their former colleagues. A typical case occurred when Representative Billy Tauzin put his services up for bidding even before he left office. After announcing he would retire from Congress at the end of his term in 2004, he received a $2 million offer to direct the Pharmaceutical Research and Manufacturers of America (PRMA), the lobbying arm of the drug industry. Former staffers and members of Congress such as Billy Tauzin retire and are quickly hired as lobbyists by industry because they bring expertise and access. One critic of the practice complained, "Hiring a well-connected staffer can run a firm something like $300,000 to $600,000 a year, and for a member of Congress, it's anywhere from $1 million to $3 million. The only businesses that can really afford that are those that are very wealthy, but clearly these companies are getting their money's worth."[11]

Table 5.1 shows PRMA's $150 million budget in 2004. (These expenditures do not include the millions of dollars that individual pharmaceutical companies planned to spend on their own.) In justifying its budget, PRMA warned that the industry needed to prepare for "the perfect storm" that included the threat of price controls, initiatives by states to make drugs more affordable, and access to cheaper drugs from abroad. To prepare for the approaching tempest, PRMA planned to spend $1 million to "produce an echo chamber of economists," that would speak against price controls, contribute $2.5 million to sympathetic research and policy organizations that could pose as "credible sources," and earmark $12.3 million to develop alliances with doctors, minority groups, patients, and universities in an effort to shape public opinion.

All of this was preparation for when the perfect storm actually did make land in the form of President Obama's proposal to increase health-care coverage for Americans and restrict insurers from "cherry-picking" clients and denying their claims. In response, the largest insurers, hospitals, and medical groups hired more than 350 former members of Congress and staff people to lobby their former colleagues. The health-care industry as a whole spent $267 million in lobbying in 2009, more than any industry has ever spent on behalf of a

TABLE 5.1

PRMA PROPOSED BUDGET FOR FISCAL 2004

Division	In Millions
Federal affairs	$14.4
Alliance Development	12.3
Pursues strategic alliances with economists, doctors, patients and influential members of minority groups to shape public opinion.	
State government affairs	11.7
Legal	9.7
Public affairs	9.4
Policy and research	9.4
International	6.3
Scientific and regulatory affairs	4.3
Finance and operations	4.3
Office of the president	1.5
SUBTOTAL	$83.3
OTHER EXPENSES	$66.7*
TOTAL	$160.0

*Includes an additional $6.3 million for a contingency fund and an addition to reserves.
SOURCE: *New York Times,* 1 June 2003, p. 33.

single issue in a single year. PRMA led the pack in terms of both spending and employing former government officials as lobbyists. It devoted $26 million to lobbying in 2009, hired forty-eight lobbying firms to work alongside its in-house operation, and employed 137 former government officials among its 165 lobbyists working the halls of Congress.[12]

As the examples from Google and PRMA demonstrate, lobbying is a sophisticated, multifaceted activity today. It involves more than simply giving members of Congress campaign contributions, taking them to dinner, or providing them with reliable facts and convincing analyses of legislation. All of these strategies for exerting influence remain essential but are increasingly regarded as insufficient. Contemporary lobbying now goes out in all directions to include not only the media, by providing reporters and editors with information, but also the public, by trying to shape its perception of an issue. Interest groups are now as active in trying to frame how issues are perceived as they are in trying to influence what policymakers should do about them. Success at grassroots strategies that shape the political agenda paves the way for success in how Washington policymakers react to it. A consequence of **all-directional lobbying**, pursuing "insider" and "outsider" strategies simultaneously, is to ratchet up its cost. As lobbying becomes more extensive, it becomes more expensive. It now costs more to play competitively, thus giving an advantage to those groups, such as business, that have the resources to do so.[13]

In addition to their resource advantage in interest group competition, business leaders have social connections with policymakers that other groups do not have, and they enjoy a mobilization of bias in their favor based upon their control of the means of production that is not available to other groups. The result is a privileged position for business that is seen as so natural that business is often not regarded as a special interest at all.[14] But just because business is "bigger, stronger, and faster" than other groups, that does not mean it always wins. The size advantage of business is canceled out when different firms and industries—some representing importers and others exporters, some representing producers and others distributers—are arrayed against one another. For example, in the struggle over President Obama's health-care bill, the U.S. Chamber of Commerce opposed a mandate on employers to provide health insurance; but Wal-Mart and the temp firm Kelly Services supported it. A similar divorce occurred in response to President Obama's climate change bill designed to limit greenhouse gas emissions. Major oil companies opposed the bill while natural gas producers supported it. Utilities with access to hydroelectric or nuclear power were in favor of it, and coal-dependent utilities lobbied against it. A once monolithic industry was divided in its approach to climate change legislation because of the differential impact it would have on energy producers. Coal-fired utilities and oil companies that emit large amounts of greenhouse gases would be hurt by the bill while cleaner energy producers, such as natural gas and the renewable power industry, would be favored.[15]

Moreover, even when business interests are unified, they may not execute their political strategy well. Sometimes they adopt the wrong game plan and find themselves outmaneuvered in the struggle over policy by more agile and creative opponents. And sometimes business has to play in the hostile court of public opinion that neutralizes its advantages. For example, public resentment over excessive executive pay made it more difficult for members of Congress to support giving bailout money to banks and other Wall Street firms. Policymakers did not want to be perceived by the public as coddling wealthy bankers and consequently were less inclined to accede to banker's demands. Although organized business interests may be bigger, stronger, and faster, the power of democracy is sometimes sufficient to overcome the many advantages that they enjoy.[16]

THE CHANGING QUALITY OF MEMBERSHIP

In 1831 a young French aristocrat came to the United States to examine how the new democracy worked. He spent two years touring what were then the twenty-six states of the Republic and came away impressed with Americans as "a nation of joiners." In his brilliant account, *Democracy in America*, Alexis de Tocqueville wrote: "Americans of all ages, all conditions, and all dispositions constantly form associations. They have not only commercial and manufacturing companies, in which all take part, but associations of a thousand other kinds, religious, moral, serious, futile, general or restricted, enormous or diminutive."[17]

Tocqueville left readers with the impression that forming organizations is easy and natural. People with common interests simply get together to pursue their shared goals. But forming organizations is not so straightforward. Someone has to invest time, provide leadership, and commit resources to make it happen. Such skills and resources may not exist and certainly are not evenly distributed among groups. For this reason, organizations of poor people, who lack time, resources, and leadership skills, are very rare while those of higher-status groups are more common. In addition, organizations face the **free-rider problem**. That is, if people acted rationally, they would not contribute to groups if they could still receive the benefits. They would free ride, let others go to meetings and pay dues to the Sierra Club, and then just sit back and enjoy the benefits of clean air and water that environmentalists worked for. Of course, if everyone behaved like this, the Sierra Club would not exist.

But the Sierra Club does exist. And it exists partly because groups offer a variety of incentives that entice people to join them. Some groups, for instance, offer material benefits to recruit members. Members receive some tangible reward for joining. For example, the American Association of Retired Persons (AARP), which represents the interests of the elderly and is the second-largest membership organization in the United States after the Catholic Church, recruits members by offering medical, insurance, and travel discounts to those who join.

Other groups depend upon **purposive incentives**, rather than **material incentives**, to recruit members. Such organizations give people an opportunity to express their common values and realize their common goals. Membership in these organizations—such as the National Right to Life Committee (NRLC), which opposes abortion rights, and the National Abortion and Reproductive Rights Action League (NARAL), which supports them—is an expression of one's values.[18]

Much of the interest group surge in the 1970s involved groups that recruited on the basis of purposive as opposed to material incentives. This focus has given contemporary interest group political activity a more ideological, partisan, and aggressive character. Political conflict becomes harsher and less compromising when people are organized on the basis of their convictions.

Another interesting shift among interest groups has been a change in the quality and class character of their memberships. Traditional mass membership organizations, such as the National Association for the Advancement of Colored People (NAACP), had state and local chapters and required members to pay dues. Members engaged in politics by participating in the life of their organization, developing civic values and organizational skills in the process. And these organizations reached down to include workers and promote their civic and political engagement. But such organizations now face increased competition from more professionally managed advocacy organizations, such as the Children's Defense Fund or MoveOn.org, that do not have dues-paying members or local chapters. These types of organizations are funded by foundations, direct mail, or Internet fund-raising appeals as opposed to membership dues.[19]

The emergence of these new professionalized organizations has increased existing class inequalities in terms of which types of citizens are represented politically through interest groups. Wealthy and well-educated citizens have always been disproportionately represented through interest groups, but this is particularly true of these new professionalized advocacy organizations. A higher proportion of their supporters are drawn from the middle and upper class than was true of more traditional mass membership organizations. As a result, the predominance of these new professionalized advocacy organizations amplifies the voice of the well-off and well educated, who find their minimal demands congenial, while the voice of the lower classes has been muted as the traditional mass membership organizations they were accustomed to declined.[20] Thus, the impact of these new organizations on the quality of American democracy has been somewhat paradoxical. The proliferation of these centralized, **professional advocacy groups** has brought new voices into the political arena but has exacerbated class-based inequalities in terms of who is speaking. They have increased the number of views expressed in the political process without broadening the base of who expresses them.[21]

E-MEDIA, INTEREST GROUPS, AND POLITICAL PARTICIPATION

The rise of new professional advocacy organizations has been given added impetus by the emergence of the Internet. The Internet has been conducive to their growth because these types of organizations require only weak ties between supporters and organizers that can be managed through the web at low cost. According to the political scientist Mark S. Bonchek, "electronic forms of communication reduce communication, coordination and information costs, facilitating group formation, group efficiency, membership recruitment, and member retention."[22] A website that may cost only $100 to create can be used by political organizers to recruit members, appeal for contributions, inform supporters, coordinate their activity, and mobilize them for action. With the click of a mouse, supporters can send public officials a message through e-mail links that interest groups provide. Furthermore, software packages are available that permit interest groups to sign up their supporters for e-mail alerts, follow who responded, and track how many e-mail appeals were received by each targeted official. The Internet has increased the reach of interest groups at the same time it has reduced their costs. The bureaucracy that membership organizations once found necessary to carry out basic functions of recruitment and coordination is less necessary because these tasks can now be done quicker and cheaper through computer-mediated communication.

No group reflects the brave new world of interest groups in the Internet era more than MoveOn.org. In 1998, spouses Wes Boyd and Joan Blades formed MoveOn.org in their basement using a standard Internet account. They e-mailed friends, requesting them to visit their website and sign a petition that urged Congress to "move on" and censure President Clinton for his sexual escapades as opposed to impeaching him. They also suggested that friends forward their appeal to their friends. Within a short period, the site accumulated 500,000 signatures. The website also solicited money for candidates running against pro-impeachment incumbents in Congress. The appeal broke records for online political fund-raising, hauling in $13 million by the end of 1999. From humble beginnings, MoveOn has become a formidable advocacy group for liberal causes and a major fund-raiser for progressive Democratic candidates. It continues to use electronic media to communicate with and mobilize supporters as well as bring people together in their neighborhoods for local political activity.

Like previous technological breakthroughs such as radio and television, the Internet has had a transformative effect on politics. Because it is so effective at reducing the organizational costs of recruiting and coordinating supporters, the Internet facilitates collective action. **Political entrepreneurs** can now at very low cost mobilize a virtual community for political action, leading to more activity by more groups. E-media, which includes the Internet, chat rooms, websites, blogging, e-mail, and other electronic forms of communication, broadens the range of interests represented, making collective action accessible to those who lack financial and institutional resources.

E-media also quickens the pace of politics, accelerating the process of recruiting and mobilizing supporters. New groups can form and deploy rapidly using electronic media. Furthermore, the Internet makes the interest group universe less stable. Just as easily as new groups form, as e-media reduces their organizational costs, so can they dissolve. Internet-based groups travel light. The virtual community that is built around an issue requires little commitment and is easily shed once an issue is exhausted.[23] Finally, e-media permits people to communicate more directly with one another, independently of leaders and formal organizations. Collective action no longer requires bureaucratic structures to organize and coordinate activity, which can now be done through e-mail, chat rooms, and a website. E-media alters not only the way in which interest groups mobilize, but their internal structures as well.

A COMPARATIVE PERSPECTIVE ON AMERICAN INTEREST GROUPS

Rich democracies, such as the United States and many countries in Europe, differ in the nature of their interest group politics. Some countries, like the United States, have a plethora of interest groups. Interest groups proliferate in the United States because the divided and decentralized structure of the state provides so many access points and opportunities for groups to influence policymakers: in committees and subcommittees within both the Senate and the House, in the courts, and in the various agencies of the executive branch. The permeable, open structure of the policymaking process invites groups with a stake in policy to organize and exert their influence upon it. In addition, the weak party system in the United States encourages interest group formation. Legislators are more open to outside influences when party discipline is weak, and interest groups can provide them with campaign assistance that parties are unable to supply.

The sheer number of interest groups leads them to compete fiercely for members. Consequently, interest group membership is unstable and turnover is high. Furthermore, American interest groups successfully recruit only a relatively small proportion of their potential constituency and are less "encompassing." For instance, only a small proportion of workers belong to unions, and only a small proportion of businesses belong to the U.S. Chamber of Commerce. Finally, American interest groups tend to be weaker and more decentralized than those found in other rich democracies. They lack the power to sanction members or to coordinate and direct their activity.

Political systems with interest groups that have qualities like those in the United States are referred to as pluralist interest group systems. Political systems with interest groups that are more encompassing, fewer in number, less competitive, and more centralized are commonly referred to as corporatist interest group systems. Examples include interest group systems in Sweden, Austria, and Germany. In corporatist systems, interest groups are often licensed by the state with a monopoly in their market, and membership in them may even be compulsory. Such interest groups are normally included in the policy-making process as opposed to having to influence it from the outside, as American interest groups do. As one can see from Table 5.2, the U.S. interest group system is considered the least corporatist of any of the rich democracies.

Corporatist and pluralist interest group systems differ in their political effects. Groups in pluralist systems tend to press their demands single-mindedly. Competition for members leads to a bidding war among them, which tends to make them adversarial and uncompromising. In contrast, corporatism tends to moderate interest group demands. With larger and broader memberships to consider, corporatist interest groups have to synthesize their members'

TABLE 5.2

INTEREST GROUP SYSTEMS

Country	Corporatist Scores
Austria	5.000
Norway	4.864
Sweden	4.674
Netherlands	4.000
Denmark	3.545
Germany (West)	3.543
Switzerland	3.375
Finland	3.295
Japan	2.912
Belgium	2.841
Ireland	2.000
New Zealand	1.955
Australia	1.680
France	1.674
United Kingdom	1.652
Portugal	1.500
Italy	1.477
Spain	1.250
Canada	1.150
United States	1.150

SOURCE: Alan Siaroff, "Corporatism in 24 Industrial Democracies: Meaning and Measurement," *European Journal of Political Research* 36 (1999): 198.

demands and articulate only the most general interest among them. Moreover, participation in the policymaking process forces contending groups to consider the big picture and compromise their own interests for the greater good. Groups in corporatist systems can afford to do so because they do not have to fear that members will defect to a rival group or worry that that they will be unable to enforce their agreement upon their members.

Interest groups in the United States are extensive today, covering all the policy bases. There are few issues on which interests groups are not active, influencing policy. But political participation sometimes escapes their boundaries into less organized, more spontaneous forms of political expression. Social movements form, raising the stakes considerably for participants because social movements require a higher level of commitment from them than interest groups. The relatively sedate and ordered world of interest groups gives way to the more active, intensive, and confrontational world of social movements.

SOCIAL MOVEMENTS

On December 1, 1955, Rosa Parks, a forty-two-year-old grandmother, boarded a bus headed home after a hard day's work at a store in downtown Montgomery, Alabama. All thirty-six seats on the bus were filled; blacks were by law seated in the back and whites in the front. When a white man got on, the bus driver asked the four black passengers seated just behind the last row of whites to move so he could be seated. No one got up to offer a seat. The driver then insisted more firmly that the four blacks vacate their seats. Three of them complied and moved to stand in the back of the bus, but Parks remained seated. The driver told her she was now illegally in the white section of the bus. She calmly replied that she had taken her seat in the back of the bus behind whites, just as the law required. The bus driver countered that the white section of the bus was where he said it was, and that he had the power to enforce local segregation laws. He notified Parks that she was under arrest, and the bus stopped until two Montgomery police officers arrived to take Parks to jail.

Parks's defiance precipitated the Montgomery bus boycott, in which blacks walked, carpooled, shared rides, and took taxis to get to work, visit relatives, and go shopping. Initially, the boycott was to last just one day and its demands were timid, negotiating the etiquette of segregation on the city's buses. But the boycott was so successful that it was extended. As it stretched into weeks and then months, the emboldened black community began to demand an end to segregation on buses. A new organization, the Montgomery Improvement

Rosa Parks sitting in the front of a bus in Montgomery, Alabama after the Supreme Court ruled segregation illegal on the city's bus system in 1956.

Association (MIA), was created to provide leadership, coordinate activity, and raise money. And a new pastor who had arrived in Montgomery just a year earlier, the twenty-five-year-old Reverend Martin Luther King, was chosen by default to lead the MIA. The white community responded viciously with bombings, mass arrests, and police harassment. But on November 15, 1956—almost a full year after Parks's arrest—the U.S. Supreme Court upheld a lower court decision declaring state and local laws requiring segregation on buses unconstitutional. Segregation on city buses was now illegal, and blacks in Montgomery celebrated their victory by ending the boycott.[24]

The Montgomery bus boycott was one of the early struggles in the budding civil rights movement. It is an example of a social movement; as we mentioned previously, social movements are not as hierarchical or formally organized as interest groups and political parties, tend to be more ideological and contentious, and move participation up to a more active and demanding level than other forms of political expression. Social movements share certain qualities that we highlight below.[25]

Social movements rarely begin with radical demands. Their original claims are usually quite limited and conciliatory, which leads supporters to expect that they will be granted. It is the denial of what are regarded as reasonable claims that escalates challenges and radicalizes groups. Such was the case, for example, with the Montgomery bus boycott. Only when the MIA's initial effort to negotiate the etiquette of segregation—whether blacks were entitled to any seats when the white section filled up—was rejected by whites did the group call for an end to segregation itself.

Second, social movements arise in response to changes in the political environment that create new opportunities groups can exploit. For example, new openings for political participation may arise as a result of the dimming repressive power of the state, or allies may emerge who can provide groups with new resources that permit them to mount challenges they otherwise would not have been able to make. Finally, splits among political elites also encourage groups to engage in collective action.[26] In the case of the Montgomery bus boycott, conflict over racial policy between the federal and state governments gave hope to activists. The federal government had just outlawed school segregation in *Brown v. Board of Education*, signaling activists that it would not support Alabama's segregation laws. The Supreme Court decision legitimized civil rights demands and emboldened activists to challenge state segregation laws.

Third, social movements empower their followers as well as develop a sense of moral legitimacy among them that their demands are justified and right. They tend to create a collective self-confidence in place of typical feelings of resignation and deference, and they offer a new way of interpreting events in place of the self-serving explanations that the dominant culture offers.[27] King gave voice to this alternative culture when he addressed the Montgomery black community on the eve of the bus boycott. Imploring his listeners to have faith in themselves and their collective power, he assured them: "If we are wrong—the Supreme Court of this nation is wrong. If we are wrong—God Almighty is wrong. If we are wrong—Jesus of Nazareth was merely a utopian dreamer and never came down to earth! If we are wrong—justice is a lie."[28]

Fourth, social movements require organizations that can develop and disseminate an alternative culture. Most social movements are built on organizations that cultivate identities, raise resources, and coordinate activities. Harry Boyte referred to such organizations as **free spaces**, where an oppositional culture could be elaborated that was insulated from the disapproval and reproach of the dominant culture. The Black Church offered such a haven for the Montgomery bus boycott by providing a physical space that was autonomous from white control where meetings could be held and an affirming message of hope and moral worth could be articulated. It was an expression of the black community that served as the base of operations for the bus boycott.

Finally, social movements flourish when they are able to enlarge the scope of conflict and mobilize people who were previously bystanders to become involved in the conflict.[29] They do so because protest and disruption are the strategies of people who lack more conventional political resources. Enlarging the scope of conflict draws new groups into the struggle in order to circumvent an unfavorable balance of power. For example, in the Montgomery bus boycott, the MIA used tactics designed to dramatize the issue for the press and television in order to reach a broader audience beyond Montgomery and replaced its initial modest demands with a sweeping challenge to segregation, thereby drawing in national civil rights groups as allies.

In the next section we offer an extended case study of the labor movement followed by shorter, capsule accounts of the women's movement, the Christian Right, and the environmental movement. The labor movement, encompassing the struggle to form unions and give workers a voice in their wages and working conditions, is typical of social movements that form around class and occupation. But new social movements have arisen that are not based on shared economic circumstances, but on shared identities as women, blacks, or gays. And they tend not to raise economic demands but to organize around moral values, as the Christian Right does around abortion, or quality-of-life issues, as environmentalists do around air and water pollution.

The interest group universe has become larger and more complicated as traditional economic interest groups are now being joined by other types of groups; the same is true of social movements. Older social movements based around work and occupation have been joined by new social movements organized around people's identities, moral values, and quality-of-life concerns. Following our discussion of the labor movement, we feature two groups on the left, the women's and environmental movements, and one on the right—Christian fundamentalists—to highlight these new social movements.

The Labor Movement

The modern American labor movement began with a punch. In 1935, at the American Federation of Labor (AFL) convention in Atlantic City, New Jersey, John L. Lewis, president of the United Mine Workers of America (UMWA), beseeched delegates to launch an aggressive organizing campaign among industrial workers. The time was ripe, he argued, for workers everywhere were on the march, looking to the AFL for leadership and direction. Textile workers in the South, longshoremen in the West, and autoworkers in the North struck and stopped production. Moreover, new political opportunities had opened up with

President Roosevelt's election and his promise of a New Deal, especially passage of the National Industrial Relations Act (NIRA) that declared workers had the right to form unions. But the AFL, which organized skilled workers such as carpenters and machinists, was reluctant to seize the opportunity and welcome into its ranks unskilled workers in the burgeoning mass production industries of auto, steel, rubber, electrical appliances, and textiles. Lewis could abide the AFL's dithering no longer. As the convention came to a close, Lewis's patience gave out. After an exchange of words with the powerful AFL traditionalist William B. Hutcheson, president of the United Brotherhood of Carpenters (UBC), Lewis jumped to his feet, leaped over a row of chairs, struck the Carpenters president with his fist, and sent him sprawling against a table. Afterward, journalists reported, "Lewis casually adjusted his tie and collar, relit his cigar, and sauntered through the crowded aisles."[30] Two weeks later, Lewis led six affiliated unions out of the AFL to form a rival federation called the Congress of Industrial Organizations (CIO). The modern American labor movement was born.

When the Depression first began, workers initially looked to their employers for help, and many placed their faith in company unions that employers sponsored. But such hopes were quickly disappointed, and workers began to form their own unions. They believed that only a legally binding **collective bargaining** agreement negotiated by an independent union could protect them from managerial favoritism and arbitrariness. Employers resisted these efforts fiercely. In response, workers occupied factories, fought with police, engaged in mass picketing, and staged industry-wide strikes in support of their demand for union recognition.

Responding to the groundswell of militancy and protest, Congress asserted jurisdiction over labor policy, taking it over from unsympathetic courts that were insulated from ripening public opinion. In 1935 Congress passed the National Labor Relations Act (NLRA), guaranteeing the right of workers to form unions. Union membership surged. By 1941, the new CIO included 3 million members; AFL unions displayed even greater growth, adding 4 million to their membership rolls. The labor movement could also point to achievements in the arena of social policy. Roosevelt's New Deal included the passage of social security, unemployment compensation, and minimum-wage laws that provided workers some security and protection from the vagaries of the market. Finally, labor was now regarded as a formidable political force. Unions devoted more resources to political activity once it became apparent that success in organizing and collective bargaining depended on the rules governing them. Unions not only increased their level of political activity, but directed more of it through the Democratic Party. This gave labor influence within the new governing coalition as the Democrats rose to become the majority party.

Economically and politically, then, the rise of the CIO and growth of the AFL in the 1930s transformed the politics of power. Greater industrial democracy, in the form of unions to check the unilateral power of management, was fused with greater political democracy in the form of more working-class influence. New relations of power were evident on the shop floor, where workers in many industries now had rights codified in collective bargaining agreements, and on the floor of Congress, where workers were now able to achieve legislative victories through their alliance with the Democratic Party.[31]

In the 1940s, unions consolidated many of the gains they had made during the previous decade. Even some of the most recalcitrant employers, who had withstood the militancy of the thirties, now capitulated and recognized unions. Anti-union strongholds at Ford and Bethlehem Steel fell to new organizing campaigns. In addition, union contracts became more elaborate, covering such issues as wage rates, grievance procedures, promotions, hiring, and layoffs. The dictatorial power of the foreman was now replaced by the workplace rule of law. World War II accelerated these advances. With firms hiring as many workers as they could find to fulfill wartime orders, union membership reached its peak in 1945 at 35 percent of the workforce.

WHAT DO YOU THINK?

Was the New Deal a Victory or Defeat for Workers?

Some view the New Deal as a lost opportunity in which an insurgent labor movement was channeled into support for unions and the Democratic Party. More radical change that challenged the structure of American capitalism was compromised in favor of cosmetic bureaucratic reforms that, in the end, strengthened it. Others argue that workers achieved remarkable gains during the New Deal. Stable unions were created, and the modern American welfare state was established. Should the New Deal be condemned for pacifying insurgent workers and channeling their demands into mere bureaucratic reforms, or should it be celebrated as a working-class victory that improved working-class lives?

At the end of the war, employers wanted to roll back the gains labor had made in the preceding years; for their part, workers were intent on protecting their standard of living. The result was the largest wave of strikes in American history, as hundreds of thousands of meatpackers, autoworkers, and steelworkers walked off their jobs. Not only did the unions survive this massive strike wave, but many new contracts included significant wage increases. But the strike wave also provoked a political backlash in the form of new antilabor legislation. In the 1946 elections, Republicans won majorities in both the House and the Senate and proceeded to pass the Taft-Hartley Act, which contained various provisions designed to constrain union organizing and strikes.

For the next twenty years, through the 1950s and 1960s, many managers bowed to the facts and reluctantly accepted unions as legitimate bargaining agents for their workers. In 1955, the AFL and CIO merged to become the AFL-CIO, thus uniting the two wings of the labor movement. Collective bargaining became routinized, even as its scope expanded to include new items such as pensions and health insurance. It also became increasingly centralized; negotiations no longer occurred plant by plant or even firm by firm, but across whole industries. Unions negotiated industry-wide with committees of employers in an effort to take wages out of competition. And in what was referred to as pattern bargaining, settlements from one industry became the standard for contracts in other industries. Although some analysts view the routinization and centralization of collective bargaining during this period as evidence of labor's bureaucratization and loss of militancy, these developments were actually the rewards of hard-earned victories. They were real achievements that were not won easily, but attained through strikes whose rate of incidence was higher than in any other Western democracy. Such high rates of industrial conflict indicated not only that employers were still testing for weakness, but that unions now had the organizational strength to survive such contests and even prevail in them.

As a result of union efforts, workers enjoyed more security, higher standards of living, and greater political influence in the postwar era. Their lives improved as citizens and as employees. But the foundation for such improvements was fragile. Union membership was increasing in absolute numbers but declining as a percentage of the workforce. Regions (e.g., the South) and occupations (service sector work) where unions were weak were growing while areas and industries where unions were strong were declining. Moreover, American business was facing more market pressure. As competition increased due to deregulation, globalization, and the growth of the nonunion sector, managerial attitudes toward unions hardened. To restore profits, management began to take back the slack they believed existed in labor relations; they demanded lower wages, cuts in benefits, longer contracts, fewer work rules, and less job protection. In many cases, demands for such concessions were a pretext for trying to eliminate unions altogether. In 1978, United Auto Workers President Douglas Fraser charged business with waging "a one-sided class war in this country" and complained that "the leaders of industry, commerce and finance in the U.S. have broken and discarded the fragile, unwritten contract previously existing during a period of growth and progress."[32]

The new employer offensive forced the unions to retreat. Unions signed concessionary contracts that rolled back gains they had achieved in previous negotiations. The new contractual terms reduced work rules, giving management more flexibility in deploying labor. Collective bargaining agreements were no longer conducted on an industry-wide basis; they were now decentralized to the plant level, thus subjecting workers to whipsawing in which workplaces competed with each other to offer lower wages so as not to put their employer at a cost disadvantage. Finally, standard wage increases with inflation adjustments that permitted some income security were replaced by new forms of compensation, including bonuses and profit sharing, that tied workers' welfare more closely to that of the firm.[33]

Retreat was also apparent in the decline of strikes. Strikes became less frequent because unions did not believe they could win them anymore. The strike weapon was neutralized by automation, the increasing ratio of managers to workers, the use of replacement workers for those out on strike, and the ineffectiveness of picket lines. *Fortune*, a business journal, reported, "Managers are discovering that strikes can be broken, that the cost of breaking them is often lower than the cost of taking them, and that strikebreaking doesn't have to be a dirty word."[34] For unions that still dared to call their members out on strike, success was no longer measured by their ability to prevent concessions but by the more humble criterion of avoiding elimination.

Finally, labor's decline was evident in its waning membership. Today, in comparing the United States to other Western democracies, only France has a lower proportion of its workforce that belongs to unions.[35]

From a peak of 35 percent in 1945, the percentage of workers who belong to unions plummeted to only 12.4 percent in 2008. And even this grim statistic overstates the degree of unionization in the United States. If one looks only at private sector workers, the unionization rate in 2008 was just 7.4 percent. The drop in membership can be attributed to three factors. First, changes in labor law made it harder to organize. As a resurgent Republican Party pulled American politics to the right, labor law increasingly was interpreted in a way that made it more difficult to organize new members. Second, employers have become more antagonistic to unions. Finally, union membership fell as a result of a sharp drop in manufacturing jobs due to plant closings and pressure from imports.

Labor today is depleted and disarmed. But there is still movement in the labor movement. In retreat, it has looked to new leaders, organizations, and strategies to stem its decline. In 1995, dissident unions deposed a stodgy AFL-CIO leadership in the first contested presidential election in the organization's forty-year history. The new leadership promised a departure from business as usual by devoting more resources to organizing and increasing labor's political influence. But some affiliated unions felt that even this new leadership was not aggressive or daring enough. They disaffiliated from the AFL-CIO to form a rival labor federation called Change To Win. Regardless of which labor federation a union belongs to, most union leaders realize they cannot afford to be complacent and are pursuing a variety of new strategies. First, unions recognize that traditional strikes at the point of production are no longer effective, and so they are conducting corporate campaigns outside of it. **Corporate campaigns** try to raise the stakes for business by informing authorities of regulatory violations that employers have committed, publicizing unsavory corporate conduct, or pressuring banks to withdraw lines of credit to recalcitrant firms. For example, unions have bankrolled efforts to embarrass and harass Wal-Mart in order to soften the company's anti-union policies.

Second, unions are now more willing to appeal to allies, such as community groups, students, and religious leaders, for support. Unions that were previously skeptical of outsiders and avoided issues beyond immediate workplace concerns are now more likely to participate in coalitions with such groups and support their demands. When the BASF chemical company tried to drive out a union from one of its plants in Louisiana, workers there successfully made common cause with environmentalists to protest the company's environmental infractions and the threat BASF posed to the health of local residents.[36] The new social unionism was also evident in the successful Justice for Janitors campaign in Los Angeles in 1990, when unions mobilized the local Hispanic community to support the predominantly Hispanic striking workforce. This model was then utilized to organize janitors in subsequent campaigns in cities like Houston and Miami, which have large Hispanic populations. Finally, unions have circumvented labor laws in which they have lost confidence to organize workers. This was the successful strategy followed by the Hotel and Restaurant Workers Union in organizing Las Vegas, which boasts the highest unionization

WHAT DO YOU THINK?

The Future of Unions

Is the decline of the labor movement reversible? Some argue that the future for unionism looks bleak everywhere, not only in the United States. Union membership is declining in almost all Western democracies; the United States is unusual only to the extent that the decline of unionism happened first and fastest here as opposed to elsewhere. Modern trends such as the shift from industrialism to postindustrialism, the growth in values of individual expression, and globalization are supposedly just too powerful for unions to overcome. Others argue that the same reasons why people joined unions in the past still exist, only more so. So long as workers lack a meaningful voice in their conditions of work, there will always be a demand for unions. Nothing fundamental has changed. The current decline of the labor movement is simply a temporary defeat in the long war between labor and capital. Do you think unions are still necessary and viable?

rate of any city in the United States.[37] Some of these strategies have begun to pay dividends as unions in 2008 experienced their largest membership gains in over a quarter-century.

Socially and politically, unions can also see signs of renewal. The number of people who report in surveys that they would like to belong to a union has gone up 25 percent since 1984; over half of all respondents now indicate they would like to join one.[38] And union households continue to be a dependable and distinctive voting bloc. In 2008, they comprised about one-fifth of all voters and were more likely than their nonunion peers to turn out and vote Democratic. Obama received two-thirds of the vote from union members, compared to a bare majority (51 percent) he won among nonunion voters. The pulse is weak within the labor movement. But the heart is still beating.

The Women's Movement

Historians often separate the women's movement into three waves of activism. The first wave, which began in 1848, owed a large debt to the antislavery movement in which many women participated. They saw parallels between the

oppression of slaves and that of women, and their participation in the aboli-
tionist movement also gave women an opportunity to develop leadership and
organizational skills that they then applied to their own movement.

Following the Civil War, when the Reconstruction Congress passed constitutional amendments giving blacks the right to vote, it pointedly failed to do
the same for women. Consequently, an independent women's movement developed whose goal was female **suffrage**. By the 1890s, groups such as female tem-
perance workers, social reformers who worked with women in immigrant
slums, and middle-class women involved in charitable volunteer work began
to coalesce around the demand for female suffrage because they increasingly
recognized that their own diverse interests could be advanced through it. The
National American Woman Suffrage Association organized and concentrated
the considerable power of these diverse groups into a movement that successfully pressured Congress to pass the Nineteenth Amendment, which enfran-
chised women in 1920.

The second wave of activism began in the 1960s. Like the first wave, in
which the emergence of women's activism was connected closely to the antislavery movement, women's liberation in the second wave was closely tied to
the struggle for black equality. Parallels were again drawn between discrimination against women and discrimination against blacks, and women gained
organizing and leadership skills through their participation in the civil rights
movement. But female activists realized they needed to act independently
because their own grievances often were dismissed as trivial in comparison
to those of blacks, and they were frequently victims of sexism within the civil
rights movement.

Second-wave activism moved along two fronts. The first was to win political equality for women, which led to the creation of the National Organization
of Women (NOW). NOW was founded in 1966 as a civil rights organization
for women, and its mission was to lobby and litigate on behalf of equal rights
for women. It enjoyed many successes, such as outlawing pay and employment
discrimination on the basis of sex. It also lobbied on behalf of the equal rights
amendment to the Constitution, which passed Congress but fell three states
short of the two-thirds required for ratification. By 1975, *Time Magazine*
awarded its "Person of the Year" award to American Women in celebration of
the women's movement's many achievements.

But legal, formal change was not sufficient. Many female activists opened a
second front in the war against sexism, claiming that the personal was political. Laws needed to be changed; but people's consciousness also needed to be
raised. For example, women joined consciousness-raising groups in which expe-

riences were shared and patriarchic values challenged. Consciousness raising provided the free space in which women developed the confidence and ideological clarity to become political activists. Part of revealing the personal as political involved challenging female stereotypes and gender roles. For example, activists protested the Miss America pageant as a sexist objectification of women, and women began to demand that men do their fair share of the housework. Feminists argued that women's liberation began at home.

Feminism flourished during the second wave and was expressed in many tendencies and groups. It included liberal feminists who defined women's liberation in terms of formal legal equality for women, socialist feminists who perceived women's subordination as part of a larger system of racial and class inequality, and radical feminists who defined male domination itself as the root of the problem. Despite the ultimate failure of the Equal Rights Amendment, the movement enjoyed so many successes—making discrimination against women illegal, getting women admitted to such male bastions as the military academies, and creating women's studies departments on college campuses— that the amendment's defeat was almost irrelevant. Success in the second wave posed the question, "Where do we go from here?" which dominated third-wave feminism.

Third-wave feminism marked a generational change as much as it did a change in goals and strategy for the women's movement. It emerged in the 1990s among young women who, some argue, grew up taking the achievements of second-wave feminism for granted. Third-wave feminists tend to be less invested in issues of equality than in exploring their own identities and promoting individual empowerment for women. Women should be free to pursue their lives unhindered by traditional stereotypes about women as well as by feminist demands to prove that women are the opposite of such myths. Third-wave feminists want to move beyond those who would put women on a pedestal and those who would portray them as victims.[39]

The Religious Right

The New Deal forged the modern labor movement, and it was the crucible that gave birth to modern conservatism. Writing in the 1960s, Frank Meyer, a leading conservative essayist, attributed "the crystallization . . . of an American conservative movement . . . to the revolutionary transformation of America that began with the election of Franklin Roosevelt in 1932."[40] New Deal federal programs antagonized those who believed in small government and free markets; the emergence of ethnic working-class voters threatened southern control of the

Democratic Party; and the new majority New Deal Democratic coalition relegated the Republican Party and their business supporters to minority status.

But modern conservatism was also influenced by the emergence of the Religious Right, which was composed of white evangelical and fundamentalist Christians. These groups mobilized politically in response to social issues such as sex education, gay rights, and most importantly, abortion rights. They deplored what they regarded as the moral decay of American life, which they attributed to the government's failure to maintain Christian values as derived from the Bible. For example, they believed government policy should reflect biblical injunctions that marriage was supposed to be only between a man and a woman; that life began at conception and pregnancies should not be terminated; and that gender roles are God-given and should not be muddled. These views led the Religious Right to oppose gay marriage, abortion rights, and the Equal Rights Amendment, respectively. Moreover, their views on social issues were now part of a sophisticated, ideologically coherent conceptual framework. Given their position on one social issue, it was now possible to predict that they held conservative positions on other issues as well.[41] For example, the sociologist Kristen Luker found that antiabortion activists not only defended the moral claims of the fetus but also shared broader values regarding the proper role of women as mothers and the view that women's work inside the home should be valued as much as it is outside of it.[42]

The Religious Right shares many attributes of the leftist social movements we detailed earlier. First, like the civil rights movement of the 1960s, the Religious Right is able to attract support across the class spectrum, from plumbers to professors. Indeed, the Religious Right is one of the few cross-class social movements existing today. Second, the Religious Right has its own version of free spaces. The Religious Right generates its own alternative subculture through a dense organizational infrastructure of megachurches and independent fundamentalist churches. These organizations cater to the worldly and religious needs of their members by providing religious camps and schools for children as well as religious books and videos for adults. They also provide such services as fitness classes, saunas, day care, and radio stations.[43] The church offers not only a haven in a heretical world but also a site where fundamentalist Christian ideas can be developed, exchanged, and disseminated among the faithful. It provides a bulwark and ideological alternative to the seductive allure of a permissive secular culture.

Second, the Religious Right uses tactics culled from the same playbook used by leftist social movements. It has engaged in dramatic, disruptive forms of political participation. In addition to conventional forms of political activity,

Religious Right anti-abortion activists at a 2007 rally in Washington, D.C., protesting the thirty-fourth anniversary of the *Roe v. Wade* Supreme Court decision decriminalizing abortion.

such as lobbying legislators, filing briefs, and mounting register-and-vote drives, it engages in rallies and marches. The Religious Right has blocked entrances to abortion clinics, held disorderly street demonstrations, and filled courtrooms and legislative halls with intimidating supporters.

Finally, the Religious Right arose as a result of shifting political opportunities. Conservative political entrepreneurs, such as Howard Philips, head of the Conservative Caucus, and Paul Weymouth, director of Committee for the Survival of a Free Congress, encouraged and tutored religious leaders in political strategy and tactics. They acted as the vanguard, guiding the Religious Right's political activity. At the same time outsiders brought more political sophistication, the resources of the Religious Right also increased. Churches became megachurches with 50,000 members, and television evangelists raised money and recruited and mobilized believers through the airwaves. Finally, the legacies of the 1960s created a heightened sense of grievance among the Religious Right. Thus, the emergence of the Religious Right as a powerful social movement was the product of a perfect storm as political entrepreneurs from conservative political organizations came on board to provide direction, resources to support collective action increased, and government policies regarding abortion, school prayer, gay rights, and the separation of church and state fed the

Religious Right's sense of grievance. The result was one of the most powerful social movements of our time; it flowed through the Republican Party and was critical to that party's resurgence.

The Environmental Movement

Like the women's movement, the history of the environmental movement can be divided into waves of activism. The first wave appeared during the Progressive era at the beginning of the twentieth century. The early environmental movement included **conservationists** who wanted the country's natural resources to be managed efficiently by the government and **preservationists** who wanted to retain the land in its natural state. The former believed that the country's natural resources should be managed with an eye to the future and that resources in the public domain should serve public, not private interests. The latter believed that nature should be left unspoiled to preserve its scenic beauty and provide unique recreational opportunities. Both groups found their champion in President Theodore Roosevelt, who enlarged the national forest system from 41 to 109 million acres, established five national parks, and created the first wildlife refuges.

Conservationists and preservationists joined together to oppose reckless abuse of the land and its resources. Although their interests frequently overlapped, they were not identical. Conservationists believed in using the land and its resources wisely; preservationists opposed using them at all. These two principles clashed most famously in the conflict over Hetch Hetchy, which we discussed in opening this chapter. Conservationists supported San Francisco's plan to dam the valley because they thought it was more practical than other alternatives for bringing water and electricity to the city; moreover, the plan would break the grip of private monopolies over the city's utilities. Preservationists, on the other hand, opposed the dam and decried the beauty and recreational opportunities that would be lost.

Urban elites, middle-class women, and rod and gun enthusiasts composed the narrow base of the early environmental movement. Urban elites tried to preserve their culture against industrial blight and consumerism by supporting conservation and preservation. Middle-class women were attracted to environmentalism as an extension of their domestic duties. Pollution and filth threatened the health of their families and attractiveness of their homes. And sportsmen joined the fray in order to preserve wilderness areas for game and birds to hunt. They formed organizations such as the Sierra Club to demand that the public domain, "the commons," be managed in the public interest, something that could be done only through government. Hence, a by-product of the early environmental movement was to expand the scope of government, especially the executive branch, to include responsibility for the environment.

When the environmental movement reemerged after World War II, it had a different focus and constituency. While one group of critics protested the environmental dangers of radioactive fallout from nuclear tests, another objected to the use of toxic pesticides by farmers. Their critiques shifted the movement's attention away from conservation and preservation to **ecology**, to an appreciation of the fragility and interconnectedness of nature. Toxic pesticides and radioactive isotopes could be carried through the air and the food chain to poison people and animals. This new ecological perspective broadened the movement's goals beyond simply preserving wilderness areas or using resources efficiently to new issues such as ensuring clean air, pure water, and safe food. It also broadened the base of the movement beyond elites to newly affluent middle-class people who were concerned about the damage being done to nature and its potential for deadly repercussions.

The next wave of environmental activism occurred in the 1960s as the environmental movement drew energy from the emergence of the New Left. The "Give Peace a Chance!" slogans of Vietnam War protesters became "Give Earth a Chance!" chants of environmentalists. Just as New Left protesters engaged in acts of guerilla theater to dramatize their grievances, so did environmentalists engage in eco-sabotage, such as disabling construction equipment that was used to cut down forests. And just as the New Left held teach-ins to inform the public and challenge the dominant culture, so did environmentalists. In April 1970, the first Earth Day teach-ins were held across the country in colleges, schools, and parks that reportedly included 20 million people participating in discussions about the environment.[44] The environmental movement became more provocative and radical as it absorbed New Left activists and their critiques of consumerism and corporate power as well as their demands for authenticity and fundamental change. A movement that was previously known for blocking legislation through genteel lobbying was now known for blocking logging roads through direct action.

The environmental movement had grown, especially among the middle class, during a period of postwar affluence. But beginning in the 1970s, affluence was replaced by recession and unemployment. Environmentalism was no longer perceived as an outcome of economic growth, in which people could now afford to be concerned about the quality of their lives, but as a threat to it. Environmentalists were increasingly ridiculed as elitists who were more interested in protecting spotted owls than in preserving people's jobs. More ominously, the Republicans who took power were less concerned with reducing the carbon footprint of industry than with reducing the regulatory footprint of government.

As economic and political conditions became more challenging, the environmental movement became more theoretically and politically diverse. The ecological perspective introduced earlier now defined the movement, especially in the fight against global warming. It also found expression in such developments as deep ecology, which held that people were part of nature's order and not the other way around. The movement also began to address issues of environmental justice, which looked at environmental issues through the prism of racial and class inequality. This perspective was expressed by grassroots activists in working-class and minority neighborhoods who protested the placement of toxic waste dumps in their communities as opposed to richer and whiter neighborhoods.

While some elements of the environmental movement became more radical in theory and practice, the old, mainline environmentalist organizations such as the National Wildlife Federation, Sierra Club, and Audubon Society became more pragmatic. They continued to lobby for green policies, but now they also performed important oversight of existing environmental legislation. This role required them to develop scientific and legal expertise so they could propose their own technical solutions to environmental problems and challenge polluters and administrative agencies in court. Environmental reform through the political system was now being pursued in a more professional and sophisticated manner. Indeed, one study found that environmental advocacy groups in Washington were very similar to other Washington-based interest groups in terms of their organization and activities, although they were more litigious. Environmental groups were more likely to turn to federal courts to make their case.[45]

The environmental movement currently has a fundamentalist and a pragmatic wing. Fundamentalist deep ecology theorists and Earth First! activists vie with pragmatists who want to lobby Washington and work with industry to help it become greener. Fundamentalists regard environmental pragmatists as "risk averse, depersonalized, overly analytical, humorless, access-driven, intolerant, statistical, centralized, technocratic, deal-making, passionless, sterilized, direct-mailing, jock strapped, [and] lawyer-laden," while pragmatists dismiss environmental fundamentalists as irrelevant, silly, and immature.[46] The issue for contemporary environmentalism is whether its fundamentalist and pragmatic wings will augment or detract from each other; that is, whether the movement's theoretical and political diversity will make it stronger or weaker.

CONCLUSION

In contrast to authoritarian regimes, citizens in the United States can participate and influence the laws that govern them. They can vote, join interest groups, participate in social movements, contribute money to political campaigns, and write letters to their representatives. In principle, anyone can use these means of political expression. But some citizens are in a better position to take advantage of these opportunities than others. Political participation may be open, but it is not free. It is greatly facilitated by class-related factors such as time, money, education, civic skills, self-confidence, and contacts with broader social networks. The uneven distribution of these politically relevant resources leads to uneven levels of political participation.

Inequalities in political participation are significant because they lead to inequalities in political outcomes. Policymakers respond to demands that are expressed. What they hear influences what they do. Consequently, what issues are considered and what is done about them reflect the interests of those who have the resources to make their views heard as opposed to those who do not.

But inequalities in political participation are not inevitable, nor are the inequalities in outcome that result from them. Citizens can develop their political voices and by doing so change the policies that govern them. The previous chapter showed how citizens can use elections to change leaders who will take the country in a different direction. This chapter has shown how citizens can also use interest groups and social movements to the same effect, to influence policy. Joining interest groups and participating in social movements are alternative and supplemental means of political expression to the ballot box. The quality of democracy and the output of government would be poorer without their contribution.

CHAPTER SUMMARY

Introduction

Political participation can take various forms, from voting and contributing money to election campaigns to joining an interest group or participating in a social movement. Citizens participate in different forms of political activity depending on their level of commitment, the resources available to them, and the opportunities and constraints they face in using them.

Interest Groups

More interest groups are more active on more issues than in the past. Interest group activity increased in response to procedural changes in Congress that made it more accessible to lobbyists, new policy initiatives by government that created new stakeholders, and the institutionalization of social movements from the 1960s.

David and Goliath

Despite the addition of new players, interest groups representing business have more resources for influencing policymakers than do other groups. Yet, being bigger, faster, and stronger does not guarantee that business always prevails. Sometimes groups representing business oppose each other, business interests may adopt the wrong political strategy, and sometimes they may find public opinion arrayed against them.

The Changing Quality of Membership

More interest groups today rely on purposive, as opposed to material, incentives to attract members. And more contemporary interest groups are centralized, professional advocacy groups as opposed to mass membership organizations. These new professional advocacy groups tend to attract wealthier supporters and do not provide their members the same civic lessons as do more traditional mass membership organizations.

E-Media, Interest Groups, and Political Participation

E-media has reduced the cost of recruiting, coordinating, and mobilizing interest group activity, thus permitting new groups to form rapidly. Although startup costs for web-based advocacy groups are low, so is the commitment of members to them.

A Comparative Perspective on American Interest Groups

American interest groups are of the pluralist, as opposed to corporatist, variety. This means they are less encompassing, more competitive with each other, and weaker in relation to their members. In contrast, corporatist interest groups, such as those found in many European countries, are fewer in number, larger and more centralized, and able to sanction their members.

Social Movements
Social movements arise when changes in relations of power permit previously passive groups to mount a challenge. These groups develop organizations that articulate an alternative culture that legitimates their demands and attract ideologically committed supporters who are willing to engage in more demanding forms of political participation.

Critical Thinking Questions

1. Which form of political expression—voting, interest group activity, or social movements—do you believe has been most effective in the United States?

2. Business interests enjoy many advantages in interest group competition, yet they do not always win. What conditions are most conducive to defeating business interests in policy debates?

3. Has the rise of the Internet and the decline of membership-based organizations been healthy for American democracy?

4. Do you think environmentalists should adopt the perspective of pragmatists or of fundamentalists?

5. What are the advantages and disadvantages of each form of political expression: voting, interest group activity, and social movements?

Suggested Readings

Frank Baumgartner et al., *Lobbying and Policy Change: Who Wins, Who Loses, and Why*. Chicago: University of Chicago Press, 2009.

Jo Freeman, *We Will Be Heard: Women's Struggles for Political Power in the United States*. New York: Rowman & Littlefield, 2008.

Joseph Lowndes, *From the New Deal to the New Right: Race and the Southern Origins of Modern Conservatism*. New Haven, CT: Yale University Press, 2008.

Theda Skocpol, *Diminished Democracy: From Membership to Management in American Civic Life.* Norman: University of Oklahoma Press, 2003.

Thomas R. Wheelock, *Preserving the Nation: The Conservation and Environmental Movements, 1870–2000.* Wheeling, IL: Harlan Davidson, 2007.

Robert Zieger and Gilbert Gall, *American Workers, American Unions,* 3rd ed. Baltimore: Johns Hopkins University Press, 2002.

PART III

POLITICAL INSTITUTIONS

The Constitution lays out the architecture of government. By *architecture*, we mean the design of political institutions—notably, the three branches of the federal government: the executive, legislative, and judicial. The Constitution also specifies how political authority is distributed among these different institutions as well as between the federal and state governments. With over 88,000 governmental units of all types nationwide—from familiar state legislatures to obscure special district authorities—the design is complicated. Much overlap and jurisdictional conflict occur among different government bodies. The design of the American political system is quite distinctive because of the degree to which the Constitution disperses authority widely among a variety of political institutions. Authority is divided in two ways. First, the United States is a federal system, which means that authority is divided between national and state governments. This is commonly described as the division of powers. The Tenth Amendment to the Constitution specifies that all powers not expressly delegated to the national government by the Constitution are reserved to the states. For much of American history, state governments exercised the bulk of governmental power. In comparison, the national or federal government was lean and mean, primarily engaged in enforcing laws, arbitrating conflicts, issuing currency, and defending the country.

Today, considerable power has gravitated to the federal level, although state governments continue to formulate, implement, and finance programs in vitally important domains like education, transportation, and property rights. Although the Constitution created a federal system with power distributed between national and state governments, one cannot neatly distinguish which level of government is responsible for which function. Sometimes there is a nearly complete separation of functions: the national government alone decides whether to commit troops abroad; state governments are primarily responsible for regulating marriage and divorce. But the typical situation is more complicated because federal and state governments are operating in the same policy areas. Political scientist Morton Grodzins challenged what he called the layer cake image of federalism, in which the national and state governments are neatly separated from each other and perform different tasks. He suggested that despite this common impression, American federalism in fact resembles a marble cake, in which governmental functions are interwoven and shared among the different levels of government.[1]

The Constitution fragments governing authority in a second way. Political power is divided not only vertically between different levels of government but also horizontally between different branches of government. Rather than uniting power within a single powerful agency, as in what political scientists call the "Westminster model" of British parliamentary government (Westminister Palace is the home of the British parliament), power is divided among the legislative, executive, and judicial branches of the federal government. The term *separation of powers* is often used to describe this dispersion of power among the different branches of government. But like the layer cake image of federalism, the concept of the separation of powers can be misleading if taken to mean that each branch of government has exclusive authority in certain domains. In fact, the opposite is the case. A better term to describe how power is distributed within the federal government would be *shared* or *overlapping powers*, as opposed to separation of powers. For example, both the Congress and the president share power in the realm of foreign policy. The president can make treaties with foreign governments, but these must be ratified by a two-thirds vote in the Senate. The president can command the military, but Congress appropriates the necessary funds for military operations. Similarly, all three branches share power when it comes to legislation. Congress can pass a law, but the president is authorized to approve or veto it. Congress can then override a presidential veto with a two-thirds vote in both the Senate and the House. Finally, the Supreme Court can nullify the law by finding it unconstitutional. But Congress can override the decision by amending the Constitution. Suggesting that the three branches share responsibility and power with regard to many governmental functions does not mean that they possesss equal power. Although the balance of power among the three branches has varied through time, it is generally agreed that the executive, directed by the president, has become the preeminent branch nowadays.

The architecture of shared or overlapping powers creates the famed system of checks and balances, according to which each branch of government has the power to check the actions of the other branches and must depend on their cooperation to achieve its goals. Again, we do not mean to imply by checks and balances that the three branches have equal power, only that government is designed in such a way that many policies and activities require the tacit or explicit support of all three institutions. Unlike a parliamentary system, where the executive and legislative branches are fused, the system of divided, yet shared, powers ensures that each branch possesses autonomous power.

The process of policy formulation, especially when it involves legislation, must run a difficult gauntlet in a political system where each branch of government can check the other and success depends on the cooperation of all of them. Chances of completing this obstacle course are made even smaller by having each elected branch of government represent different constituencies. The president is elected nationally, senators are elected from each state, and members of the House of Representatives are elected from districts within states. In effect, our constitutional design requires legislation to win three different types of majorities—nationally, by state, and by district. That is, shared powers require groups to build overlapping, simultaneous majorities at the level of the presidency, the Senate, and the House. Legislation must run the equivalent of a triathlon (neglecting the courts for the moment), a series of three different athletic events requiring three different kinds of skills: running, cycling, and swimming—but with one important difference. In a triathlon, a contestant can lose one event but still be declared the winner so long as he or she has the highest combined score at the end of the contest. This would be insufficient under our system of government. The Constitution requires contestants to win all three events *outright*. Groups that desire political change must win at every step of the process, but those groups that want to defend the status quo have to win just once to block a bill. Legislation must pass the House, be approved by the Senate, and then be accepted by the president (excluding the difficult task of overriding a presidential veto), or it will fall short of passage. The first years of Barack Obama's presidency provide a perfect illustration of the conservative bias of these institutional arrangements. Despite Obama having been elected by a solid majority and enjoying large Democratic majorities in both houses of Congress, he encountered immense obstacles in attempting to persuade Congress to pass several of his signature reforms.

The design of government in the Constitution, with its system of shared powers among independent institutions representing different constituencies, thus has highly conservative implications. This bias is no accident: it was intended by the Founders who created it. On the one hand, the designers of the Constitution embarked on a remarkable political experiment in 1787. They proposed to create the first republic in which political authority would be located in the hands of the people instead of a king. The architects of the Constitution were intent on protecting the government against tyranny, which they had just fought a revolution to defeat. On the other hand, the Founders were frightened by the audacity of their own democratic inclinations. They believed that democracy, if left to its own devices, posed a threat to the natural hierarchy in society. Political scientist Robert Dahl observes that the Founders were "alarmed by the prospect that democracy, political equality, and even political liberty itself would endanger the rights of property owners to preserve their property and use it as they please."[2] They thus devised checks and balances as a way to protect the unequal social order without taking away any of the majority's democratic rights. Checks and balances, they believed, would protect the rich by requiring workers and farmers to build concurrent majorities at every level of government. Majorities would have to be built in the House of Representatives by districts based on population, in the Senate according to states, and in the presidency across the entire country. The Founders anticipated that the result would be deadlock and government paralysis, for majorities would find it difficult to win at every level required of them.

The Founders sought to create a government powerful enough to promote market-based economic development but not so powerful that it could be used as an instrument of popular forces to restrict the rights of property. They brilliantly achieved this task of constitutional engineering. When public power is unable to rule because it is gripped by deadlock, private power rules in its place.

The next three chapters, covering the presidency, Congress, and the courts, respectively, examine the institutional structure of government and how power is distributed within and among the three branches. The structure of government, the relationships among the different institutions of government, and the formal and informal rules that govern how they work internally have important consequences for policy. In other words, institutions count. Policy is not simply a reflection of economic and social forces; rather, these social forces are refracted through institutions whose rules and relationships affect the outcome of their struggle. Some groups win and some groups lose, depending on the structure of government. But the structure of government, the relationship among institutions, and their formal and informal rules are not set in stone and are themselves subject to political conflict. The Constitution may have created the architecture of government more than two hundred years ago, but the design is constantly being remodeled. The executive branch does not look like it did fifty years ago, nor is its relationship to Congress the same as it was fifty years ago. Groups struggle over not only who will occupy the government but also what it will look like. The institutional form of government changes as a result of political conflict. Political institutions—through their relationships to each other and their internal procedures—reflect the larger distribution of power in society at the same time they help to shape it. The focal point of the federal government, and therefore the place we begin our study of political institutions, is the presidency.

6

THE PRESIDENCY

INTRODUCTION

Delegates to the Constitutional Convention arrived in Philadelphia in 1787 with many complaints about their form of government. One of their objections to the Articles of Confederation, which established the first American government after the Revolutionary War in 1776, was that it did not provide for a single official responsible for directing the executive branch who would be independent of Congress. Many of the Founders believed that a new government required an autonomous and energetic presidential office, as opposed to the weak executive that labored under the Articles. But the Founders disagreed over the powers that should be invested in this new presidential office and how it should be filled. Alexander Hamilton, a brilliant thirty-year-old delegate from New York, shocked the gathering by praising the British monarchy—against whom the colonies had revolted a mere decade before—as a suitable model to emulate. Recognizing that hereditary monarchy would never be accepted in America, Hamilton suggested that the new federal government be directed by an elected monarch who would hold office for life.

Hamilton's view was an extreme one among the delegates in Philadelphia. But it made the arguments of those who proposed strengthening the executive appear moderate. A strong executive was needed, advocates argued, because elected assemblies were too easily swayed by popular pressure. The constitutional architects specifically designed the newly created office of the president to be independent of Congress in order to check what they perceived as the latter's democratic excesses.

The creation of an executive branch largely independent of Congress and directed by a single person—the president—is a key institutional innovation of the American Constitution. It distinguished the new form of government under the Constitution from that under the Articles and, indeed, from any other government in the world at that time. Yet while the delegates to the Constitutional Convention agreed that a more powerful and independent executive was necessary, they differed about the extent of the president's powers. As a result, the Constitution leaves them relatively ambiguous and incomplete.[1]

In addition to uncertainty and conflict concerning the powers to invest in the president's office, delegates to the Constitutional Convention also disagreed over how presidents should be chosen. James Wilson of Pennsylvania proposed that the executive be directly elected by the people. But the delegates rejected this proposal because it would make the president responsive to the very democratic spirit they were intent on taming. After creating an executive independent of Congress, delegates were not about to propose selecting the president through direct election. James Wilson fretted that the question of how the president should be chosen was "in truth the most difficult of all which we have had to decide."[2] With more desperation than confidence, the convention delegates devised a plan by which a newly created Electoral College, a council of wise statesmen (of course, women did not have the suffrage at this point) would elect the president. As with so many other provisions of the Constitution, this plan was a compromise. It tried to create a procedure for reconciling the desirability of having wise, dispassionate men select the president with popular participation in the selection process (because citizens would elect state delegates to the Electoral College, or they would elect state legislators who in turn would elect the state's delegates). Quite quickly, however, the role of the Electoral College changed. When citizens began to vote for slates of delegates pledged to one candidate or another, votes in the Electoral College merely ratified the outcome of the statewide popular vote. The Constitution specifies that states have as many votes in the Electoral College as they have senators and representatives in Congress. (Citizens of Washington, D.C., also elect delegates to the Electoral College.) As a result, the Electoral College tends to overrepresent small states. For example, with 3 electoral votes, one for its sole representative and two for its senators, Wyoming has one electoral vote for every 166,000 citizens in the state while California, with 55 electoral votes, has one electoral vote for every 600,000 citizens.

To be elected president, a candidate must first gain the nomination. There are no constitutional rules for doing so—not surprising, given that the Constitution does not recognize the existence of political parties. In the current era, the Republican and Democratic national parties are the gatekeepers whose nomination is essential for someone to be considered a serious candidate. The parties hold conventions every four years to nominate the party's presidential and vice presidential candidates, adopt a party platform, select party officers, and review party rules. Party conventions were once significant because they decided which of the contending candidates for the party's presidential nomination would be chosen. Today, however, the parties' presidential nominees are effectively chosen in statewide primaries by party members who vote to select the party's candidate. National party conventions have become made-for-TV events. They simply crown the candidate who won a majority of convention delegates during primary season and provide a stage to introduce him or her to a nationwide audience. Indeed, the last time either the Democratic or the Republican Party convention needed more than one ballot to select a presidential nominee was in 1952. Presidential primaries have so reduced the drama and spectacle of the party conventions that the television networks have vastly reduced their coverage of them.[3]

Following the nominating conventions and the presidential campaign, the election is held on the first Tuesday of November. For a candidate to be elected president, he or she must receive an absolute majority of votes in the Electoral College; that is, presently, 270 votes. In the rare case when no candidate clears this threshold, either because of a tie or because some votes go to third-party candidates, the House of Representatives selects the president by majority vote.

By 1836, every state but South Carolina had decided to cast all its votes as a unit for the candidate who received the most votes within the state, regardless of how narrow the margin. As discussed in Chapter 4, this practice is known as the unit rule. Nowadays, all states but Maine and Nebraska cast their entire electoral votes for the candidate who receives a plurality in their state's presidential election. As a result, the Electoral College vote for president usually diverges significantly from the popular vote. For example, in 2000, the presidential election hinged on several hundred votes separating Al Gore and George W. Bush in Florida. Bush was awarded all of Florida's 25 electoral votes even though he won the state by only 537 votes out of almost 6 million votes cast statewide. By the same token, Al Gore benefited from the unit rule when he won all the electoral votes from Iowa (7), New Mexico (5), Oregon (7), and Wisconsin (11), even though he carried these states by less than 1 percent of the popular vote.

Because of the unit rule, a presidential candidate can win the popular vote nationwide and lose in the Electoral College—where the outcome is decided. This is precisely what happened in 2000, when Al Gore received 550,000 more popular votes than George W. Bush but lost 271–267 in the Electoral College. Usually, however, the effect of the unit rule is to magnify the result of the popular vote. For example, in 2008 Barack Obama won a comfortable majority of the popular vote—53 percent—but a resounding 68 percent majority of the Electoral College vote.

The Twenty-second Amendment to the Constitution specifies that no president can serve more than two terms. Most first-term presidents seek reelection. Among recent presidents, Ronald Reagan, Bill Clinton, and George W. Bush were reelected to a second term; Jimmy Carter and George H.W. Bush were defeated for reelection.

The Constitution specifies a procedure known as **impeachment** for removing a president from office. According to the Constitution, the grounds for impeachment are that the president must commit "high crimes and misdemeanors." Removal from office involves a two-stage process. First, a simple majority of the House of Representatives must vote to impeach the president. Second, two-thirds of the Senate must meet as a judicial body, presided over by the chief justice of the Supreme Court, and vote to convict an impeached president. Two presidents in American history have been been impeached: Andrew Johnson in 1868 and Bill Clinton in 1998. In neither case did the necessary two-thirds of the Senate vote to convict the president. As a result of the Watergate scandal, Richard Nixon resigned in 1974 to avoid near certain impeachment, when taped conversations were released documenting that the president had orchestrated a cover-up of a break-in at the Washington headquarters of the Democratic National Committee.

THE HISTORICAL PRESIDENCY

In the debates over the Constitution in Philadelphia, Alexander Hamilton defended the office of the president as one that would give "energy" to the government. He believed that a strong executive was necessary to provide leadership and decisiveness to a government that could otherwise drift and be stalemated in a system of checks and balances. According to political scientist Stephen Skowronek, the "energy" that Hamilton sought to invest in the office has made the president a powerful source of political change. More than any other government official, presidents routinely "disrupt systems [and] reshape political landscapes."[4] Regardless of whether they are liberal or conservative, Democrat or Republican, all presidents, according to Skowronek, are agents of change. They seek to set the wheels of government in motion in order to remake it according to their own concept of what it should be.

Today the president has become the energy center of the government, just as Hamilton envisioned it. Congress is often too decentralized and fragmented to compete for leadership with the president. But there are no constitutional or political guarantees that the president will be successful in wielding power.

Presidential power must be constructed; it cannot be taken for granted. The system of separated powers constitutes a powerful brake on presidential initiatives. Thus, it is the exceptional president who succeeds in accomplishing reforms. This means that the federal government's policies tend to reflect rather than reshape the existing distribution of economic and political resources. Thanks to the mobilization of bias described in Chapter 2, the result of the federal government's action and inactions is to favor affluent Americans and business interests.

Before the Civil War, most presidents exercised relatively few powers because the responsibilities of the national government itself were quite limited. According to one scholar, chief executives in the nineteenth century were "chief of very little and executive of even less."[5] Bold innovators like Andrew Jackson and Abraham Lincoln were isolated exceptions, not the rule. When a young Princeton professor published an influential study of American politics in 1885 entitled *Congressional Government*, which demonstrated that Congress was the foremost policymaking institution of American government and that the president was powerful only to the extent that he could **veto** bills passed by Congress, this did not challenge received wisdom. Twenty-three years later, however, the scholar changed his mind and, in *Constitutional Government in the United States*, developed a far more expansive view of the presidency. Soon after, by his actions as president, Woodrow Wilson—the former Princeton professor— contributed even more directly to the creation of a powerful presidency. Presidential scholar Jeffrey Tulis considers that Wilson helped to invent the "rhetorical presidency" by making speeches directly to the American people and bypassing Congress.[6]

Throughout the nineteenth and early twentieth centuries, there were swings between strong and weak presidents, between presidential and congressional supremacy. But as giant corporations developed in the twentieth century, the federal government grew in size and power, and the presidency as an institution expanded along with it. First, the regulatory role of the federal government increased because corporations outgrew the narrow boundaries of mere states. Only federal law could regulate the behavior of firms that now operated nationally, and the president directed the executive that performed the work of regulation. Although presidents did not directly control the **independent regulatory commissions (IRCs)** created by Congress to regulate the economy, they nominated IRC commissioners. Second, during the Great Depression of the 1930s the federal government, under the president's direction, became responsible for economic management as business, labor, and consumers sought federal action to prevent the boom-and-bust swings of the business cycle. Third, during the same period the federal government took on new social responsibilities, creating a welfare state that would distribute resources to the elderly, unemployed, and disabled who could no longer provide for themselves. Finally, the federal government grew in response to the global character of capitalism and the rise of the United States as a global power. In particular, presidential power increased substantially as a result of the two world wars of the twentieth century and the Cold War that followed World War II. The president was the commander in chief of the military and responsible for mobilizing the nation's resources to bolster military power. Thus, there has been a mutually supportive relationship between the growth of big government and capitalism, the emergence of the United States as a world power, and the expansion of presidential power.

Accompanying the growth of the federal government's role was a change in the balance of power among the three branches of government: power tilted decisively toward the president during Franklin D. Roosevelt's presidency from 1933 to 1945. The New Deal and World War II supersized the presidency and executive branch. Since the New Deal, the modern presidency is looked upon as "the preeminent source of moral leadership, legislative guidance, and public policy."[7] Roosevelt actively encouraged people to look to the federal government to guarantee economic health and to rely on the president to direct the effort. Roosevelt's "fireside chats" beamed his radio message into millions of homes and enabled him to establish a personal connection with the public.[8] One scholar observes: "The New Deal and World War II permanently established the president as the single most powerful figure in both the legislative and administrative processes of government, as well as the elected official

President Franklin D. Roosevelt conducting a "fireside chat."

charged, in the eyes of the public, with primary responsibility for initiating and securing policies in the public interest."[9] The executive branch expanded with the creation of an array of regulatory and administrative agencies that provided the president with tools to pursue policies quite apart from Congress, the courts, and political parties.

THE IMPERIAL PRESIDENT

The symbolism and substance of presidential power are vast. Presidents draw an annual salary of $400,000 and are provided with an additional account of nearly $200,000 for travel, entertaining, and other personal expenses. The White House staff numbers over five hundred, and the president travels in presidential limousines, helicopters, and jetliners (dubbed Air Force One). The presidential family resides in the 123-room White House at the most exclusive address in the world—1600 Pennsylvania Avenue. A staff of about one hundred attends to the First Family's personal needs at a cost of over $8 million per year. To escape the buzz of Washington, the president can repair to Camp David, a 180-acre retreat in the mountains of Maryland reserved for use by the presidential family.

Although the material rewards of the presidency are substantial, they are modest compared to the compensation of presidents of even medium-sized corporations—not to mention CEOs of large corporations, corporate lawyers, and high rollers on Wall Street. Those seeking the presidency are far more motivated by ideological commitment and the desire to wield power than by a lust for wealth. What presidents do possess in abundance is power, prestige, and authority.

There are several sources of presidential power. A place to begin is what the Constitution delegates to the president. However, the Founders, as we discussed previously, were reluctant to provide a detailed enumeration of presidential powers. Article II of the Constitution, which defines the power of the presidency, has been referred to as "the most loosely drawn chapter of the Constitution."[10] It is far shorter and more general than Article I, which defines the powers of Congress. And its location in the Constitution—in second position, with Congress having pride of place—is richly symbolic.

The Constitution empowers the president to approve or veto legislation passed by Congress, act as commander in chief of the armed forces, faithfully execute the laws, pardon criminals, make treaties, call Congress into special session, appoint government officials, and recognize foreign governments. These are substantial prerogatives. For example, the power to take care that the laws are faithfully executed, in the words of the Constitution—that is, to supervise the implementation of laws—potentially provides an invitation to exercise expansive power. But the formal powers enumerated in Article II do not begin to exhaust the total powers that presidents exercise nowadays. They are so great that historian Arthur Schlesinger Jr. coined the term *imperial president* to describe the expansion of presidential power in the modern epoch.[11]

The president's greatest political resource is that, along with the vice president, he or she is the only official selected by a nationwide election. Thus, the president embodies the nation, and all the emotional and patriotic symbolism that this evokes. Unlike parliamentary regimes, where prime ministers direct the government and monarchs or indirectly elected presidents perform ceremonial duties as heads of state but have little political power, the president is both **head of state** and **head of government**. By fusing real and symbolic power, the presidency serves as "the focus for the most intense and persistent emotions in the American polity," in the words of presidential scholar James David Barber.[12]

Thanks to unlimited media access, presidents have a unique opportunity to deliver their message. The media is endlessly fascinated with the president, ranging from the first family's choice of a puppy to far-reaching policy decisions. Media coverage reinforces the impression that the presidency is the essential institution at the center of political life. Presidents go to extraordinary lengths to dramatize their message, for example, by delivering speeches in carefully selected settings. To evoke reminders of U.S. participation in World War II, President Obama chose Berlin, Germany, and Normandy, France, as sites for major addresses in 2009. And he traveled to Cairo, Egypt, to deliver a highly publicized speech praising the contributions of Muslims to U.S. society and calling for more harmonious relations between the United States and the Muslim world. When President Obama was engaged in a make-or-break attempt in 2010 to sway public opinion and round up congressional votes to pass health reform legislation, he convened a day-long televised meeting with congressional leaders of both parties. He sponsored the meeting to demonstrate his determination to forge a consensus on health-care legislation and more generally to provide a graphic example of presidential leadership.

Political scientist Bruce Miroff writes that, by enjoying unlimited access to the media, "the president gains an unparalleled advantage in defining political reality for most Americans. . . . Press or partisan criticism may challenge a president . . . but the outline of reality that he has sketched is usually left intact."[13] A graphic illustration of Miroff's point: for years after the September 11 attack on the United States, seven out of ten citizens believed that Iraq's dictator Saddam Hussein was linked to the bombings. Yet there was never credible evidence of such a connection.[14] Why were so many Americans misled? Because President George W. Bush and members of his administration repeatedly claimed that such a link existed.

Presidential power is considerably bolstered by management of the federal bureaucracy, which includes over 2.7 million employees and a 2009 fiscal year budget of $3.52 trillion. By directing the executive branch, presidents influence how federal policy is made, interpreted, and implemented. We discuss this question later in the chapter.

Presidents deploy extensive resources to influence private citizens and officials outside the executive branch. They can make skillful use of patronage, including the power to nominate federal judges and ambassadors. They can issue invitations to the White House to reward supporters and supply friendly persuasion to holdouts. They can make deals by offering inducements in return for votes.

Presidents also have sticks to punish opponents. They can deny members of Congress access to the president and other officials, starve their districts of federal largesse, and mobilize friendly lobbyists to apply pressure.

Because presidents are party leaders, they can appeal for support from fellow party members in Congress and elsewhere. In return, presidents can make appearances on behalf of elected party leaders, raise money for them, and support their pet projects. However, the separation of powers limits the utility of the party card. Members of Congress owe primary loyalty to voters and groups in their home districts, who provide the votes and contributions necessary for a representative to gain the party's nomination and win in the general election. Representatives mostly run their own election campaigns. If support for the president means damaging their electoral prospects, they will be strongly tempted to jump ship. For example, despite enjoying large Democratic majorities in both houses of Congress, President Obama was unable to persuade some Democratic representatives to support his proposed reform of health care in 2009 and 2010. Many so-called Blue Dog Democrats—Democratic members of Congress from relatively moderate districts—feared an electoral backlash if they supported a measure opposed by health insurance companies and regarded by many constituents as risky and radical.

Finally, presidents have benefited immensely from the rise of the United States as a global power. As the United States has become the dominant actor on the world stage, presidents are in a privileged position to write the script because they are uniquely situated to speak for the national interest. As the world shrinks, as foreign policy decisions touch people's everyday lives, from war and threats of terrorism to economic globalization and climate change, presidents become larger than life. The more foreign policy matters, the more presidents matter.

Writing in the 1960s, Richard E. Neustadt, the most influential scholar on the modern presidency, described the trajectory of presidential power as follows: "In instance after instance, the exceptional behavior of our earlier 'strong' Presidents has now been set by statute as a regular requirement."[15] Presidential powers once thought to be extraordinary have become routine.[16] However, as we describe below, the past several decades have not simply continued the trend toward ever greater presidential power. Important reversals have also occurred.

The most recent attempt to expand presidential power occurred during the presidency of George W. Bush. For several years, he was highly successful in expanding the scope of presidential and executive powers. However, opposition to several initiatives increased during the course of his presidency and some were reversed or scaled back by Congress, the Supreme Court, and his successor, President Obama. The most important innovations of the Bush presidency included the following:

- President Bush issued a record number of **signing statements**, that is, documents that provide the president's interpretation of the meaning of laws just passed and are intended to provide guidance to courts and administrative agencies. A *New York Times* journalist observed that "Mr. Bush transformed signing statements from an obscure tool into a commonplace term."[17] Bush's statements directed administrative officials to disregard provisions of legislation that he considered to infringe on his prerogatives as commander in chief or chief executive. For example, one signing statement ordered government officials to ignore a law banning the torture of detainees when the administration decided that the nation's security was threatened.

- President Bush invoked a doctrine known as the **unified executive** to assert sole and unlimited control over the executive branch. Whereas Congress traditionally exercised oversight over executive agencies, and agencies possessed significant autonomy as a result of statutes and administrative regulations, President Bush claimed that the Constitution granted him undivided control over the executive branch. President Bush also claimed that the War on Terror required an unprecedented exercise of presidential power. He invoked the doctrine of **state secrets** to suppress the release of information and prevent judicial challenges to executive decisions. He asserted that his role as commander in chief enabled him to ignore existing laws and treaties, including prohibitions on torture. There is credible evidence that the president's actions were illegal, unconstitutional, and may constitute crimes against humanity.[18] We discuss this issue further in Chapter 11.

- During President Bush's first term, Republican control of Congress considerably bolstered his power, especially because (as described in Chapter 4) congressional Republicans firmly supported the president. A key instance was the USA Patriot Act, passed by Congress after 9/11, which provided the executive branch with wide latitude relatively unconstrained by congressional or judicial oversight. For example, it authorized the government to seize citizens' financial records and carry out warrantless searches. The government was also given greatly expanded power to imprison and interrogate those deemed to pose security risks. The revised guidelines developed by the Justice Department provided legal justification for actions that, as noted earlier, are considered by legal scholars and others to constitute torture. We explore this question further in Chapter 11.

When the Democrats gained control of the Senate in 2004 and the House of Representatives in 2006, pushback began. Further, beginning in 2004, several Supreme Court rulings blocked the president's attempt to curtail civil liberties and judicial scrutiny of the executive.

During the 2008 presidential campaign, Barack Obama criticized what he characterized as President Bush's abuse of presidential power. When he became president, Obama partially reversed the trend toward a hyperpowerful president. He announced his intention to close the prison at Guantánamo Bay, Cuba, that was created after 9/11. The prison held many detainees for years without judicial protection. (However, delays in closing the prison occurred because of a failure to resolve the issue of where to transfer detainees.) Obama ordered administration officials to cooperate with requests for information made under the provisions of the Freedom of Information Act. He made an active effort to involve Republican members of Congress in shaping legislation. The Obama administration emphasized that it sought to respect traditional checks and balances.

In important respects, however, the Obama administration did not fully relinquish the newly expanded powers of the executive. For example, the government continued to invoke the doctrine of state secrets in an attempt to quash judicial proceedings when it feared that embarassing information would be disclosed and that the case would go against the government. It successfully opposed congressional efforts to restore civil liberties weakened by the USA Patriot Act. Although candidate Obama criticized President Bush for issuing signing statements, President Obama adopted the same practice, albeit less frequently. For example, when Obama signed a bill in 2009 appropriating funds for international financial institutions (IFIs), he announced that he would ignore a provision mandating him to seek to pressure IFIs to adopt labor and environmental standards. Complying with this provision, he stated, would "interfere with my constitutional authority to conduct foreign relations."[19] Disappointed Democratic congressional leaders wrote President Obama, "During the previous administration, all of us were critical of the president's assertion that he could pick and choose which aspects of Congressional statutes he was required to enforce. We were therefore chagrined to see you appear to express a similar attitude."[20]

The modern presidency (which, as we will describe, extends far beyond the president) commands the most powerful military in the world, manages a vast bureaucracy, sets the agenda of government, defines the national interest, dominates the media, provides party leadership, and can reward its supporters with ample benefits. If this were the whole story, the president would be a modern Leviathan. But it is far from the whole story.

THE PERILS OF PRESIDENTIAL POWER

In *Gulliver's Travels*, Jonathan Swift's satire on the modern condition, Gulliver found himself not only standing over the Lilliputians, towering above them, but also, at times, being tethered by them. Presidents, for all their awesome powers, may find themselves in a comparable position and be unable to achieve their goals. This paradox was conveyed in a remark by President Harry Truman as he imagined what would happen when his newly elected successor, the World War II hero General Dwight D. Eisenhower, took office. Truman predicted, "He'll sit here and he'll say, 'Do this! Do that!' *And nothing will happen. Poor Ike*—it won't be a bit like the Army. He'll find it very frustrating."[21] Truman knew from bitter experience that presidents often exercise power not by giving orders, as occurs in the military chain of command. Instead, presidential power often requires persuading other powerful officials that their own best interest lies in complying with what the president requests. Although we will explore the question further, for now the important distinction to keep in mind is between *command* and *persuade*.

Throughout the 1970s, the presidency was a beleaguered institution. The power and majesty of the presidential office were weakened by the debacle in Vietnam under President Lyndon Johnson and the criminality involved in Watergate under President Richard Nixon. Both events exposed presidential fraud and deception. During the Vietnam War, the Department of Defense conducted classified research that charted the dismal progress of the war. Yet at that very moment, President Johnson was publicly announcing that the United States was making substantial progress in subduing the Vietcong. After Daniel Ellsberg, a young Pentagon analyst who helped conduct the classified research, became outraged by Johnson's mendacity and opposed to U.S. policy, he leaked the studies to the *New York Times*. When the *Times* published what came to be known as the Pentagon Papers, it created a major scandal that rocked the Johnson administration and hastened its downfall.

The Watergate scandal also revealed presidential deception. During the 1972 presidential campaign, Republican Party operatives broke into the headquarters of the Democratic National Committee, apparently seeking documents to help the Republican cause. The matter would have been forgotten if not for a brilliant series of investigative reports by *Washington Post* reporters Bob Woodward and Carl Bernstein, who followed the trail of wrongdoing to the Oval Office. For months, President Nixon strenuously denied knowledge of or participation in the criminal scheme. However, his deception was dramatically revealed when the Supreme Court ordered the release of confidential tape recordings of Nixon's conversations with close aides. The tapes revealed that Nixon directed an attempted cover-up of the burglary. Faced with the near certainty of impeachment, Nixon resigned from office in disgrace. For years after these events, the media and Congress became more ready and willing to challenge presidential leadership.

The end of the golden age of capitalism in the 1970s further weakened the presidency. Since the Great Depression and the New Deal, the president's fortunes have been closely tied to the fate of the economy. The power and prestige of the president (as well as that of the entire government) flourish when corporate capitalism prospers; and the president's popular and professional standing falls when the economy stagnates, as it did in the 1970s and after 2008.

Recent presidents have also been confronted by a resurgent Congress, often led by the opposing party. In the 1950s and 1960s, Congress was willing to follow the president's lead because it agreed with his policies. For example, during the Cold War, Congress often deferred to the president because it shared his goal of containing communism. But when Congress and the president began to disagree over substantive issues of domestic and foreign policy beginning in the 1970s, Congress sought to recover its lost prerogatives. Congress tried to legislate limits on presidential powers in the War Powers Act of 1973. It created the Congressional Budget Office in 1974 to provide it with economic expertise to counter that available to the president.

Congress became more assertive beginning in the 1970s because of the almost routine development of divided government, in which different parties controlled Congress and the presidency. Democrats controlled Congress throughout much of the Republican presidencies of Richard Nixon, Ronald Reagan, and George H.W. Bush, whereas the Republicans held majorities in Congress through six of Bill Clinton's eight years in the White House. Divided government gives Congress an incentive to challenge the president; this point is illustrated by the greater challenge President George W. Bush faced in his second term, when Democrats regained control of Congress.

An increase in partisan polarization, both in Congress and the country, made it difficult for President Obama to gain congressional approal for his initiatives even though he could count on solid Democratic majorities in both houses. Rather than an imperial president, scholars now highlight the importance of institutional gridlock in Washington.

Presidents have also been weakened by the recent proliferation of interest groups. According to Stephen Skowronek, the institutional universe of political action that presidents face today has "gotten thicker all around." He asserts that "there are more organizations and authorities [for presidents] to contend with, and they are all more firmly entrenched and independent."[22] Presidents may seek to go over the heads of interest groups and build their own personal coalitions, both to get elected and to govern once they reach the White House. Although this reduces their obligations to other political actors, the flip side is that interest groups are similarly less obliged to remain loyal members of the president's team.

In brief, there is no consistent trend in the amount of power that modern presidents possess. If presidents in the 1970s appeared weak, Presidents Reagan (1981–89) and George W. Bush (2001–09) deployed presidential power to the limit—and in some cases beyond. The presidency is the most powerful institution within American government, but presidents encounter immensely powerful obstacles to the pursuit of their goals within American government and society as well as abroad.

Whether presidents are strong or weak depends on particular circumstances and the ability of presidents to take advantage of them. Some presidents are more fortunate than others. They encounter a less resistant environment when the opposition is in disarray, and their party commands a working majority in Congress. Or they may occupy the White House at a time of national crisis, when there is widespread public support for vigorous presidential leadership. The personal factor can also weigh heavily. Some presidents are more skillful than others at playing the hand they have been dealt.

Presidential Styles

Presidents construe their role in quite different ways. Presidential style is a function of the particular skills and aptitudes each person brings to the office. John F. Kennedy was supremely confident to the point of arrogance, Lyndon Johnson was beset by profound insecurity—although his long experience in the Senate and close friendship with influential senators enabled him to exert considerable legislative influence—and Richard Nixon was suspicious by nature. Ronald Reagan had little patience for the details of policy but was brilliantly effective at communicating their broad themes to the public. Jimmy Carter was just the opposite. He brought his training as an engineer to the presidency and was intensely interested in the details of policy. George W. Bush, on the other hand, delegated authority to trusted subordinates and tended to view issues in stark, moral terms. A *New York Times* reporter noted that "Barack Obama was able to rise from the Illinois State Senate to the presidency in large measure because of his ability to explain complex issues and then to make a persuasive argument."[23] However, the opposition almost managed to stonewall Obama when he tried to gain congressional approval for health-care reform. Some analysts claimed that Obama's relatively low-key approach, and his deferring to congressional leaders to shape the legislation, contributed to his difficulties. Other analysts praised his skill in gaining support for a reform that had eluded presidents stretching back to Harry Truman. (Some idea of the enormous range of issues that Obama deals with can be gleaned from Figure 6.1.)

FIGURE 6.1

A PRESIDENT'S DAY

Thursday, March 11, 2010

President Obama generally begins the day with a forty-five-minute workout and arrives in the Oval Office at about 9 a.m.

10:00 a.m.	Received the presidential daily briefing
10:30 a.m.	Received the economic daily briefing
11:15 a.m.	Addressed the Export-Import Bank's Annual Conference
1:00 p.m.	Met with grassroots leaders of the movement for comprehensive immigration reform
1:45 p.m.	Met with members of the Congressional Black Caucus
3:00 p.m.	Met with Senators Chuck Schumer and Lindsay Graham
3:45 p.m.	Met with Secretary of State Hillary Clinton
4:15 p.m.	Met with senior advisers
5:05 p.m.	The president and Michelle Obama hosted a screening of *The Pacific*
6:20 p.m.	Met with members of the Congressional Hispanic Caucus

After his scheduled itinerary, Obama typically spends time with his family from 6:30 p.m. to 8:30 p.m., and then turns to briefing papers and other paperwork until approximately 11:30 p.m.

SOURCES: Politico, "Thursday, Mar. 11, 2010," at http://www.politico.com/politico44/index.html?refresh=1 (accessed April 30, 2010); Jon Meacham, "A Highly Logical Approach," at http://www.newsweek.com/id/197891/ (accessed April 30, 2010).

Presidents shape the office in their own image. Some are hands-on managers; others prefer to delegate authority. Some are comfortable with a rigid chain of command; others prefer to improvise. Journalist Elizabeth Drew writes that the Clinton White House was so unstructured during his first term that one White House aide described it as an "adhocracy."[24] The opposite was true of George W. Bush, who ran a tight ship in which loyalty and teamwork were prized over brilliance and freelancing. If Clinton's White House team resembled a jazz ensemble where the musicians go off on their own riffs, Bush's resembled a military drill team in which the musicians play the music they are given and march together in lockstep. Barack Obama sought to strike a balance between the anarchy of Clinton's White House and the rigidity of Bush's.

Presidential leadership is exercised in contexts with particular features. As mentioned already, crisis and war permit presidents to overcome blockages that would normally compromise presidential power. The attacks of September 11, 2001, provide an illustration. Before 9/11, the Bush administration was floundering. Poll numbers were low and the economy was in recession. After 9/11, a presidency that had appeared small now loomed large. Approval ratings for President Bush soared. Congress deferred to the president. The system of checks and balances became seriously imbalanced as President Bush used the threat of terrorism to increase presidential power. Fears generated by the attacks were also manipulated to justify launching a preemptive, aggressive war against Iraq, further consolidating power in the executive branch. The president's role as symbolic leader of the country was used to rally public opinion.

As a general matter, presidential power is exercised most decisively and effectively when the president opposes some action. For example, the Constitution authorizes the president to veto bills passed by Congress. Vetoing a bill does not require the cooperation of any other political actor—just a pen that works. The veto is usually effective because it is rare that the required two-thirds majority can be assembled in each chamber to override it.

However, presidents who make historians' lists of great presidents do so not by preventing change but by promoting it. The presidents most likely to be remembered are those who have sponsored bold and successful initiatives. Congress, the federal bureaucracy, and special interest groups often resist presidential direction. Yet no other office in the political system can muster comparable initiative, coherence, and resources on behalf of a concerted course of action.

WHAT DO YOU THINK?

Are Checks and Balances Alive and Well?

The president's power has generally increased as the size and power of the federal government grew in the twentieth century. Has the growth of presidential power made the concept of checks and balances invalid? Further, what do you think should be the optimum extent of presidential power? How does your proposal compare with the power that recent presidents have exercised, and why do you propose that the president should have more, less, or the same power as recent presidents?

DIRECTING THE EXECUTIVE

The agencies comprising the federal executive are the largest single organization in the United States. The nearly 3 million civilian officials on the federal payroll perform a range of jobs that defy description—from postal clerks delivering mail to the secretary of defense, who directs 700,000 civilian employees and over 2 million enlisted personnel. Taken together, federal bureaus, agencies, commissions, and executive departments represent the greatest concentration of power in the world. But the key words are *taken together*, for the executive is far from a unified and coherent entity. The enormous size, diversity, and fragmentation of the federal bureaucracy makes it a lumbering giant.

To the extent that a center directs the vast executive, it is the chief executive—that is, the president. The size of the presidential office dramatically increased over the past century. When Herbert Hoover served as president, from 1929 to 1933, his staff consisted of a personal secretary and two assistants. Today the president's White House staff and Executive Office of the President (EOP) number in the thousands.

However, presidents have a hard time getting the different parts of the executive branch to cooperate. Presidents do not have a monopoly of legal authority or political influence over the bureaucracy. They appoint about 3,000 officials, a small number compared to the millions of career civil servants. Congress defines most agencies' organization and mission, appropriates the funds they depend upon, approves (or rejects) presidential nominees for key executive positions, and can summon administrators to testify before congressional committtees. As a result, presidents share control of the executive with Congress. Further, bureaucratic agencies also have a life of their own. Each agency has its own interests, and its employees are vigilant to protect the agency's turf (jurisdiction). Presidents often regard agencies within the executive—or even the bureaucracy as a whole—not as instruments to do their bidding or allies in a common struggle, but as opponents. Commands issuing from the top (i.e., the president and presidential staff) often have a curious way of being distorted or ignored at the bottom. For example, one study found that two years after President Jimmy Carter issued an order on a topic requiring 75 administrative agencies to issue their own implementing regulations, only 15 had done so.[25] Presidents may be located at the top of the bureaucratic chart, but they must compete with other actors for influence over federal agencies.

As mentioned earlier, the key institution by which presidents seek to impose their will is the **Executive Office of the President (EOP)**. This collection of specialized agencies with about 1,600 staff members includes the White House

Office (the president's personal staff and closest advisers), National Security Council, National Economic Council, Council of Economic Advisors, and Office of the Vice President. The largest unit in the EOP is the Office of Management and Budget (OMB), which prepares the president's budget.[26]

The EOP provides the president with expertise and performs management tasks on his or her behalf. It is the first in a series of concentric circles surrounding the presidency (Figure 6.2). Members of the EOP, especially the White House staff, are passionately loyal to the president, owe their position to him or her, and share the president's goals. Many staffers in the EOP are political appointees and likely to have been close associates of the president before their appointment. For example, FOBs ("Friends of Bill") were distributed throughout the Executive Office under the Clinton administration. According to one estimate, 80 percent of the White House staff under President George W. Bush had served in his campaign organization.[27] President Obama appointed to the EOP many members of his entourage from the days when he was an Illinois state legislator from Chicago. A *New York Times* report noted that "The Obama White House is now populated with as many Chicagoans as it previously housed Texans."[28]

Until recently, the office of vice president warranted only passing mention in a survey of the presidency. The vice president's main job was usually described

President Obama conferring with his advisers.

FIGURE 6.2

EXECUTIVE BRANCH

Executive Office of the President (EOP)
includes
Council of Economic Advisors
National Economic Council
National Security Council
Office of Management and Budget

Cabinet Departments
Agriculture
Commerce
Defense
Education
Energy
Health and Human Services
Homeland Security
Housing and Urban Development
Interior
Justice
Labor
State
Transportation
Treasury
Veterans Affairs

Independent Regulatory Commissions
includes
Federal Reserve Board
National Labor Relations Board

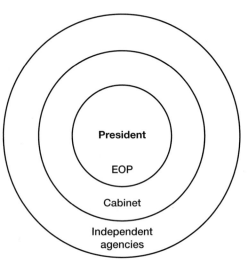

as waiting in the wings for the president to die in office. However, the office of vice president became more important when President Bill Clinton delegated Vice President Al Gore authority to supervise important policy sectors, including technological development and climate change.

Yet Gore's power paled in comparison with that of his successor. Richard Cheney, vice president during George W. Bush's two terms in office, was indisputably the most powerful vice president ever. Cheney helped shape policy in many areas and played an especially influential role regarding energy, foreign, and security policy. He was deeply involved in counterterrorism activities, the decision to invade Iraq, the conduct of the war, and the treatment of prisoners captured in Afghanistan and Iraq. Although not part of the formal chain of command, Cheney issued directives to the CIA, including orders to keep certain activities secret from executive officials and congressional committees charged with oversight.

According to political scientist Shirley Anne Warshaw, "Dick Cheney was not just the vice president, but in reality the unelected co-president of the United States."[29] Indeed, Warshaw's description of their respective spheres of influence suggests that Cheney was the more important of the two. "Bush managed his faith-based agenda, moved forward his compassionate conservatism, and served as the public face of the administration. Cheney managed the larger portfolio of economic, energy, and national security policy and worked to expand the power of the presidency."[30]

President Obama delegated responsibility to Vice President Joseph Biden Jr. for directing some limited features of economic and foreign policy. Biden is reported to play an important role in policy discussions within the administration, but he exercises substantially less power than Cheney did.

Another important position within the presidential orbit is that of presidential spouse. The official office of First Lady was created for Edith Roosevelt during President Theodore Roosevelt's presidency. However, presidential wives (so far no husbands have served as first spouse) historically were supposed to be seen but not heard. Eleanor Roosevelt, the wife of Franklin Delano Roosevelt (FDR), broke the mold. She was a commanding figure and a powerful voice for women's rights, children's rights, and human rights. After FDR's death, President Harry Truman named her the first American representative to the newly created United Nations, and she played a key role in formulating the UN Declaration on Human Rights.

Presidential spouses have their own staffs to help them pursue projects in which they have particular interests and expertise. Bill Clinton appointed his wife Hillary to direct a task force charged with proposing a plan to reform the health-care system. She also championed women's rights and advocated increasing public resources for families and child care. Laura Bush, a former librarian, sponsored events to highlight the value of books and reading.

Michelle Obama has been especially prominent, partly because of intense public curiosity about the first African American presidential family and partly because of her own strong personality. Ms. Obama has focused on promoting healthy eating. She provided the media with some fine photo ops when the Obama family pitched in to create a vegetable garden on the White House grounds. She also sponsored events that, for the first time, brought together official Washington and the predominantly black population of the city. And she often meets with military families to convey the government's gratitude for their service.

The next ring out from the presidency and vice presidency is the "permanent government," consisting of the fifteen departments in the executive branch, including the Department of Defense, State Department, Department of Commerce, and Treasury Department. Departments are umbrella organizations containing most of the agencies and bureaus that comprise the federal bureaucracy. For example, the Department of Commerce includes over two dozen diverse offices and agencies, including the Bureau of the Census, the Patent and Trademark Office, and the National Oceanic and Atmospheric Administration.

Executive agencies often tend to identify their interests with those of the powerful business interests in the particular economic sector that they regulate. Different federal agencies can therefore promote diametrically opposite policies. For example, the Department of Agriculture has historically subsidized and promoted the interests of corn farmers and agribusiness by encouraging the use of corn syrup as a sweetener in soft drinks and other products. At the same time, the Surgeon General, a federal official whose mandate is to promote public health, has warned (thus far to no avail) that sweeteners like corn syrup cause obesity, tooth decay, and diabetes.

Because they represent different interests, executive agencies frequently compete with each other for power and resources. The ones that promote an administration's agenda are likely to be rewarded with fatter budget increases from one year to the next. Consistent with their policy priorities, President George W. Bush starved the National Labor Relations Board (the agency charged with enforcing labor laws), and President Obama substantially increased its budget.

The president appoints a secretary to lead each department, and the fifteen department secretaries (along with a few other officials, including the vice president and, under President Obama, the small business administrator), compose the president's **cabinet**. The cabinet as a collective body is less than the sum of its parts; that is, it rarely plays an important role in presidential decision making. For example, President Clinton met with his cabinet only eighteen times over the course of his entire first term and had even fewer cabinet meetings in his second term. The classic story about presidents' relations with their cabinet involves Lincoln's announcement, following a vote of his cabinet: "Eight votes for and one against [the president's]; the nays have it."

Presidents have substantial control over the size, scope, and resources of federal agencies, although they share this power with Congress. The president's proposed budget can seek to starve an agency whose activities he or she dislikes and to pamper an agency whose activities the president favors. However, presidents are not all-powerful, because Congress must approve these proposals. Presidents can also issue **executive orders** requiring or authorizing federal agencies to act. By this means, according to one scholar, presidents can "establish policy, reorganize executive branch agencies, alter administrative and regulatory processes, [and] affect how legislation is interpreted and implemented."[31]

The third ring out from the president enjoys more autonomy from the president than do the departments. This ring consists of the independent regulatory commissions (IRCs), such as the National Labor Relations Board (NLRB), the Federal Trade Commission (FTC), and the Federal Reserve Board. Presidents appoint commissioners to direct these agencies, subject to confirmation by Congress; but unlike secretaries of departments, the appointees serve for a fixed term and cannot be fired by the president. Because the terms of independent regulatory commission appointees often straddle administrations, newly elected presidents must wait for commissioners' terms to expire before replacing them. Although IRCs are mandated to regulate the participants in a given sector, the IRC often is informally captured by the powerful interests within the sector. This represents another example of how government tends to reflect inequalities of power and wealth rather than redistribute them.

As this description of the federal bureaucracy makes clear, the federal government is not organized hierarchically but rather in concentric circles that surround the president (see Figure 6.2). The federal bureaucracy is like a solar system in which some planets orbit closer than others to the presidential sun. But federal agencies are also under the magnetic pull of other suns in the galaxy that threaten to draw them away from presidents' directions. For one thing, the system of shared powers endows Congress with influence over federal agencies and exerts a gravitational pull on them that competes with the force of the president. Federal agencies depend on Congress for appropriations, and Congress provides their legislative mandate—their job description. Congress also performs oversight to ensure they comply with their mandate. Further, in a manner similar to the process described earlier by which IRCs are captured by their "clients," federal bureaus and agencies often seek to promote the interests of their powerful constituents, including lobbies, interest groups, and other economic actors. Thus, presidential control of the bureaucracy is weakened by private groups that develop mutually supportive, friendly—sometimes called clientelistic—relationships with federal agencies. Interest groups gravitate to federal agencies because the agency has legal authority to provide sanctions and benefits to the group. Thus, clients seek to "rent" the agency for their own benefit. In exchange for tax breaks, subsidies, and favorable rulings, clients give an agency political support in bureaucratic struggles over turf, OMB budgeting, and congressional appropriations. Groups with superior resources—often large corporations, as well as interest groups and lobbies that are dominated by the largest members in a sector—are, of course, best situated to succeed at the politics of power.

Finally, the bureaucracy itself may resist presidential direction. Federal agencies are the repositories of vast amounts of expertise that can be mobilized to sabotage presidential policy. Presidential appointees are often dependent on the information that bureaucrats possess. Presidential appointees typically become advocates of the agency they are charged with directing. Rather than acting as the president's agent, the appointee becomes a double agent who represents the agency's interests to the president.[32]

Given the many challenges to their management of the executive branch, presidents often prefer to circumvent the bureaucracy altogether. They concentrate policymaking inside the EOP, relying on staff assistants whom they know and trust and who are personally loyal to them. In related fashion, the president may appoint "czars" in the EOP to supervise policy development and implementation in high-priority sectors. President Obama, for example, appointed czars with responsibility for drug policy and for executive compensation for banks receiving government bailout funds. This survey of the federal executive indicates its enormous size and wide scope. We now analyze the ways that modern presidents have used this power.

THE EXERCISE OF PRESIDENTIAL POWER

Because of the president's central position within American government, and because the position is so poorly defined in the Constitution, scholars have engaged in many attempts to understand the basis of presidential power. Presidential scholar Clinton Rossiter identified ten presidential "hats" or roles: chief of state, chief executive, commander in chief of the armed forces, chief diplomat, chief legislator, chief of the party, voice of the people, protector of the peace, manager of prosperity, and world leader.[33] Political scientist Thomas E. Cronin reduced Rossiter's list to four spheres or subpresidencies: foreign policy, economic management, domestic policy, and symbolic or moral leadership.[34] Aaron Wildavsky, a specialist in public policy, suggested a still simpler classification by distinguishing two presidencies, one for foreign affairs and the other for domestic affairs.[35]

These classifications are a useful point of departure. We reconfigure them to suggest three broad purposes on behalf of which contemporary presidents exercise power: making capitalism work at home, defending America at home and abroad, and maintaining political stability.

Making Capitalism Work at Home

The presidency is at the center of the sprawling bureaucracy responsible for the stable functioning of an immense, highly complex, and interdependent political economy. No other institution can present a coherent program, mobilize public support for it, and implement policies to stabilize and strengthen capitalism and democracy. Presidential planning is an essential feature of modern capitalism, no less under a laissez-faire ideologue like Ronald Reagan than under "New Democrat" Bill Clinton, "compassionate conservative" George W. Bush, or "post-partisan" president Barack Obama. A major presidential goal is to promote a vibrant capitalist economy.

As we analyze in other chapters, concepts like economic health, stability, and growth are not neutral. Differently put, one can ask: whose economic health, stability, and growth? How are the benefits of economic health, stability, and growth distributed? During the economic crisis of 2008–09 (described in Chapters 2, 3, and 9), presidents gave highest priority to stabilizing capitalism. This was the rationale for massive expeditures to bail out the auto industry, banks, and financial institutions as well as for deficit spending to stimulate the sagging economy. Government leaders repeatedly emphasized that these extraordinary measures were designed to enable private markets to function again with minimal possible government intervention.

During periods of economic stability, government assistance to the market system is less visible. Although the smooth functioning of the economy depends on government intervention during good times as well as bad, intervention is less dramatic when it does not take the form of massive bailouts. Nonetheless, making capitalism work is a major task carried out 24/7 by the president and the EOP economic team, including the Office of Management and Budget, the National Economic Council, and the Council of Economic Advisors. An illustration of the importance of this function of presidential leadership is that President Obama directed the head of the White House National Economic Council, within the EOP, to provide him with a daily economic briefing as a counterpart to the briefing he receives from his National Security Advisor.

Moving outside the EOP, a wide array of government agencies have major economic responsibilities. These agencies include the Departments of the Treasury, State, Agriculture, Commerce, Labor, Energy, and Interior as well as the Small Business Administration, Federal Reserve Board, Environmental Protection Agency, and independent regulatory commissions like the Securities and Exchange Commission. This partial list suggests how much of the federal executive's activity involves economic matters.

High on the agenda of most executive agencies is the goal of promoting the interests of particular business sectors. For example, as described in Chapter 3, the Federal Reserve Board is beholden to bankers. The Agriculture Department tailors its policies to favor agribusiness. The Interior Department is concerned with the welfare of mining interests. On the other hand, agencies whose mandate is to represent groups and interests at the periphery of corporate capitalism, such as the Labor Department and Department of Education, have far less power and occupy a relatively low rank in the informal hierarchy of federal agencies.

Defending America at Home and Abroad

The power of the presidency has increased in tandem with the rise of the United States as a superpower and in response to threats to its domestic security. A president's first job is to keep Americans safe, and presidents are granted immense power and initiative to do so. When it comes to pursuing objectives abroad, presidents seek to maintain a stable international framework in which the United States occupies the preeminent place and American values are reflected. More concretely, presidents seek to promote American business interests abroad. They direct American representatives to international organizations like the United Nations (UN) and International Monetary Fund (IMF) to safeguard the interests of American business. Next in importance, presidents attempt to mobilize American power to promote human rights and democratic regimes, so long as these regimes do not challenge American interests. Thus, the tension we have analyzed in previous chapters between supporting capitalism and supporting democracy is evident in the president's conduct of foreign policy. (These issues are further explored in Chapter 11.)

Presidents rely on multiple sources of power to pursue the ambitious agenda of defending America at home and abroad. First, the Constitution grants the president the power to negotiate treaties, receive ambassadors from foreign countries (which implies the right to recognize or refuse to recognize the government of a particular country), and, above all, command the armed forces.

Second, presidents use crises, and sometimes even manufacture them, as a pretext to boost their power. Third, presidents have at their disposal the staff resources of the entire defense and foreign affairs establishment, and they enjoy unique access to the media to defend their actions. Fourth, Congress generally defers to the president when it comes to foreign affairs.

Particular mention should be made of the president's command of the armed forces. The framers of the Constitution intended the president's power as commander in chief to be confined to the limited occasions when hostilities begin. The Constitution granted Congress, not the president, the power to declare war and appropriate funds for military expenditures.

Presidents have expanded the power of the presidency by broadly interpreting their authority as commander in chief. Supreme Court Justice Robert Jackson once warned that, thanks to serving as commander in chief, the president essentially has the power "to do anything, anywhere that can be done with an army or navy."[36] Presidents have often deployed American troops to pursue their preferred foreign policy objectives. For example, President James K. Polk provoked war with Mexico in 1846 by sending American troops into disputed land between Texas and Mexico. When Mexican forces fired on the troops, Polk quickly extracted from Congress a declaration of war. Polk's actions brought forth an angry reaction from a young Illinois congressman: "Allow the president to invade a neighboring nation, whenever *he* shall deem it necessary to repel an invasion . . . and you allow him to make war at his pleasure. Study to see if you can fix *any limit* to his power in this respect."[37]

The words of the young congressman, Abraham Lincoln, proved prescient indeed; Lincoln himself substantially expanded presidential power during the Civil War. He refused to call Congress into special session in the first months of the war. He directed southern ports to be blockaded without congressional authorization, expanded the armed forces beyond their congressionally prescribed size, and spent money for purposes not approved by Congress.

Contemporary presidents, like their predecessors, have often dispatched troops first and sought congressional approval later—if they bothered to seek approval at all. In 1983, President Reagan ordered U.S. armed forces to invade the tiny Caribbean nation of Grenada and overthrow its government without seeking authorization from Congress. After Saddam Hussein of Iraq invaded Kuwait in 1991, President George H.W. Bush sent 200,000 troops to neighboring Saudi Arabia to protect its oil fields without seeking congressional approval. When he later did so, two political scientists observe, Congress "had little choice except to grant the president the authority he requested." They comment, "As most legislators were doubtless aware, withholding such approval would mean that the United States stood in real danger of incurring a serious diplomatic and military defeat in the Middle East. This was an outcome for which few legislators were willing to take responsibility."[38]

Following the bombing of the World Trade Center and Pentagon in 2001, Congress passed the USA Patriot Act authorizing the executive to engage in a greatly expanded array of activities to fight terrorism. Only later did Congress protest at being bypassed and try to recover its constitutional authority. When the Bush administration refused to consult with Congress or share information with it, Republican Representative Dan Burton, chair of the House Government Reform Committee, complained, "This is not a monarchy. His title is President George Bush, not King George."[39]

Maintaining Political Stability

Capitalist production, and more generally the functioning of a large, complex, and diverse society, generates dislocations, inequalities, and discontent. This provides the structural context for the third arena of presidential activity: mediating the challenges resulting from the collision of democratic politics and capitalist production. Thomas E. Cronin suggests that "calibration and management of conflict is the core of presidential leadership."[40] A major presidential concern is to prevent conflict from threatening political and economic stability.

When discontented groups express grievances, presidents often take to the media. For example, President Clinton excelled at empathizing. He famously assured an AIDS activist during the 1992 presidential campaign, "I feel your pain."[41] Sometimes presidents try to defuse an issue by forming commissions to study it. "These commissions," according to one skeptic, "study the situation and, in due course, issue a report, which after a flurry of publicity, is filed away, its recommendations unimplemented and forgotten."[42]

Presidents may drape themselves in the flag and appeal to patriotic sentiments as a way to unify the nation in face of challenge. President Bush's appearance at Ground Zero of the World Trade Center following the 9/11 attack helped identify the president with this national calamity. In the United States, patriotism can be considered as a functional substitute for a state religion in which the president acts as high priest.

The media are a key tool that presidents use to maintain political stability. As described earlier in the chapter, no other person in the world enjoys comparable media access. Almost one-third of the White House staff works on packaging the president for media consumption. Speechwriters, press

President Bush at Ground Zero in the week following the attack on the World Trade Center on September 11, 2001.

secretaries, pollsters, and media consultants seek to portray presidents and their policies in a favorable light. The job of delivering the president's message is vastly more complicated nowadays due to the explosion of new media, a topic described in Chapter 4.[43]

In recent years, presidential campaigning and governing have blended. During the Clinton presidency, political consultants more actively participated in policy discussions than had been the case under previous presidents. George C. Edwards described the Clinton administration as "the ultimate example of the public presidency—a presidency based on a perpetual campaign to obtain the public's support and fed by public opinion polls, focus groups, and public relations memos."[44]

Politics determined policy to an even greater extent during the Bush presidency. When John DiIulio Jr. (Bush's director of the Office of Faith-Based and Community Initiatives) resigned, he criticized the influence of political advisors on policymaking and warned that policy was being sacrificed to image and political calculation.[45] *New York Times* columnist Thomas Friedman claimed that the Bush administration's policy toward Iraq was driven more by domestic political concerns in the United States than by the stated aim of bringing democracy to Iraq. Friedman wrote, "That is why, I bet, Karl Rove [President Bush's political advisor] had more sway over this war than Assistant Secretary of State for Near Eastern Affairs Bill Burns. Mr. Burns knew only what would play in the Middle East. Mr. Rove knew what would play in the Middle West."[46]

President Obama relies heavily on the media. He has held numerous press conferences, authorized countless photo ops, and granted an endless number of "exclusive" interviews with talk-show hosts and journalists.

Today the public face of the presidency is highly managed and contrived. The administration chooses what news to reveal and when to reveal it. When asked why President Bush waited until September to begin beating the drums of war against Iraq, his chief of staff explained, "From a marketing point of view you don't introduce new products in August."[47]

Of course, presidents sometimes wish that their actions would escape the media spotlight. They cannot always control the spin that the media give to a story. Off-the-record remarks may end up as the lead story on network TV or being scanned by millions on YouTube.

Sometimes presidents find that expressions of concern, blue-ribbon commissions, and other symbolic gestures are not sufficient to maintain stability. At these times, if the challenge to the existing order is sufficiently great and appears to be escalating, a president can attempt to reestablish control in two additional ways. Although diametrically opposite, the two courses are not mutually exclusive. First, the president can propose to provide benefits to aggrieved groups. In their historical analysis of social policy, Frances Fox Piven and Richard Cloward found that welfare funding increased "during the occasional outbreaks of civil disorder produced by mass unemployment" and then con-

WHAT DO YOU THINK?

The President: Between Capitalism and Democracy

Previous chapters of this book have analyzed the tension within the American political system between the undemocratic organization of the capitalist economy and the democratic organization of elected political institutions. As the most powerful official in the government and the entire country, the president's selection, policies, and conduct in office might be expected to reflect this tension. Is this the case? How? Further, is the tension manifested in different ways, depending on particular issues, as well as from one president to another? Select two presidents from the period since World War II, and suggest how the tension referred to earlier helps illuminate their conduct in office; or, conversely, how their conduct in office helps clarify the approach summarized in this and earlier chapters.

tracted when stability was restored. For example, one response by the federal government to labor unrest in the 1930s and black militancy in the 1960s was to sponsor new social programs.[48]

Presidents, and state and local authorities, may also choose to respond to acute challenges to social stability by calling out the National Guard, mobilizing the armed forces, engaging federal marshals, and using the FBI to maintain political order. Force represents the iron fist cloaked by the velvet glove of presidential symbolism, media glorification, and policy concessions. Following 9/11, for example, federal agents arrested approximately 1,200 foreign nationals, refused to release their names, detained them in secret locations, and held deportation hearings for many without allowing them access to an attorney. Presidents have often cooperated with local authorities in using violence to break strikes by workers and to quell urban protests.

CONCLUSION

Political power is centralized in the executive branch, and within the executive branch, it is concentrated in the Executive Office of the President. The presidency is at the apex of the government and is uniquely qualified to coordinate the different parts of the government through a coherent program. It is a key institutional site where conflicting demands in society are sifted to promote policies of economic performance and social stability. The presidency enjoys this exalted position by virtue of the constitutional power vested in it and because, along with the vice presidency, it is the only office elected on a national basis.

At the same time, presidential power is highly contingent. Presidents must contend with countervailing pressures from citizens, business firms, interest groups, and social movements. They must also work within the system of checks and balances, which allots independent powers to the legislative and judicial branches. Given the constitutional architecture of the separation of powers, presidents cannot command; they must persuade. Presidential success requires obtaining the cooperation of the legislative and judicial branches, which are independent and may not be acquiescent. Further, federal agencies in the executive branch often resist presidential direction because they are subject to a variety of conflicting influences. In such circumstances, presidents tend to move policymaking inside the EOP, where staff are more loyal and subject to their direct control, and to rely on techniques that bypass Congress and minimize bureaucratic obstruction.[49]

Presidential success comes from making change, not preventing it. Presidents themselves encourage the expectation that they will provide leadership and initiative to the entire government. Ironically, presidential power is most effective when it is least important (preventing change) and least effective when it is most important (creating change). Even with immense political resources at their disposal, presidents often cannot overcome interest group opposition, congressional resistance, adverse court rulings, and bureaucratic resistance. Yet, despite the daunting obstacles that presidents encounter, they are in the best position to provide government with energy and direction. Presidents attempt to provide initiative and coherence to the federal government in order to make capitalism work at home, defend America at home and abroad, and maintain political stability when threatened by the dislocations generated by policies in the first two arenas. It is not surprising that they rarely achieve all of these goals.

CHAPTER SUMMARY

Introduction

There was no precedent for the office of the president when the Constitution was written. The Founders designed the presidency to provide energy to the executive branch. At the same time, they sought to limit the risk of executive tyranny by constructing a system of separated powers in which the executive would play a secondary role to Congress. They also limited the extent of popular participation in selecting the president by creating the Electoral College. Delegates to the Electoral College were supposed to represent the more prosperous and conservative section of the community. However, the president soon began to be elected by popular vote following the growth of the party system and the extension of suffrage. The Electoral College remains important because of the unit rule, according to which all of a state's delegates to the Electoral College vote for whichever presidential candidate obtains a majority of the state's popular vote. The result is to provide very small and very large states with disportionate influence in presidential elections.

The Historical Presidency

The Founders designed the presidency to provide energy to the executive branch. At the same time, fear of tyranny led the Founders to construct a system of separated powers in which the executive would play a secondary role to Congress. For over a century, the presidency was a relatively weak institution, both because the federal government had limited power compared to state governments and because Congress was the more assertive branch of the federal government. Important changes in the twentieth century, including the growth in size and complexity of the American economy, economic crises, and war, thrust the president onto center stage. The most decisive changes occurred in response to the Great Depression and World War II. The presidency assumed a central role because of FDR's New Deal, wartime mobilization, and the Cold War that followed. Since then the federal government, especially the executive branch directed by the president, has exercised vast powers.

The Imperial President

Presidents are endowed with an ample array of powers, including constitutional grants of powers in domestic and foreign affairs. They have extensive informal powers, including legitimacy that they enjoy as the only official (along with the vice president) elected by the entire nation. Additional power derives from their unique access to the media and their power to direct the federal bureaucracy. They also can appeal to the loyalty of congressional and other officials who share their party affiliation. They enjoy additional power because the United States is the most powerful country in the world. President George W. Bush sought to further extend presidential power by relying on the concept of the unitary executive as well as the president's role as commander in chief. President Bush justified an extension of the president's power by referring to the War on Terror and the wars in Afghanistan and Iraq. Many analysts claim that his actions violated international laws and treaties and may have amounted to crimes against humanity.

The Perils of Presidential Power

Despite having enormous powers, the president faces many obstacles to the exercise of presidential leadership. One factor is the U.S. system of separated powers, which gives Congress and the Supreme Court powers independent of the president that can be used to check the president's power. Another is that economic difficulties reduce the scope for presidential initiative. And the growth of interest groups represents yet another countervailing power to presidential leadership. Given these strong constraints, presidents are more able to block change than promote it. Yet presidents who are rated as outstanding gain this reputation from initiating change rather than preventing it. A final factor relating to the exercise of presidential leadership is the personal style of the president.

Some presidents closely supervise subordinates and are involved in the details of policy formulation and implementation; other presidents delgate major responsibility for these matters.

Directing the Executive

The president's principal tool for formulating and implementing policy is the executive branch. The president is not only a person but an institution—the presidency. The institutionalized embodiment of the president, the Executive Office of the President (EOP), is itself a large and powerful multi-agency operation. The EOP's mission is to assist the president in directing the executive branch and leading the country. The EOP includes the president's principal advisers on economic, social, security, and foreign policy. Outside the EOP are located the major executive departments of government. Each department is headed by a secretary chosen by the president. Each department is a giant agency in its own right, possessing substantial administrative authority, several bureaus, and a large budget. The secretaries of the major departments comprise the Cabinet and are under the president's direction. Further removed from presidential control are independent regulatory commissions and other semi-autonomous agencies. Presidential control is limited over federal agencies because they possess distinctive interests, expertise, and power. Moreover, they often have close and supportive relations with their clients or constituents within their jurisdiction, who are likely to be powerful economic interests. Therefore, the executive branch is at the same time sprawling, complex, divided, and also generally inclined to support economically powerful and affluent interests.

The Exercise of Presidential Power

Presidential power is exercised on behalf of three major goals. First, the president is responsible for making capitalism work at home. This task involves using the vast range of resources within the executive branch to maximize economic stability and growth. Second, the president seeks to defend America at home and abroad. This goal involves protecting American citizens from attack as well as seeking to maintain American economic, political, and military dominance abroad. Third, the president seeks to maintain political stability. Doing so involves using the government's administrative, financial, and military resources to overcome challenges to the status quo.

Critical Thinking Questions

1. President Obama has compared changing the orientation of the federal government to changing the direction of an ocean liner. What did he mean by this claim? Was it accurate? How can it be done?

2. Do you agree with President George W. Bush's claim that the War on Terror justified the use of exceptional measures? Identify two such measures that he sponsored, and discuss whether you consider them legitimate in light of the situation since 9/11.

3. Periodically, historians are polled to identify great presidents. Who do you consider the best and the worst president since World War II? Why? What criteria have you used in making your selection, and why are these criteria the most useful ones?

Suggested Readings

Joel D. Aberbach and Mark A. Peterson, eds., *The Executive Branch*. New York: Oxford University Press, 2006.

Jonathan Alter, *The Promise: President Obama, Year One*. New York: Simon & Schuster, 2010.

Theodore J. Lowi, *The Personal President: Power Invested, Promise Unfulfilled*. Ithaca, NY: Cornell University Press, 1985.

Richard E. Neustadt, *Presidential Power and the Modern Presidents: The Politics of Leadership*. New York: Simon & Schuster, 1991.

Richard M. Pious, *The American Presidency*. New York: Basic Books, 1979.

Stephen Skowronek, *The Politics Presidents Make: Leadership from John Adams to George Bush*. Cambridge, MA: Harvard University Press, 1993.

Jeffrey K. Tulis, *The Rhetorical Presidency*. Princeton, NJ: Princeton University Press, 1987.

Garry Wills, *Bomb Power: The Modern Presidency and the National Security State*. New York: Penguin Press, 2010.

THE CONGRESS

INTRODUCTION

Although Congress is just one of three branches that compose the federal government, Article I, Section 8 of the Constitution assigns it especially substantial responsibilities. These include the capacity to declare war; to build, support, and control the Army and Navy; to collect taxes, borrow money, and pay debt; to control immigration; to regulate commerce and set rules for overseas trade; to create courts inferior to the Supreme Court; to establish networks of post offices and roads; and, more generally, to "make all laws which shall be necessary and proper for carrying into execution the foregoing powers, and all other powers vested by this Constitution in the government of the United States, or any department or officer thereof." In addition, the House of Representatives was given the power to impeach—that is, bring charges against—members of the executive branch and the judiciary. The Senate then acts as a trial court for all impeachments, requiring a two-thirds majority of those voting in order to convict. Article II, Sections 2 and 3, further instructs the president to report to Congress on the **State of the Union** and to secure approval from the Senate for treaties negotiated with other countries and for appointments to high governmental positions, including justices of the Supreme Court.

By lodging these vast powers in Congress as the country's national representative body, the United States fulfilled the demand posed a century earlier by the political thinker, John Locke, who had announced in his *Second Treatise of Government* that "the *first and fundamental positive* Law of all Commonwealths *is the establishing of the Legislative Power*. . . . This *Legislative* is not only *the supream power* of the Common-wealth, but sacred and unalterable."[1] In almost every other democracy, the national legislature lacks the kind of authority the American separation of powers system places in Congress. Elsewhere, parliaments largely confirm what the government of the day wishes

WHAT DO YOU THINK?

The Importance of Congress

In *Leviathan*, a great seventeenth-century work of political theory, Thomas Hobbes placed the king at the center of his vision of a stable political order. In the *Second Treatise of Government*, another great seventeenth-century text, John Locke placed the legislature at the center of his vision for a good political system. The United States, of course, has no king; but it does have a large and capable executive branch that is headed by the president. The country also has the globe's most independent legislature, the result of its separation of powers. Which of these works by Hobbes and Locke, contrasting the role of the executive with the role of the legislature, seems most compelling today? Can the two perspectives be reconciled and combined?

to achieve, for not to do so can cause a government to fall and thus require new elections.

In 1885, twenty-eight years before he became the president of the United States, Woodrow Wilson wrote an analysis of "the essential machinery of power" in America and concluded "that, unquestionably, the predominant and controlling force, the center and source of all motive and regulative power, is Congress."[2] As the representative body that is expected to bring into government the wishes of the people, members of the House and Senate are elected to represent districts and states, and thus to transport the preferences of the people who live there to Washington. With senators and representatives exercising powers delegated to them by the people, Congress was designed to be the government's most popularly legitimate institution.

And yet, there is a long tradition of doubt and distrust. Woodrow Wilson was suspicious of congressional power. He thought Congress to be too unwieldy, too unpredictable, and too interested in patronage and spending to produce good government. Many Americans have shared such misgivings. Though most citizens tend to support their own members of the House and Senate, they consistently express less confidence in Congress than in the presidency or the Supreme Court. In July 2009, only 22 percent of Americans thought Congress was doing a good or excellent job (an increase from the single-digit ratings of the prior year). Perhaps thinking about a raft of recent scandals (including the 2005 resignation of Republican California House member Randy ["Duke"]

Cunningham, who pleaded guilty to accepting $2.4 million in bribes, and the 2009 conviction of former Democratic Louisiana House member William Jennings ["Bill"] Jefferson on eleven counts of bribery), a third thought Congress to be corrupt. Fully seven in ten believed that members of Congress are more interested in advancing their own careers than in helping the country.[3]

This chapter probes this puzzling and paradoxical situation. Congress is the most open and accessible of the three branches of the federal government. Its elected members have to stay alert to shifts in the public mood. Their jobs depend on it.[4] Congress thus is often responsive to pressures from less privileged groups because, according to Elizabeth Sanders, its members are "bound to local constituencies," making them "exquisitely sensitive to the economic pain and moral outrage of their electorates."[5] Although both the presidency and Congress are more responsive to groups that have wealth and power, they often are attuned to hear different voices. Congress, according to the Founders, was supposed to represent local constituencies while the president, in Thomas Jefferson's words, was "the only national officer who commanded a view of the whole ground."[6] Some members of Congress, of course, develop national concerns and followings. In chairing the House Finance Committee, for example, Democrat Barney Frank has responsibilities that extend far beyond the interests of his Boston suburb; and as an openly gay member of Congress, he often has articulated the concerns of that large national constituency. Yet even individuals whose positions induce them to take on broad national concerns can never stray far from the particular **preferences** and specific interests of their districts and their electorates.

Why, then, is the public so skeptical about Congress and the legislative process? These reservations and suspicions about Congress, we argue, are not a reaction to specific public policies but to patterns of influence and the unevenness of political representation that affect how congressional procedures operate and what they produce. Many people perceive these practices to be unfair. As political scientists John Hibbing and Elizabeth Theiss-Morse write, "[T]he people believe they see processes that are not just, processes that are not equitable. A minority—the extremists, the special interests—are seen as having more access and influence than 'the people.' Lobbyists are in and ordinary people are out, so there is a clear injustice present."[7] The public often lacks respect for Congress because it often appears to be captured by special interests that generously contribute to congressional campaigns, employ vast numbers of well-funded lobbyists to influence legislation, and enjoy special access to congressional members. More likely to vote, contact their senator or representative, donate money, and belong to interest groups, those who command wealth and organization are best positioned to take advantage of access to Congress. Congress tends to hear these persons and groups more clearly than other Americans because their money, their votes, and their access amplify their voices.

What happens inside Congress, however, is not simply the work of outside forces that bring their influence to bear in the form of lobbying, campaign contributions, and election results. Senators and representatives come to office with their own beliefs and ideological orientations. They are not blank pads on which outside interests simply inscribe their views. Public policy, moreover, also is a product of the structure, rules, and procedures of Congress. The most important aspect of congressional structure is its division into two parts, the Senate and the House of Representatives. Each chamber of Congress represents different kinds of constituencies. The Senate represents states, which have broad and varied populations. Each state elects two senators. The six-year terms for senators are staggered so that only one-third of all senators face election every two years. The House of Representatives, by contrast, represents districts within states based on the size of their population. These smaller constituences tend to be less diverse. Though the entire House must stand for election every two years and is thus exposed as a body to electoral swings, two-thirds of the Senate is not up for reelection and, at any given moment, is more insulated from its voters. Electoral forces thus wind their way through the Senate more slowly than they do the House. With only 100 members—compared to the House, which has 435—the Senate is a more intimate chamber, providing more latitude for action by individual members. In addition, because senators represent large, diverse constituencies, they must moderate their politics. Senators have to reach out and satisfy broader electorates, and that tends to push them more to the political center than House members. Each chamber, moreover, is governed by its own formal and informal rules that affect how they consider laws, certify appointments, conduct investigations, and remove officials from office.

To probe why a significant and open legislature based on elections and representation often receives harsh reviews, this chapter reviews the origins and history of Congress, discusses patterns of congressional influence and the nature of the legislative process, considers the relationship of the House and Senate to the wider society, and discusses the powers of Congress within the political system.

THE ORIGIN OF TWO LEGISLATIVE CHAMBERS

James Madison put the matter bluntly to the delegates at the Constitutional Convention in Philadelphia in 1787. The problem confronting them was to devise a political formula that would guard against the "inconveniences of democracy" in a manner that was still "consistent with the democratic form of government."[8] The Founders, who believed in sovereignty by the people, also were concerned that democracy would threaten the social order. They perceived their task as one of "preserving the spirit and form of popular government" while avoiding what experience under the Articles of Confederation had taught them was its consequence: that the majority would use their democratic rights to pursue their economic interests through the government—what many Founders condemned as "the leveling spirit" that could threaten the stability of the social order.

To protect the government against what the Founders perceived as the excesses of democracy, they created the presidency (as we saw in Chapter 6). But they did not stop there. The Founders also sought to check too strong a popular voice in the government by creating a legislature with two separate chambers: a House of Representatives, whose members would be elected by popular vote; and a Senate, whose members would be chosen by the various state legislatures. Without a Senate with two members for each state, moreover, small states and slaveholding states might not have ratified the Constitution, for these states gained protection for their interests by securing this form of assured representation.

It was widely assumed at the convention, political scientist Robert Dahl has written, that a popularly elected House of Representatives with small districts and frequent elections "would be the driving force in the system; that the peo-

WHAT DO YOU THINK?

The Senate's Role

The United States Senate was fashioned to cool the heat of popular pressures and demands and to slow down the legislative process to make it more deliberative, based on reason rather than emotion. Some will argue that it operates all too well, thwarting the wishes of the people by over-representing small states and by having rules, including the filibuster, that give a minority of senators the ability to block legislative progress. Others believe this situation leads to better lawmaking and gives minorities who feel intensely about a subject a welcome capacity to resist majorities that are less intense. Which of these arguments do you find most persuasive?

ple's representatives would be turbulent and insistent; that they would represent majorities and would be indifferent to the rights of [elite] minorities; that the people would be the winds driving the ship of state and their representatives would be the sails, swelling with every gust."[9] The Founders also believed that the will of the majority expressed in the House of Representatives needed to be modified and checked by a Senate.[10] The House might be filled by commoners, but the Senate was to be composed of society's natural aristocracy: its wealthy, educated, cultivated elites.[11] Senators were not to be elected directly but were to be appointed by state legislatures that were presumed to be more favorable to mercantile, financial, and business interests than the electorate as a whole. The Founders sought to further ensure the autonomy of senators by permitting them to serve for a term three times longer than that of members of the directly elected House of Representatives. The independence, character, and virtue of senators, the Founders believed, would stand as a bulwark against what they feared would be the irresponsible democratic tendencies of representatives. The Senate, in the words of George Washington, would be "[t]he cooling saucer into which the hot coffee from the cup of the House should be poured."[12]

The most enduring protection against democratic excess that the Founders designed into the Senate was the way seats in that chamber were to be apportioned. Each state, regardless of whether it was large and populous or small and barely inhabited, was entitled to two members in the Senate, no more and no less. This deliberate malapportionment, in which voters in less populated states are more represented within the Senate than voters in more populated states, violates democratic principles of political equality. The 480,000 people in Wyoming, our least populous state, receive the same two votes in the Senate as the 32 million people who live in California, our most populous state. When the Senate is measured by the one person, one vote standard, political scientist Arend Lijphart found it was the most malapportioned legislative body in the world. Forty percent of all U.S. senators come from the smallest states in terms of population, together comprising just 10 percent of the population; more than 80 percent of all senators come from states that together account for just one-half of all Americans.[13] If they joined together, these forty senators, plus just one more, could block any new law and stymie any treaty or presidential appointment by conducting a **filibuster**, utilizing the Senate's rules for unlimited debate that a supermajority of sixty is needed to end. Not only is unequal representation greater in the Senate, but its effects are more meaningful. In other countries with two separate legislative houses, the chamber not based on population—such as the House of Lords in Britain and the Senate in France and Canada—is always the weaker of the two. By contrast, the U.S. Senate is never less than equal in power to the House of Representatives, and even possesses powers not granted to the House, such as approving presidential appointments and foreign treaties.[14]

The inequalities between large and small states reflected in the Senate are not innocent.[15] For example, large urban states are disadvantaged compared to smaller rural states. In addition, because racial minorities are concentrated in the most populous states, such as California and New York, those populations are the least well represented by the equal number of votes given to both large and small states in the Senate. By contrast, demographically homogenous small states like Wyoming and North Dakota are given more weighted votes.[16]

CONGRESS: PAST AND PRESENT

The House of Representatives reached the height of its powers in the early years of the twentieth century, appearing to confirm the Constitutional Convention's conception of the House as the driving force of the government. The House's power lay in its structure, which was highly centralized and concentrated in the Speaker, who led the majority party in the House. Joe Cannon, Speaker of the House from 1903 to 1911, was considered by many to be even more powerful than the president. The Speaker led his party's caucus, which adopted a formal legislative agenda that was then passed by disciplined party majorities.

The House of Representatives thrived during this period of party government. But the centralization of power in the Speaker and his ability to provide effective leadership to the majority party in the House came at the expense of individual representatives, who were reduced to near impotence. The House of Representatives as an institution may have been powerful, but individual members outside the leadership enjoyed little of it. By 1910, the rank and file of the House rebelled and stripped Cannon of much of his power. Ironically, the big winner from this revolution inside the House of Representatives was the presidency. Party unity imposed by the Speaker once brought representatives together; now it gave way to the tug of diverse local interests that pulled them apart. With power now decentralized and the majority party unable to act in a disciplined fashion in support of a common program, it was easier for the president to seize the initiative and exercise legislative authority. Once the era of party government came to an end in the House of Representatives, the presidency assumed legislative leadership by setting the agenda of issues to be considered, offering policy proposals, and rallying public opinion.

During the second decade of the twentieth century, the Senate's character changed quite dramatically. Until 1913, its membership was chosen by the legislatures of each state rather than by popular election. That year, upon ratification of the Seventeenth Amendment to the Constitution stipulating that "the Senate of the United States shall be composed of two Senators from each state, elected by the people thereof," the Senate became a more democratic body. The elections of 1914, 1916, and 1918—each one selecting a third of the Senate—replaced appointed senators with elected senators.

The significant shift in the congressional-presidential balance of power, marked by a shift to presidential leadership, first began to unfold during Woodrow Wilson's presidency (1913–21). This trend accelerated during the New Deal of President Franklin Delano Roosevelt (1933–45). Elected in 1932 during the Depression, Roosevelt presented an ambitious program to address the crisis of the Great Depression in his first one hundred days. Congress largely followed his lead. When Congress occasionally balked at taking presidential direction, Roosevelt went over its head and appealed directly to the public through press conferences and radio "fireside chats" (discussed in Chapter 6) for support of his New Deal.

Into the 1960s, Congress continued to play a mostly subordinate role to the presidency in initiating policy proposals and setting the agenda of government. Congress was content to let the president provide leadership, and even encroach on congressional powers, because it largely agreed with the president's policies. Having left the broad design of policy to the president and the executive branch, the role of Congress, according to Samuel Huntington, was "largely . . . reduced to delay and amendment."[17]

But the uneasy consensus on foreign and domestic policy that had existed in previous decades began to collapse in the 1960s. Racial issues, which had been kept off the domestic agenda to create the appearance of a satisfied consensus, exploded in the streets of Birmingham, on the roads of Mississippi, and in the slums of Detroit, Newark, and Los Angeles. Concurrently, college campuses erupted in protest to the war in Vietnam, shattering the prior consensus about foreign policy. Disagreements between the presidency and Congress soon were reflected in institutional combat between the two branches. By the late 1960s and early 1970s, Congress was appropriating funds for domestic programs that President Richard Nixon refused to spend, and Nixon pursued a covert war in Cambodia despite congressional action proscribing it. Moreover,

divided government, in which different parties are in control of the presidency and one or both houses of Congress, became the norm (Table 7.1). When government is divided between the parties, congressional leaders have more incentive to pursue agendas independent of the president.

Reasserting itself in the 1970s, Congress began to reclaim the authority it had ceded to the president. Congress tried to restrict the president's encroachment on the legislature's war-making powers through the War Powers Resolution of 1973. It matched the president's budgetary powers by revamping its own budgetary procedures, challenging claims of presidential prerogatives, scrutinizing presidential appointments more carefully, and altering the president's legislative proposals. A series of internal reforms initiated by House Democrats in the 1970s vested power in party leaders within the House of Representatives. The Speaker of the House; the House majority leader, who assists the Speaker in setting strategy; and the majority whip, who lines up votes among the party's rank and file, were empowered to promote goals supported by the Democratic House caucus.[18] Other reforms also were geared to make Congress more open. Previously, committee chairs had been free to act as petty tyrants who ruled independently of their party's leadership—even independently of the majority sentiment of their own party's members. That era's reforms also prohibited hearings closed to the public and increased the number of subcommittees, with the aim of making it easier for the public to influence lawmaking and to make members of Congress more equal in power to each other.

The shift in power to the party leadership that began under the Democrats accelerated when Republicans became the majority in 1994 for the first time in forty years. Republicans had drafted a "Contract with America," a ten-point legislative program aimed at lowering taxes and reducing the size of the federal government that they pledged to enact if elected. The new Republican Speaker of the House, Newt Gingrich, claimed the election was a mandate to enact the Republican agenda, even though polls revealed that most voters had never even heard of it. After a hiatus of eighty-five years going back to Speaker Joe Cannon, party government had returned to the House of Representatives.

But this moment of party government was brief. President Bill Clinton successfully portrayed the House Republicans and their leadership as extremists willing to hold the government hostage if he did not capitulate to their demands to dramatically cut the scale of federal spending. A government shutdown in late 1995, when Congress refused to pass a budget advocated by the president, turned the public against the Republican House leadership and broke the party's

WHAT DO YOU THINK?

Unified or Divided Government: Which Is Preferable?

Some argue that the country does best when the same political party is in charge in Congress and the presidency, because that pattern facilitates getting a legislative program accomplished. Others contend that a split in party control is better because it forces moderation. Which pattern is likely to secure a larger public interest?

momentum. With House Republicans on the defensive, the legislative initiative passed to the president once again.

After the traumatic attacks on the World Trade Center and the Pentagon in September 2001, the nation and Congress looked to President George W. Bush for strong leadership. His administration's international and domestic agenda—including wars in Afghanistan and Iraq, and the Patriot Act that dramatically widened the ability of the federal government to conduct intelligence gathering within the United States, listen to phone calls, read e-mails, and look into medical, financial, and library records—tolerated few compromises. Congress increasingly was eclipsed as a site of policy innovation and decision making. Moreover, after Congress passed laws that administration had reservations about but that the president did not want to veto, President Bush frequently issued signing statements. As discussed in Chapter 6, these written pronouncements may accompany new statutes and in some cases order the executive branch to implement the statute according to the president's interpretation of the Constitution. The effect would be either to ignore or undercut some, or even most, of the law's provisions.

The first decade of the twenty-first century primarily has been a period of **unified government**. In May 2001, Senator Jim Jeffords of Vermont switched his party affiliation from Republican to Independent. His decision to join the Democratic Party caucus erased the Republican majority, but it was regained in the election of 2002 and held through 2006, when the Democratic Party secured control of both chambers. With the election of President Obama in 2008, unified government was again in place. Under unified government, the Obama White House entered into more robust collaborative relationships with the majority in Congress in crafting the details of key legislation, including the stimulus package and health-care reform.

TABLE 7.1

PARTY CONTROL OF CONGRESS AND THE PRESIDENCY

Year	Congress	President	Senate (100)	House (435)
2009	111th	D	D–60*	D–256
2007	110th	R	D–51**	D–233
2005	109th	R	R–55	R–232
2003	108th	R	R–51	R–229
2001	107th	R	D***	R–221
1999	106th	D	R–55	R–223
1997	105th	D	R–55	R–228
1995	104th	D	R–52	R–230
1993	103rd	D	D–57	D–258
1991	102nd	R	D–56	D–267
1989	101st	R	D–55	D–260
1987	100th	R	D–55	D–258
1985	99th	R	R–53	D–253
1983	98th	R	R–54	D–269
1981	97th	R	R–53	D–242
1979	96th	D	D–58	D–277
1977	95th	D	D–61	D–292
1975	94th	R	D–60	D–291
1973	93rd	R	D–56	D–242
1971	92nd	R	D–54	D–255
1969	91st	R	D–57	D–243
1967	90th	D	D–64	D–247
1965	89th	D	D–68	D–295
1963	88th	D	D–66	D–259
1961	87th	D	D–64	D–263

*Three Independents caucused with Democrats, including Arlen Specter (R–PA), who switched to Independent status, effective May 2009.
**Independent Senator Bernard Sanders (VT) gives the Democrats a one-seat majority.
***There were 50 Ds and 50 Rs until May 24, 2001, when Senator James Jeffords (R–VT) switched to Independent status, effective June 6, 2001; he announced that he would caucus with the Democrats, giving the Democrats a one-seat advantage.

CONGRESSIONAL CAREERS AND THE ELECTORAL CONNECTION

Senators and representatives have desirable jobs. They are treated with respect, they have a chance to influence policy, they meet interesting people, and their work is varied and stimulating. Their salary in 2009 was $174,000 (the Speaker of the House earned $223,000, and the majority and minority leaders in the House and Senate earned $193,400). Members of the House and Senate also receive generous pensions (if they last at least five years in office), inexpensive life insurance, tax breaks (if they own two homes), allowances for their offices, almost unlimited mailing privileges, nearly free medical care, free parking, frequent trips abroad at government expense, and a large staff. But such benefits are available also to high-priced lawyers and corporate managers in the private sector who hold just the sort of jobs many people leave to run for Congress. What being a member of Congress provides that cannot be found in the private sector is the capacity to act directly in shaping public affairs. The job, though constrained by all sorts of pressures from constituents and organized interests, offers politically informed persons the chance to act on their belief that they will serve the public well. This is immensely satisfying.[19] So, too, is the deference accorded to members of the House and Senate. "The most seductive part of it," a congressman from the Midwest acknowledged, "is the deference. My God, it's amazing how many people can never seem to be able to do enough for you, here or when you go home. . . . Maybe I could and maybe I couldn't make more money in private business, but I do know this: I'd never have my ego fed half so grandly."[20] Or as former Senator Larry Pressler from South Dakota commented regarding his return to private life after twenty-two years in Congress: "I feel like Cinderella after the ball. Poof! . . . Overnight my staff dropped from more than 100 down to one. My personal assistants disappeared into thin air. . . . Christmas season is an eye opener. The traditional flood of holiday cards has dwindled to about one-fourth of the senatorial level. And speaking of cards, I now hand out business cards. United States Senators don't do business cards. Everyone knows who they are."[21]

Some members of Congress who retire complain that the job of representative is not as rewarding as it used to be, but there is no lack of applicants to replace them. The House and Senate continue to be filled with professional politicians who view their job in Congress as their career. Even those members elected promising to leave after serving for a certain number of terms frequently find the office so enticing that they want to extend their stay. Political scientist David R. Mayhew argues that the behavior of representatives and senators follows from the objective of getting reelected. In pursuit of this goal, members of Congress try to generate favorable publicity and claim credit for benefits that they bring back to their district.[22] In this respect, no one else in Congress quite matches Senator Robert C. Byrd of West Virginia—the longest-serving member in the chamber's history—in the amount of federal projects, many of them bearing his name, he has directed to his state. There is the Robert C. Byrd Courthouse in Charleston, the Robert C. Byrd National Aerospace Education Center in Bridgeport, and the Robert C. Byrd Locks and Dam at Gallipos Ferry, as well as health clinics, highways, bridges, and academic buildings that also bear the Byrd name and were paid for in whole or in part with federal money.

In the first presidential debate of 2008, the Republican candidate, Senator John McCain, strongly opposed such **earmarks** (the practice of inserting authorization for a specific project in a bill), referring to them as a "gateway drug . . . to out of control spending and corruption." Although not all members of Congress support the pork barrel politics of earmarking, the Arizona Republican has been in the minority on this issue. When Senator McCain offered an amendment in 2009 that would have stripped an omnibus appropriations bill of some nine thousand earmarks, his proposal was defeated 63 to 32. Among his fellow Republicans voting with the majority was Senator Lindsey Graham of South Carolina, who told reporters, "I think I should have the ability as a United States Senator to direct money back to my state as long as it is transparent and it makes sense."[23]

The **electoral connection** between voters and Congress is also based on members of Congress intervening with the bureaucracy on behalf of their constituents to solve problems with Social Security, passports, immigration, veterans benefits, and other matters. More and more members of Congress, according to political scientist Morris Fiorina, prefer "to be reelected as an errand boy than not be reelected at all."[24] One House member told Richard F. Fenno Jr., who studied what representatives did back in their local districts, "This is a business, and like any other business you have to make time and motion studies" as to what activities are most electorally rewarding.[25] Because the first order of business is to stay in business by getting elected, representatives develop what Fenno called a "home style," calculated to make members identify with voters in their district.

Above all, maintaining the electoral connection has come to require money . . . lots of money. The success of candidates for Congress depends in no small part on how effective they are at generating campaign funds. In 2008, the average cost of running a House race was nearly $1.1 million, and almost $6.5 million for a Senate seat (Table 7.2). In the tightly contested Minnesota Senate seat that year, Republican Norm Coleman and his successful challenger, Democrat Al Franken, each spent nearly $20 million. Across the country, the candidate who raised the most money won over 90 percent of the time. The high cost of running is often prohibitive to new challengers, and it helps assure that many races remain uncompetitive. Fully one in four incumbents in the House are left without an opponent.

As Will Rogers once quipped, "It takes a lot of money to even get beat nowadays."[26] In comparison, when Abraham Lincoln ran for Congress in 1846, he returned all but 75 cents of the $200 supporters had raised, reporting that "I

TABLE 7.2

MOST EXPENSIVE CONGRESSIONAL RACES, 2008 ELECTION

Senate

1.	Minnesota Senate	$46,071,475
2.	Kentucky Senate	$33,956,959
3.	North Carolina Senate	$28,511,493
4.	Georgia Senate	$27,057,327
5.	Texas Senate	$26,950,952
6.	Massachusetts Senate	$20,716,841
7.	Oregon Senate	$20,674,392
8.	Colorado Senate	$20,073,534
9.	New Hampshire Senate	$18,090,181
10.	Louisiana Senate	$16,111,862

House

1.	New York District 20	$12,170,225
2.	California District 04	$11,762,110
3.	Illinois District 14	$11,323,032
4.	Colorado District 02	$10,749,234
5.	Illinois District 10	$9,672,621
6.	New Mexico District 02	$7,873,615
7.	Connecticut District 04	$7,610,761
8.	Texas District 22	$7,510,436
9.	Pennsylvania District 10	$7,415,290
10.	Washington District 08	$7,193,397

SOURCE: Center for Responsive Politics, "Most Expensive Races," at http://www.opensecrets.org/bigpicture/topraces.php?cycle=2008&Display=allcands (accessed March 16, 2010); based on data released by the Federal Elections Commission, May 1, 2009.

did not need the money. I made the canvass on my own horse; my entertainment being at the houses of friends, cost me nothing; and my only outlay was seventy-five cents for a barrel of cider, which some farm-hands insisted I should treat them to."[27] Candidates today need to raise so much money not because they want to, but because they are afraid not to. Today, campaign fund-raising follows the same logic as an arms race: Incumbents and challengers alike try to build up their arsenals and raise more money to prevent their opponent from gaining a financial advantage. Fear ratchets up the cost of campaigns to higher and higher levels. Most of these funds are spent for television advertisements designed to enhance name recognition and image rather than discuss substantive issues. "Half the money you spend in a campaign is wasted," admitted one old-time politician. The only problem is "you just don't know which half."[28]

WHAT DO YOU THINK?

Congressional Campaign Finance

Because congressional elections are so expensive, can you think of alternatives to the current system of financing campaigns that are likely to make American democracy work better? Should there be restrictions on levels of spending? Should campaign financing come from public rather than private funds? Are regulations about campaign finance restrictions on, or aids to, free speech?

The sheer cost of running for office has many consequences. The need to raise money gives donors privileged access to members of Congress. The list of congressional donors is very long, and it reflects local as well as national interests. Four of the five leading donors to Senate Majority Leader Harry Reid's election coffer of $7.7 million in 2008 (two years before his term was up) were Las Vegas casinos, a key industry in his home state of Nevada. Minority Leader Mitch McConnell, from Kentucky, in turn raised a whopping $21 million, including tens of thousands from his state's energy companies and legal firms. Money, though, often flows into a representative or a senator's campaign coffers from beyond the district or state he or she represents. Senators Reid and McConnell raised funds from health professionals, real estate investors, and securities and investment firms from around the country. Interest groups contribute money to members of the House and Senate who sit on committees and subcommittes with jurisdiction over policy areas and issues that affect them. Most of these sources of funds are unknown to the average voter, and most of them help gain access to Congress on behalf of issues that are of narrow concern to a particular group.

Congressional candidates are on the circuit continuously, asking for money, attending fund-raisers, and appealing to lobbyists. It usually does not matter whether a member of Congress has a safe seat and faces only token opposition, or whether he or she won by a narrow margin in the last election and can expect another close contest. Either way, the member will be out raising money relentlessly. Even Charles Rangel, the Democratic chairman of the House Ways and Means Committee who is regularly reelected with 90 percent of the vote in his New York City district, raised $5 million in 2008 to protect his seat from potential challengers within his own party.

Money is particularly critical to making a race more competitive when an incumbent seeks reelection in a district where the challenger has a reasonably

Democratic Party donors applaud President Barack Obama as he participates in a fund-raiser for Senate Majority Leader Harry Reid (D–NV) in the Colosseum at Caesars Palace in Las Vegas on May 26, 2009.

good chance to begin with. Incumbents have many advantages. Voters have good reason to back them because they have experience at their jobs, and their seniority makes them more likely to influence legislation in ways that advantage their constituents. But there is a direct relationship between the amount of money challengers raise and their chances of meaningfully competing. Without sufficient funds, few challengers can raise enough money to escape obscurity and get known sufficiently to be recognized by voters.[29] The fund-raising advantage incumbents enjoy explains, in part, why such a large proportion of them win and why most congressional elections are not really competitive.[30] While members from competitive seats raise money to hold off capable rivals, those from safe seats build up war chests to discourage opponents. Most of the time, they succeed.

Elections are mechanisms designed to hold Congress accountable to the voters. In 1787, George Washington endorsed the two-year term for members of the House of Representatives, expecting the House would turn over rapidly in membership. Power, he wrote in a letter to his nephew Bushrod Washington in November 1787, "is entrusted for certain defined purposes, and for a certain limited period . . . and, whenever it is executed contrary to [the public] interest, or not agreeable to their wishes, their servants can and undoubtedly will be recalled." Washington's expectation has not been borne out. In the nineteenth century, congressional turnover was very high; in 1870, more than half of the representatives sent to the House were newly elected. But by 1900, new members comprised less than one-third; by 1940, less than one-quarter; and by 1988, less than one-tenth. Congress has become a career in which representatives and senators expect to serve long tenures. Even in relatively high-turnover congressional elections—like those of 2006 and 2008, in which the Democratic Party made significant gains, recapturing control of the House and Senate by gaining 31 seats in the House and 6 in the Senate in 2006 and netting a further 21 seats in the House and 8 in the Senate in 2008—only 23 incumbents lost their bid for reelection, including 4 who lost their primary battle. In Figure 7.1, we can see the substantial job security members of Congress enjoy.

New blood is more likely to arrive in Congress by winning open seats in which the incumbent is not running than by defeating a sitting member seeking reelection. Incumbency is a powerful electoral asset because incumbents enjoy an enormous financial advantage over their opponents. In addition, incumbents have access to perquisites such as mailing privileges and staff with which to contact and serve voters back home, and they come from districts that have been carefully drawn to include voters already disposed to vote for members of their party.

FIGURE 7.1

PERCENTAGE OF INCUMBENTS (SEEKING REELECTION) REELECTED TO CONGRESS

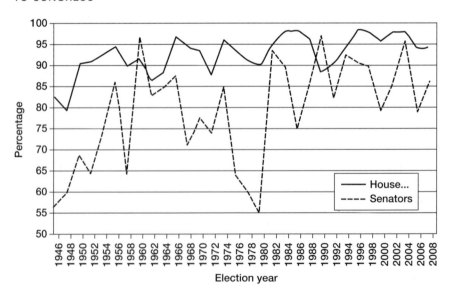

When elections become mere rituals, turnout can decline, voters become cynical, and representatives feel less accountable. Senate elections tend to be more competitive and the incumbency advantage less powerful than in the House. Senate incumbents face more experienced, better-financed opponents, and their statewide constituencies are large enough that one party does not dominate them so clearly, as is often true in smaller House districts.

MEMBERS OF CONGRESS

The ideal representative body mirrors the population as a whole. John Adams, the second president of the United States, once said that the legislature should be "an exact portrait in miniature, of the people at large."[31] No legislature in the world, of course, has the exact demographic profile of the citizens its members represent. Nor is perfect symmetry necessary for the interests of the population to be represented. But a disproportionately unrepresentative legislature is likely to leave many members of the population without representatives who even minimally comprehend their life situations and needs, while others who are overrepresented are likely to have their views taken into account as a matter of course.

It is emphatically *not* the case that, just because someone comes from a certain social background, he or she will necessarily promote the interests of that group: former car dealers in Congress will not necessarily promote the interests of car dealers, and wealthy members of Congress will not necessarily defend the interests of the rich. For example, Senator Jay Rockefeller of West Virginia comes from a very wealthy family, yet has been among the leading advocates of social programs for the poor. Similarly, a white member of Congress can do a very good job representing a black-majority district, as Steve Cohen of Memphis, Tennessee, has been doing in the House since 2006; and a black member of Congress can do a good job representing a district where whites significantly outnumber blacks, as Barack Obama did for the state of Illinois when he served after his 2004 election to the Senate.

The effects of social background on congressional decision making are subtler than that. The social background of members of Congress is important because they bring assumptions to their work based on their life experiences. Inasmuch as members of Congress are more likely to have some life experiences than others, they are likely to be sensitive to, perhaps intuitively aware of, some issues more than others. Consequently, it matters whether the social backgrounds of members of Congress are roughly similar to those of the people they ostensibly represent. It is certainly true that members of Congress, like all of us, are able to appreciate and understand issues that go beyond their own limited experience. But social background makes a difference in whether Congress members will have to make an extra effort or will gravitate naturally to the responses and issues they are familiar with based on their life experiences. See Table 7.3 for a demographic breakdown of the 111th Congress.

It is ironic that Congress, our most democratic institution, is so demographically unrepresentative. Congress does not look like America. Congress contains a much higher proportion of white, male, educated, rich, professional, and business people than the population as a whole. Congress is less male and less white than it used to be, but the average social background of members of Congress still differs strikingly from that of the rest of the population. For example, blacks comprise 12 percent of the electorate. In the Congress that convened in 2009, they occupied 7 percent of the seats in the House and only 1 percent

---

TABLE 7.3

DEMOGRAPHIC COMPOSITION OF 111TH (2009–10) CONGRESS*

	House	Senate
Gender		
Male	360	83
Female	75	17
Race/Ethnicity		
White	364	96
Black	40	1
Hispanic	23	1
Asian	7	2
Native American	1	0
Religion		
Christian	393	86
Jewish	31	13
Muslim	2	0
Buddhist	2	0
Unspecified	7	1
Age**		
<40	22	0
40–59	243	42
>60	170	58

*These numbers represent the 435 voting members of the House and the 100 voting members of the Senate.
**The numbers in this category are based on the age of the senator or representative at the beginning of the 111th Congress (January 3, 2009).

of all Senate seats (and that only after the outgoing governor of Illinois, shamed by a corruption scandal, appointed an African American to replace Barack Obama as junior senator from Illinois). Hispanics are 9 percent of the electorate, and they occupied 6 percent of the seats in the House and only 3 percent of all Senate seats. Women make up 52 percent of all eligible voters, and they made up about 18 percent of the seats in the House and held 17 percent of the seats in the Senate. Such imbalances have policy consequences. Female and minority representatives bring unique perspectives to Congress. Their disproportionate absence means that the concerns of minorities and women are not always pursued as vigorously as they might have been had their numbers in Congress better reflected their numbers at large.[32] Not only is Congress unrepresentative of the American people with respect to race, ethnicity, and gender, but a great gap exists in class position as well. The vast majority of members of Congress are lawyers, bankers, or businesspeople. Very few people from working-class occupations are ever seated.[33]

In circumstances marked by targeted fund-raising and campaign spending, higher turnout among affluent voters, and their greater ability to mobilize and command attention, it is harder for the less well represented to be heard. Recent research by political scientist Larry Bartels compared the responsiveness of U.S. senators to the preferences of constituents who are wealthy, middle class, or poor. "In almost every instance," he concluded in a study of **roll call voting** in the House and Senate regarding government spending, abortion, civil rights, and the minimum wage, "senators appear to be considerably more responsive to the opinions of affluent constituents than to the opinions of middle-class constituents, while the opinions of constituents in the bottom third of the income distribution have *no* apparent statistical effect on their senators' roll calls."[34]

REALIGNMENT AND POLARIZATION

During the past four decades, two especially noteworthy changes in congressional membership have occurred. There has been a dramatic change to patterns of partisanship in the South, and a growing polariztion has come to characterize the relationship between the Democratic and Republican parties. These developments are closely related.

The civil rights movement precipitated an electoral realignment in the South, which shifted its partisan sympathies from Democratic to Republican. In 1960, before the great civil rights struggles of that decade, the southern delegation included only six Republican members in the House and no Republican members in the Senate. Since then, Republicans have become dominant in southern congressional elections, and they now comprise a significant majority of the southern House and Senate delegations. In the 111th Congress that began to serve in January 2009, 72 of the 132 southern House members were Republican, as were 14 of the 22 southern members of the Senate (Figure 7.2).

The result of this transformation in southern political representation has been a growing polarization between the two parties in Congress. Southern Democrats today are more liberal and more likely to vote with their party than were their conservative Dixiecrat forebears.[35] Southern Democrats have become national Democrats. By contrast, southern Republicans are among that party's most conservative members. The radical growth in their number has moved the Republican congressional party to the right. Southern Republicans "form an almost monolithic bloc" across a wide range of issues in Congress and score higher on conservative tests of ideological purity than do nonsouthern Republican legislators.[36]

With the replacement of most southern Democrats (the least partisan and least ideological group of legislators) by southern Republicans (the most partisan and most ideological group of legislators), the parties have grown increasingly divided and are characterized by an "incredible shrinking middle," as one senator referred to the decline of moderates in Congress.[37] Further, there has been a dramatic decline in the presence of Republicans in the Northeast. In

FIGURE 7.2

PROPORTION OF SEATS HELD BY DEMOCRATS IN ELEVEN SOUTHERN STATES

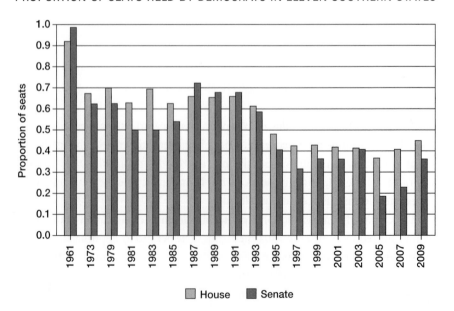

2010, there were no Republican members of the House from the New England states. In 1960, for New York State, 27 out of 43 members of the House were Republicans. The 2008 election reduced this number to three. The now dominant northern liberal wing of the Democratic Party has acted as a pole of attraction, pulling southern Democrats in the House to the left; at the same time, the southern conservative wing of the Republican Party has acted as a pole of attraction pulling the rest of the GOP to the right.

The division between Republicans and Democrats has grown considerably. The average Democrat, who tends to represent urban areas populated with ethnic and racial minorities, has become more liberal on social and economic issues during this period. Meanwhile, the average Republican, who tends to represent more rural and suburban districts, has become more conservative. The political differences *within* the parties have declined, and the political differences *separating* the parties in Congress have grown. In both the House and the Senate, parties have become more cohesive and more polarized.

Two leading students of the ideological positions of members of Congress, Keith Poole and Howard Rosenthal, have tracked the degree of polarization in Congress over the course of the country's history. They have created a scoring system, known as NOMINATE, that emplaces members of Congress in an ideological position based on their roll call voting pattern (Figure 7.3). The system puts the scores together by party, so it is possible to see how the parties diverge, over time, from the median ideological position (scored as zero) in a conservative (scored as positive) or liberal (scored as negative) direction, thus giving us a visual image of an increasing pattern of polarization in both the House and the Senate.

The regional and ideological circumstances in Congress thus are very different today than they were even at the start of the Clinton administration in 1993. Then, southern members were still an important force in the Democratic Party, whereas today they constitute less than a quarter of the party's members in the House and just 12 percent of its senators. For Republicans, southerners have become more dominant. Despite some losses in the two most recent elections, southern Republicans in 2009 numbered 45 percent of the party's membership in the House and 48 percent in the Senate. As we have seen, these changes have ideological consequences. Presently, even the least liberal Democrats in Congress, the Blue Dog Coalition, are significantly less conservative than the bloc of more conservative Democrats that President Clinton had to deal with. And in the Republican Party, virtually all the moderates have disappeared.[38]

As a result of this mounting divergence between the parties, politics in Congress has become more divisive, and the impact of the political parties on

FIGURE 7.3

NOMINATE SCORES FOR HOUSE OF REPRESENTATIVES AND SENATE

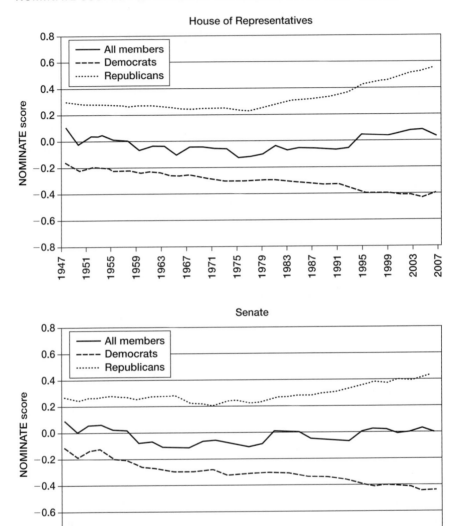

congressional voting has increased. Partisan voting, in which a majority of Democrats vote against a majority of Republicans, is now more evident, as is the degree of party discipline.[39] A by-product of this partisan identification and conflict has been a greater centralization of power in the hands of party leaders. They control their party caucuses and the course of legislation by deciding who they assign to committees, by rewarding the most loyal, by controlling access to the floor for legislation that committees advance, and by promoting roll call behavior that either supports or opposes the president in as uniform a way as possible. All these levers of control have been enhanced by increasing ideological likeness within each party. When members of the majority party agree on policy, strengthening party leaders increases the chances that the majority's policy goals will prevail.[40]

Growing polarization also has an affinity with campaign contributions by issue-oriented groups. Since 1990, advocates of gun rights have contributed campaign donations totaling $20.4 million, of which $17.5 million has been directed into Republican coffers. By contrast, gun control proponents have given $1.8 million, of which all but $100,000 has gone to Democrats. In the same period, pro-life abortion policy advocates have donated $6.3 million, sending $5.9 million to Republicans, while pro-choice abortion groups have donated $17.3 million, of which 14.1 million has supported Democratic candidates. Overall, campaign donations by lobbyists, totaling $157.6 million, have been divided to give $83 million to Democrats and $74 million to Republicans.[41]

THE LEGISLATIVE PROCESS

The quest for money, the social background, the patterns of electoral connection, and the ideological commitments of members of Congress all influence what they do when legislation navigates the labyrinth of formal and informal rules that govern congressional decision making. But the fate of legislation often is determined by seemingly archaic and technical procedural rules, such as the terms under which the Senate and House consider a bill. Representative John Dingell of Michigan reportedly said, "If you let me write the procedure and I let you write the substance, I'll [beat] you every time."[42]

Although each member of Congress has only one vote, some members are more powerful than others. Legislators have different amounts of power depending on which committee they sit on, whether they are a committee or subcommittee chair, whether they are a member of the majority party, and whether they are a party leader. The procedures and rules of the House and the Senate determine the powers invested in these positions and are never neutral. Some groups win and some groups lose, depending on how the rules distribute power within Congress.

The legislative process begins with the submission of a bill to both the House and the Senate. Most bills are introduced without any expectation of success, often to appeal to particular groups of constituents. More than 6,000 pieces of legislation are introduced into Congress each year, and fewer than 400 actually have a chance of passage. Only members of the Senate and the House may submit bills. When legislators introduce a bill in Congress, they often are acting on behalf of constituents, interest groups, a federal agency, the president, or even on their own personal convictions.

The bills that have the greatest chance of success and that generally define the agenda of Congress are those submitted by legislators on behalf of the president. The Office of Management and Budget (OMB), together with the congressional liaison staff in the Executive Office, coordinates the executive's legislative efforts. OMB acts as a clearinghouse, reviewing legislative requests from federal agencies and departments to ensure they conform to the president's program, while the legislative affairs officers in the White House coordinate presidential lobbying of Congress.

Once a bill is introduced in the House and the Senate, it is referred to a committee for consideration. Most committees dealing with the substance of public policy mirror Cabinet agencies. Farm bills go to the House Agriculture Committee and the Senate Agriculture Committee, tax bills go to the House Ways and Means Committee and the Senate Finance Committee, and so on.[43] Committee referrals made by the House Speaker and Senate Majority Leader thus are generally routine. When issues cut across existing committee lines, Senate and House leaders have more discretion in referring bills to committee. This could affect the bill's chances of success because a legislative proposal might receive a warmer reception in one committee than it does in another.

Congress at work, Woodrow Wilson once said, is Congress in committees. Committees are legislative gatekeepers, "little legislatures," that perform the bulk of the legislative work in Congress. They collect information through hearings and investigations, they draft legislation in what are called markup sessions, and they report legislation to the floor of their respective chambers.[44] More than 90 percent of all bills submitted to Congress do not make it out of committee.

Once a bill leaves the committee, it is placed on the House and Senate calendars. In the House, the Rules Committee determines which bills will come to the House floor, when they will be scheduled, and under what conditions they will be debated. Such rules can put up obstacles or ease a bill's path to passage. Whereas the ratio of members on congressional committees from the majority party to those from the minority ordinarily reflects the ratio in each chamber, this ratio is much greater on the Rules Committee so that the majority party can control the flow of legislation on the floor of the House.

The rules under which the House considers legislation began to change in the 1970s. Previously, legislation often came to the House floor under open rules from the Rules Committee with no restrictions on germane amendments. But as the House became more partisan and divided after the 1980s, both parties with the majority on the Rules Committee have been attaching more restrictive rules to more and more legislation. Such rules limit the time for debate and the amendments that can be offered on the floor of the House; approximately three in four bills coming out of the Rules Committee prohibit amendments.

The Senate has no equivalent committee to schedule and set the terms of debate on the Senate floor. Scheduling is largely the work of the Senate majority leader, but he or she requires **unanimous consent** to bring up a bill for Senate consideration. Individual senators who want to prevent passage of a bill can filibuster—that is, hold the Senate floor and not give it up until the offending bill is removed from consideration—unless sixty members vote to end debate. Often, the threat of a filibuster, rather than an actual extended debate, is used to make it impossible to pass legislation unless a supermajority of sixty senators are prepared to vote for the bill. Nor does the Senate limit and set the terms of debate on the Senate floor, as the Rules Committee does for legislation considered by the House. The rules of the Senate are much more freewheeling than those for the House.

Taken together, these various rhythms and traits produce different patterns of representation in each chamber. Members of the House are more likely than senators to work hard on behalf of specific local interests depending on the makeup of their district, whether they be requests by farmers for better subsidies, by specific businesses who want less regulation or higher tariffs to restrict overseas competion, or by unions in their constituencies wishing to have a less difficult time organizing workers. Senators, representing larger constituencies with all kinds of crosscutting pressures, tend to be more attuned to the demands of large groups that operate at the level of the states or the nation as a whole. In that way, they serve as more of a bridge between Congress and the president. Over time, however, the differences between the character of representation in the two chambers have been reduced because the size of House districts has grown. Since 1928, the size of the House of Representatives has been fixed at 435 members (as well as five nonvoting representatives). In 1928, the average size of each House district was 275,000 persons; today, it is just over 700,000.

Even when the versions of a bill introduced in both the Senate and the House are the same, they may look very different after they come out of the committee process in both chambers. House and Senate committees mark up a bill without conferring with each other, and amendments to it on the floor of the House and the Senate proceed independently. As a result, the version of the bill passed by the House may not look the same as the one passed by the Senate.

The president can sign only bills that have been passed in identical form by both houses of Congress. Differences between the House and Senate versions of the bill are resolved in conference committees. **Conference committees**, composed of House and Senate members selected by the Speaker and the Senate majority leader, respectively, meet to reconcile differences in the versions of a bill passed by the House and the Senate. If conference can resolve the differences between the House and Senate versions of the bill, the new, reconciled version of the legislation is then sent back to the House and the Senate to be voted up or down, without amendment. If both houses vote to accept the conference report—that is, to accept identical versions of the bill—the final bill is then sent to the president for signature. The bill becomes law when the president signs it; or it becomes law without the president's signature ten days after the president receives it, provided Congress is still in session. The president may also veto the bill, but that veto can be overridden by two-thirds votes in both the House and the Senate.

This legislative process is noteworthy for the number of choke points, or opportunities to block legislation, that it contains. "It is very easy to defeat a bill in Congress," President John F. Kennedy once observed. "It is much more difficult to pass one."[45] A bill can be waylaid at the subcommittee and committee levels; it may never be scheduled for consideration on the floor of the Senate or the House; it may fail to pass either the Senate or the House; conference may not be able to reconcile differences between Senate and House versions of the bill; the Senate or House may find the conference bill objectionable; the president may veto the legislation; and the Senate and House may be unable to marshal the two-thirds majority necessary to overturn a presidential veto. And all of these potential choke points must be successfully negotiated within the two-year life span of a single Congress, or else the measure has to be reintroduced and the whole procedure repeated again when a new Congress is seated.

Following passage of a campaign finance reform bill in the Senate in 2001, Senator John McCain of Arizona, one of its principal sponsors, warned of the many dangers still ahead: "I think this is a victory, but I want to emphasize, I have no illusions about the House [of Representatives], about a conference, about the White House. We've just taken the first step, and as we enjoy this moment, tomorrow we'd better fully understand that we've got a long way to go."[46] His warning was prophetic, at least in the short term. That year, the campaign finance reform bill passed in the Senate but later died in the House. In 2002, the Bipartisan Campaign Reform Act, sponsored by Senators McCain and Russell Feingold of Wisconsin, did successfully overcome procedural roadblocks and became federal law.

A legislative process loaded with many points where new legislative proposals can be stopped is not politically neutral, but broadly serves to protect the status quo. The legislative process puts innumerable roadblocks in the way of those who seek to use the government to bring about change. Groups that are systematically disadvantaged and depend on political power and public policy to offset their lack of power in the marketplace often find themselves stymied by a legislative process that creates so many opportunities for blockage and defeat. They must build winning coalitions within both the House and the Senate at the subcommittee level, at the committee level, on the floor of each chamber, at conference, and then within the executive branch. Opponents, on the other hand, need to win only once at any level to defeat the bill. A legislative process that creates so many opportunities for obstruction, that promotes failure rather than success, makes it difficult for the disadvantaged to enlist public power against corporate private power.

The procedures of Congress, its rules of the game, are constantly in flux as groups seek to adjust them and thus advance their interests. Political struggles about rules vitally affect prospects for legislative outcomes. Congress frequently reforms itself as legislators seek to change the process by which legislation is made in order to change the results. The most important of such recent rules changes concerns what is known as the **reconciliation** process, a procedure that was created mainly to deal with how the federal budget is approved.

The president submits a budget for the coming fiscal year. After amending it, Congress passes a budget resolution. This resolution is not signed by the president, because it is not a law; rather, it acts as an authorizing guideline for subsequent appropriations (which are signed into law by the president). Created by the Congressional Budget Act of 1974, reconciliation was first designed as a narrow procedure to bring revenue and direct spending under existing laws into conformity with the levels set in the annual budget resolution by directing various committees to bring out legislation that is consistent with its priorities. A reconciliation bill follows these instructions. When it is reported out, the legislation is limited to twenty hours of debate in the Senate (ten hours on the conference bill) and thus cannot be blocked by a filibuster.

Over time, the use of this procedure has extended to major substantive lawmaking. During the Reagan presidency, reconciliation was employed to cut social welfare spending. Later, in the Carter years, reconciliation was deployed by Democrats to successfully reverse many of President Reagan's cuts to the welfare state, particularly Medicaid. President Clinton failed to overcome the objections of Senate stalwart Robert Byrd to using the reconciliation strategy for his comprehensive health-care reform in 1993. But in 1996, Clinton and a

Republican Congress successfully used reconciliation to pass welfare reform; and in 1997, they amended Medicaid to create SCHIP, a health-care program for children. President George W. Bush and congressional Republicans later used reconciliation to pass nearly $1 trillion in tax cuts during his administration, and the Obama administration utilized the procedure to pass health-care reform.[47]

Overall, the legislative process is so daunting that Congress deviates from it quite often to avoid gridlock. According to congressional scholar Barbara Sinclair, unorthodox lawmaking has become routine as Congress increasingly circumvents its own procedures. Committees are bypassed more frequently; bills are now more likely to be reworked after they emerge from committee; the content of legislation is more likely to be worked out in summits among executive and legislative leaders; and omnibus legislation, in which disparate bills are offered together in one legislative package, is now more common. Sinclair argues that it is no longer accurate to speak of one legislative process; rather, there are now many.[48] The legislative process has become a maze in which bills may now take many different paths through Congress on the way to enactment.

Legislating, though, does not exhaust what Congress does. When we considered the presidency, we observed that the president manages the federal bureaucracy but that Congress creates it. Each new federal agency originates with an act of Congress, which describes what the agency is supposed to do and provides the funding to do it. Congress is usually quite vague in its legislative instructions for agencies because it cannot anticipate all the contingencies an agency might encounter, and because Congress hopes to avoid criticism and controversy by not being too specific. As a result of this delegation, agencies have a great deal of discretion in interpreting the mandate they receive from Congress. Thus, to help ensure that federal agencies interpret and implement the law as the legislature intended, Congress engages in **oversight** of the bureaucracy.

As government has grown, Congress has come to spend more time on oversight, especially during periods of divided government when it is less sure that the president and the executive branch will act in ways that reflect its intentions. Oversight is performed by congressional subcommittees and committees, which review the activities of agencies under their jurisdiction. They hold hearings at which members of Congress remind agency heads that Congress is the boss, that they get their appropriations from Congress, and that Congress expects deference from them.

SEEKING INFLUENCE

This maze and this pattern of oversight, combined with the reforms that made Congress more open to scrutiny and influence, have had the ironic effect of exposing the complicated legislative process to special interests that have the ability to fund **lobbying** efforts. The very openness of Congress to the social forces outside it means that the diversity and inequalities of the larger society are reflected within it. Those with the most political resources outside of Congress are in the best position to take advantage of Congress's accessibility, to cultivate relationships with its members, committee and subcommittee chairs, and party leaders. The legislative process is scrutinized carefully by a small army of lobbyists who seek to influence legislation. Spending on lobbying is immense, and it has been increasing by leaps and bounds. In 1998, total spending on lobbying reached $1.4 billion. Ten years later, in 2008, lobbing by companies, unions, and other interest groups cost $3.3 billion, as 15,220 registered lobbyists perfomed their work. Some special interests have their own in-house lobbyists, and the majority hire specialized lobbying firms located in Washington, D.C. (many of them on K Street).

On his way to vote in the Capitol on July 8, 2009, Congressman John Adler (D–NJ) briefly says hello to lobbyists from a New Jersey pharmaceutical company.

Inasmuch as business has more political resources than other groups, it can best take advantage of Congress's openness to influence the legislative process. When political scientists Kay Lehman Schlozman and John T. Tierney examined interest group presence in Washington, they found that 70 percent of all the organizations represented in their sample were either businesses and trade associations or law and public relations firms hired by corporations to represent them in Washington.[49] The largest Fortune 500 companies were the best represented. They maintained their own lobbying arms in Washington, were members of their industrial trade group, and participated in peak organizations like the Business Roundtable. Moreover, the Washington corporate office was no longer a dumping ground where corporate executives placed their incompetent relatives to keep them out of harm's way. To the contrary, managers of corporate public affairs departments gained status within the corporate hierarchy. The *Wall Street Journal* found "the post of government-affairs executive has taken on added luster. A tour through the government-affairs department can be a quick route to the top."[50] Indeed, many corporate lobbyists are former government officials who can offer their new employers privileged access to former government colleagues and knowledge of agency or congressional procedures. Almost one-third of all retiring members who had served in the previous Congress, and Cabinet-level officials from the departing Clinton administration, signed with lobbying or government relations firms during the Bush administration. A comparable process is at work today.

Compared to other interest groups, business is the most organized, hires the most lobbyists, has the most contact, and devotes the most money to influencing policymakers. Between 1998 and 2009, labor unions spent $359 million on lobbying. By contrast, the finance, insurance, and real estate sectors of the

WHAT DO YOU THINK?

Pressure Group Lobbying

Lobbying, it is thought, provides legislators with information about the interests that care about bills, the content of legislation, and the intensity of preferences among members of the public. Lobbying, it also is thought, twists the democratic process out of shape by giving too much influence to those with the most vested interests. How can lobbying be made more fair and more effectively democratic? Would the legislative process be better if there were no lobbyists at all?

economy spent over $3.4 billion, a sum nearly matched by health insurance and pharmaceutical companies. Single companies also spend princely sums to influence legislative outcomes. In 2008, Exxon Mobil invested $29 million; General Electric $19 million; Verizon $18 million; the aircraft manufacturers Boeing and Lockheed $16.6 million and $15.8 million, respectively; and General Motors, just before it went bankrupt and was bailed out by the federal government, $13.7 million.[51]

Lobbying firms often specialize by party. Seeking clients, one such company, Parven Pomper Strategies, Inc., advertised in 2009 how "our team of Democratic lobbyists and strategists . . . develop and implement winning strategies," boasting that "our relationships with key policymakers . . . means that we have the connections necessary to open the doors to the important public policy decision-makers. Our years of legislative and political experience in Washington means that we know the key decision-makers in Washington, how and when the decisions will be made, and how to best lobby on your behalf." Groups that have retained the company include FedEx, Chevron, Monsanto, Pfizer, and Visa.[52]

Lobbying is a sophisticated, multifaceted operation that requires an extraordinary amount of money to be effective. Take, for example, the case of Microsoft Corporation, which initially ignored politics. Prior to 1998 it employed one lobbyist, working out of an office in a suburban Washington shopping mall, and contributed less than $10,000 to candidates running for federal office. But Microsoft soon realized it needed friends on Capitol Hill when Congress began to consider legislation affecting the technology industry and the Justice Department sued the company for violating antitrust laws. Today, Microsoft invests a lot of money to influence policy. It contributes hundreds of thousands of dollars to parties and candidates, has hired a "dream team" of lobbyists, financed the writing of supportive op-ed pieces, and underwritten the work of academics and research groups that advocate Microsoft's positions.[53] Just in case legislators miss Microsoft's message in the media, the company gives money to local organizations that support Microsoft to make it appear that the company enjoys grassroots support. It also creates new trade groups that generate support for the company through websites and arranges meetings between Microsoft executives and congressional leaders.

Such lobbying efforts cost Microsoft tens of millions of dollars, much more than their opponents who lobby for public interest groups can afford to match. But this expense pales in comparison to what industry trade groups spend to influence policy. The pharmaceutical industry has more registered lobbyists than there are members of Congress. When they go to work, they often find themselves lobbying former colleagues because more than one-half of all drug lobbyists are either former members of Congress or former staff members. Thomas A. Scully, who ran Medicare for President Bush, left government soon after Medicare reform passed to take a job with a law firm that represents companies in the health-care industry. Tom Daschle, the former Senate Majority Leader, a Democrat from South Dakota, lost his seat in 2004 and then went on to earn about $5 million over the course of the following four years, largely by consulting for health-care industries.[54]

There is no guarantee, of course, that efforts to secure influence will achieve the intended results; but frequently they do. Consider the passage in the House of Representatives of a comprehensive climate bill in late June 2009. The *New York Times* reported that the bill "grew fat with compromises, carve-outs, concessions, and out-and-out gifts intended to win the votes of wavering lawmakers and the support of powerful industries" that had lobbied hard to revise the legislation. The result "would funnel billions of dollars in payments to agriculture and forestry interests. Automakers, steel companies, natural gas drippers, refiners, universities, and real estate agents all got in on the fast-moving action."[55] The cumulative impact of these concessions—including the largest, which guaranteed that utilities could continue to build and operate coal-burning power plants without incurring new costs—sharply reduced the environmental impact of the legislation aimed at dealing with global warming.

CONCLUSION

In a democratic ideal, society is made up of relatively equal interests, each pursuing their own political goals and with government responding in an even-handed way. The representative qualities of Congress—sharpened by regular elections, open hearings and procedures, and visible forms of debate—make the national legislature more responsive to public participation than do the bureaucracies of the executive branch or the Supreme Court. But political representation is contested on an uneven playing field. Few groups can match Microsoft or PRMA in the amount and variety of resources devoted to lobbying public officials. Few can donate substantially to political campaigns. Few can mobilize press attention. Even fewer can develop close ties with individual members of Congress.

Representation thus tends to be both genuine and profound, yet deeply uneven. The very structure and rules of Congress, and the multiplicity of pathways by which a bill becomes a law, can become sources of uneven advantage in gaining access and influence. Further, with incumbency strong, the need to raise money inhibiting challengers, the parties polarized quite deeply, and members of Congress drawn largely from—and responsive to—the higher strata of society, it is no wonder that so many Americans judge the institution harshly. Many citizens are disaffected because they do not see their backgrounds, ideas, or their wish that a broad public interest be served reflected with sufficient regularity in congressional affairs. The local representation they get often is skewed to the most vocal, the best off, the leading interests. Yet these are not the only influences. Members of Congress and their constituents have preferences and goals that often are shared, and no member can afford to simply represent the powerful while needing the support of a majority. The politics of power in Congress thus are tense, charged, and contradictory. And the stakes are high.

CHAPTER SUMMARY

Introduction
Congress is both the most accessible branch of the federal government and the one that often scores highest in public distrust. This paradox is explained by how influence is wielded and why many Americans believe these patterns are not fair.

The Origin of Two Legislative Chambers
The Constitutional Convention, concerned that it was necessary to protect the country from excessive democracy, created a Senate that gives each state, large and small, two seats, and that elects its members to serve for six-year terms. It also created a House of Representatives, whose members serve two-year terms and are intended to more directly reflect popular preferences.

Congress: Past and Present
The actual capacity of Congress compared to the presidency, and the relative abilities of each house to legislate, have changed over the course of American history. Such changes are often a result of key procedural reforms; but they are also the product of the kinds of issues that come to the fore at any given moment, and of how much power Congress is willing to delegate to the executive branch.

Congressional Careers and the Electoral Connection

Members of Congress are almost constantly running for office or raising large sums of money in order to do so. Elections are designed to hold Congress accountable to voters. Election campaigns are expensive and thus tilt influence in the direction of those capable of funding them. In an age of polarization, most incumbents are reelected, therefore making the process less competitive than in the past.

Members of Congress

The social backgrounds of members of the House and Senate imperfectly reflect those of the population as a whole. They are unrepresentative with respect to gender, ethnicity, race, and class. Very few members come from working-class backgrounds.

Realignment and Polarization

Two closely related changes have altered the congressional landscape. The southern states, which persistently voted Democratic before the civil rights revolution, have increasingly supported conservative Republicans. In turn, each party has moved away from the political middle and from each other: Democrats, on average, have become more liberal; and Republicans, on average, are now more conservative.

The Legislative Process

The complex labyrinth any proposed legislation must travel before becoming a law contains many choke points and opportunities to block legislation, thus advantaging the status quo and providing many opportunities to influence the results.

Seeking Influence

The very openness and complexity of the congressional process makes it possible for those interests with the most resources to sway how the legislature acts by organizing active and expensive lobbying campaigns. The number of lobbying firms has recently grown rapidly. They tend to specialize by party and by subject.

Critical Thinking Questions

1. What role has the South played in lawmaking at different moments in American history? How and why has this role been distinctive?

2. Why are American citizens so often skeptical about Congress and the work it performs?

3 How important are political parties in shaping the legislative process?

4. Does it matter when members of the House and Senate are different in class, race, and gender from the voters they represent?

Suggested Readings

E. Scott Adler and John Lapinski, eds., *The Macropolitics of Congress.* Princeton, NJ: Princeton University Press, 2006.

Robert A. Caro, *Master of the Senate: The Years of Lyndon Johnson.* New York: Random House, 2003.

Keith T. Poole and Howard Rosenthal, *Congress: A Political-Economic History of Roll Call Voting.* New York: Oxford University Press, 2000.

Elizabeth Sanders, *Roots of Reform: Farmers, Workers, and the American State, 1877–1917.* Chicago: University of Chicago Press, 1984.

Eric Schickler, *Disjointed Pluralism: Institutional Innovation and the Development of the U.S. Congress.* Princeton, NJ: Princeton University Press, 2001.

Steven S. Smith, Jason M. Roberts, and Ryan J. Vander Wielen, *The American Congress,* 6th ed. New York: Cambridge University Press, 2009.

Charles Stewart III, *Analyzing Congress.* New York: Norton, 2001.

THE COURTS

INTRODUCTION

Although Christmas was only two weeks away, there was little evidence of it on the taut, grim faces of the Supreme Court justices as they left work on December 12, 2000. Their pained expressions registered the burden of the momentous and extraordinary decision they had just reached. They had good reason to feel anxious because their ruling was remarkable not only for what the Court had to say in this important case, but for how the Court said it and how it reached its decision. For example, although petitioners often ask the Court to accelerate its schedule, it rarely does so. But in this case, the justices expedited hearings and proposed a schedule for submitting briefs and arguing before the Court that was even faster than what the parties proposed.[1]

Another unusual aspect of the decision was that it created a new constitutional principle. But this was followed by an astonishing disclaimer announcing that this new principle would not apply to future cases. Such a stipulation was surprising because the Supreme Court normally tries to articulate rules that can serve as precedents for future decisions. But in this instance, the Court went out of its way to indicate that its ruling applied only to this one case, this one time, to this one set of circumstances.

Moreover, individual members of the Court are pretty consistent in their views across cases. But in this case, some justices appeared to violate their own legal principles in order to reach the outcome they wanted. Justices normally concerned with states' rights and deference to lower courts set those views aside in this case to rule the other way. They overruled state courts, state laws, and local canvassing boards to reach the verdict they wanted.

Lastly, the Court is generally reluctant to get dragged into unseemly election disputes and nasty partisan quarrels. But in this case, in *Bush v. Gore*, No. 00-949, a five-to-four majority of the Court decided to suspend a recount of

Supreme Court Justice David Souter leaves court a few hours before it releases its ruling in the Florida case that decided the 2000 presidential election.

disputed presidential votes in Florida, effectively making George W. Bush the forty-third president of the United States. Summarizing the extraordinary role that the one-vote majority on the Supreme Court played in deciding the outcome of the 2000 presidential election, the comedian Mark Russell mused, "We have a new president. In this democracy of 200 million citizens, the people have spoken. All five of them."[2]

Federal courts interpret the Constitution, the supreme law of the land. They get to say what the law is, and their judgment is final. "We are under a Constitution," Chief Justice Charles Evans Hughes once remarked, "but the Constitution is what the judges say it is."[3] The principle of **judicial supremacy**, that the courts are the law's final arbiter, was asserted as late as 2000 in *Dickerson v. United States*, when Chief Justice William Rehnquist wrote, "Congress may not legislatively supercede our decisions interpreting and applying the Constitution."[4]

The principle of judicial supremacy gives the courts the power of **judicial review**, which permits them to nullify or overturn any federal, state, or public law that conflicts with the Constitution. As a result of judicial review, the courts have invalidated state laws mandating segregation, presidential orders depriving alleged terrorists of their constitutional rights, and laws passed by Congress making it a federal crime to carry guns near schools.

The power of the courts is reflected not only in judicial review, but in the extraordinary independence granted federal judges. They are appointed to life terms, cannot have their salaries reduced, and cannot easily be removed from office. Consequently, they can decide cases without fear for their job security and do not have to tailor their decisions to suit donors, interest groups, or voters. They are protected from political retribution, so they can issue rulings without worrying about how their decisions might affect their careers.

Yet, for all the judiciary's power and prestige, leading political observers have pointed to its limitations since the founding of the Republic. Alexander Hamilton put his view bluntly: "Of the three powers . . . the judiciary is next to nothing."[5] He described the courts as the "least dangerous branch," having "no influence over either the sword or the purse; no direction either of the strength or of the wealth of the society." That is, the courts may rule on a case but must depend on other branches of government to implement their decision and put their judgment into effect. For example, when President Andrew Jackson disagreed with a Supreme Court ruling, he reportedly snickered, "[Chief Justice] John Marshall has made his decision, now let him enforce it."[6] A vivid and recent example of the Court's helplessness occurred in 2007 when it ruled against the Environmental Protection Agency (EPA), requiring it to determine whether greenhouse gas emissions pose a health hazard and, if so, to issue regulations limiting them. Reluctant to comply, the EPA director rejected a finding of the agency's own scientists indicating that greenhouse gases did indeed pose a health threat. It then thumbed its nose at the Court and said that it was not prepared to issue any regulations limiting greenhouse gases. The contrast between a court system that, on the one hand, can nullify laws passed by other political institutions and, on the other, find its decisions stymied by them, could not be greater.

The courts are also hindered by a lack of democratic legitimacy. Unlike presidents or members of Congress, federal judges are appointed, not elected. Consequently, they cannot appeal to election results as the basis for why citizens should obey their decisions. Instead, Justice Tom C. Clark explained, "We have to convince the nation by the force of our opinions."[7]

Finally, the courts are at the mercy of the other branches of government for their budget, staff, and jurisdiction. Their dependence on the other branches of government for resources weakens the courts in relation to them.

The powers and limits of the courts place them in creative tension with the other branches of government. Another source of tension for the courts is managing their role as both legal and political institutions. As a legal institution, the courts are supposed to be guided by precedent in neutrally and passively interpreting the law. Judges are supposed to be objective; they must not interpret the law to satisfy whoever is in power or issue rulings that reflect their own personal beliefs. Reason, not power, is supposed to guide them. Chief Justice John G. Roberts Jr. articulated the view of the courts as legal institutions at his confirmation hearings, when he told the Senate Judiciary Committee: "Judges and justices are servants of the law, not the other way around. Judges are like umpires. Umpires don't make the rules; they apply them."[8]

But, in practice, judges do make rules; and thus courts act as political as well as legal institutions. Unlike umpires, judges do not simply apply the rules to what occurs on the field; instead, they actually decide what the rules are through their decisions. If the rules were always clear, there would be no need for judges to resolve differences over what they are. And just like other political actors, judges have their own policy goals and are influenced by public opinion, election results, and their own worldviews when they issue rulings. The courts reflect broader social values that judges convey through their decisions. The courts' legitimacy depends upon being independent of larger political forces as well as ensuring they are taken into account.

The courts' relationship to equality is similarly ambiguous and conflicted. On the one hand, the law is an arena of equality: the same rules apply to everyone. No one is above the law, and justice is supposed to be blind to whether a person is white or black, male or female, rich or poor. On the other hand, formal, legal equality is compromised when it operates within a society marked by racial, gender, and class inequalities. For example, the individuals who sit on death row are poor, almost to a person—not because rich or middle-class individuals never commit murder, but because rich defendants can afford to hire high-priced legal talent to represent them whereas poor suspects must depend on overworked and underpaid public defenders. The same basic procedures of trial by jury may apply to all Americans who are charged with murder, but the results are strongly shaped by a defendant's ability to pay for defense lawyers.

Finally, whether the law is a conservative or progressive force is also hard to pin down, because the courts may reflect both. On the one hand, the law may be dismissed as mere pretense, a tool used by the powerful to enforce their domination behind the law's false promises and pretty phrases. But the formal framework of rights and procedures provided by the law also creates tangible resources that ordinary people can draw upon to make claims on the rich and the powerful.[9] It is the law under the Constitution that grants people freedom of speech and assembly, protects citizens from unreasonable search and seizure, and requires the government to follow certain procedures and respect people's legal rights when charging them with crimes. And ordinary citizens can appeal to the law in asserting these rights, as civil rights activists did in the 1960s, and as those imprisoned without due process did during the Bush administration's War on Terror.

This chapter explores judicial power and weakness, and the tension between the courts as legal and political institutions. It also clarifies how the law can both promote equality and offer an illusion of it, and how it can be both a balm for the strong and a resource for the weak.

WHAT DO YOU THINK?

Was *Bush v. Gore* Justified?

The majority on the Supreme Court believed that it did the right thing intervening in the 2000 presidential election. In essence, the majority argued that the country simply could not afford the delay and indecision entailed by a prolonged recount of challenged votes in Florida. The minority thought the Court brought dishonor on itself through its ruling. Justice Stevens wrote that while we may never know with certainty who the winner of the presidential election was, "the identity of the loser is perfectly clear. It is the Nation's confidence in the judge as an impartial guardian of the rule of law." Do you think the Court acted wisely or precipitously in intervening in the 2000 presidential election?

A DUAL COURT SYSTEM

If we are to understand the court's many ambiguities, we need first to understand how the courts are organized.

The United States has a **dual court system**; state and federal systems of justice exist side by side. Each of the fifty states and the federal government maintain their own system of courts. The federal court system is divided into three levels. The base of the federal system is comprised of ninety-four district courts. District courts are where full trials are conducted: witnesses are examined, and exhibits are entered into the record. Most federal cases begin and end here. But a litigant unhappy with a decision at district court can appeal to the next level, the court of appeals. There is one court of appeals for each of the twelve judicial circuits. Most cases are heard on appeal from district courts in the states under their jurisdiction by panels of three judges (rather than by a single judge, as at the district level). Only about one in ten cases make it to this level. At the top of the federal court system stands the Supreme Court. It is the court of last resort; there is none higher.

States are free to organize their courts as they please, name them as they wish, and establish their jurisdictions as they see fit.[10] Consequently, many states' court systems are modeled on the federal organization, but others are not. For example, many states follow the federal system and refer to their court of last resort as the supreme court. But in Maryland and New York, the highest court is called the court of appeals. Some states confusingly refer to their trial courts, the lowest-tier courts, as circuit or superior courts; and some states have only two levels of courts, with no intermediate or appeals court as in the federal court system.

Another important difference between federal and state court systems is the method of selecting judges. Federal judges are appointed by the president subject to confirmation by the Senate, but 87 percent of all state judges are elected. Appointing judges is hard to reconcile with democratic theory because judges selected in this manner are not accountable to voters. Citizens cannot judge the judges and remove them.

But electing judges, as is done in 39 states, entails its own risks that may compromise judicial legitimacy. Running for office is not cheap and becoming a state supreme court judge has never been so expensive. Campaign contributions in state supreme court elections reached $34 million, an all-time high, in 2008.[11] As the cost of campaigning increases rapidly, judges may be tempted to rule in favor of lawyers and litigants that contribute to their election campaigns. John Grisham's novel, *The Appeal*, in which a chemical company receives a favorable ruling from a judge in return for campaign contributions is, unfortunately, ripped straight from today's headlines. In West Virginia, one member of the state's supreme court received $3 million in campaign contributions from a coal company executive, and another judge was photographed vacationing with him. Both judges had twice ruled to throw out a $50 million verdict against the coal executive's company. The losers in state court then petitioned the U.S. Supreme Court, claiming that the executive's campaign spending had created such a sense of impropriety that it denied the petitioner's due process. The Supreme Court ruled in their favor, claiming that excessive campaign contributions to a judge create an unconstitutional threat to a fair trial. As the example from West Virginia shows, when judges are elected there is the appearance, if not the fact, that justice is for sale to the highest bidder.[12] Electing judges can also taint decisions because the candidates may try to curry favor with the public. Two political scientists found that judges who were up for reelection tended to give harsher sentences in order to display their law-and-order credentials to the public.[13]

Federal courts hear about 400,000 cases each year. But this is less than 2 percent of the total U.S. caseload, and state courts handle all the rest. In 2007, over 103 million cases were filed in the nation's 15,500 state and local courts. The cases ranged from traffic infractions and custody disputes to criminal cases involving murder and rape. Given the amount of litigation at the state

WHAT DO YOU THINK?

How Should Judges Be Selected?

What is the best process for selecting judges? Electing judges, as is done in many states, has the virtue of permitting citizens to hold judges accountable for their decisions. At the same time, however, the pressure to raise money for election campaigns, or issue decisions that are popular, may taint judicial independence. Appointing judges to life terms, as is done at the federal level, may have the opposite effects. It promotes judicial independence at the expense of accountability. Which process do you prefer: the way many states elect judges, or the federal system of appointing them?

compared to the federal level, it is no surprise that about 90 percent of all people in prison, as well as 99 percent of those on death row, have been convicted in state court.

Federal court rulings interpret the Constitution and apply federal laws that govern all Americans. In addition, federal courts have the power to review the decisions of state courts to ensure they comply with federal law. But the United States is a federal system of government that reserves some powers to the states. They have their own laws, constitutions, and courts. Where does state law end and federal law begin? For example, take the case of marijuana use. According to federal law, the Comprehensive Drug Abuse Prevention and Control Act of 1970, it is a crime to manufacture, distribute, dispense, or possess substances such as marijuana. But in 1996, California approved by referendum the Compassionate Use Act, which permitted the use of marijuana for medicinal purposes. Pursuant to the passage of the California law, Diane Monson, who suffered from severe chronic pain, was prescribed marijuana by her physician; and her condition improved dramatically. In 2002, agents of the U.S. Drug Enforcment Administration (DEA) raided her home and confiscated her stash. Monson then went to court for an injunction to prevent the federal government from enforcing drug laws that apply to the use of marijuana for medicinal purposes. California, not Congress should rule in this area, she claimed. The case made it all the way to the Supreme Court (*Gonzalez v. Raich*, 2005), which upheld the federal government's authority to prohibit the local cultivation and use of marijuana because it affected interstate commerce.

As a result of the Court's ruling, the federal government can still prosecute patients who consume marijuana for medicinal purposes, but the California law did not completely go up in smoke. It still offered pot users protection from prosecution by state authorities. Because 99 percent of all pot arrests are by local police officers and not by DEA federal agents, California has a thriving business of marijuana production and distribution for medicinal use (estimated value: $14 billion). It has also been joined by twelve other states that now permit the use of pot by prescription.[14] When President Obama was elected, his Attorney General, Eric Holder Jr., reversed the policy of the Bush administration and said the federal government would not prosecute marijuana distributers who complied with state law, even though it was still illegal. Subsequently, more states passed medical marijuana laws because the threat of federal prosecution for growing, selling, and using pot was lifted.

THE FEDERAL COURT SYSTEM

Each of the three tiers of the federal court system—district and appelate courts, as well as the Supreme Court—plays an important policymaking role. District courts, readers may recall, are trial courts, where the record and facts of a case are established. Following the trial, judges apply the law to the case at hand. Because the Supreme Court generally restricts itself to articulating general principles, district court judges enjoy a great deal of discretion in how to apply Supreme Court rulings and to decide which rulings apply to which cases. For example, in *Brown v. Board of Education of Topeka, Kansas*, which outlawed state-sanctioned racial segregation, the Supreme Court did not fix a date for ending segregation but instead instructed the district courts to "act with all deliberate speed." But many district courts in the South reflected the region's opposition to *Brown* and used their discretion to forestall desegregation. Consequently, ten years after *Brown*, only 1 percent of all southern black children were in nonsegregated schools. The courts acted with "entirely too much deliberation and not enough speed," according to Justice Hugo Black, in requiring southern school districts to comply with the Court's ruling.[15]

Courts of appeals (see Figure 8.1 for the jurisdiction of different courts of appeal) also are important policymakers. Most of their decisions are final because the Supreme Court takes up so few cases that have been decided by these courts. Appellate courts hear more than 28,000 cases a year; the Supreme Court normally hears fewer than 100. Consequently, in the real world, federal appeals courts have the final say in most matters of law. One important difference, however, between the Supreme Court and courts of appeals is that decisions by appellate courts apply only to the specific states covered by the deciding court, whereas Supreme Court decisions apply to the entire country. For example, in 1996, the Fifth Circuit Court of Appeals (covering Texas, Louisiana, and Mississippi) ruled that the University of Texas Law School discriminated against other applicants when it gave preference in admissions to Latinos and blacks. The appellate court ruled that schools may not discriminate in admissions on the basis of race. This left the appeals court decision standing as the law in those states included within Fifth Circuit jurisdiction. Six years later, in 2002, the Sixth Circuit Court of Appeals (covering Michigan, Ohio, Kentucky, and Tennessee) ruled just the opposite to the Fifth Circuit on an identical question. It decided that the University of Michigan Law School could give preferential treatment to minority applicants. As a result of the two appeals court decisions, the law was different in one part of the coun-

FIGURE 8.1

COURTS OF APPEALS CIRCUIT BOUNDARIES

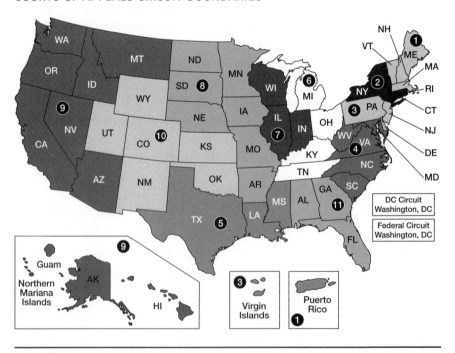

SOURCE: Robert A. Carp and Ronald Stidham, *The Federal Courts*, 2nd ed. (Washington, DC: CQ Press, 1991), 18.

try than it was in another. Schools were prohibited from giving preference in admissions to minorities in southern states covered by the Fifth Circuit, but they could do so in midwestern states covered by the Sixth Circuit.

More recently, in 2009, the Ninth Circuit Court of Appeals in San Francisco ruled that the Constitution's Second Amendment on the right to bear arms applied to the states, and the Seventh Circuit Court of Appeals in Chicago found that it did not. This left citizens in Alaska, Arizona, California, and other western states covered by the Ninth Circuit Court with the right to bear arms despite state laws outlawing them; but citizens in Illinois, Indiana, and Wisconsin who were covered by the Seventh Circuit had to respect local laws limiting guns.

When federal appeals courts disagree, as occurred with regard to affirmative action in higher education or whether local laws limiting guns are in breach of the Second Amendment, the Supreme Court often takes up the case and renders a decision that applies nationally to all federal courts.[16] In 2003, the Supreme Court ruled in *Grutter v. Bollinger* that it was legal for colleges and universities to take race into account in their admissions decisions. The Supreme Court decision invalidated the previous ruling by the Fifth Circuit that had outlawed affirmative action programs by schools under that court's jurisdiction.

Article II of the Constitution empowers the president to nominate federal judges, subject to the "advice and consent" of the Senate. This gives the Senate a veto over presidential appointments much like the veto power the president enjoys over bills passed by Congress. Appointments to the federal bench are especially consequential because federal judges have lifetime tenure. Unlike an administration's legislative successes that can be undone in the next Congress, the effect of a president's judicial appointments is long term and enduring. Lifetime tenure of federal judges permits presidents to leave a legacy regarding how laws are interpreted through the judges they appoint to the federal bench. Because judges remain on the bench long after the presidents who appointed them are gone, presidents can extend their reach beyond their term of office through the judges they appoint. As Table 8.1 reveals, President Ronald Reagan was very successful at leaving his stamp on federal courts, appointing half of all federal judges by the time he left office. In this sense, the courts tend to lag other political institutions and act as a drag on political change. Judges appointed by long-departed presidents may still be issuing decisions based on values that are considered obsolete or have since been repudiated by voters at the polls.

As the courts have become more active in recent years, setting policy in areas such as abortion, guns, and religious practice, the selection process of federal judges has become more public, divisive, and intense. Under President Ronald

TABLE 8.1

PRESIDENTIAL LEGACIES ON FEDERAL COURTS

The table depicts the number of judges appointed by each president and shows how quickly a president can make an impact on the makeup of the courts.

President	Appointed to Supreme Court	Appointed to Courts of Appeals*	Appointed to District Courts**	Total Appointed	Total Number of Judgeships***	Percentage of Judgeships Filled by President
Johnson (1963–69)	2	40	122	164	449	37
Nixon (1969–74)	4	45	179	228	504	45
Ford (1974–77)	1	12	52	65	504	13
Carter (1977–81)	0	56	202	258	657	39
Reagan (1981–89)	3	78	290	368	740	50
Bush (1989–93)	2	37	148	185	825	22
Clinton (1993–2001)	2	66	305	373	841	44
G.W. Bush (2001–09)****	2	57	287	344	866	40

*Does not include the U.S. Court of Appeals for the Federal Circuit.

**Includes district courts in the territories.

***Total judgeships authorized in president's last year in office.

****George W. Bush data through September 1, 2008.

SOURCE: "Imprints on the Bench," *CQ Weekly Report* (January 19, 2001): 173.

Reagan, for the first time in American history (and under his successor, George H.W. Bush), White House aides were involved in the process of reviewing the credentials of potential judges and screening them to confirm their conservative values.[17] Under President Clinton, the White House staff did not participate in the selection of judges as actively as its predecessors had, nor were his appointees as liberal as his predecessor's were conservative. As one Clinton aide explained, "We don't see courts as a vehicle for social change. It's enough to put people of demonstrated quality on the bench. We've done this across gender, race, and national origin lines. And that is a legacy the president is proud of."[18]

Yet, despite selecting a politically moderate group of judges, the Clinton terms were marked by a dramatic increase in Senate scrutiny of judicial nominations. When Republicans gained control of the Senate in 1994, one-third of Clinton's appointments to appellate courts were blocked by the Republican majority on the Senate Judiciary Committee, and the average time to confirmation for an appointment to federal district and appellate courts more than doubled.[19] (See Figure 8.2 for the percentage of judical nominees confirmed by the Senate over time.)

When George W. Bush became president, he moved quickly and aggressively to follow the same strategy that previous Republican administrations had adopted. Bush announced that he would no longer consult with the American Bar Association on judicial appointments, as past presidents had done. Rather, judicial appointments would be reviewed by a White House team, which would seek advice from members of the Federalist Society, a group of conservative legal jurists, lawyers, and academics. This resulted in Bush submitting a list of extraordinarily conservative and highly controversial judges for Senate confirmation. Democrats proceeded to filibuster and prevent consideration of some of Bush's judicial nominees in the same manner that Republicans had previously obstructed Clinton's appointments. But the Bush administration's efforts to transform the judiciary in its own conservative image proceeded apace. By the time Bush left office in 2009, he had appointed 40 percent of all sitting federal judges. Compared to previous presidents, Bush's judical appointees were regarded as "the most conservative on record," especially in the area of civil liberties and rights.[20]

The thorough political screening that judicial appointments were subject to under the Bush administration extended to the entire work of the Justice Department under Bush's attorney general, Alberto R. Gonzales. Nine U.S. attorneys were dismissed for reasons that had little to do with their job performance and more to do with being insufficiently loyal to the Republican Party. Immigration judges were selected on the basis of their politics and not their

FIGURE 8.2

PERCENTAGE OF NOMINEES CONFIRMED BY FULL SENATE

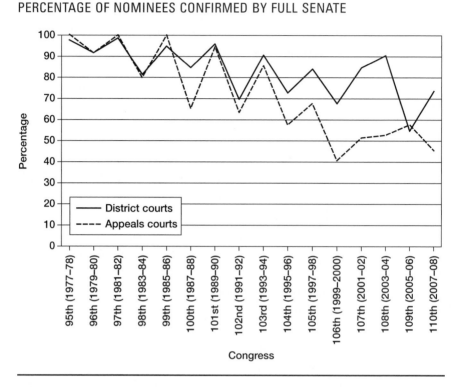

Congress

SOURCES: Lauren Cohen, *Warring Factions: Interest Groups, Money, and the New Politics of Senate Confirmation* (Columbus: Ohio State University Press, 2002); Robert A. Carp and Kenneth Manning, Presentation at Roundtable, Annual Meeting of the Midwest Political Science Association, Chicago, Illinois, April 2009; and Sheldon Goldman, "Obama and the Federal Judiciary: Great Expectations but Will He Have a Dickens of a Time Living Up to Them?" *The Forum 7*, no. 1 (2009).

credentials; and candidates for the attorney general's prestigious honors program, as well as the department's summer intern program, were chosen on the basis of their political affiliations rather than their merits. Once judges become subject to political litmus tests, it is hard for administrations to resist extending that practice to the entire apparatus of justice itself.

Compared to its predecessors, the Obama administration has shown little inclination to use its power of appointment to shape the federal judiciary. When President George W. Bush took office, he moved quickly to infuse the courts with conservative judges. In his first year, he submitted 64 nominees for confirmation by the Senate. In contrast, President Obama made only 31 appointments in his first year in office and only 12 of them were confirmed. Senate Republicans placed "holds"—threats to filibuster—on many of his nominees, thus preventing the Senate from ever voting on them. Early on, Obama's effort to fill vacancies on the lower courts with judges who reflect his values was the victim of his administration's lethargy in putting forward nominees as much as it was the target of Republican zeal in opposing them.

THE SUPREME COURT

At the top of the judicial system is the Supreme Court. The late Justice Robert H. Jackson said judgments by members of the Supreme Court are "not final because we are infallible; we know that we are infallible only because we are final."[21] The Court receives the vast majority of its cases from the federal district and appellate courts. As Table 8.2 reveals, many more cases are filed with the Court each year than it has the time or inclination to hear. The number of petitions to the Court has increased while the number of cases on which the Court issues signed, written opinions has declined. In 2007–08, the Court received over 9,600 petitions but agreed to fully review only 75 of them. The Court carefully chooses which cases to hear, applying what is called the **rule of four**. That is, the Court will consider only those cases that at least four justices want to hear.[22] In choosing which cases to hear, Chief Justice William Howard Taft (1921–30) explained that the Court should devote its resources to cases "that involve principles, the application of which are of wide public importance or governmental interest, and which should be authoritatively declared by the Court."[23] In 1949, Justice Fred Vinson provided a fuller statement of the guidelines the Court has followed in selecting which cases to review:

> The Supreme Court is not, and never has been, primarily concerned with the correction of errors in lower court decisions. . . . The function of the Supreme Court is . . . to resolve conflicts of opinion on federal questions that have arisen among lower courts, to pass upon questions of wide import under the Constitution, laws and treaties of the United States, and to exercise supervisory power over lower courts. If we took every case in which an interesting legal question is raised, or our *prima facie* impression is that the decision below is erroneous, we could not fill the Constitutional and statutory responsibilities placed upon the Court. To remain effective, the Supreme Court must continue to decide only those cases which present questions whose resolution will have immediate importance far beyond the particular facts and parties involved.[24]

TABLE 8.2

U.S. SUPREME COURT CASES FILED AND DISPOSED: 1980–2007

Action	1980	1990	1995	2000	2003	2004	2005	2006	2007
Total cases on docket	5,144	6,316	7,565	8,965	8,882	8,588	9,608	10,256	9,602
Total cases available for argument	264	201	145	138	140	128	122	108	125
Cases argued	154	125	90	86	91	87	88	78	75
Number of signed opinions	123	112	75	77	73	74	69	67	67

SOURCE: U.S. Census Bureau, "The 2010 Statistical Abstract," at http://www.census.gov/compendia/statab/2010/tables/10s0322.pdf (accessed March 17, 2010).

The Supreme Court has had as few as five justices, when it was first organized in 1789, and as many as ten. Its membership, set by Congress, has been fixed at nine since 1869. The head of the Court is the chief justice of the United States, who is appointed by the president—subject to confirmation by the Senate. The chief justice may be the official leader of the Court but is only first among equals in his relationship to the other eight justices. In a 2006 interview, Chief Justice John G. Roberts Jr., who had been on the job just one year, acknowledged, "There is this convention of referring to the Taney Court, the Marshall Court, the Fuller Court, but a chief justice has the same vote that everyone else has. . . . The chief's ability to get the Court to do something is really quite restrained."[25]

The chief justice is in effect the leader of the orchestra, but he cannot tell the other justices what music to play. Some chief justices, however, are better than others at being conductors and can get the other justices to play the same tune. For example, Chief Justice Earl Warren used every personal and political argument he could think of to convince two reluctant members of the Court to sign a unanimous opinion in the *Brown* decision. Other chief justices have not been so successful. The Court sometimes leads, more than it is led by, the chief justice.

Decision making on the Court begins after lawyers on each side plead their case in oral argument before the assembled justices. Like students having to suffer a bad presentation in class, the justices' attention may flag while listening to the lawyers. To divert themselves, the justices sometimes pass notes to one another commenting on the courtroom proceedings or news from the world outside. On October 10, 1973, in the midst of the baseball playoffs and an investigation of Vice President Spiro Agnew, Justice Potter Stewart passed this note to his colleague Harry Blackmun during oral argument: "V.P. Agnew just resigned! Mets 2 Reds 0."[26]

Following oral argument, the justices discuss the case in private conferences. No law clerks or secretaries may attend. Confidentiality is designed to promote a frank and full exchange of views among the justices. The chief justice leads the discussion, during which the justices reveal how they would decide the case and the reasons for their position. According to Justice Antonin Scalia, "[N]ot much conferencing goes on" at conference anymore.[27] Views are stated rather than argued. There is less collective deliberation and more expounding of individual views. After the conference reveals each justice's tentative vote on a case, the chief justice, if in the majority, assigns the writing of the Court's opinion to one of the justices who voted with the majority. Chief Justice Roberts referred to his ability to assign opinions when in the majority as "not my greatest power, it's my only power."[28] (If the chief justice is not in the majority, the senior member of the majority assigns the opinion.) Chief justices value the power to assign cases. It allows them to select the justice most likely to make an argument that can retain the tenative majority from conference. Selecting who writes the majority opinion is regarded as so important that Chief Justice Warren Burger was suspected by the other justices of voting frequently with a majority he disagreed with, so that he might select who would write the majority opinion.

Justices assigned to write the majority opinion circulate a draft to their colleagues, who review it and respond. As a result of written exchanges among the justices, the rationale for the decision may be modified and votes may be switched, so that a completely different decision emerges from the process. For example, the 1989 *Webster v. Reproductive Health Services* case threatened to overturn the 1973 *Roe v. Wade* decision establishing a woman's constitutional right to an abortion. A majority of five justices at conference voted to uphold a Missouri law that would have placed restrictive conditions on abortions. Chief Justice William H. Rehnquist assigned himself the task of writing the majority opinion. But as memos circulated among the justices in response to Rehnquist's draft, Justice Sandra Day O'Connor switched her vote. What once was a 5–4 majority at conference to effectively overturn *Roe* became, after an exchange of views among the justices, a 5–4 majority to reaffirm *Roe* (while still upholding some of the restrictions in the Missouri law). A similar shift occurred in an otherwise inconsequential case called *Huddleston v. United States* (1974), in which a 5–4 majority for Huddleston at conference turned into an 8–1 majority against him after briefs circulated among the justices. Justice Lewis F. Powell Jr., who had voted to acquit Huddleston at conference, sent a note to Blackmun (who wrote the dissenting opinion): "Although I voted the other way at Conference, upon a mature consideration and in light of your excellent opinion, I am persuaded to join you."[29]

The process in the *Webster* and *Huddleston* decisions reveals that conference votes are tentative and not carved in stone. Indeed, Supreme Court scholars Lee Epstein and Jack Knight contend that justices change their minds frequently regarding how they will rule as a case proceeds from conference to final decision.[30]

In the early days of the Republic, presidents would select justices who shared their views; but they also nominated them with an eye to regional balance on the Court. An informal tradition developed in which seats on the Court were reserved for people from New England, New York, and the South. As regional conflicts dissipated and immigration increased, diversity on the Court was defined in religious, not regional terms. A new informal tradition emerged in which there was a Catholic and a Jewish seat on the Court to reflect the emergence of these groups. Today, presidents are much less concerned with regional and religious balance because those bases of conflict in society have been replaced with new issues based on gender and race. For example, if Elena Kagan, who President Obama nominated to replace the retiring John Paul Stevens, is confirmed by the Senate, no Protestants would be left on the Court even though they are the largest religious group in the United States, and New Yorkers would occupy four of the nine seats. Concern about religious and geographic diversity has given way to ensuring gender and racial balance. Consequently, more attention is paid to ensuring that women and blacks are represented on the Court. Thurgood Marshall was the first black to join the Court in 1967, and Sandra Day O'Connor was the first woman appointed to the Court in 1981. The notion of diversity on the Court continues to be modernized and redefined to reflect a changing society. Hispanics are now the largest and fastest-growing minority group, and President Obama acknowledged their emergence in 2009 when he appointed Sonya Sotomayor, a Latina of Puerto Rican descent, to replace David Souter.[31]

Although the notion of diversity on the Court is constantly being updated, ideology continues to drive the selection process. Presidents select justices who share their values and policy preferences. And far from being friendly or familiar with presidents prior to their nomination, many had not even met them before interviewing for the job.

Although presidents appoint members to the Supreme Court whom they believe will reflect their views, sometimes they are spectacularly wrong in their predictions. President Harry Truman, for example, did not mince words over his disappointment with Justice Tom Clark: "Tom Clark was my biggest mistake. No question about it. . . . I don't know what got into me. He was no damn good as Attorney General, and on the Supreme Court . . . it doesn't seem possible, but he's even worse. He hasn't made one right decision that I can think of. . . ."[32] When asked what his biggest mistake was while in office, President Dwight Eisenhower replied, "The appointment of. . . Earl Warren."[33] More recently, conservatives were often disappointed by the liberal decisions of Justice David Souter, whom President George H.W. Bush, a Republican, appointed to the Court in 1990. Sometimes presidents guess right, only to have appointees change their views over time. Justice Harry Blackmun voted with his friend Chief Justice Warren Burger, another conservative Nixon appointee, 90 percent of the time when he first came on the Court. But his views changed, and by the time he retired from the Court in 1994, he had become its most liberal member.[34] Judicial scholars have noted that Supreme Court justices are more likely over time to vote in ways that deviate from the values of the president who appointed them, but the differences are not great.[35] Most justices reflect pretty well the politics of the president who appoints them.

Presidential appointments to the Supreme Court are more contentious today than they were in the past. Prior to the Senate rejection of two of President Richard Nixon's Supreme Court nominees in 1969 and 1970, one has to go back to 1930 and the Hoover administration to find the last time the Senate rejected a presidential appointment to the Supreme Court. Most Senate confirmation hearings resembled that for Justice Whizzer White in 1962: the Senate Judiciary Committee hearing lasted a total of 90 minutes, the committee then met in executive session for another 5 minutes, and White's nomination was confirmed on the floor of the Senate that same afternoon. In contrast today, Senate confirmation hearings are long, contentious affairs that are more like fierce rugby scrums than polite cricket matches. Pitched battles occurred in 1987 over President Reagan's appointment of Robert Bork, and in 1991 over President George H.W. Bush's nomination of Clarence Thomas. The former was rejected as too conservative by a Democratic Senate, and the latter was confirmed by the Senate despite charges of sexual harassment against him. Supreme Court appointments have drawn increasing scrutiny in part because more political issues are being placed at the Court's door. Groups are litigating what they cannot legislate. The Court increasingly is being called on to choose between competing policies in areas of profound disagreement. This, in turn, calls attention to the people appointed to the Court, who are increasingly perceived as making public policy when they decide cases. The frequency of divided government between Congress and the president, and the partisan and ideological polarization within Congress, have also contributed to the frequent and contentious battles over judicial appointments.

Judicial Activism and Restraint

We have seen how the Constitution established the Supreme Court and left it to Congress to create lower federal courts as they might be needed. But the Constitution did not stipulate the number of members of the Supreme Court or what its specific powers would be. For example, the power of judicial review, in which the courts can nullify any federal, state, or public law that they believe conflicts with the Constitution, is not explicitly granted by the Constitution and cannot be found within it. This power first was asserted by the Supreme Court in the landmark case of *Marbury v. Madison* (1803), in which the Court ruled that Thomas Jefferson's secretary of state, James Madison, had failed to properly convey the commission appointing William Marbury to a government post as a last-minute act of President John Adams. In his *Marbury* decision, Chief Justice John Marshall wrote, "It is emphatically the province and duty of the judicial department to say what the law is. . . . A law repugnant to the Constitution is void; . . . courts as well as other departments are bound by that instrument."[36] Even after *Marbury*, however, judicial review was slow to institutionalize. The Court waited another fifty-four years before attempting to invalidate another act of Congress, in its infamous *Dred Scott* decision confirming black slavery, and it was not until the late nineteenth century that the principle was fully established.

The principle of judicial review is in tension with democratic theory inasmuch as it gives unelected judges the power to overrule laws made by a majority of elected officials. When courts overrule legislatures, it is regarded as an expression of **judicial activism**. Although judicial activism may be hard to reconcile with democratic theory, in some circumstances it may actually enhance democracy—such as when legislation violates a provision of the Bill of Rights or subjects minorities to the tyranny of the majority, as was the case in *Brown*.[37]

Opponents condemn judicial activism as an example of unelected judges making law, whereas advocates praise it as an example of judges protecting the weak from oppressive majorities. The opposite of judicial activism is **judicial restraint**, which occurs when courts defer to the will of the people expressed through legislative majorities. Justice Oliver Wendell Holmes, for example, believed that democratic politics produced many bad laws that judges had no business changing. If his fellow citizens wanted to go to hell, Holmes once remarked, it was his job to help them on their way.

Most expressions of judicial activism, of courts failing to defer to elected officials, have been conservative, preserving and protecting property rights. The Supreme Court's 1905 *Lochner v. New York* decision, which vacated a state law that restricted working hours, and its initial rulings that struck down New Deal legislation, are examples of judicial review acting to overturn progressive social and economic legislation. But there is no automatic identification of judicial activism with conservative results or, correspondingly, of judicial restraint with liberal outcomes. Law professor Philip B. Kurland has suggested that "[a]n 'activist' court is essentially one that is out of step with legislative or executive branches of the government" and that it is liberal or conservative "depending which role its prime antagonist has adopted."[38] Activist judges are more likely to be concerned with the consequences of their decisions—which can be either liberal or conservative—while justices who practice restraint are more likely to be concerned with the legal consistency of their decisions, which likewise can have either liberal or conservative consequences. The political complexity of the issue was recently apparent when President George W. Bush celebrated the fiftieth anniversary of the *Brown* decision—in which activist judges nullified state segegration laws. That same day, his office issued a press release criticizing the Massachusetts Supreme Court's ruling in favor of gay marriage on the grounds that "The sacred institution of marriage should not be redefined by a few activist judges."[39] Like President Bush, most people do not support judicial activism or restraint in principle; rather, they support one or the other depending upon whether they agree or disagree with the Court's ruling in a particular decision.

The Supreme Court in History

Marbury v. Madison settled a question that had divided the country along clear partisan lines. Judicial review was supported by the Federalist Party, which was dominated by northern manufacturing, finance, and mercantile interests. Southern and western agrarian, planter, and small landowning interests in the Republican Party favored the principle of legislative supremacy and opposed judicial review. But Federalists and Republicans were also divided over the scope of national as opposed to state power. This question came before the court in the form of *McCulloch v. Maryland* (1819). In *McCulloch*, the Court ruled that federal law was supreme. State law would have to give way when federal and state laws were in conflict. But not until *McCulloch* did the Court decisively rule in this manner. Thus, the *Marbury* case confirmed the power of the Supreme Court, and the *McCulloch* case confirmed the power of the national government. Both marked a triumph of national industrial interests in the Federalist Party over local agrarian interests in the Democratic Party.

After Chief Justice John Marshall's death in 1835, President Andrew Jackson appointed Roger Taney to lead the Court. The Court over which he presided, in contrast to the Marshall Court, tilted toward states' rights and southern interests. This was particularly evident in its *Scott v. Sanford* (1857) decision, when the Court, by a 7–2 vote, ruled that no black could be an American citizen, that a black was "a person of an inferior order," that no individual of African descent was a "portion of this American people," and that blacks were slaves and possessions of their owners no matter whether they were in a slave or a free area of the country. The *Dred Scott* decision provoked an outcry in the North and hastened the onset of the Civil War.

Following the Civil War, the Court was in the hands of northern Republicans, who were chiefly concerned with safeguarding property and providing a legal environment for the development of capitalism. For example, the Fourteenth Amendment, adopted in 1868, was intended to protect black civil rights from hostile state actions. But its famous due process clause—no state shall "deprive any person of life, liberty, or property, without due process of law"—served corporate interests more than it did blacks following Reconstruction. The courts held that many laws regulating business were unconstitutional because they deprived business of due process, and this stance precipitated a wave of judicial activism by the Court.[40] The Court used its laissez-faire interpretation of the Constitution to nullify so many laws that Justice Oliver Wendell Holmes complained there "was hardly any limit but the sky to the invalidating of [laws] if they happen to strike a majority of the Court as for any reason undesirable."[41] Not only did the courts protect business from most government regulation, but they limited the reach of antitrust laws and restricted the ability of unions to organize and to strike. In recognition of the Supreme Court's service to business, a New York bank president told an audience of capitalists in 1895: "I give you, gentlemen, the Supreme Court of the United States—guardian of the dollar, defender of private property, enemy of spoliation, sheet anchor of the Republic!"[42]

But the Court's defense of property rights and freedom of contract could not withstand the popular momentum of Franklin Roosevelt's New Deal. Initially, the Court repeatedly struck down New Deal legislation. It outlawed the Agricultural Adjustment Act, a New York State minimum-wage law, and the National Industrial Recovery Act, which were enacted to relieve the Depression. The outlook was grim for other New Deal legislation whose constitutionality was also being challenged, such as the Social Security Act and the National

Labor Relations Act. The more the Court stood as a roadblock in the way of the New Deal, the more popular frustration with the Court's undemocratic character grew. Senator George Norris of Nebraska expressed this common complaint when he denounced the Court on the Senate floor, saying, "The members of the Supreme Court are not elected by anybody. They are responsible to nobody. Yet they hold dominion over everybody."[43]

Never before had a president been so stymied by the Court in implementing his agenda. Yet Roosevelt was unable to alter the Court's decisions, because he had no chance to change its composition. Roosevelt had the misfortune in his first term to be the first president ever to serve a full four years and not appoint someone to the Supreme Court. Unable to change the Court through appointment, he proposed "court packing" legislation, which would have permitted the president to appoint a new justice, up to a total of fifteen, for each justice who reached age seventy and did not retire. Because six of the nine justices were over seventy at the time, this legislation would have enabled Roosevelt to add six new like-minded justices to the Court. Roosevelt lost the battle to reform the Court in Congress, but he won the war. While Roosevelt was seeking acceptance for his plan to reform the Court and more court-curbing bills were proposed in Congress than ever before, Justice Owen Roberts, who had previously voted against New Deal legislation and had written some key opinions striking them down, now voted to uphold such legislation as constitutional.[44] One member of Congress noted that Justice Roberts had effectively amended the Constitution and changed the lives of millions simply "by nodding his head instead of shaking it."[45] Justice Roberts's about-face is often referred to as the "switch in time that saved nine." This reversal gave Roosevelt a majority on the Court, one he later expanded on. By the end of his presidency in 1945, he had filled more Court vacancies than any president since George Washington.

This reform episode reveals much about the power and limits of the Supreme Court. The Court can nullify the will of the people, as it initially did regarding New Deal legislation. But if the Court stands too hard and too long against public opinion, the Court's decisions risk losing legitimacy in the eyes of the public. The prestige and stature of the Court will suffer. This is particularly damaging because the Court does not derive legitimacy from democratic theory. Supreme Court justices are not elected and are not accountable to those affected by their decisions—or to anyone, for that matter. Instead, the justices must depend on their eminence and prestige as the reasons their decisions should be respected. The Court must constantly keep its reputation aloft, appearing above the political and partisan fray, because it cannot draw legitimacy for its decisions from democratic theory as other American political institutions claim to do.

After 1936, the Supreme Court upheld every New Deal statute whose constitutionality was challenged. Judicial activism was replaced with judicial restraint. In the course of confirming the New Deal, the Court initiated a constitutional revolution that greatly expanded the power of the federal government over business and the states. Previously, the Court had narrowly construed the definition of interstate commerce, so that many business operations were not subject to federal law. But now the Court defined interstate commerce so broadly that federal law applied to virtually all business transactions. When lawyers for business argued, for example, that the federal government lacked the right to regulate working conditions, the Court ruled that Congress did have authority to legislate in this area, explaining, "When industries organize themselves on a national scale . . . how can it be maintained that their industrial relations constitute a forbidden field into which Congress may not enter?"[46] The Court now interpreted the reach of the federal government so expansively that there were almost "no social welfare or regulatory statutes that the Courts would not validate."[47]

This constitutional revolution in 1937 replaced classical legal doctrines based on freedom of contract with a new jurisprudence based on government regulation of business. Freedom of contract was just, according to the old **classical legal theory**, because it reflected results arrived at in a neutral market among free and willing parties. But as the legal scholar Roscoe Pound argued in 1903, the freedom of contract doctrine represented a conception of equal rights that was fraudulent to "everyone acquainted at first hand with actual industrial conditions."[48] Employers enjoyed much more market power than did individual workers in bargaining, for example, over the employment contract. Moreover, the Depression made it painfully clear that the interpretation of contractual freedom the Court wanted to protect rested on false assumptions about the ability of unregulated markets to satisfy people's needs. The formal, abstract, detached quality of classical legal doctrine was now replaced with one that was realistic and grounded in results. If the market was not neutral, if its results were harmful to society, then it was appropriate for government to intervene. The constitutional revolution of 1937 marked the rise of a new legal theory that could justify government interference in freedom of contract so as to require firms to pay minimum wages, bargain with their unionized workers, and prevent them from hiring child labor. The Court finally acknowledged what had long been recognized everywhere else: that laissez-faire capitalism was dead.

THE MODERN COURT: FROM WARREN TO ROBERTS

On March 16, 1948, twenty black citizens assisted by the National Association for the Advancement of Colored People (NAACP) filed suit in U.S. district court in Florence County, South Carolina. They claimed that racial segregation practiced by the Clarendon County Board of Education violated the equal protection clause of the Constitution's Fourteenth Amendment. Simple justice, they believed, required the government to give black children the same educational opportunities it provided to whites. In Clarendon County, the local board of education spent $673,850 to maintain 12 schools for whites in 1949–50 and less than one-third of that amount for 61 schools for blacks. White schoolchildren rode to school in buses, often passing black schoolchildren who had to walk because the school board provided no buses for them.

The suit was filed under the name of Henry Briggs, the first plaintiff in alphabetical order, who worked in a gas station. Before the litigation was over, he would be fired from his job. Maisie Solomon, another plaintiff, also lost her job. John McDonald could not get a loan for his tractor, Lee Richardson could not secure credit for his farm, and no one would rent land to William Ragin for growing cotton. The doors of justice may be open to everyone, but sometimes it requires uncommon courage to walk through them.

After two years of delay and defeat in the lower courts, this school segregation case reached the Supreme Court of the United States. There, the suit joined two other school segregation cases, from Delaware and Virginia, that the Court was also hearing on appeal. These cases were consolidated with a fourth school segregation case from Kansas: *Brown v. Board of Education of Topeka*. This case was listed first because the justices did not want the issue of segregation to appear as purely a southern matter.

On May 17, 1954, Chief Justice Earl Warren read the Supreme Court's unanimous opinion in the group of school segregation cases known collectively as *Brown*. He told the assembled spectators and reporters that the Court had asked itself if racial segregation in public schools deprived black children of equal opportunity. "We believe that it does," he declared. His closing remarks left no doubt where the Court stood: "We conclude that in the field of public education, the doctrine of 'separate but equal' has no place. Separate educational facilities are inherently unequal. Therefore the plaintiffs . . . have been . . . deprived of the equal protection of the laws guaranteed by the Fourteenth Amendment."[49]

The *Brown* decision was only one of many decisions the Warren Court made that resonated across the country and whose principles still stand today. The issues the Warren Court wrestled with no longer involved government regulation of business, as had been the case for the New Deal that preceded it. Since 1937, the Court had decisively settled such issues in favor of regulation. Now the Court concerned itself with issues of civil liberties and extending the principle of political equality to new areas. From just 9 percent of the Court's agenda in 1933, cases involving civil rights and civil liberties accounted for 65 percent of the Court's docket in 1971. The Rights Revolution had begun.[50]

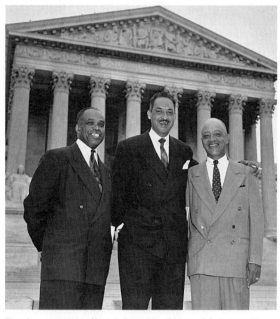

The three attorneys (from left to right, George E.C. Hayes, Thurgood Marshall, and James Nabrit Jr.) who argued the case against school segregation, standing and smiling in front of the U.S. Supreme Court building after the Court issued its *Brown* decision.

The Warren Court created a more inclusive meaning of democracy through its civil rights decisions, its rulings expanding freedom of speech and press protections, its voting rights decisions, and its application of the Bill of Rights to the states. These decisions provoked tremendous controversy. But the Warren Court prevailed because it was in tune with the activist, liberal wing of the Democratic Party, which was the governing coalition at the time.[51]

The Warren Court's effort to realize the promise of legal equality for all Americans was evident in a number of landmark decisions. *Brown*, of course, led the way in civil rights. But the Court was reluctant to pursue its civil rights agenda until Congress took the lead with the Civil Rights Act of 1964. Once Congress showed intiative, the Court announced that time had run out for school districts to show deliberate speed in desegregating schools (*Griffin v. County School Board of Prince Edward County*). Four years later, in *Green v. County School Board of New Kent County*, the Court required school districts that had practiced segregation in the past to stop discriminating and take affirmative action to achieve racial balance in their schools.

The Warren Court also acted to expand the notion of legal equality and ensure the effectiveness of each citizen's vote by requiring equally apportioned legislative districts. Some state legislative districts included many more voters than others. In *Baker v. Carr* (1962), the Court ruled that it was appropriate for federal courts to hear cases challenging malapportioned state election districts. Two years later, in *Reynolds v. Sims*, the Court took the next step to making the promise of political equality a reality. It declared that the "one person, one vote" principle, which governed congressional districting, should also apply to state legislatures. Writing for the majority on the Court in requiring states to apportion their legislative districts fairly by population, Warren wrote, "Legislators represent people, not trees or acres."[52]

The Warren Court also was responsible for extending the boundaries of democracy by requiring states to abide by virtually every provision of the Bill of Rights. State law enforcement and criminal procedures would now have to meet federal due process requirements, giving defendants charged with crimes certain procedural rights and protections enumerated in the Bill of Rights. In *Mapp v. Ohio* (1961), the Court ruled that the police could not conduct searches for evidence without a court order. Two years later, in *Gideon v. Wainwright* (1963), the Court declared that states must provide legal counsel to all defendants charged with serious crimes. In 1966, the Court handed down the *Miranda* decision, which stated that a confession obtained from a criminal suspect during interrogation is not admissible as evidence in court unless the accused person has been informed of his or her rights to remain silent and to be represented by a lawyer. But the Rights Revolution extended beyond banning states from trying defendants without lawyers, allowing police to conduct searches without court authorization, or eliciting confessions without informing defendants of their rights. It also meant states could no longer outlaw the sale of contraceptives, prohibit abortions, or segregate schools. State laws that did so were now regarded as violations of fundamental constitutional rights.[53]

Some of the Warren Court's decisions have become national standards. It is hard to imagine the law today tolerating government-sanctioned racial segregation, as it once did, or deviating from the principle of one person, one vote, as it once also did. Even Chief Justice William Rehnquist, who was opposed to much of the Warren Court's jurisprudence, acknowledged in 2000 that some of its rulings were now so embedded that respect for precedent weighed heavily against overruling them. Although subsequent Supreme Court decisions have chipped away at the Warren Court's jurisprudence in recent years, its legacy lives on.

The Burger Court

Conservatives attacked the Warren Court for coddling criminals, tying the hands of police and prosecutors, being irreligious, violating states' rights, and promoting civil unrest. Richard Nixon pledged to remold the Court in his 1968 presidential campaign, and within a year of his election, he had a chance to deliver on that promise. In 1969 Earl Warren retired, and President Nixon appointed Warren E. Burger, a known critic of many Warren Court decisions, to replace him as chief justice. By the end of Burger's service as chief justice in 1986, Republican presidents had appointed six members to the Supreme Court. Only two members of the liberal bloc from the Warren Court, Justices William Brennan and Thurgood Marshall, remained on the bench, along with the moderate Byron White.

Circumstances were ripe for conservatives to undo the work of the Warren Court. But the counterrevolution many anticipated never happened. The power of judicial precedent, the lack of leadership provided by Burger, and the skill of liberal Justice William Brennan in coaxing a majority of justices to follow the Warren Court's rulings were enough to hold the line. In a review of the Burger Court, political scientists Mark Silverstein and Benjamin Ginsberg concluded in 1987: "The most controversial decisions of the Warren era involving school prayer, reapportionment, desegregation, and criminal procedure remain the law of the land. The Burger Court nibbled at the edges of several Warren Court precedents, often seeking to confine their application, but overt attempts at overruling were either avoided or defeated."[54]

Nowhere was the Burger Court more faithful to its predecessor than in the area of civil rights. In *Swann v. Charlotte-Mecklenburg County Board of Education* (1970), the Court made clear there would be no retreat from *Brown*. The Court unanimously upheld the use of busing to achieve racially balanced schools. The Court also gave constitutional approval to affirmative action plans as a way to remedy past discrimination against minorities and other protected groups. But the Burger Court's most famous decision, *Roe v. Wade* (1973), most clearly expresses the degree to which the Court drew on the legal reasoning of the Warren Court. The Warren Court first recognized a constitutional right to privacy in *Griswold v. Connecticut* (1965) when it stuck down a state law barring the use of contraceptives. In *Roe v. Wade*, the Burger Court applied the Warren Court's logic of a right to privacy in order to strike down state laws denying a woman's right to an abortion.[55]

But as the number of liberal holdovers from the Warren Court decreased and the decline of the Democratic governing coalition became more evident, the Burger Court, over time, became more conservative. The drift to the right was particularly apparent in criminal law, where the Burger Court began to chip away at the Warren Court's revolution in due process and reduce defendants' procedural rights and protections.

The Rehnquist Court

In 1986, Republicans pulled the equivalent of a double steal in baseball. Justice Burger retired and was replaced as chief justice by William Rehnquist, the most conservative member of the Court. Controversy over his nomination to chief justice erupted at his Senate confirmation hearings. Questions regarding Rehnquist's integrity, honesty, and respect for minority rights distracted attention from the appointment of Antonin Scalia, who was even more conservative, to the seat Rehnquist formerly occupied.[56]

William Brennan, the most liberal member of the Court, stepped down in 1990. President George H.W. Bush replaced him with David H. Souter. Thurgood Marshall, the last liberal holdover from the Warren Court, resigned a year later in 1991. President Bush replaced him with another African American, Clarence Thomas. Skin color may have been the only thing that Marshall and Thomas had in common. Marshall opposed the death penalty and supported affirmative action and a woman's right to an abortion. Thomas, on the other hand, favored the death penalty and opposed abortion and government programs to remedy the effects of discrimination. Marshall was esteemed within his profession, but the American Bar Association's judiciary committee gave Thomas the lowest rating ever given a confirmed justice; none of the members rated him well qualified.[57]

Scalia and Thomas perceive their role as undoing what they regard as the perfidious work of the Warren and Burger Courts. Both Scalia and Thomas regard the law as moving dangerously away from its original meaning as the Founders intended, and they hope to restore it. Other Supreme Court justices appointed by Republican presidents to the Rehnquist Court—Sandra Day O'Connor, David Souter, John Paul Stevens, and Anthony Kennedy—were conservative but not counterrevolutionaries like Scalia and Thomas and resisted too great a turn away from the precedents set by their predecessors. To simply discard the legal legacy of those Courts, this group believed, would damage the Supreme Court as an institution. Thus, in 1991, Justices O'Connor, Souter, and Kennedy wrote an unusual joint opinion upholding *Roe* in the abortion case *Planned Parenthood of Southeastern Pennsylvania v. Casey*. This trio of Republican appointees to the Court was aware that if the Court overturned *Roe*, this decision would be perceived, quite accurately, as due simply to the change in membership on the Court. It would expose the Court to the charge that its decisions reflect election results rather than the Constitution. The joint opinion of O'Connor, Souter, and Kennedy argued that, since *Roe* had been decided, people "had ordered their thinking and living around that case," and that no legal principle weakening *Roe*'s constitutional basis had emerged since 1973. "A decision to overrule *Roe*'s essential holding under the existing circumstances," their opinion continued, would be "at the cost of both profound and unnecessary damage to the Court's legitimacy and to the rule of law."[58]

President Bill Clinton was the first Democrat to appoint a justice to the Supreme Court in twenty-six years. In 1993, Byron White retired. President Clinton replaced him with Ruth Bader Ginsburg, the second woman appointed to the Court after Sandra Day O'Connor. In 1994 Harry Blackmun retired, giving Clinton the chance to make another appointment. He chose Stephen Breyer.

That the Supreme Court follows the election returns was as true of the Rehnquist Court as it was of the Warren Court. The former reflected the shift in public opinion to the right and the Republican Party's resurgence, just as much as the Warren Court reflected Democratic Party dominance and popular demands to increase democratic rights. The Rehnquist Court's record was a conservative one but not overly so. It revived states' rights, was suspicious of affirmative action, liked the death penalty, was willing to approve restrictions that states set on abortions, was not sympathetic to the rights of defendants, and was less vigilant of the separation of church and state. It did not overturn Warren and Burger Court precedents but instead hollowed them out, limiting their application—or, in Justice Brennan's generous term, giving them a "cramped interpretation."[59] For example, a woman's right to an abortion still stands, but the Court permitted states to place more obstacles in the way of women who sought one. The principle of affirmative action was still intact, but the legal bar such programs must pass was raised higher. The due process rights of criminal defendants, such as access to a lawyer, still existed; but the Court was much more tolerant of the evasive ways that law enforcement officials followed these rights.

On the other side of the ledger, the Rehnquist Court struck a blow for long-established legal rights when it rejected President George W. Bush's arguments that he had the power as commander in chief to detain suspected terrorists indefinitely without knowledge of the charges against them or even access to a lawyer. The Court, in effect, ruled that the president was not above the law. The Rehnquist Court also compiled a strong record on First Amendment cases. According to legal scholar Burt Neuborne, the Rehnquist Court has "echoed and deepened the powerful First Amendment doctrine [it] inherited . . . and has been among the strongest free speech courts in the nation's history."[60] Its most famous ruling in this arena was *Texas v. Johnson* (1989), which held that burning the flag is protected by the First Amendment. And in *Lawrence v. Texas* (2003), the Court strongly reaffirmed the right-to-privacy doctrine first enunciated in *Griswold* and culminating in *Roe* to strike down a Texas antisodomy law. The Court declared that to the same degree as heterosexuals, gays are "entitled to respect for their private lives" by the government. This ruling was a constitutional watershed that provided a due process guarantee to gay men and women for their private sexual behavior and overruled the Court's previous 1986 *Bowers v. Hardwick* decision.

The Rehnquist Court drew the ire of liberals for undermining in practice, if not in principle, the Warren Court legacy. But it also disappointed conservatives who expected it to spark the counterrevolution that the Burger Court had failed to produce. Although pleased with the general drift of the Court to the right, conservatives condemned it for lacking the courage of its convictions.

The Roberts Court

Rehnquist died in 2005, and President Bush nominated John G. Roberts Jr. to fill his post. Roberts had impeccable legal and political credentials. He graduated from Harvard law school, served as a Supreme Court clerk for Rehnquist, and worked in the Reagan Justice Department before becoming a successful corporate lawyer. In 2000, he advised the Bush team on its legal challenges to the contested presidential election; three years later, he was appointed by President Bush to the United States Court of Appeals for the District of Columbia.

The Court continued to experience turnover following Rehnquist's departure when Sandra Day O'Connor retired. She was replaced in 2006 by Samuel Alito, who served on the U.S. Third Circuit Court of Appeals. The irony of Alito's appointment as a replacement for O'Connor did not escape veteran court-watchers. In Alito's first major opinion on the appeals court, he was the only one of three judges hearing the case to uphold all abortion restrictions of a new Pennsylvania law, including spousal notification requirements. When the state law eventually came to the Supreme Court in *Planned Parenthood v. Casey*, this was the only restriction that the Court struck down, and O'Connor wrote a blistering critique of the law's requirement that husbands be notified. Now she was being replaced by a judge whose views on abortion she had ridiculed earlier.[61]

In 2009, David Souter announced his retirement, permitting President Obama to make his first Supreme Court appointment. He chose U.S. Court of Appeals Judge Sonya Sotomayor as Souter's replacement. Sotomayor's appointment was historic because she is the first Hispanic justice ever to serve on the Court. A year later, in 2010, Justice John Paul Stevens announced his reitrement and President Obama nominated Elena Kagan, the former dean of Harvard law school and the solicitor general of the United States, to replace him.

A 2010 photo of the members of the U.S. Supreme Court, taken before the retirement of Justice John Paul Stevens. Standing (left to right): Justice Samuel Anthony Alito Jr., Justice Ruth Bader Ginsburg, Justice Stephen G. Breyer, and Justice Sonia Sotomayor. Seated (left to right): Justice Anthony M. Kennedy, Justice John Paul Stevens, Chief Justice John G. Roberts Jr., Justice Antonin Scalia, and Justice Clarence Thomas.

The Roberts Court is still young, and its jurisprudential legacy is not yet clear. It has rewarded the faith of conservatives with sympathetic rulings in most cases, and it has also disappointed them at times. This is particularly true in regard to the limits it has placed on presidential powers. It has repeatedly, if only by the slimmest of margins, ruled that "no prisoner is beneath the law, and no president above its limits."[62] In four separate decisions, the Roberts Court has ruled that detainees—alleged enemy combatants whom the Bush administration imprisoned in its War on Terror—are entitled to due process, and when Congress tried to restrict the Court's jurisdiction by suspending rights for detainees, the Court struck down that provision as well.

For a time, the Roberts Court was the most professionally homogenous court in American history. All of its members were former judges who served on U.S. courts of appeals, although this may change with Elena Kagan, who had no judicial experience, being nominated in 2010 to replace John Paul Stevens. Their resumes shine with degrees from the best Ivy League law schools, but no members of the Roberts Court have ever served in a legislature or run for public office. And though their backgrounds as brilliant legal technicians are supposed to reassure the public that the Court is nonideological and will be modest in its rulings, the Roberts Court has been as divided as any other Court and not at all shy about overturning precedents and public laws.[63] In its 2009 term, for example (as discussed in earlier chapters), the Court ignored legal precedents and by a 5–4 vote in *Citizens United v. Federal Election Commission* overturned federal laws limiting corporate campaign activity on behalf of candidates, claiming such laws limited corporations' free speech rights under the First Amendment. The decision is likely to encourage even more spending by business in elections, and it drew an unusual rebuke from President Obama in his 2010 State of the Union address when he criticized the Court for opening up elections even more to the influence of special interests.

The backgrounds of the Roberts Court members are strikingly similar, but the Court itself is split ideologically. The Court was exquisitely balanced between its right (Alito, Roberts, Scalia, and Thomas) and left wings (Breyer, Ginsburg, Sotomayor, and Stevens), with Justice Kennedy often enjoying the swing vote between them. In 2006, the Court decided one-third of its cases by a 5–4 vote, and Kennedy voted with the majority in every one of those decisions. In its 2008–09 term, the Court again decided about one-third, or 23 of its 74 signed decisions, on a 5–4 vote. Kennedy again provided the deciding vote in all but five of those cases. The Court's political balance will likely not be disturbed by Justice Stevens's retirement in 2010 as President Obama will simply nominate another liberal to replace him.

But this familiar description of the Court as evenly balanced between its right and its left, with Kennedy in the center casting the deciding vote, is flawed for three reasons. First, it fails to capture how much the center of gravity of the Court has moved right. Compared to the Warren Court, the left on today's Court would be considered moderates, the center would be on the right, and those now on the right would be off the scale entirely.[64] When Justice Stevens retired in 2010, he noted that every justice appointed since he joined the Court in 1975 was more conservative than the person he or she replaced. The shift is especially evident in cases involving business wrongdoing. Not only has the Roberts Court frequently ruled in favor of business, but many of these decisions were either unanimous or involved few dissenting votes. There are no economic populists among the "liberal" wing of the Court, as there were in the past. Previously, progressive and consumer groups used lawsuits to challenge corporate wrongdoing; but those petitions now receive little encouragement from liberals on the Court, to say nothing of the other members.[65]

Second, the left-right image of the Court does not take into account how ambitious its rulings are. So far, rulings from the Roberts Court have been limited in their impact because justices continue to go off in their own direction, issuing several **concurring opinions** that minimize the reach and impact of their decisions. Thus, what Mark Silverstein wrote of the Rehnquist Court is equally true of its successor: even when the conservative bloc wins, "their victory is undercut by a multiplicity of concurring opinions that strive to emphasize precisely how little new law is being created."[66]

Finally, like the Courts preceding it, the Roberts Court will be shaped by its political environment. Courts speak to the nation, but they also listen to it. In 2007, for example, the Court imposed strict time limits on workers' ability to file pay discrimination suits. This ruling brought a strong rebuke from many groups and an attempt by Congress to overturn the decision by amending the statute the Court had interpreted. The next year, in the following term, the Roberts Court was much more solicitous of employee rights and favored workers in five discrimination cases.[67]

The political context of the Roberts Court was changed dramatically by the 2008 elections. The Court now must calibrate its conservative inclinations to reflect the more liberal results of the election returns. The election put into office a president who is a former professor of constitutional law and takes a keen interest in it. The 2008 elections also created the potential to change the political complexion of the Court by altering its membership. So far President Obama has not been able to take advantage of this opportunity despite having the good fortune to appoint two justices in his first two years in office. Since no conservative members of the Court have retired, Obama has only been able to replace one liberal with another, leaving the Court's political balance unchanged despite extensive turnover.

As the political environment shifts, the Court cannot help but follow, albeit imperfectly. The Roberts Court's decisions, like those of Courts before it, will be a "function of what they prefer to do, tempered by what they think they ought to do, but constrained by what they perceive is feasible to do."[68] Linda Greenhouse, former judicial affairs reporter for the *New York Times*, wrote in her farewell column covering the Court: "The court is in America's collective hands. We shape it; it reflects us. At any given time, we may not have the Supreme Court we want. We may not have the court we need. But we have, most likely, the Supreme Court we deserve."[69]

POLITICS BY LAWSUIT

Americans are known to be litigious, settling their disputes in court rather than among themselves. About 100 million suits are filed in court each year. The degree to which Americans engage in lawsuits is not a cultural trait, but a reflection of the many rights they enjoy and the openness of the judicial system to their assertion. Recently, corporate America has tried to reduce the prevalence of lawsuits, claiming they are often frivolous and expensive. Lobbyists for business have encouraged members of Congress to pass bills that would cap punitive damages awards by juries and discourage lawsuits by making plaintiffs pay if they lose. The most commonly cited example of a justice system that is out of control is the 1994 case of a woman who won a multimillion-dollar award from McDonald's after she spilled coffee on herself. But the general perception that her claim was trivial is a myth. In fact, McDonald's had received over seven hundred complaints about burns from their coffee, which was twenty degrees hotter than in most other restaurants; and the woman in question required skin grafts for third-degree burns that took more than a year to heal. Moreover, the woman had offered to settle before the trial, and despite encouragement from the judge, McDonald's refused to do so. Only after it lost did McDonald's claim hypocritically to be the victim of a process that it chose to pursue. While the $2.9 million jury award received extensive coverage in the media, not many newspapers covered the story of how the woman actually received $600,000 after the judge reduced the jury's punitive damages award. Although the law may serve the interests of corporations, it can also be used to hold them accountable for coffee that burns enough to require hospitalization as well as for unsafe cars, cancerous cigarettes, and dangerous drugs.

Victims of corporate wrongdoing are not the only ones turning to the courts for restitution. More and more groups are looking to the courts to settle political issues. This is particularly so during extended periods of divided government when Congress and the executive branch are deadlocked. Political actors then look to the courts to settle issues in the absence of a stable political coalition to do so. But groups also go to court to settle issues when they believe they will get a more favorable response from them than from the other branches of government. For example, when George W. Bush became president, environmentalists began filing expensive lawsuits against polluters because they had little faith the Bush administration would enforce environmental regulations that were designed to police them.[70] The courtroom has become simply another extension of the political battle once it moves past the electoral, legislative, and administrative arenas. Nor is this exclusively a recent development. More than 150 years ago, Alexis de Tocqueville noted this peculiar trait when he observed, "There is hardly a political question in the United States that does not sooner or later turn into a judicial one."[71]

Nor have the courts passively accepted their new popularity. They have actually encouraged it. Previous restrictions regarding the kinds of cases that could be brought in federal court, and the parties who could bring them, have been relaxed. This change, according to the political scientists Benjamin Ginsberg and Martin Shefter, has "given a wider range of litigants access to the courts, has rendered a broader range of issues subject to judicial settlement, and so has greatly increased the reach of the courts in American life."[72] The new openness of the courts has contributed to a broader involvement of the courts in policy and politics. For example, federal district courts have gone so far as to take over local school systems, constructing elaborate plans for their desegregation when local school boards have dragged their feet. Courts have become involved in such matters as what schools would close, where new ones would be constructed, and which schools students would attend. In the 1970s, people in Alabama joked that the real executive leader of the state was Federal District Court Judge Frank M. Johnson Jr., and not Governor George Wallace. Johnson earned such notoriety because his appointees oversaw Alabama schools, prisons, mental hospitals, and elections when state agencies failed to perform their constitutional duties. State courts also have moved into policy areas normally reserved for the other branches of government. Some state courts have found grossly unequal school funding across local districts illegal because it was not in compliance with state constitutional requirements to provide "high quality" or "uniform and general" education. They have required reluctant state legislatures to equalize school funding, even going so far as to mandate how much money needs to be redistributed among school districts.

Finally, the courts' growing involvement in policy and politics is evident in the lack of deference courts now show to federal administrative agencies. Courts today are less willing to defer to the expertise of administrative agencies in how legislation is to be interpreted and implemented. Of course, the more courts substitute their judgment for that of administrative agencies, the more they invite litigation. Groups seeking vigorous enforcement of the law and those resisting regulation now engage in politics by lawsuit, appealing to the courts to overturn administrative decisions they oppose.[73]

Although groups have had some success in appealing to the courts and getting policies changed, what happens in the real world is often a different matter. Fifteen years after the *Brown* decision that began with a suit in Clarendon County, South Carolina, that district's public school system enrolled three thousand black children and just a single white child. In 1979, twenty-five years after the *Brown* decision, a new school desegregation suit was filed in Topeka, Kansas, by Linda Brown—the original plaintiff in the school desegregation case that bears her name—on behalf of her children! The same story is true with regard to abortion. Despite the victory in *Roe*, the number of abortions actually grew faster in the years preceding that landmark decision than they did in those afterward.[74] Legal victories can confirm changes that have occurred in the halls of Congress, at elections, and in the minds of citizens, but they are no substitute for them.

THE COURTS IN COMPARATIVE PERSPECTIVE: INCARCERATION NATION

The American justice system is distinctive in numerous ways. Many other countries grant their courts the power of judicial review, but few others do so through the regular court system. In Germany and France, constitutional questions are handled by special courts created for that specific purpose. By contrast, in the United States the question of whether a law is constitutional or not is heard in the same court where all other types of cases are tried. Another unusual quality of American courts is the way that judges are chosen. Few other countries select judges through elections, as is typically done at the state and local levels in the United States. Instead, other countries try to insulate judges from political influences at the appointment stage by having their peers select judges on the basis of professional criteria, as opposed to having more politically inclined legislators or chief executives choose them. In still other systems, when politicians do appoint judges, political influences are mitigated by making their term of appointment nonrenewable. When judges know they are appointed for only one term, they do not have to look over their shoulder and worry how a ruling will affect their career when they decide cases.

But in no respect is the United States more unique than in its criminal justice system. No other developed country has such a vast prison complex to warehouse such a large number of prisoners; no other country inflicts such harsh and punitive sanctions on offenders. Even as the state was being rolled back in other arenas beginning in the 1970s, it was expanding dramatically in terms of prison and punishment. The number of prisoners has increased five-fold since 1973, and sentences meted out by judges have become longer and less proportional to the crime. With more than 2 million adults in jail, the United States has a larger proportion of adults in prison than any country in the world. More than half of those in prison are black, and more black men are behind bars than are enrolled in college. And the cost of creating this vast penal colony has not been cheap. In 2001, the criminal justice system accounted for 7 percent of state and local government spending—roughly equal to what these jurisdictions spent on health care and hospitals. They allocated more money to constructing prisons than to new college buildings, and in some states there was a clear relationship of increased outlays for prisons and decreased outlays for higher education.[75]

The American criminal justice system is not simply of a different scale than that found elsewhere. It is also harsher and more punitive. Nonviolent offenders in Europe comprise a smaller proportion of the prison population than they do in the United States. Offenders in the United States receive longer sentences than they would receive for the same crime committed elsewhere. Moreover, many people lose their rights as well as their freedom when they enter prison. For example, in many states a citizen with a prison record cannot vote and is ineligible for social services, such as student loans.

Finally, the United States is unique in regard to its use of capital punishment. Europe had its last execution in 1977. In contrast, about three thousand people currently sit on death row in American prisons, awaiting execution. The appetite for the death penalty has declined worldwide, and more countries are abolishing capital punishment; but the United States remains a leader, in such dubious company as Iran and China, in executing its own citizens.[76]

The preference of the American criminal justice system for retribution over rehabilitation can be traced to a variety of factors. First, law-and-order politicians have stoked the public's taste for vengeance. Politicians trolling for issues and votes promise to get tough on crime. Second, the prison-industrial complex—comprised of private corporations that supply and run prisons, prison guards and staff, and local communities that depend on prisons for jobs and income—drives the the prison boom. It is a powerful interest group that promotes and profits from prison expansion. Third, the prison boom arose as a means of crime prevention, of removing offenders from the street and thereby making society more secure. Finally, the victims' rights movement also contributed to the race to incarcerate by pitting the rights of victims against the rights of offenders. Victims' rights has framed the issue as a zero-sum game in which punishing offenders is designed to compensate victims for their loss, as opposed to providing social services and aid to assist them.[77]

CONCLUSION

The courts are mostly conservative institutions that support the status quo. Their decisions usually follow and confirm reforms rather than cause them. Based on a study of civil rights, women's rights, and reapportionment, among other subjects, political scientist Gerald Rosenberg concluded that, in the United States, "courts can *almost never* be effective producers of significant social reform. At best, they can second the social reform acts of other branches of government."[78] The law usually follows politics, not the other way around. In addition, the social reform potential of the courts is diminished because the courts need to respect precedent, must fit their rulings to the specific contours of a case, must wait for cases to be brought to them, and require the cooperation and support of other political actors to implement their decisions. They cannot go much further than the other institutions they depend upon are willing to go.

Yet, as we argued in the introduction to this chapter, it would be a mistake to dismiss the significance of the courts or the degree to which the law can be a tool of social change. The *Brown* decision, for example, gave impetus and legitimacy to black demands for political equality. Blacks were more willing to challenge segregation when they had the law behind them. In addition, new legal principles expounded in one circumstance can be applied in a different context to win new rights. For example, the right to privacy that was first expounded in a case permitting the use of contraceptives became the constitutional basis for a later case that made abortions legal. Constitutional principles can take on a life of their own, applying to issues beyond the specific circumstances in which they were first articulated. Finally, courts are an important check that the weak can appeal to in challenging those who have power. After all, even the powerful cannot do as they please but must submit to the rule of law. Presidents cannot simply ignore citizens' rights when ordering them to be detained; companies cannot pollute in violation of environmental laws; and employers cannot simply indulge their prejudices when hiring and firing workers. Citizens can appeal successfully to the courts to assert their rights of due process, the public can sue companies that violate environmental laws, and workers who are the victims of discrimination can go to court for restitution. Of course, successfully asserting these rights in court depends upon the resources people have outside of them. Still, as much as the law may reflect and confirm the powers that be, it can also be a tool to hold them accountable.

CHAPTER SUMMARY

Introduction
The courts are riddled with ambiguity. First, they are both powerful and weak in relation to the other branches of government. Courts have the power of judicial review, and federal judges enjoy lifetime tenures ensuring their independence. But the courts must depend on other branches of government to implement their decisions, and their decisions lack democratic legitimacy because judges are not elected. Second, the courts are both legal and political institutions. They are supposed to follow the letter of law but also must be mindful of the political context in which they decide cases. Third, the courts reflect both equality and inequality. Citizens have equal rights, but they also have unequal resources to take advantage of those rights. Finally, the courts can act as both a conservative and a progressive force. The law often reflects the interests of the powerful, but it is also a resource people can use to make legal claims against them.

A Dual Court System

All fifty states have their own court system, with their own laws, courts, and constitution, alongside that of the federal government. State courts are the real workhorses of the judicial system, because most cases are decided here rather than in federal courts. One important difference between state and federal courts is the way judges are selected. Most states elect judges, but federal judges are appointed.

The Federal Court System

The federal court system is divided into three tiers. District courts are the lowest level, where trials are held, followed by courts of appeals that hear cases on appeal from district courts. The U.S. Supreme Court is the highest court, the court of last resort. Federal judges are appointed by the president but must be confirmed by the Senate. Today, more judicial appointments to federal courts are challenged and delayed by the Senate than in the past, and the judicial appointment process to federal courts has become increasingly partisan and contentious.

The Supreme Court

The Supreme Court hears cases that are approved by four justices and often involve important constitutional issues. The Court has nine members and is led by the chief justice, who is only first among equals. Presidents appoint justices who share their values, but sometimes justices issue decisions that unpleasantly surprise those who appointed them. The Supreme Court has been activist at times, nullifying laws, and has shown restraint at others, deferring to Congress and upholding the consitutionality of its laws. For example, during the New Deal a conservative Court struck down legislation passed by a liberal Congress and administration. But the Court soon reversed itself in order to fend off critics and approved of New Deal legislation that greatly expanded the power of the federal government over business and the states.

The Modern Court: From Warren to Roberts

The Warren Court during the 1960s greatly expanded citizen rights and conceptions of political equality. But as the country shifted from liberal to conservative, so did the Court. The Rehnquist Court did not overturn many of the Warren Court's precedents, but it did limit them in practice. The current Court is led by Chief Justice Roberts and is now balanced between four moderates and four conservatives. In its short tenure so far, the Roberts Court has been friendly to business, which has pleased conservatives; but it is also skeptical of presidential claims of power, which has disappointed many of its supporters.

Politics by Lawsuit
More U.S. citizens bring suit in court than do those in other countries because American courts have relaxed restrictions on the kinds of cases they will accept and who can bring them. Consequently, the court's openness has encouraged groups to achieve through lawsuit what they could not achieve through legislation.

The Courts in Comparative Perspective: Incarceration Nation
Most countries do not have judicial review or elect judges, as is done in the United States. But the United States is most distinctive compared to other developed countries when it comes to its criminal justice system, which is more punitive, puts more people in prison, and still has the death penalty.

Critical Thinking Questions

1. In 1996 the U.S. Circuit Court of Appeals for the Fifth Circuit held that the equal protection clause of the Fourteenth Amendment did not permit schools to establish preferential, race-based admissions policies. Four years later, the Sixth Circuit took the opposite view and ruled that schools could consider race and ethnicity in admissions to achieve a diverse student body. Which ruling do you think should guide college admissions?

2. Should the Senate interpret its "advise and consent" role in judicial appointments as an equal partner to the president that does not hesitate to use its veto power, or should it restrict itself to an advisory role in which it defers to the president except in extraordinary circumstances?

3. Is judicial review compatible with democracy or antithetical to it? Supporters argue that it is necessary to curb majorities from depriving minorities of their rights. Opponents argue that it thwarts democracy by permitting judges to overrule the people's representatives.

4. Was Roosevelt correct in trying to pack the court? Some argue that Roosevelt threatened the constitutional system of checks and balances when he

did so. Others believe it was necessary because the Court thwarted popular legislation that was designed to address the problems posed by the Depression.

5. Should the courts have acceded to the Bush administrations' arguments that enemy combatants are not entitled to due process normally given to those charged with crimes? Or did the court rule correctly that President Bush exceeded his powers in depriving prisoners of their due process rights?

6. Are prisons an effective deterrent to crime? Is punishment an appropriate form of retributive justice for victims of crime? Under what circumstances, if any, should the death penalty be invoked?

Suggested Readings

Charles Epp, *The Rights Revolution: Lawyers, Activists and Supreme Court Cases in Comparative Perspective.* Chicago: University of Chicago Press, 1998.

Lee Epstein and Jack Knight, *The Choices Justices Make.* Washington, DC: Congressional Quarterly Press, 1998.

Linda Greenhouse, *Becoming Justice Blackmun: Harry Blackmun's Supreme Court Journey.* New York: Times Books, 2007.

Gerald N. Rosenberg, *The Hollow Hope: Can Courts Bring About Social Change?* Chicago: University of Chicago Press, 1991.

Bernard Schwartz, *A Basic History of the U.S. Supreme Court.* Princeton, NJ: Van Nostrand, 1968.

Jeffrey Toobin, *The Nine: Inside the Secret World of the Supreme Court.* New York: Doubleday, 2007.

PART IV

PUBLIC POLICY

I f political participation is the motor that drives the machine of political institutions, public policy charts the direction the machine moves. Some policies reduce inequality, and others generate new and deeper inequalities. Some extend the scope of public responsibility, and others contract government's role. Some advance extreme market capitalism, and others modify its operations. Some project American power abroad, and others offer a more modest global role. Part IV analyzes three of the most important areas in which the federal government acts to influence what the country does, how it acts, and the shape its economy and society will take. Economic policy creates the framework within which capitalism operates and allocates resources. Social policy and the welfare state determine how patterns of risk and the distribution of income and wealth will be modified by democratic decision making. Foreign policy orients how the United States deals with global affairs. Because these policy domains are so important, they are among the most important and contested sites of a politics of power.

Public policies are both a result and a cause. They result from battles among citizens, groups, and public officials. They help determine who gets what, where, and how. Policies also matter because they help shape future outcomes. They create arrangements that confer advantages to some political actors and disadvantages to others. Citizens come to new struggles over the proper scope and role for government armed with the weapons that previous policies have given them.

Public policy is not made in a vacuum. In the United States, it occurs in a context of tensions between capitalism and democracy, which are analyzed in Chapters 2 and 3, and within the settings of political participation and institutions that are analyzed in Chapters 4 through 8. Because policies are debated openly and determined within democratic institutions, outcomes often are responsive, at least in part, to what public opinion wishes and mobilized groups demand. At the same time, the democratic features of American government are constrained and sometimes distorted by the advantages capitalism confers, by patterns of inequality, and by uneven access to political institutions.

ECONOMIC POLICY

INTRODUCTION

For some Americans, the recession that began in 2008 has been distressing. Families have had to tighten their budgets and delay plans that involved major expenses, such as sending children to college or scheduling major surgery. For other Americans, the recession has been a catastrophe. Jobs have been lost, houses foreclosed, and cars repossessed. They have been left with no income and no assets. One group is less secure and less well off than before but is feeling lucky to have weathered the storm. The other group has absorbed the full fury of the recession.

The onset of recessions and the extent of their pain are influenced by economic policies. Indeed, no actions by government—except, perhaps, mobilizing for war—touch the lives of more Americans more profoundly than economic policies. Jobs, incomes, and standards of living depend on government performance in this area. Americans prosper when the government's economic policies succeed. They seek refuge and try to avoid becoming a victim when the policies do not work.

This chapter reviews economic policy through which the government sets the rules and influences the environment in which private production takes place. It concentrates on three ways that government tries to shape economic performance: fiscal policy, which entails taxes and spending by the government; monetary policy, which involves setting interest rates; and regulation, which mandates or prohibits certain activities.

THE GOVERNMENT AND THE ECONOMY

In 2008, governments at all levels—state, local, and federal governments taken together—collected $4 trillion in revenues and spent $4.7 trillion in outlays.

When revenues and expenditures are combined, the total amount of money passing through the government was about 60 percent of **gross domestic product (GDP)**, the total value of goods and services produced in the United States. These figures have given rise to the common belief that the government is too big, that it confiscates too much money in the form of taxes and spends too much in the form of wasteful programs. Indeed, government has grown dramatically since 1950, as Table 9.1 indicates. State, local, and federal government revenues accounted for just 20.7 percent of GDP in 1950, reached their high of 30.1 percent of GDP in 1999, and fell back to 28.1 percent in 2008 as a result of President George W. Bush's tax cuts and declining tax receipts due to the recession. When government outlays or expenditures at state, local, and federal levels are taken together, they were just 22.7 percent of GDP in 1950, were 29.2 percent of GDP fifty years later in 2000, and grew to 33 percent by 2008. As the

TABLE 9.1

GOVERNMENT SPENDING AS A PERCENTAGE OF GDP

Year	Total Government Receipts	Government Receipts % of GDP	Total Government Expenditures	Government Expenditures % of GDP
1950	56.4	20.7	62.0	22.7
1955	90.8	22.9	97.6	24.7
1960	130.7	25.2	135.8	26.2
1965	172.6	25.1	181.9	26.5
1970	286.5	28.3	298.3	29.5
1975	428.9	27.5	499.8	32.0
1980	756.7	27.8	853.5	31.3
1985	1,117.9	26.9	1,347.4	32.5
1990	1,585.7	27.6	1.862.1	32.5
1995	2,092.7	28.6	2,318.3	31.6
2000	3,006.2	31.0	2,834.0	29.2
2001	3,012.2	29.9	2,986.9	29.7
2002	2,887.1	27.8	3,209.9	30.9
2003	2,060.2	26.5	3,415.0	31.6
2004	3,040.0	26.4	3,594.8	31.2
2005	2,421.2	28.0	3,846.9	31.4
2006	3,758.3	28.9	4,115.0	31.6
2007	3,999.4	29.3	4,297.3	31.5
2008	3,995.2	28.1	4,669.9	33.0

SOURCE: *Historical Tables: Budget of the U.S. Government, Fiscal Year 2011* (Washington, DC: Office of Management and Budget, 2010), 21–26, tables 1.1 and 1.2.

activities of government have increased from 1950 to the present, especially in the realms of social welfare and defense, so have the expenses and revenues to pay for them.

Despite these increases and frequent complaints about "big government," the size of the public sector in the United States is actually quite small when viewed comparatively. For example, the tax burden on American citizens is actually quite light compared to that in other advanced industrial countries. The United States collects a lower proportion of its GDP in the form of taxes than any other advanced industrialized country (Figure 9.1). It also spends less as a percent of GDP than any other affluent country except for Australia, Ireland, Japan, and Switzerland (Figure 9.2).

The smaller public sector in the United States, both in terms of revenue collected and money spent, is reflected in leaner benefits and fewer public services available to Americans. For example, in many other rich democracies, the

FIGURE 9.1

TOTAL ESTIMATED TAX REVENUE IN 2006 AS PERCENT OF GDP

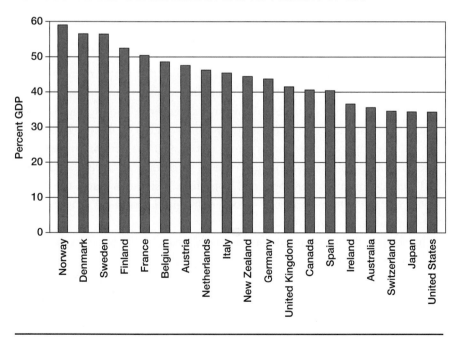

SOURCE: *Government at a Glance 2009* (Paris: OECD, 2009), table 1.1.

FIGURE 9.2

GENERAL GOVERNMENT DISBURSEMENTS AS PERCENT OF GDP
(2006 OR CLOSEST YEAR AVAILABLE)

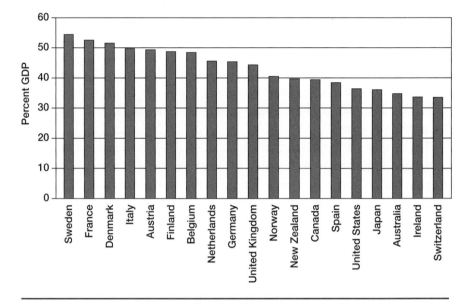

SOURCE: *Government at a Glance 2009* (Paris: OECD, 2009), table 4.1.

government either provides child-care services directly or gives more generous subsidies for child care than American families receive.

The comparatively small size of the government in relation to the economy is also apparent when one measures it by jobs as well as by money. Public sector employees in the United States comprised about 15 percent of total employment in 2008, about 23 million government workers at all levels—state, local, and federal—out of a workforce of 137 million. Again, this places the United States near the bottom compared to other affluent democracies in terms of its share of public sector employment.

Not only is the government comparatively small, but it also lacks the power to manage the economy effectively and influence the behavior of private firms significantly. Corporate managers in the United States enjoy more autonomy to run their business without interference from the government than they do elsewhere.[1] Compared to their counterparts in other advanced economies, U.S. firms are subject to fewer and less invasive government regulations that proscribe or require certain activities. Nowhere else, for example, does the absence of government regulations give employers so much power to fire or lay off workers and leave them unprotected from summary job loss.

Alongside weak regulatory controls, the government also relies on indirect mechanisms, notably fiscal and monetary policy, to intervene in the economy. The government uses **fiscal policy** to manage the economy by adjusting the government's budget, and it uses **monetary policy** to influence the economy by adjusting interest rates. But the ability of policymakers to effectively utilize even these tools is undermined by their institutional design. Control over fiscal policy is divided between Congress and the president; control over monetary policy is vested in the Federal Reserve Board (popularly known as the Fed). Because fiscal and monetary policies are assigned to different institutions that are independent of each other, there is no assurance that fiscal and monetary policy will be coordinated—that is, that they will push in the same direction at the same time.[2]

Like foreign and domestic policy, economic policy is subject to a politics of power. In response to the recent recession, the government has flexed its economic muscles and even developed new ones. The government's modesty with respect to the normal measures of size must now be put alongside a new aggressiveness it displays in coping with a steep rise in unemployment and a decline in economic activity. The government has brokered marriages between failing and healthy banks, supervised the reorganization of the automobile industry,

---

WHAT DO YOU THINK?

What Is the Right Size for Government?

Where should the line between governments and markets be drawn? Are Americans better or worse off because government spending and revenues account for such a small percentage of gross national product (GNP) compared to that for other affluent democracies? Some argue that too much government intervention in the economy chokes off innovation, promotes inefficiency, and leads to decision making based on what yields the biggest dividends for politicians, not for society. Others believe that the market is too unstable and leads to outcomes that are too unequal without the moderating and guiding hand of government. Are Americans better off with less or more government?

become the majority owner of mortgage companies, and guaranteed corporate loans. Policies of minimal intervention based on the premise that government was the problem created a financial meltdown to which government is now depended on to provide as the solution.

FISCAL POLICY

Fiscal policy manipulates the total amount of government revenue and spending so as to manage overall demand in the economy. Government can either stimulate the economy by running a **budget deficit** or restrain it by running a **budget surplus**. Budget deficits pump money into the economy, encouraging more spending, while surpluses take money out, discouraging investment and consumption. Fiscal policy envisions government budgets as thermostats, adjusting automatically to counteract the economy's market swings. But the budget is more than a fiscal tool to bring the economy into balance, cooling it down when **inflation** gets too high and revving it up when employment gets too low. It also establishes the priorities and values of the government. The budget depicts in black and white who the winners and losers in society will be. It reveals relationships of power in society by the way it distributes costs and benefits among different groups. Some groups will shoulder a larger share of the tax burden while others will receive more in government benefits. For example, the shift in the politics of power from President Bush to President Obama is evident in their budgets. The budgets submitted by President Bush gave the wealthiest Americans the largest tax cuts, but President Obama's first budget proposed to impose the largest tax increases on them. Spending priorities also shifted as Bush's budgets devoted proportionally more money for defense while Obama's budget called for a higher proportion of spending for health care and education.

The budget process is a long, difficult, and intensely political affair that involves partisan conflict between Democrats and Republicans as well as institutional conflict between the legislative and executive branches, jurisdictional conflict within each of these branches, and interest-group conflict among an immense array of pressure groups. The budget process begins in the Executive Office of the President (described in Chapter 6), where the Office of Management and Budget (OMB) formulates the president's budget. OMB negotiates with federal agencies to reconcile differences between their requests and the president's projections. It then submits a draft budget to the president for review and approval. Presidents then make whatever changes they think are necessary

The production of President Obama's 2010 budget by the U.S. Government Printing Office.

before presenting their budget proposal to Congress. The 2010 budget that President Obama submitted to Congress for consideration consisted of five volumes and weighed in at over eleven pounds.

The president's budget, reflecting the administration's preferences and priorities, becomes the point of departure for consideration by Congress. According to the Constitution, Congress has the power to make laws regarding taxing and spending, and it can thus reject or amend the president's budget. The president and Congress, in effect, share power over the budget; conflict is inevitable between them as each branch tries to impose its own priorities. Conflict over the budget between the two branches of government is particularly intense when the presidency and Congress are controlled by different parties. In 1995, when Bill Clinton, a Democrat, occupied the White House and Congress was controlled by the Republicans, disagreement over the budget led to a temporary shutdown of the federal government. Federal offices and national parks were closed for twenty-six days because without a budget agreement between Congress and the president, there was no authority to pay federal workers to keep them open.[3]

Relations between Congress and the president do not often deteriorate to the point of shutting down the federal government for lack of funds. Rather, the president's budget becomes the starting point for consideration by Congress, which begins when the budget committees in both the House and the Senate adopt a budget resolution. This specifies the total amount of money the government intends to raise and spend. Expenditures are distributed across twenty broad categories of government activity, such as defense, energy, and agriculture. The budget resolution is a general plan of spending and revenue targets. Committees within Congress are then charged with amending existing law to reflect tax and spending changes consistent with the totals called for in the joint budget resolution. "For example," Daniel J. Palazzolo writes, "it is one thing to agree that $35 billion in tax breaks will go towards tuition assistance for higher education; it is another thing to determine who is eligible, how much each person will be eligible for, how the tax credits will be structured and the like."[4] The appropriations committees in both the House and Senate review these changes and stipulate the actual funding levels for particular programs with an eye to keeping total spending within the guidelines set by the joint budget resolution. Appropriations bills are then submitted to presidents for their signature or veto.[5]

The final budget agreed to by the president and Congress is simply an estimate of what the government will spend and how much revenue it will collect. No one really knows for sure, for example, what the final cost of disaster relief will be in any given year, whether the United States will be in a war that it did not anticipate fighting when the budget was first drafted, or exactly how much revenue certain taxes will raise. Budgets are intentions that the future sometimes respects and at other times mocks.[6]

TAXES

Nobody likes taxes. Americans, like citizens in other countries, complain that they pay too much, that the tax system is too complicated, and that the system is unfair.[7] Yet, taxes are necessary to pay for government: for the services we receive from it, such as police protection; and for the benefits we collect from it, such as Social Security. Taxes are the oil that keeps the machinery of government running. Just as no one likes paying money to fill up their car with gas, no one likes paying taxes. But cars cannot run without gas, and government does not work without taxes. "Taxes," Chief Justice Oliver Wendell Holmes once wrote, are "the price we pay for civilized society."[8]

Tax policy is highly contentious as groups seek to influence what the overall level of taxation should be, what types of taxes should be imposed, and what share of these taxes different groups should pay. All these aspects of tax policy have changed over time as a result of political conflict. Federal tax receipts rose steadily from 1983 to 2000 to 20 percent of GDP. But President Bush's tax cuts reversed trends, and tax revenues fell to just 16.5 percent of GDP by 2003. The last time the ratio of federal taxes to the economy was that low was in 1955. Tax receipts proceeded to recover somewhat; but the recent recession reduced economic activity, and tax receipts fell back to 17.7 percent of GDP in 2008.

Bush's tax cuts precipitated a decline in federal revenue that contributed to rising federal deficits. The deficit is expected to rise even faster under President Obama due to all his spending programs to revive the economy in the midst of recession. Deficits require the government to borrow money to pay its bills, and creditors charge interest for the money they lend it. The government then must dip into current revenues to pay off interest charges on the debt it owes, thus leaving less money in the budget to support vital services such as health care, environmental protection, and homeland security. In fiscal year 2008, the federal government paid $226.6 billion in interest to holders of the national debt. This was 8.5 percent of all federal outlays, more than the federal government spent on any agency or department except for defense and health and human services.

Deficits are not necessarily bad; at times, they are even appropriate. It depends on how well the economy is doing and what the government spends the money on. Governments can borrow money and invest in programs that contribute to social welfare and economic growth, or they can borrow money for programs that have little payoff except to the special interests that receive it. Some investments yield a high social and economic return that makes borrowing money worthwhile; others generate little value and only add to the debt burden of future generations. Whether deficits are good or bad depends on the state of the economy as well as on how wisely the money is invested.

The amount of taxes the government collects as a proportion of GDP has changed, but so has the composition of taxes. There are different streams of tax revenue. State and local governments, for example, rely primarily upon sales and property taxes to raise revenue. The federal government, however, relies upon different kinds of taxes to raise money. As Table 9.2 indicates, the federal government raises more money from individual income taxes than it does from any other revenue source. From 1950 to the present, it has collected between 40 and 50 percent of all its money from this one source. Although the proportion of all federal revenues collected from individual income taxes has remained fairly steady, the same cannot be said of other revenue streams. The contribution of corporate income taxes to total tax revenues has declined over time. Corporate income taxes accounted for one-quarter of all federal tax receipts in 1950. By 2008, they accounted for less than half that amount: only 12.1 percent of federal revenue. The federal tax rate for big corporations is supposed to be 35 percent on profits, but loopholes, credits, and accounting gimmickry have cut the effective corporate tax rate to about 20 percent. Sometimes tax shelters permit corporations to avoid taxes altogether.

Along with corporate taxes, the proportion of taxes the federal government raises through excise taxes (i.e., federal sales taxes on such items as alcohol, cigarettes, and gasoline) has also fallen. The federal government collected about one-fifth of its money through these kinds of consumption taxes in 1950. By 2008, they amounted to a negligible 2.7 percent of total revenue.

The decline in the proportion of federal revenue raised through corporate and excise taxes has been compensated for by a rise in the proportion of taxes

TABLE 9.2

PERCENTAGE COMPOSITION OF TAX RECEIPTS BY SOURCE

Year	Individual Income Tax	Corporate Income Tax	Social Insurance and Retirement Receipts	Excise Tax	Other
1950	39.9	26.5	11.0	19.1	3.4
1955	43.9	27.3	12.0	14.0	2.8
1960	44.0	23.2	15.9	12.6	4.2
1965	41.8	21.8	19.0	12.5	4.9
1970	46.9	17.0	23.0	8.1	4.9
1975	43.9	14.6	30.3	5.9	5.4
1980	47.2	12.5	30.5	4.7	5.1
1985	45.6	8.4	36.1	4.9	5.1
1990	45.2	9.1	36.8	3.4	5.5
1995	43.7	11.6	35.8	4.3	4.6
2000	49.6	10.2	32.2	3.4	4.5
2001	49.9	7.6	34.8	3.3	4.3
2002	46.3	8.0	37.8	3.6	4.3
2003	44.5	7.4	40.0	3.8	4.3
2004	43.0	10.1	39.0	3.7	4.2
2005	43.0	12.9	36.9	3.4	3.8
2006	43.4	14.7	34.8	3.1	4.1
2007	45.3	14.4	33.9	2.5	3.9
2008	45.4	12.1	35.7	2.7	4.2

SOURCE: *Historical Tables: Budget of the U.S. Government, Fiscal Year 2011* (Washington, DC: Office of Management and Budget, 2010), table 2.2.

collected by social insurance receipts. The Social Security payroll tax, which finances retirement and health benefits for the elderly and disabled, accounts for the largest portion of these contributions. Social insurance contributions have replaced corporate income taxes as the second-largest revenue stream to the federal government, after individual income taxes. Social insurance contributions amounted to about 10 percent of all taxes in 1950. In 2008, they amounted to more than one-third of all tax receipts.[9]

Taxes are collected from many different sources. They are also distributed among many different groups. Some pay more than others in taxes. Some argue that the tax system should be **progressive**, requiring the rich to pay a larger proportion of their income in the form of taxes. Others believe the tax system should be **regressive**, that tax rates should not increase as personal income rises. As Figure 9.3 reveals, when all types of state and federal taxes are considered together—federal and state income taxes, Social Security contributions, sales

FIGURE 9.3

SPREADING THE TAX BITE AROUND

Taking all types of government taxes into consideration, the tax burden, as a percentage of pretax income, is roughly the same for all income groups.

Income group	Average pretax income		Total government tax receipts		As a percentage of income
Bottom 20%	$7,946	▪	$1,449	▮	18%
Second 20%	20,319	▪▪	2,847	▪	14
Middle 20%	35,536	▪▪▪	6,622	▪	16
Fourth 20%	56,891	▪▪▪▪	9,835	▪▪	17
Top 20%	116,666	▪▪▪▪▪▪	21,632	▪▪▪	19

Government receipts include federal and state income taxes, Social Security contributions (employee's share), property taxes, utility taxes, federal and state tobacco taxes, federal and state alcohol taxes, federal and state gasoline taxes, and state sales tax.

SOURCE: From Daniel Altman, "Doubling Up of Taxation Isn't Limited to Dividends," *New York Times*, 21 January 2003, C1. Data from Consumer Expenditure Survey of the Bureau of Labor Statistics; R. J. Reynolds Tobacco; Beer Institute; Wine America; Wine and Spirits Wholesalers of America; American Petroleum Institute; Tax Foundation.

taxes, property taxes, and others—the distribution of the tax burden among the rich, poor, and middle class is quite similar. That is, for each quintile of income, earners pay the same proportion of their income in the form of taxes. The bottom 20 percent of income earners paid $1,449 in taxes, or 18 percent of their average pretax income, while the top 20 percent paid $21,623 of their average pretax income in taxes—just 1 percent more than the bottom fifth paid. All income groups pay roughly the same proportion of their average pretax income in the form of taxes when all different kinds of taxes are lumped together.[10]

Finally, tax policy is not simply about how much money to raise, how to do it, and who should pay for it. It is also about creating incentives for certain types of behavior by offering tax exemptions, rebates, and deductions. For example, the government encourages home ownership by permitting home-owners to deduct the interest they pay on their mortgage from their taxes. It encourages investment by permitting businesses to deduct from their taxes the cost of depreciation for equipment. It encourages people to save for retirement by permitting citizens to shield income they contribute to a retirement account from taxation. That is, government often makes policy by subsidizing certain activities through the tax code. Policymakers often prefer to offer what are called **tax expenditures**—public subsidies through favored tax treatment—rather than authorize normal expenditures for the same purpose. The cost is the same to taxpayers in either case, whether it takes the form of direct spending or tax revenue that would otherwise be collected. But the political consequences are very different. Making policy through the tax code by giving favored tax treatment to certain activities is not as visible as new spending for programs. The costs of tax expenditures are diffuse, and their effects not easily traceable. Policymakers prefer what Jacob Hacker called the "subterranean politics" of tax expenditures over appropriating money for new programs because they are less likely to arouse conflict.[11] As a result, the use of tax expenditures as a way to make policy has increased. This has resulted in a very complex tax code that is now filled with an array of exemptions, deductions, and rebates to encourage citizens and businesses to act in certain ways. The tax code that was once perceived simply as a way to raise government revenue has now become a more concealed and more frequent means by which government makes policy.

SPENDING

Taxes are one side of the government budget. The other side is composed of spending. Political conflict is as pervasive and bitter over spending as it is over taxes. Groups struggle over how much money the government should spend and what it should be spent on. Evidence of these conflicts is apparent in how government expenditures have changed over time. Federal expenditures that were just $42 billion (just 15.6 percent of GDP) in 1950 had increased to almost $3 trillion, or 21 percent of GDP, by 2008. The federal government spends more today because it does more than it did sixty years ago. Social Security coverage was not as broad as it is today, Medicare for seniors and Medicaid for the poor did not exist, and such offices as the Environmental Protection Agency had not yet been created.

The federal government accounts for about two-thirds of all government expenditures, and state and local governments spend the rest. Just as the revenue sources from which the federal government raises money have changed, so have the categories in which the national government spends it. Some federal activities that once captured a large share of the federal budget now get less, and other activities now get more. Consider, for instance, how spending for national defense and the welfare state—the two largest charges on the federal budget—have changed through the years (Table 9.3). Not only do defense and the welfare state together capture more of all federal money than they did in the past, but the balance between them has changed dramatically. In 1954, in the midst of the Cold War, 69 percent of all federal outlays were devoted to defense spending. From that peak, the share of federal spending committed to the military declined steadily to 16.1 percent in 1999, until increases tied to the wars in Afghanistan and Iraq saw military spending increase to 20.7 percent of federal spending in 2008. In the interim, the percentage of the federal budget dedicated to welfare state spending, which includes federal expenses for health care, education, income support, Social Security, and veterans' benefits, increased considerably. Welfare state expenses that comprised only 15.6 percent of the federal budget in 1954 accounted for nearly two-thirds (63.6 percent) of all federal spending by 2008.

Although the balance between welfare and warfare has shifted over time, these two items, along with paying interest on the debt, accounted for 93 percent of all federal outlays in 2008. All the other tasks the federal government performs, from maintaining the national parks to paying the salaries of federal judges, are accounted for by the remaining 7 percent of federal spending.

Another way of looking at how federal money is distributed is to divide it between mandatory and discretionary accounts as opposed to separating expenditures by government activity or function. Two-thirds of all federal spending is mandatory. Spending for these programs, Daniel J. Palazzolo writes, is "governed by formulas or criteria set forth in authorizing legislation" passed by Congress "rather than by appropriations."[12] These programs are the result of

TABLE 9.3

FEDERAL OUTLAYS FOR DEFENSE AND THE WELFARE STATE (IN MILLIONS OF DOLLARS)

Year	Defense	% of Federal Expenditures	Welfare State	% of Federal Expenditures
1954	49,266	69.5	13,076	18.5
1955	42,729	62.4	14,908	21.8
1960	48,130	52.2	26,184	28.4
1965	50,620	42.8	26,576	30.9
1970	81,692	41.8	75,349	38.5
1975	86,509	26.0	173,245	52.1
1980	133,995	22.7	313,374	53.0
1985	252,748	26.7	471,822	49.9
1990	299,331	23.9	619,329	49.4
1995	272,066	17.9	923,765	60.9
2000	294,495	16.5	1,115,481	62.4
2001	305,500	16.4	1,194,409	64.1
2002	348,555	17.3	1,317,437	65.5
2003	404,920	18.8	1,417,707	65.7
2004	455,847	19.9	1,485,870	64.8
2005	495,326	20.0	1,586,122	64.2
2006	521,840	19.7	1,672,076	63.0
2007	551,286	20.2	1,758,493	64.4
2008	616,097	20.7	1,895,740	63.6

SOURCE: *Historical Tables: Budget of the U.S. Government, Fiscal Year 2009* (Washington, DC: U.S. Government Printing Office, 2010), 47–55.

previous commitments that Congress is obligated to meet. For example, **mandatory spending** includes payments on the national debt. To retain its access to credit, the government must pay off its debt when it comes due. But the most expensive form of mandatory spending takes the form of **entitlement programs**. Entitlement programs provide benefits to citizens as long as they meet certain eligibility requirements. Their cost is open ended. The government will provide benefits to all those who qualify, regardless of how many there are or what the final cost may be. Social Security, for example, is an entitlement program. Citizens who have contributed to the Social Security program receive Social Security checks from the government when they apply and become eligible. Food stamps and Medicare are other examples of entitlement programs.

Mandatory spending consumes so much money that not much is left over for discretionary spending. Unlike entitlement programs, discretionary spending is under the jurisdiction of the House and Senate Appropriations Committees, which provide authority for "federal agencies to incur obligations and make payments out of the treasury for specified purposes."[13] The largest expense of any discretionary program is defense. Defense spending consumes one-half of all discretionary spending by the federal government. The other half is composed of nondefense spending, which includes everything from highway maintenance to grants and loans for those attending college to managing the national forests. The small share of federal outlays devoted to discretionary programs means that it is very hard for Congress to direct expenditures through its annual appropriations process. Only one-third of all federal spending is really up for grabs each year. It also means that it is difficult for Congress to control spending without reducing the cost of entitlement programs. Government outlays increase each year because the cost of entitlement programs grows each year. And that growth is automatic as more people qualify for such programs as Social Security and Medicare, the two largest and most expensive entitlement programs.

MONETARY POLICY

Along with fiscal policy, the government tries to manage the economy through monetary policy. Monetary policy attempts to fine-tune the economy by manipulating interest rates, the cost of money. High interest rates tend to slow down the economy by discouraging spending. Low interest rates, on the other hand, encourage borrowing and spending by making credit cheap and easy to obtain. Like fiscal policy, monetary policy is used to counteract tendencies toward economic instability. If the economy is tending toward inflation or excessive demand, raising interest rates will cool it down. Conversely, if a recession is likely to occur and demand is slack, reducing interest rates will help revive the economy by making loans more attractive for consumers who want to purchase new goods and for businesses that want to make new investments.

But manipulating interest rates is not simply about trying to counteract tendencies toward inflation and recession. Like fiscal policy, monetary policy affects different groups in different ways. For example, affluent people with savings in the bank generally benefit from high interest rates—tight money—because it increases the value of their investments, but the opposite is often true for working-class people, who are more likely to go into debt than to have savings. Lower interest rates on loans reduce the interest charges they have to pay on their debt. Similarly, entrepreneurs who need credit to start or expand a business do better when interest rates are low, whereas their lenders profit more when

The Federal Reserve Building in Washington, D.C.

interest rates are high. Thus, whether to err on the side of setting interest rates high or low is not simply a technical matter of managing the economy but a political one of rewarding some groups at the expense of others. A key question then is who decides, and on what basis, if the economy needs higher or lower interest rates?

Monetary policy is in the hands of the Federal Reserve Board, whose mandate is to maximize employment, stabilize prices, and moderate long-term interest rates. The Federal Reserve Board (or Fed) determines the rate of interest that the Federal Reserve Bank charges American banks to borrow funds. When the Federal Reserve Bank raises the rate it charges banks for loans, banks increase the rate they charge their customers to borrow money. The result is that fewer loans are made, and economic growth slows. Similarly, when the Fed lowers the interest rate it charges banks for loans, banks can give their customers easier credit terms, increasing the flow of money in the economy. For example, in 2008 as unemployment rose and stock prices dropped sharply, the Fed reduced interest rates at the fastest pace in its history to keep up—at one point even hurriedly arranging an unscheduled meeting to cut rates. The discount or interest rate it charges banks dropped from 5.75 percent in August 2007 to an unprecedented 0.50 percent by December 2008. By dropping rates so low and so fast, the Fed was trying to revive the economy by virtually giving money away free to banks in hopes of easing the lending terms that banks charge their customers.

Aside from lending money to banks, the Fed affects the money supply via open market operations, in which the Federal Reserve Bank buys or sells government bonds. Bonds are loans that the government promises to repay with interest when the debt is due. Buying government bonds puts more money into circulation; selling bonds withdraws money from the economy. Finally, the Fed influences the money supply by setting the reserve rate that banks must hold on deposits. The reserve rate is the proportion of money that banks must keep on hand in the event that depositors withdraw funds from their accounts. An increase in the reserve rate means that banks have to hold more of their funds in reserve and thereby have less money to lend out. This situation decreases the money supply. Lowering the reserve rate has the opposite effect. It permits banks to lend out a higher proportion of their deposits as loans to creditors, thereby increasing the money supply. These different methods the Fed uses to manipulate the money supply send ripples through the economy, affecting the direction of the stock and bond market, the rate of interest that banks charge on mortgages, and the rate of interest that credit card companies charge on unpaid balances. But the ripples continue far beyond, affecting whether companies hire more employees or prune their payrolls, whether wages and salaries go up or down, and, most generally, whether the economy expands or contracts. The fact that so little is known about the operation of the Federal Reserve Board is an extraordinary feature of American politics. Henry Ford Sr. once observed, "It is well enough that the people of the nation do not understand our banking and monetary system for, if they did, I believe there would be a revolution before tomorrow morning."[14]

According to journalist William Greider, the Fed is "the crucial anomaly at the very core of representative government, an uncomfortable contradiction with the civic mythology of self-government."[15] When the Fed was created in 1913, it was deliberately insulated from democratic pressures and the influence of elected politicians. Of all the government agencies, the Fed enjoys the most political independence from both Congress and the president. It does not have to depend on Congress for money, because it is self-financing through the interest it collects on government bonds it holds; and members of its board of governors are appointed for lengthy fourteen-year terms. It enjoys this enviable position because, ostensibly, monetary policy—adjusting interest rates—is a technical matter beyond politics. The Fed was deliberately given substantial autonomy in order to insulate monetary policy from democratic control. The fear (not completely unjustified) was that the government would simply print money because it was politically expedient to do so. Easy credit greases the wheels of commerce but may also lead to inflationary spirals and speculative bubbles. On the other hand, putting monetary policy beyond democratic accountability does not mean that politics has disappeared. In the absence of democratic control, monetary policy may be captured by banks, which have the most interest in it.

The Fed tends to adopt the perspective of banks because they are its primary constituency: over two thousand banks are members of the Federal Reserve System, and most Federal Reserve Board members either previously worked for banks or are economists trained in finance. The Fed, after all, is a bank itself, the central bank of the United States. Moreover, representatives from the banking community participate and vote when the Fed deliberates over monetary policy. Interest rate targets are set by the Federal Open Market Committee (FOMC). The FOMC is comprised of the seven members or governors who form the Federal Reserve Board, in addition to the presidents of the twelve District Federal Reserve Banks. Commercial banks in each district select the president of each Federal Reserve Bank, and five of the presidents have voting privileges on the FOMC. In 1993, Representative Henry B. Gonzalez, chair of the House Committee on Banking, wrote an open letter to President Clinton deploring the presence of bankers on the FOMC and the lack of influence the public has over its composition. Gonzalez wrote:

> In general, the Federal Reserve decision makers are bankers or friends of bankers. Decision makers representing the concerns of agriculture, small business, labor, and community groups are almost unheard of. . . . Last week, the Fed selected one of their [sic] own, William J. McDonough, as president of the New York Federal Reserve Bank. Mr. McDonough's qualifications and his views on monetary policy . . . will not be debated in public. His expertise in central bank monetary policy will not be questioned in Senate confirmation hearings. However, because he has been selected through the Fed's internal private mechanisms, he will manage our nation's money supply without ever going before the American people or their representatives.[16]

But the direct influence of representatives from the banking community actually participating in and voting in policymaking discussions of the FOMC is only insurance. The Fed tends to promote the interests of banks because it believes that what is good for banks is good for the economy. After all, banks supply money to the industrial muscles of the economy. If the muscles don't receive the blood they need, they will not work. Thus, there is a structural basis for why the Fed supports banks. The health of the economy, the Fed believes, depends on the health of the banks that pump money through it.

Nowhere was this structural dependence on banks more apparent than in how the Fed responded to the recent financial crisis when major Wall Street investment banks threatened to go under. Willem H. Buiter, a professor of finance at the London School of Economics, argues that the Fed was so accommodating to Wall Street's distress—offering to come to its rescue in exchange for very little—because it has "internalized the objectives, concerns, world views and fears of the financial community."[17] The Fed wasn't bought, blackmailed, or bribed when it offered to save Citigroup, Bear Stearns, Bank of America, and other financial institutions that were about to collapse due to bad loans they had made. Rather, the Fed provided a lifeline because it has internalized the "objectives, interests, and perceptions" of the financial community as its own. It viewed the needs of the broader economy through the needs of the banking community it was supposed to regulate.

The independence and authority of the Federal Reserve has elevated its chair to what some regard as the second most powerful position in the government. No one earned that reputation more than Alan Greenspan, who chaired the Fed from 1987 to 2006. He was called "the Maestro" and received rock star coverage for the way he guided the economy through recessions and financial crises. But Greenspan's tenure as chair has come under more critical scrutiny lately. It's as if the curtain has been pulled back, revealing the wizard to be an ordinary mortal at best, or a fraud at worst. He endorsed Bush's tax cuts, which contributed to the deficit, kept interest rates too low and thus contributed to the bubbles in the housing and credit markets, and opposed regulations that would have prevented banks from taking on too much risk. As the recession deepened, even Greenspan came to admit "a flaw in [his] model of how . . . the world works" when he told the House Committee on Oversight and Government Reform that "Those of us who looked to the self-interest of lending institutions to protect shareholders' equity—myself included—are in a state of shocked disbelief."[18] In other words, Greenspan acknowledged that government regulation was necessary and that banks could not be trusted to regulate themselves, because the self-interest of banks is not enough to ensure safe, prudent lending practices.

In 2006, President Bush appointed Ben Bernanke, Chair of the President's Council of Economic Advisors, to succeed Greenspan as the new chair of the Fed. Bernanke was a protégé of Greenspan's, but he has diverged from many of Greenspan's policies in response to the meltdown of the financial sector and the gravest economic crisis since the Great Depression of the 1930s. First, Bernanke reversed course and now supports more regulation of the financial sector. Second, he is more tolerant of dissent within FOMC meetings and more candid in explaining Fed policy than Greenspan ever was. Finally, he has transformed the Fed into the lender of last resort. To avert financial panic, The Fed extended loans to banks and insurance companies that were about to collapse but were deemed too big and too interconnected to fail. But then the Fed proceeded to extend credit to a wider variety of patients that were not in critical condition at all, but were still sick because the normal medicine the Fed prescribed was no longer working. Even though the Fed cut interest rates to almost zero, this was not enough to get credit flowing. Businesses could not get credit lines they needed to meet payrolls, make purchases, or roll over debt. The Fed proceeded to purchase assets other than traditional treasury bills in order to pump money into the economy. It offered loans to companies in exchange for stock; bought securities containing home mortgages, auto, credit card, student and small business loans; lent money to banks; and guaranteed money market funds that underwrite short-term loans to businesses. The amount of money devoted to these purchases and investment guarantees—over $5 trillion—far outstrips any bailout money approved by Congress. After learning that the Fed had committed the U.S. government to investments in the real estate, insurance, banking, automobile, and other industries, one Republican was so appalled that he complained, "I thought I woke up in France. But, no, it turned out it was socialism here in the United States of America."[19]

This is not your father's Fed anymore. The Fed has become more active, stretching its authority into new realms. It has gone beyond its traditional tools of influencing the money supply to engage in more regulatory oversight of the financial sector, such as engineering mergers of failing with healthy banks. It has improvised and been so aggressive in pumping money into the economy that its activity blurs the line between monetary and fiscal policy. The new types of investments the Fed has made—purchasing stock in companies, issuing short-term loans to businesses, and making investment guarantees—are the kinds of policy decisions normally reserved for Congress and the president. But this new assertiveness is not without risk to the Fed. As the Fed becomes more involved in the process of picking winners by deciding which industries to support and which ones not to, it becomes more of a target for lobbying and congressional appeals. It loses its sense of majesty, standing above the fray, and jeopardizes its independence.

WHAT DO YOU THINK?

Should the Fed Be More Democratically Accountable?

Critics of the Fed's independence believe that it is too important not to be accountable to the public. Moreover, in the absence of accountability to Congress and the president, the Fed is responsive to the interests of banks by default. Defenders of the Fed believe that greater accountability to Congress and the president will lead to bad policy. The Fed will not act prudently if it has to answer to public officials. It will always keep the money flowing, which will lead to inflation in order to satisfy political leaders. Should the Fed's independence be protected or should it be more democratically accountable?

Even though the Fed has developed new muscles, it still uses them for the same purposes. It continues to identify the welfare of the economy with the welfare of Wall Street investment houses and banks. The links between the Fed and the financial community remain strong. Until May 2009, the chair of the New York Federal Reserve Bank (the most important regional reserve bank) also served on the board of directors of the investment bank Goldman Sachs. With such close exchange of personnel and shared worldviews, it is little surprise that the Fed demanded little in return for the money and guarantees it provided the financial community. Many Wall Street executives got to keep their exorbitant compensation packages, and their companies were able to sell their toxic debt to the Fed and receive guarantees against losses from it. The change from Greenspan to Bernanke has not changed the way the Fed interprets its mandate to maximize employment and stabilize prices as one that depends upon the "stability, well-being and profitability of the financial sector."[20] It still assumes that what's good for Wall Street is good for America.

REGULATION

Fiscal and monetary policies affect economic actors indirectly by influencing the conditions in which they operate. Policymakers use fiscal and monetary policies to create a predictable environment of stable prices and high employment levels, so that economic actors can plan with some certainty about the future. But government can also use more direct means to influence what economic actors do. When authorized by Congress to do so, the bureaucracy can engage in regulation, setting explicit rules of behavior that firms and workers must follow. Regulations dictate what economic actors can and cannot do. For example, regulations stipulate that firms cannot sell products that are unsafe, issue misleading financial statements, engage in deceptive advertising, or discriminate. Other regulations require firms to accurately label foods and drugs, post safety notices, and pay a minimum wage to their workers.

Complaints about "big government" often refer to regulation. Conservatives and business grumble that the American economy is overregulated. They suggest that rules governing firms are proliferating, imposing unnecessary costs in terms of compliance, discouraging innovation with a maze of bureaucratic requirements, and promoting inefficiency by distorting the normal operation of the market. But, again—just as we saw previously with regard to the United States having a rather small public sector—when viewed comparatively, the United States is one of the least regulated markets in the world. According to the Fraser Institute, a conservative Canadian think tank, the hand of regulation in the United States is not heavy at all, but exceedingly light. The United States ranked seventh out of more than one hundred countries surveyed in terms of having the freest credit, labor, and product markets.[21]

The government issues regulations when markets do not work to protect the public interest and when markets fail to promote or work against values that society treasures, such as clean air, safe workplaces, reliable products, and honest business practices. Unregulated markets where firms compete to maximize their profits will not produce these conditions by themselves. Instead, regulations imposed by the government are necessary to create them.

The authority of the federal government to issue regulations governing economic actors stems from the power the Constitution gave Congress to regulate commerce among states and with foreign nations. But this power was largely dormant until the late nineteenth century when, under popular pressure, Congress created the Interstate Commerce Commission (ICC) in 1887 to regulate railroad rates and routes. This office was followed by a host of regulatory agencies, created by Congress in response to popular outcries about the abuse of corporate power. In 1914, Congress established the Federal Trade Commission (FTC) to prevent firms from discouraging competition and to protect consumers from unfair business practices. The Food and Drug Administration (FDA) was created in 1931 to prevent firms from selling tainted food and harmful drugs, and the Securities and Exchange Commission (SEC) was created in 1934 to prevent investors from being defrauded by stock market manipulation. But these efforts often led to the opposite result of what reformers intended. Officials in government agencies developed close ties with the industries they were supposed to regulate as they engaged in day-to-day business with them, became familiar with industry executives, and were hired away by them.[22] The FDA became responsive to the pharmaceutical industry and the SEC to Wall Street brokerage houses. In 2008, whistleblowers alerted Congress that the Federal Aviation Administration (FAA) was permitting airlines to fly planes that had not passed mandatory safety inspections. Permitting airlines to skip inspections was part of the FAA's Customer Service Initiative, through which the agency defined its customer as the airlines and tried to save them money as opposed to serving the flying public and ensuring their safety. Watchdogs for the public had become guard dogs for industry.

The first wave of regulatory agencies created during the Progressive and New Deal eras—such as the aforementioned FDA and SEC—were engaged in **economic regulation**. Congress created these agencies to regulate specific industries, a process that often involved managing competition and setting industry standards. In the 1960s, however, a new surge of popular protest emerged and demanded **social regulation** as opposed to economic regulation by the government. The civil rights movement pressed Congress to create agencies that would enforce new civil rights laws preventing discrimination. In 1970, environmentalists succeeded in getting Congress to establish the Environmental Protection Agency (EPA) to develop and enforce environmental quality standards. That same year, under pressure from the labor movement, Congress created the Occupational Safety and Health Administration (OSHA) to establish and monitor workplace safety and health standards. And two years later, in 1972, the consumer movement successfully used its growing influence in Congress to create the Consumer Products Safety Commission.

While the earlier and later waves of regulation both stemmed from popular dissatisfaction with free markets, economic and social regulation are very different from one another. The first wave of economic regulation fixed prices, managed competition, set standards, and issued licenses for specific industries. The FDA regulated the pharmaceutical industry, the ICC regulated trucking and the railroads, and the SEC regulated stock market brokerage firms. But the second wave of social regulation cut across industries to affect businesses in virtually all of them. All firms, regardless of the industry they were in, now had to abide by antidiscrimination laws, environmental regulations, and workplace safety rules. "The result," the political scientist David Vogel writes, "was a fundamental restructuring of both the politics and the administration of government regulation of corporate social conduct."[23] Public interest activists in the

civil rights, women's, consumer, labor, and environmental movements successfully put business on the defensive. New government agencies created rules and
enforced laws that affected virtually all firms in terms of who they hired and
fired (nondiscrimination employment laws), their process of production
(workplace safety and health rules), and their environmental impact (environmental protection laws).

But the reach of these new agencies across industrial lines also helped forge
a united front by business against them. The second wave of regulation had
awakened a sleeping giant. Business mobilized to roll back what it perceived as
new, intrusive, and costly social regulations. Campaign contributions from business soared, corporate lobbying increased, and advertising campaigns to sway
public opinion in favor of what was termed "regulatory reform" were launched.
A counteroffensive by a mobilized and cohesive business community was moving across all fronts.

Ironically, the same arguments business raised against social regulations they
found so objectionable—that such rules are costly, disturb efficient markets, and
hamper innovation—were made against economic regulations that regulated
industries found so congenial. Critics criticized regulations that protected industries from competition as promoting complacency, and they condemned regulations that ensured businesses of rates of return as contributing to inflation.

In addition, business's arguments that regulations promoted big government
and thwarted free enterprise created an atmosphere of distrust and antipathy
toward all government agencies and activity, even those that protected their
industries. Political leaders seized upon this broad antigovernment sentiment
to make a popular case against entrenched regulated industries. The result was
that regulatory reform even affected agencies that business had captured. For
example, the Civil Aeronautics Board, which had been created in 1938 to prevent ruinous competition among airlines, was abolished in 1985. Deregulation
of the railroad and trucking industries followed soon after. The grip of industries over the agencies that were supposed to regulate them may have been powerful, but it was not immutable. Political circumstances surrounding the
agencies engaged in economic regulation had changed in such a way as to offset and neutralize the benefits previously offered by firms they regulated.[24]

The politics of regulation are evident not only in the presence or absence of
rules, but in how vigorously they are enforced. Like fiscal and monetary policies that are adjustable in response to economic circumstances, the zealousness
with which the government pursues regulation is adjustable in response to political circumstances. There is regulatory slack in the system that can expand or

contract depending on the political pressures brought to bear on it. The government can go out looking for environmental violations or wait for complaints to come to it; the government can issue large fines to those who violate labor laws or issue slaps on the wrist; the government can employ enough inspectors to ensure food meets safety standards, or it can employ too few; and it can set high standards for car emissions or permit higher levels of pollution. Whether regulations are enforced energetically or negligently is as much a source of political conflict among advocates and opponents of regulation as the regulations themselves. Standard setting and enforcement by regulatory agencies can stretch and bend in response to the political pressures applied to them as well as in response to the political orientation of the party controlling the government.

Take the case of the Securities Exchange Commission (SEC), which was created in 1934 to protect investors in the stock market against fraud. The SEC has often lacked the will and the means to do its job. Most recently, it failed to bring to light Bernie Madoff's Ponzi scheme, in which old investors were paid off not with actual earnings on their investment but with money coming in from new investors. Madoff's trickery fleeced his investors of over $65 billion. The SEC had been tipped off about Madoff's scam as early as 1999, and had even investigated his firm three times, but gave it a clean bill of health after each examination. Indeed, one of the lawyers who investigated Madoff and found no wrongdoing received the SEC's highest performance rating, in part for her ability "to understand and analyze the complex issues of the Madoff investigation." As if that were not embarrassing enough, Madoff then used the SEC's clearances as a selling point to assure investors that his investment practices were legitimate.[25] Nor did the SEC carefully scrutinize the finances of failing investment banks like Lehman Brothers or Bear Sterns, or the credit rating agencies who gave deceptive AAA ratings to debt-ridden companies and risky assets. Part of the problem is the close ties binding the SEC to the industry it is supposed to regulate. The SEC's director of enforcement, Robert Khuzami, was appointed in 2009 from his previous job as general counsel for Deutsche Bank. His predecessor, Linda Thomson, left the agency to become general council at JPMorgan Chase; and her predecessor left to become general council at Deutsche Bank. It is easy to imagine enforcement officers might not be aggressive in going after investment banks that they recently worked for or are hoping to cash in with as their next employer.

But the problem of poor SEC enforcement lies deeper. On the one hand, the SEC has an interest in bringing fraud to light so that investors will be confident enough to gamble in the stock market. No one is likely to invest in stock if they think the game is rigged against them or they cannot trust that "the house" is requiring the dealers to play by the rules. On the other hand, the SEC is reluctant to regulate the securities industry too aggressively because it fears that bringing too much fraud to light would cause investors to lose confidence in it. People would be reluctant to invest if they thought the stock market was rife with deceit, false information, and stock manipulation. Share prices would decline along with the careers of those who run the SEC. The agency believes that preserving

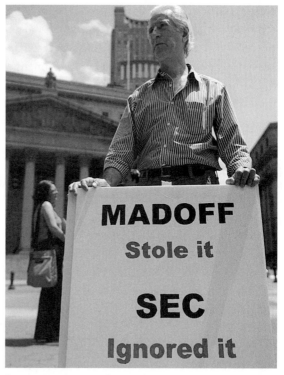

A protestor appears at the sentencing hearing for Bernard Madoff, who was convicted of eleven felonies that defrauded thousands of investors of billions of dollars.

confidence in the stock market is essential to its operation, even if that confidence may be false.[26]

CONCLUSION

In the United States, the production and allocation of goods and services is largely determined by the market. Yet, no economy, not even a capitalist one that operates according to the laws of supply and demand, can exist without government. Government is necessary to create a common currency that facilitates trade and exchange, to enforce contracts that promote security and predictability, and to supply public goods, such as police protection and highways, that society needs but the market will not provide because it is unprofitable to do so. As a congressman from Mississippi once acknowledged without a hint of irony, "The free enterprise system is too important to be left in the hands of private individuals."[27]

Economic policy sets the balance between markets and government. What is so remarkable about this in the United States is the degree to which markets are granted wide latitude to determine who gets what and how much. Despite all the complaints about "big government," the size of the government in relation to the economy is relatively quite small. The government spends less, and Americans are taxed less as a proportion of the economy than are citizens in almost any other advanced industrial society. Not only does the government direct less of the flow of money through the economy than is the case in many other countries, but it has weak levers with which to direct the economy. Fiscal and monetary policy can influence only the circumstances in which economic actors operate. They can influence the behavior of firms only indirectly. And the effectiveness of these tools of economic management is crippled by their institutional design. They are assigned to different institutions—Congress and the president in charge of fiscal policy, and the Federal Reserve Board in charge of monetary policy—without any assurance that they will work in conjunction with one another. Regulations are a more direct means of influencing what business does. But regulation in the United States is not pursued with the vigor found in other countries. Firms must comply with fewer regulations, and the regulations that do exist are often not vigorously enforced.

The pervasiveness and dependence on markets in the United States is due to the political power of business. But the latitude granted markets has to be defended constantly. Political conflict threatens continually to challenge business autonomy. Social regulations of the 1960s and 1970s, which left a legacy of environmental, workplace, consumer, and civil rights protections, rolled back the private power of business. Although business regained enormous freedom beginning in the 1980s, the recent financial crisis contributed to demands for more regulation. It revealed how lax regulation of the financial sector had become, letting banks take on too much bad debt and permitting scam artists to fleece investors.

The recent recession had a similar effect on fiscal and monetary policy. The government became much more aggressive and interventionist. Government, which was previously regarded as the problem, was now relied upon to provide the solution. The Fed bought stock in companies that buy and sell mortgages, engineered mergers between failing and healthy banks, guaranteed loans, and bought bad debts that banks carried on their books. The Obama administration became the de facto overseer of the auto industry as it supervised the bankruptcy and reorganization of General Motors and Chrysler in exchange for federal support. And Congress became more assertive by approving funds to support ailing industries and homeowners. The trench warfare of economic policy between those who advocate reliance on markets and those who want to give more power to government, as well as between those who want government to support business and those who want government to give priority to social needs, is never silent and never still.

CHAPTER SUMMARY

Introduction
The recession that began in 2008 demonstrates the significance of economic policy. When policies that influence the production and allocation of goods and services work well, families have income to pay for food, housing, health care, and some amenities. When they do not work well, unemployment rises, foreclosures increase, and the demand for government and charitable assistance grows.

The Government and the Economy
Compared to other affluent democracies, the U.S. government's role in the economy is quite small. Government revenues and expenditures are a relatively small percentage of GDP, public sector employment is a relatively small proportion of total employment, and businesses have to comply with relatively few regulations. But in response to the 2008 recession, government has become more active and interventionist, involving itself more directly in the management of firms and their strategies.

Fiscal Policy
Fiscal policy occurs when the government uses the budget to fine-tune the economy, running deficits to stimulate it and promote employment, and running surpluses to slow it down and ward off inflation. The budget is negotiated between the president and Congress. The budget is significant because it reveals relations of power in society by depicting which groups must pay a higher share in taxes and which groups receive a larger share of benefits.

Taxes
As the responsibilities of government have grown, so have revenues as a percentage of GNP to pay for them. In addition, sources of revenue have shifted from excise and corporate income taxes to payroll taxes on workers. Finally, tax policy not only is used as a means to raise revenue but

also is increasingly used to make policy. The government favors certain activities and discourages others by treating them differently through the tax code.

Spending

The government spends more money as a proportion of GNP because it does more than it did in the past. Over 90 percent of all federal outlays are accounted for by just three items: welfare expenditures, defense spending, and payments on the national debt to creditors. The little that remains is devoted to all other federal programs. Entitlement programs account for two-thirds of all federal spending, leaving only one-third of all spending to be decided through the budget appropriations process each year.

Monetary Policy

The Federal Reserve Board is responsible for monetary policy, which influences interest rates and is supposed to regulate the banking industry. The Fed is politically independent of Congress and the president, which means it is subject to very little democratic oversight. The Fed tends to identify the welfare of the economy with the welfare of banks, which leads to monetary policies that are pleasing to them.

Regulation

Regulations that require or prohibit certain activities are weak in the United States, and their enforcement is often quite lax. Regulations take the form of either economic regulations that apply to certain industries or social regulations that apply to all firms in all industries. Regulators are often captured by the businesses they are supposed to regulate.

Critical Thinking Questions

1. Why are Americans so concerned about big government when the actual size of the government is smaller than in almost any other developed country?

2. Should the government intervene more in the economy, or should it let markets rule?

3. The United States spends far more on defense and much less on welfare than other developed countries. Do you think the way we allocate our budget among these different functions is appropriate?

4. Control over economic policy is shared between the executive and legislative branches as well as the Federal Reserve Board. Are we better off with policy fragmented among so many independent institutions, or should it be consolidated in one with a subordinate role assigned to the others?

Suggested Readings

Dean Baker, *Plunder and Blunder: The Rise and Fall of the Bubble Economy.* Sausalito, CA: PoliPointPress, 2009.

William Greider, *Come Home America: The Rise and Fall (and Redeeming Promise) of Our Country.* New York: Macmillan, 2009.

Jacob S. Hacker, *The Divided Welfare State: The Battle Over Public and Private Social Benefits in the United States.* New York: Cambridge University Press, 2002.

John Howell Harris, *Right to Manage: Industrial Relations Policies of American Business in the 1940s.* Madison: University of Wisconsin Press, 1982.

Jonas Pontusson, *Inequality and Prosperity: Social Europe vs. Liberal America.* Ithaca, NY: Cornell University Press, 2005.

Allen Schick, *The Federal Budget,* 3rd ed. Washington, DC: Brookings Institute Press, 2007.

Bob Woodward, *Maestro: Greenspan's Fed and the American Boom.* New York: Simon & Schuster, 2005.

SOCIAL POLICY

INTRODUCTION

People hope to grow old. When they do, their quality of life depends in part on diet and exercise, but also on uncertain circumstances affecting their health and finances. Some risks of aging are inevitable. Some are less certain. Accidents can happen at work. Firms disappear, and with them go many jobs. Spouses die prematurely, leaving financial problems for their families. Other risks, like the chance of being poor, are strongly shaped by where persons are situated, including their family history, racial background, neighborhood location, experience of schooling, and the availability of work. Much of the time, people deal with these perils by private action. Those who can afford the cost often invest for their old age and take out private health, life, and disability insurance policies. Some adults pay for schooling to retrain and gain new skills. Private charities, both secular and religious, direct assistance to the homeless and the destitute.

For all but the wealthiest, however, private solutions are either insufficient or inaccessible. For this reason, all the democracies in countries wealthy enough to afford such policies sponsor programs to cushion risk and provide citizens with security. Across the political spectrum, almost all Americans support national policies, and much spending, that cushion citizens against the dangers that come with age, ill health, unemployment, or the death of a spouse. The federal government offers Social Security to the elderly and to surviving spouses in the form of a monthly pension. Medicare provides payments to doctors and hospitals, and prescription drugs, for people over sixty-five. Unemployment insurance cushions the blow, helping tide workers over until they land a new job. On a state-by-state basis, workers' compensation provides medical care for persons injured at work.

These programs of **social insurance** are the largest part of the **welfare state**. They step in when markets are unable to offer material security in the face of hazardous possibilities. Most welfare state spending of this type benefits the working middle class. Social insurance programs are based on contributions workers make in the form of payroll taxes to the government, which holds these funds in trust in the event of a worker's death, injury, unemployment, or retirement. These programs cover almost all those in the labor force and their families. Their benefit levels tend to keep up with the cost of living. Although there is variation in levels of support in some social insurance programs, including unemployment insurance and workers' compensation, the largest programs tend to have quite uniform benefit levels. Since the early 1970s, **Social Security** payments, which are set nationally, have been indexed; that is, they increase in step with the previous year's rate of inflation. Beneficiaries of these policies tend to be perceived as "deserving," because they worked and contributed toward their benefits through the payroll taxes they paid. Social insurance programs enjoy broad levels of support, both because large groups of Ameriecans are beneficiaries and because they are regarded as payment for the contributions that beneficiaries have made over the years.

Other social policies compensate for the limits and failures of the marketplace in more targeted ways. As we have discussed, the United States is characterized by an unusual degree of inequality as well as by significant **poverty**. To counteract and offset hardship, a cluster of programs offer a safety net to especially disadvantaged citizens. These include food stamps (coupons that the poor can redeem for food, housing assistance, and child welfare payments) and **Medicaid**, which offers health insurance to the needy. These **public assistance programs**, which help citizens missed by social insurance, are selective and means-tested. They are available only to Americans whose income or wealth is below the level set by law. Unlike Social Security, public assistance program benefits are not indexed, nor is there a national standard of support. That is, benefit levels in public assistance programs often are eroded by inflation and are unequal across the states. Under **Temporary Assistance to Needy Families (TANF)**, a federal program administered by each of the fifty states, the maximum monthly benefit for a family of three ranges from a high of nearly $1,000 in Alaska to a low of just under $300 in Georgia.[1] Such programs that lessen the burdens of poverty and deprivation are controversial. Many Americans believe that government's efforts to alleviate poverty relieve the poor of responsibility for their own situations; this belief is so strong that the very word *welfare*, despite its positive dictionary meaning as something that promotes well-being, often is used as a negative term.

Passed in March 2010, the Affordable Health Care Act, discussed later in this chapter, is notable for the way it does not fit neatly into these distinctions between public and private provisions for social welfare, and between the social

WHAT DO YOU THINK?

What Is the Proper Role of Government?

Many Americans believe that economic and social well-being is not the concern of government. How Americans deal with deficiencies in income, security, health, and education should largely be the responsibility of families, churches, and organized charities. Many others, by contrast, believe that a critical role must be played by governmental policies because only the government has the resources to effectively compensate for deep inequalities or minimize a wide range of risks, including those associated with unemployment, aging, education, and housing. Where do you stand on this question?

insurance and transfer policies of the welfare state. This significant legislation keeps the provision of health care largely in the hands of private insurance, while also expanding eligibility for Medicaid. Moreover, it utilizes public funds to subsidize the purchase of private insurance, and it increases the oversight of the federal government to regulate the type and quality of insurance private companies provide.

Government also provides for schooling. Long thought a basic feature of citizenship, education prepares children to enter the worlds of work, community, and politics by conferring knowledge and skills that are indispensable for an effective adulthood. Public school systems are primarily a state and local government responsibility, but the federal government has been playing an increasingly significant role in this area of social policy as Washington has come to provide funds, entice reforms, and set standards.

There is also what might be called a hidden or private welfare state. Although private arrangements to deal with risks are inadequate, most Americans continue to depend on welfare benefits that flow through the private sector. Some, for example, receive health insurance and a pension from their employer as part of the compensation package attached to their job. More money is distributed to pensioners from private retirement plans than from Social Security. Political scientist Jacob Hacker writes, "In no other nation do citizens rely so heavily on private benefits for protection against the fundamental risks of modern life."[2] But the private welfare state is not really so private. The government subsidizes the private welfare state through the tax code. Employer-sponsored health care and pension contributions are not taxed as income. Exempting income from taxation to support the private welfare state costs the government over $400 billion in revenue each year. The tax system also subsidizes mortages up to $1,000,000 by allowing the deductability of mortgage interest, which only homeowners may claim.

The relatively large scale of the private welfare state is a hallmark of American social policy. Many benefits that citizens in other rich democracies receive from their government are provided to Americans either through their job or personal savings and investments. The difference between these two approaches is substantial. When governments provide benefits, everyone who qualifies is eligible. But when private firms and persons are the source of benefits, only those workers who have the market power to make employers provide health insurance and private pensions receive them from their companies. Most of the health-care and pension benefits provided by employers go to those who are better off, while lower-paid employees receive less generous fringe-benefit packages. In other words, the private welfare state is more inequitable than government programs in terms of who benefits and how much they benefit.

Spending on social insurance and public assistance programs, as well as state-subsidized private welfare programs, has expanded dramatically since World War II. By 2020, the country plans to spend an additional 940 billion federal dollars on health care. Yet, the United States actually is and will remain near the bottom of the standings in terms of its welfare costs compared to European countries. Comparatively, the U.S. welfare state is small; it captures a more limited share of tax revenues and national wealth than does welfare spending in comparable advanced capitalist countries (Figure 10.1). In 2009, the United States devoted 15.8 percent of its gross domestic product (GDP) to public social expenditures. Most other rich democracies spend considerably more: some, including Italy, Finland, Germany, France, Sweden, Austria, and Denmark, devote 25 to 30 percent of their GDP to such programs. American spending is just above the level of South Korea, Mexico, and Turkey.

The American welfare state is distinctive in other ways as well. Another way to compare welfare states is by the degree to which they detach a person's well-being from dependence on the labor market. Some societies provide social rights, such as a right to health care, to all their citizens regardless of their position in the labor market. In other societies, including the United States, the amount and kind of benefits depends more heavily on one's job. Overall, Americans enjoy fewer and less generous social rights than can be found in many other industrial societies. Although some benefits (like Social Security pensions) are quite generous, many other benefits tend to be low, often stigmatizing, and of short duration. They hardly provide a reprieve from the market. An example is the long-standing system of employer-based health insurance. Those with good jobs usually have enjoyed employer-based health insurance, but an

FIGURE 10.1

PUBLIC SOCIAL EXPENDITURE AS A PERCENTAGE OF GDP

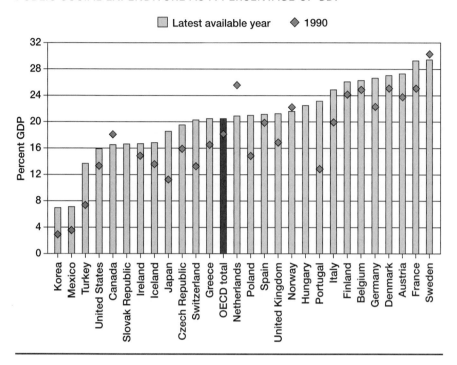

SOURCE: OECD Factbook 2009, at http://titania.sourceoecd.org/vl=1643454/cl=12/
nw=1/rpsv/factbook/10/02/02/10-02-02-g1.htm (accessed March 11, 2010).

increasing number of jobs, especially those that are poorly paid and nonunion, have lacked such insurance. This situation, which closely tied health insurance to employment, contributed to the result that more than 45 million Americans had no health insurance in 2010 (the new health-care law is aimed at changing this). Thus the interaction of the public and private welfare states often reinforces the way the marketplace distributes income and wealth, rather than offering an alternative to it.[3]

THE HISTORICAL WELFARE STATE

The perception that the American welfare state is a laggard, a late addition to the family of welfare states, is based on when key social policies—workers' compensation, **unemployment insurance**, disability insurance, and old-age pensions—first were enacted. These welfare state programs were created at the federal level in the United States with the passage of the Social Security Act in 1935, well after they were established in many European countries.

But this comparison gives a false impression that the federal government was not involved in social assistance before the enactment of Social Security. In fact, an unusual sort of welfare state, one that diverged from Europe, existed before 1935. West European welfare states were aimed at workers and provided everything from unemployment insurance in the event of layoffs to workers' compensation in case of an industrial accident. A consequence of targeting workers was that these welfare programs predominantly covered men, who were far more likely to participate in the labor force than women. In the United States, on the other hand, the early American welfare state did not target working men but rather extended social protection to veteran soldiers and mothers.

Between 1880 and 1910, the federal government spent more than a quarter of its entire budget on pensions for Union Civil War veterans and their dependents. In fact, the federal government spent more money on pensions for former Union Army soldiers and their dependents than on any other category except for interest payments on the national debt. By 1910, more than 500,000 Americans—28 percent of all men over age sixty-five—received federal benefits averaging $189 per year, which was a tidy sum at the time. An additional 30,000 Civil War orphans, widows, and dependents also received payments from the federal government.[4] Coverage rates were as high as those in some European old-age programs, and the benefits Americans received were more generous than those some pensioners received in Europe.

This unusual social assistance program in the form of veterans' pensions expired when the generation of Civil War veterans passed away. As these payments were ending, a "maternalist" welfare state developed that promoted moth-

WHAT DO YOU THINK?

Markets and Morals

Supporters of extensive welfare states offer three kinds of arguments. Some are based on making markets, especially the labor market, work more efficiently. Others are based on the rights that come with citizenship, making the case that people suffering insecurity and deprivation cannot be active participants in public life. Still others present moral arguments for the welfare state, claiming that social policy has an ethical component of responsibility for other human beings. How would you assess such arguments and choose among them?

erhood. During the Progressive era, the first two decades of the twentieth century, a program of mothers' pensions provided income assistance to single, poor mothers so they could stay home and raise their children. Providing income support to single mothers was perceived as preferable to having a woman work outside the home or give up her children to an orphanage or foster home because she could not provide for them. Each of these options would have undermined the mother's role, which advocates of mother's pensions sought to preserve.

But not all mothers were treated alike. To qualify for assistance, they had to prove themselves worthy. Widows could easily do this, because they were not perceived as responsible for their plight; but unwed mothers were often excluded. Benefits, moreover, were made contingent on the behavior of mothers. They had to display moral character by showing "intelligence, willingness to learn English, piety, celibacy," compliance with directions from social workers, and dedication to "full-time child-centered domesticity."[5] The price of accepting mothers' pensions was state regulation over the lives of women to ensure they conformed to traditional gender roles. Further, the maternalist welfare state was marked by deep racial discrimination. As the political scientist Deborah Ward has demonstrated, many states and localities, especially in the South where most African Americans still lived, excluded black mothers from the rolls of recipients.[6] Mothers' pensions thus are an example of how certain roles—in this case, roles based on gender and race—can be inscribed by social policy.

THE NEW DEAL AND BEYOND

The shock of the Great Depression provided the impetus for the most dramatic expansion of the U.S. welfare state to date. When President Franklin D. Roosevelt declared in 1937 that "one-third of [the] nation" was "ill-housed, ill-clad, ill nourished," his estimate understated the problem. The proportion of the population that fit this description in the midst of the Depression, contemporaries agreed, was actually closer to one-half.[7] The main source of this distress was the staggering unemployment that afflicted the nation. In 1933, almost 13 million workers—a quarter of the workforce—were jobless, looking for work. Unemployment bred poverty and poverty bred despair. One man wrote to relief officials in Washington and inquired, "Can you advise me as to which would be the most humane way to dispose of myself and family, as this is about the only thing that I can see left to do."[8]

Poverty, low wages, and unemployment led some to abstain from politics. But it led others to take political action. Thousands of workers occupied factories to demand union recognition, the unemployed marched to demand food and shelter, and farmers dumped their produce to demand higher prices. The Roosevelt administration responded to these challenges by offering federally funded jobs and social welfare programs to help the needy. The corporate community balked at these reforms, claiming they were a threat to private enterprise. But with the prospect of mass unrest growing, Roosevelt ignored their misgivings. The president recognized that a safety net providing citizens with a modicum of economic security was necessary both to alleviate suffering and save capitalism, even if promoting such programs meant opposing conservatives who urged thrift and passivity in the face of distress.

There was an ironic quality to this hostility to the New Deal. As the business publication *Fortune* magazine observed in 1935, "it was fairly evident to most disinterested critics" that the New Deal "had the preservation of capitalism at all times in view."[9] Social reform was part of the administration's strategy to keep the market economy functioning. When the threat of civil disorder arose, the federal government expanded work relief programs. When the threat of disorder waned, federally funded jobs diminished. Some social welfare concessions were extended when the poor disrupted the status quo and were then retracted once the threat passed.[10]

But enduring legacies, especially the Social Security Act, have continued to shape American life. Passed in 1935, this law offered pensions and unemployment compensation to qualified workers, provided public assistance to the elderly and the blind, and created a new national program for poor, single mothers, called Aid to Dependent Children (ADC; later called **Aid to Families with Dependent Children**, or **AFDC**). The protection and support the government provided through the Social Security program made it possible for the blind, the unemployed, the elderly, and poor single mothers to live with a modicum of security and dignity.

Yet even as the Social Security Act blazed new paths, it reinforced many conservative ideas about poverty from the previous period. First, it continued the American tradition of localism. States were given the authority to set benefit levels and eligibility requirements for ADC and unemployment insurance. This discretion led to wide variations in benefits between states. Citizens in identical circumstances were treated differently, depending solely on which state they lived in.

Second, benefits were set quite low. Benefit levels continued to follow the "least eligibility" principle, which held that no one should be better off on welfare than in work. Benefits should be set below the wage of the lowest-paid worker, so that the poor would rather offer themselves to any employer on any

A U.S. government poster displayed in post offices and other public buildings instructing citizens on how to apply for the old-age benefits of the Social Security Act.

terms rather than accept relief.[11] Welfare should be made as undesirable as possible in order to reinforce the work ethic and ensure an abundant supply of cheap labor.

Third, the Social Security Act institutionalized the invidious distinction between deserving and undeserving welfare recipients. Programs organized on the principle of social insurance, like Social Security, were for workers who deserved them. These programs were financed through payroll taxes on employers and employees. Recipients "earned" their benefits through their contributions while they worked. Public assistance programs, on the other hand, were financed out of general tax revenues. These programs were means-tested and stigmatized the poor. While social insurance programs for workers enjoyed political support, public assistance programs for the poor were deplored as government handouts for the unworthy.

The Social Security Act reinforced gender inequalities. The separation of the poor into public assistance programs and workers into social insurance programs distinguished how most men fared from how most women accessed the welfare state. With relatively few women in the wage labor force, men were more likely to qualify for social insurance programs like Social Security and unemployment compensation, which depended on contributions from earnings and paid benefits only to individuals who had to leave the labor force because they were laid off or retired. Women, by contrast, were more likely to receive their benefits from public assistance programs that were neither well funded nor well regarded.

Finally, Social Security, in tandem with other key policies of the 1930s and 1940s, also had a profound racial content. Inflected by the preferences of the southern wing of the Democratic Party, these policies massively advantaged American whites while often excluding African Americans, especially the majority who still lived in the seventeen states that mandated racial segregation. During Jim Crow's last hurrah in the 1930s and 1940s, when members of Congress from the abovementioned seventeen southern states controlled the gateways to legislation, policy decisions dealing with welfare, work, and war excluded or differentially treated the vast majority of African Americans. Farmworkers and maids, the jobs held by most southern blacks, were denied Social Security pensions and access to labor unions. Benefits for veterans were administered locally. For example, the famous GI Bill of 1944 provided a substantial array of educational and financial benefits to returning GIs. It adapted to "the southern way of life" by accommodating to segregation in higher education, to the job ceilings local officials imposed on returning black soldiers who came home from a segregated army, and to an unwillingness to offer loans to blacks even when they were insured by the federal government. Of the 3,229 GI Bill guaranteed home, business, and farm loans made in 1947 in Mississippi, for example, only two were offered to black veterans.[12]

With most blacks left out, the damage to racial equity was immense. Social Security, which excluded the majority of blacks until well into the 1950s, quickly became the country's most important social legislation. Perhaps most surprising and most important, the treatment of veterans after the war, despite the universal eligibility for the benefits apparently offered by the GI Bill, perpetuated the blatant racism that had marked the affairs of a still segregated military during the war itself. At no other time in American history have so much money and so many resources been put at the service of the generation completing education, entering the workforce, and forming families. At the very moment a wide array of public policies were providing most white Americans with valuable tools to insure their old age, get good jobs, acquire economic security, build assets, and gain middle-class status, black Americans were mainly left to fend for themselves, with the exception of their growing participation in public assistance programs aimed directly at the poor.

The last major New Deal social policy initiative was the Fair Labor Standards Act of 1938, a law that established the first national minimum wage (twenty-five cents per hour) and a forty-hour work week. Soon, World War II brought a halt to social reform as the country fixed its attention on defeating Germany, Italy, and Japan. When the war ended, liberals hoped to restore the momentum of the New Deal. But a politically resurgent business community, in tandem with an increasingly conservative Congress, resisted new social initiatives. Supporters of federal welfare programs were thrown on the defensive and effectively denounced in the early years of the Cold War as being the opening wedge of communism and a threat to freedom. In 1946, conservatives in Congress weakened a bill that would have committed the government to a full-employment policy. In 1949, a national health insurance bill proposed by the Truman administration was defeated in Congress.[13] No comparably broad program of national health insurance would be enacted for another sixty years. Other parts of President Harry Truman's Fair Deal—his program to extend the New Deal welfare state—met a similar fate.

Upon being defeated politically, unions and other liberals who supported national health insurance tried to obtain from employers what they could not secure from Congress. Unions in large corporations began to negotiate fringe benefits packages in collective bargaining with employers; the benefits included health insurance, employer-funded pensions, and supplementary unemployment for their members. Between 1948 and 1959, the number of workers who received health insurance and private pensions as part of their employment contracts tripled. A private welfare system, in which social protections such as health insurance and pensions were tied to jobs through labor contracts between employers and employees, began to develop. As we noted earlier, the United States is distinctive in its mix of public and private sector welfare spending, which is weighted heavily toward the private sector. Approximately 25 percent of all welfare spending in this country comes from the private sector, compared to just 5 percent in France and Sweden.

The private welfare system of employer-based benefits made workers dependent for their social protection—health insurance and pensions—on the firms that employed them. This pattern of social provision not only tied workers to their employers but also divided workers from each other. Only workers employed in the corporate sector of the economy received extensive social protections from their employers. Workers who toiled for firms in the competitive sector of the economy often did not receive such fringe benefits, because small firms could not afford to pay health insurance costs or contribute to private pensions for their workers. Consequently, workers in the corporate sector of the economy, who were receiving social protection from their employers, had less of a stake in improving, expanding, and adding new government programs that workers in the competitive sector and the poor depended on. The private welfare system of employer-based benefits siphoned off political pressure from corporate sector workers—the most organized and politically powerful section of the American working class—to increase the level of protection the American welfare state provided beyond the minimum necessary for social peace.

Although the New Deal may not have gone forward under President Truman, a Democrat, neither did it go backward under his successor, President Dwight Eisenhower, a Republican. Under Eisenhower, conservatives did not try to revoke the Social Security Act or return to the pre-Depression style of minimal government.[14] Corporations that had adamantly opposed Social Security in the 1930s now acknowledged that it could help stabilize the economy and was preferable to more radical, or conservative, alternatives. Moreover, it would have been futile to roll back Social Security, given its broad popular support. The issue for Republicans was striking the proper balance between private welfare plans run by employers and public welfare programs run by the government. Republicans were determined that the welfare state should not displace welfare capitalism in the form of private, employer-based welfare plans. According to Marion B. Folsom, an Eastman Kodak executive who became secretary of health, education, and welfare in Eisenhower's cabinet, government should provide only "basic minimum protection and it should not be intended to cover all the needs of everyone." He argued that benefits in government programs should be low and that businesses should be offered tax incentives to subsidize their own employer-based welfare plans. Limited public benefits would encourage the need for and reliance on private, corporate welfare plans. These private, corporate plans, in turn, would act as a brake on the further extension of public welfare state programs.[15]

THE NEW POVERTY

The publication in 1962 of *The Other America: Poverty in the United States*, by Michael Harrington, roused the nation's conscience. Using statistics that were widely available but had drawn little attention, Harrington exposed a disturbing truth: despite unprecedented prosperity, 40 to 50 million people—one-quarter of all Americans—remained mired in poverty. In previous decades, full employment had reduced poverty. But by the mid-1960s, the traditional correlation between low unemployment and low AFDC welfare rates no longer applied. Throughout the 1960s, in the midst of one of the most prosperous decades in the nation's history, the number of families needing income assistance grew by almost 10 percent per year.[16]

One reason that welfare caseloads grew even as the economy boomed was the changing color of poverty. A disproportionate and increasing number of the poor now were African Americans who lived in urban ghettos. Once blacks migrated from the South to join the modern industrial economy in northern cities like Cleveland, New York, and Chicago, they faced greater discrimination and larger obstacles to social mobility than did the immigrant groups, such as Italians, Poles, and Jews, who preceded them. Race proved a more visible and powerful marker of difference than ethnicity and nationality.[17]

Blacks, moreover, entered the modern industrial economy at the very moment it was passing from the scene. When previous immigrant groups had arrived with little education, the economy needed their unskilled labor to dig canals, lay railroad tracks, and work in the industrial plants of Detroit, Philadelphia, and Chicago. That was no longer true by the time blacks migrated north. Technology had reduced the need for labor in manufacturing. Capital had replaced labor in production. Economic restructuring now put a premium on education that many urban blacks lacked. In addition, factories no longer were located in cities accessible to blacks. Manufacturing plants were now located in the suburbs, where taxes and land were cheaper. This put many blue-collar manufacturing jobs beyond the reach of poor black residents located in center cities.[18] At the same time postindustrial capitalism was producing well-compensated white-collar jobs requiring education, it was also creating service sector jobs that failed to pay a living wage. Those who worked hard and played by the rules were consigned to poverty by a lack of skills, a lack of unions that could bargain for higher wages on their behalf, and a lack of government regulations that could assure them an adequate income.[19]

The color of welfare was changing, becoming darker as job discrimination and economic changes conspired to restrain black mobility, and so was its gender. Women now increasingly filled the ranks of the poor. Poverty became feminized. This development, dating back a half-century, has continued to shape the contours of poverty today. Almost one-third of all female-headed households presently are poor. These families comprise more than one-half of all families in poverty—a significant increase from forty years ago, when female-headed

WHAT DO YOU THINK?

Responsibility for Poverty

Some argue that poverty is largely caused by structural factors over which individuals have little or no control. These factors include family background, educational opportunities, the state of the job market, and differences in economic life chances in different cities and states. Others argue that poverty is mostly caused by bad choices individuals make about schooling, job training, and family formation. How would you judge these differences in emphasis?

households accounted for only one-third of all poor families.[20] Single mothers are likely to be poor either because women earn lower wages when they work or because they need to stay home to care for their children and are unable to work.

The poor also became younger—much younger than they once were. The great success of the American welfare state in reducing the poverty rate among the elderly has only underlined its greatest failure: the high and persistent poverty rate that remains among children. The poverty rate among those who are sixty-five years of age and older has declined by almost two-thirds in just four decades, from 29.5 percent in 1967 to 9.9 percent in 2007.[21] In the same period, the poverty rate among children has hovered stubbornly around 20 percent—almost twice the current poverty rate for the elderly.[22] The American poverty rate among children is three times the rate in Western Europe. Poverty among children in Europe is so much lower than in the United States because European countries spend more money on more programs for families with children, thus raising children above the poverty line who otherwise would be below it. No other developed welfare state is as generationally skewed as that of the United States, where benefits flow to the elderly through such relatively expensive programs as **Medicare** and Social Security while fewer and less expensive efforts are made to insulate children from deprivation and its corrosive effects.[23]

Poverty has remained persistent. As we show in Chapter 2, both good and bad jobs in postindustrial capitalism have been growing at the expense of blue-collar jobs in the middle. The service sector jobs available to unskilled workers (e.g., fast-food worker, maid, and security guard) are characterized by low wages, low or no fringe benefits, and irregular and temporary employment. A single parent with three children who worked steadily for 40 hours a week, 52 weeks a year at a minimum-wage job in 2009 would have earned only $15,080, which is 58 percent of what the government defined as the poverty line for such a family ($25,790). Indeed, over time, the value of the federal minimum wage has declined, as indicated in Table 10.1.

THE GREAT SOCIETY PROGRAM

The last concerted effort to grapple with poverty as a national priority, the Great Society initiated by President Lyndon Johnson in 1964, happened nearly a half-century ago. Like the first great wave of social reform, the New Deal, that was made possible by the sweeping Democratic electoral realignment spearheaded by President Roosevelt in the 1930s, this wave of reform also was the result of

TABLE 10.1

FEDERAL MINIMUM-WAGE RATES, 1959–2009

	Value of the Minimum Wage			Value of the Minimum Wage	
Year	Current Dollars	Constant (1996) Dollars*	Year	Current Dollars	Constant (1996) Dollars*
1959	1.00	5.39	1987	3.35	4.63
1960	1.00	5.30	1988	3.35	4.44
1961	1.15	6.03	1989	3.35	4.24
1962	1.15	5.97	1990	3.80	4.56
1963	1.25	6.41	1991	4.25	4.90
1964	1.25	6.33	1992	4.25	4.75
1965	1.25	6.23	1993	4.25	4.61
1966	1.25	6.05	1994	4.25	4.50
1967	1.40	6.58	1995	4.25	4.38
1968	1.60	7.21	1996	4.75	4.75
1969	1.60	6.84	1997	5.15	5.03
1970	1.60	6.47	1998	5.15	4.96
1971	1.60	6.20	1999	5.15	4.85
1972	1.60	6.01	2000	5.15	4.69
1973	1.60	5.65	2001	5.15	4.56
1974	2.00	6.37	2002	5.15	4.49
1975	2.10	6.12	2003	5.15	4.39
1976	2.30	6.34	2004	5.15	4.28
1977	2.30	5.95	2005	5.15	4.14
1978	2.65	6.38	2006	5.15	4.04
1979	2.90	6.27	2007	5.85	4.41
1980	3.10	5.90	2008	6.55	4.94
1981	3.35	5.78	2009	7.25	5.47
1982	3.35	5.78			

*Adjusted for inflation using the CPI-U (Consumer Price Index for All Urban Consumers).
SOURCE: Infoplease, at http://www.infoplease.com/ipa/A0774473.html
(accessed March 22, 2010).

a thorough Democratic electoral victory. Another key factor was the pressure exerted in each era by mobilized protests, led especially by labor during the New Deal and the civil rights movement during the Great Society.

In 1964, fifty-one freshmen Democrats were elected to Congress on President Johnson's coattails. Liberals now had enough votes to overcome the veto that the conservative coalition of Republicans and southern Democrats in Congress had exercised over social welfare legislation in the 1950s. A liberal

Democratic president with concurring supermajorities in the Senate and the House could now overcome the obstacles that opponents had used to stymie welfare state initiatives in the past.[24]

In his 1964 State of the Union address, President Johnson declared a **War on Poverty** that would result in a Great Society, free of hunger and privation. The AFL-CIO reflected the sentiment of other liberals when it crowed, "The New Deal proclaimed in 1933 has come to a belated maturity now under LBJ in 1965."[25] After a thirty-year hiatus, the federal government was building on the legacy of the New Deal and assuming new responsibilities in almost every area of social welfare. Federally funded health insurance, in the form of Medicare and Medicaid, was established for the aged and the poor. New educational opportunities for the disadvantaged, such as Head Start and Upward Bound, were enacted. Job-training programs, such as the Job Corps, were legislated. New initiatives in housing and urban development, such as the Model Cities program, followed suit. The thrust of these initiatives was to enhance opportunities for the poor, "to open up doors, not set down floors; to offer a hand up, not a handout," according to historian James T. Patterson.[26] Federal social welfare expenditures almost doubled from 1965 to 1975 in support of these efforts. Social welfare costs, which amounted to one-third of the entire federal budget in 1965, accounted for more than one-half ten years later.[27]

But like the social reform period of the New Deal, the War on Poverty was short-lived. Initially, the War on Poverty drew its moral and political energy from the civil rights movement. But as the moral power of the civil rights movement declined amidst violence and internal strife, so did the impetus behind the Great Society. Equally important, the Johnson administration became distracted by the war in Vietnam. The more the war against communism in Asia escalated, the more the war against poverty at home lost momentum. A conservative backlash toward the Great Society first appeared in the 1966 congressional election, which restored the blocking power of the conservative coalition of Republicans and southern Democrats within Congress.[28] Two years later, in 1968, Richard Nixon (a Republican) was elected president on a platform skeptical about the Great Society and the moment of social reform effectively came to an end.

According to many conservatives, the War on Poverty failed; worse, its antipoverty programs were harmful. Welfare rolls, they noted, continued to increase, not decrease; crime became worse, not better; more single mothers appeared, not fewer; and illegitimacy rates continued to rise, not decline. The country's cities burned as violent urban protests rocked the nation in the late 1960s. During his 1968 campaign, Nixon captured this sense of disappointment when he charged, "For the past five years we have been deluged by government programs for the unemployed, programs for cities, programs for the poor, and we have reaped from these programs an ugly harvest of frustration, violence and failure across the land."[29]

Backlash toward the Great Society also developed because the War on Poverty had polarized the electorate along the fault lines of the division between social insurance and public assistance programs. Workers covered by social insurance had little stake in the Great Society programs that aided the poor. As the prosperity of the 1960s turned into the stagflation of the 1970s, resentment over these expenditures and their tax burden grew. Race compounded this resentment. Many New Deal programs purposely left blacks out, but the War on Poverty purposely targeted them for inclusion.[30] The political consequences of the Great Society program pitted taxpayers, who were part of the social insurance system, against tax recipients, who received public assistance; the private sector was set against the public sector, workers against the jobless, and whites against blacks.[31] Politicians in both parties exploited and exacerbated these tensions, using *welfare* as a code word to appeal to some voters' fears concerning crime, taxes, morality, and race.

The recoil against the Great Society reached its peak during the Reagan administration (1981–89). President Ronald Reagan came to office pledging to shrink the federal government. His administration quickly aimed its fire at the poor, and the Great Society programs they depended on. Some federal programs, such as funding for public service jobs and revenue sharing for the states, were eliminated completely; other poverty programs were cut back drastically.[32]

The Reagan attack on the welfare state overreached, however. Tax cuts for the rich and spending cuts for the poor exposed his administration to charges of unfairness, even meanness. As poverty became more visible due to government cutbacks and rising unemployment, the public became more upset with the results. As David Stockman, Reagan's budget director, observed, "The abortive Reagan revolution proved that the American electorate wants a moderate social democracy to shield it from capitalism's rough edges."[33]

In fact, far from failing, the War on Poverty had succeeded in reducing the number of people living in poverty. The poverty rate dropped from 19 percent in 1964 to less than 12 percent in 1979. The number of people living below the poverty line declined until President Reagan signaled retreat in a war the country was winning. Government income-support programs, not economic growth, accounted for the largest part of this decline. Before taking such income supports into account, the number of households in poverty fell by 900,000 between 1965 and 1971. But with these programs, the number of poor families declined by 2.6 million.[34] The federal government's antipoverty programs not only lifted families out of poverty but also raised the quality of their lives by reducing malnutrition, increasing access to medical care, improving housing, and opening up educational opportunities that previously had not been available.[35]

Despite these dramatic changes, critics of the War on Poverty were suspicious of the type of difference such programs made in poor people's lives and were opposed to government "handouts" that were not earned by contributing to social insurance programs. Poverty programs, they argued, may have improved poor people's lives materially, but they did not change their behavior—welfare dependency, illegitimate babies, and family breakup. Even granting that more of the poor's basic needs may have been met as a result of Great Society initiatives, the critics insisted this success came at the cost of the recipients' character. This line of argument, however, does not hold up to close scrutiny. Larger cultural forces regarding sexuality and parenthood, not welfare policy, drove the trend toward more female-headed households. Moreover, poverty, low wages, and the growing insecurity of the market weakened the ties that bound families together. As the noted economist Lester Thurow put it, "The traditional family is being destroyed not by misguided social welfare programs coming from Washington . . . but by a modern economic system that is not congruent with 'family values.'"[36]

Inaccurate impressions of welfare dependency also abounded. In fact, of the people on welfare, most received benefits for short periods rather than over the long term.[37] People moved in and out of the welfare rolls not because they wanted to be there, but because personal and economic setbacks including divorce, abandonment, unemployment, lack of child care, or sickness placed them there. And all the disadvantages of being poor that afflict one generation affect the next. What was passed from one generation to the next among the poor was their poverty, not welfare dependency.[38] This was evident in the classic study of poor urban black men by the anthropologist Eliot Liebow, who found that they had followed in the failed footsteps of their fathers not because a *culture* of poverty had been handed down, but because the same social and educational *deficits* of poverty that had prevented their fathers from succeeding were visited on their sons.[39]

FROM REAGAN TO CLINTON

During the Reagan administration, a concerted effort to reduce the size and scope of the welfare state proved only a partial success. Welfare state spending was slowed but not reversed. Great Society poverty programs took heavy cuts, mostly surviving in truncated form, while New Deal social insurance programs emerged relatively unscathed.[40] But the Reagan administration's impact on the welfare state was more profound than can be gleaned from looking at welfare state spending alone. Republicans succeeded in placing the welfare state on the defensive as conservatives now set the terms of debate over social policy. The problem of poverty was redefined from increasing the poor's resources to changing their behavior, from blaming their circumstances on the inadequacies of the economy to blaming it on the perverse incentives of the welfare state.

The public mood changed so much that even Democrats were prepared to renounce their own New Deal and Great Society legacies. In March 1990, members of the Democratic Leadership Council (DLC), a group of moderate and conservative Democrats, announced they were ready to bury their party's past. Meeting in New Orleans, they dismissed the relevance of New Deal and Great Society programs, claiming that "the political ideas and passions of the 1930s and 1960s cannot guide us in the 1990s." At that meeting, the DLC selected a new council president to present this view, putting a little-known governor from a small southern state on the national stage for the first time. His name was William Jefferson Clinton.[41]

President Clinton's social policy was shaped decisively by these two inheritances from previous Republican administrations: a large federal deficit and a conservative definition of the welfare problem. To reassure financial markets that he was serious about cutting the federal deficit, Clinton sacrificed his 1992 campaign promise to invest in domestic programs. His failed health-care plan also fell victim to fighting the deficit, relying on government regulation to lower costs rather than raise new taxes or increase spending to pay for it. Even as the budget began to run surpluses toward the end of the 1990s, the Clinton administration continued to give priority to fiscal responsibility at the price of failing to restore cuts to welfare state programs.

The welfare state during the Clinton presidency was not simply mortgaged to deficit reduction but also conducted within a conservative definition of the welfare problem that the president adopted as his own—the view that public assistance programs undermined the character of the poor. From this perspective, the best way to build their character was to remove the welfare crutch they depended upon. This view was embodied in a major reform of the welfare system, the Personal Responsibility and Work Opportunity Reconciliation Act (PRWORA), which President Clinton signed in 1996.

Replacing the old welfare program, Aid to Families with Dependent Children (AFDC), marked a radical shift in welfare policy. The debate in Congress was charged. "This isn't welfare reform," Senator Daniel Patrick Moynihan of New York thundered in dismay as this overhaul of the existing welfare system wound its way through Congress. "This is welfare repeal."[42] Conflict on the House Ways and Means Committee over eliminating the guarantee of welfare benefits to every eligible poor American was so furious that the sergeant at arms had to be called to restore order. When the bill reached the floor of the House, the debate reached uncommon levels of acrimony. Some Democrats compared Republican welfare proposals to Nazism, and some Republicans likened welfare recipients to wild animals. This debate was overwrought because it was freighted with many meanings, from relationships between the sexes to relationship between races to relationships between the states. Eventually, the Republican Congress—seizing the initiative President Clinton gave them when he promised "to end welfare as we know it" during the 1992 presidential campaign—sent the president a welfare bill that did what he pledged, but in ways he never intended. Forced to choose between breaking his campaign promise to reform welfare and repudiating his own more generous welfare proposals, President Clinton chose the latter and signed the PRWORA. This legislation created a new welfare program, Temporary Assistance to Needy Families (TANF), to help impoverished children and their families.

AFDC had been an entitlement program that required the federal government to provide income assistance to poor families for as long as they were eligible. The amount of federal money for welfare would adjust automatically to cover some of the money that states gave to poor families, regardless of the number of families on the rolls and regardless of how long they had been there.[43] Under TANF, states now receive fixed sums of money from the federal government in the form of block grants to help pay for welfare. These sums do not increase automatically with the welfare rolls. When more people qualify, raising the number of clients, and when states spend all of their federal money but choose not to supplement it, poor families who are eligible for income sup-

WHAT DO YOU THINK?

Consensus and Controversy

Some vital public policies, including Social Security and Medicare, once were keenly opposed as inappropriate intrusions by government into private markets. Today, they have become a part of the social minimum that almost no citizen or political leader is against. What happened? How did this shift from contestation to agreement occur? And why did it not happen with regard to AFDC?

port may not receive any. TANF has given states more discretion on how to spend federal welfare money and devise their own welfare policies, but with one important condition required by Congress. The law sets a limit of two years on welfare, after which recipients must work, and it establishes a lifetime limit of five years during which people may receive welfare.

The promise of a Democratic president and a Republican Congress to "end welfare as we know it" thus was redeemed. Welfare as an entitlement was eliminated by setting time limits on benefits and by removing the guarantee that the federal government would reimburse the states for each eligible recipient, regardless of how many there were.

Proponents of this law have pointed to declining welfare rolls—they were cut in half during the program's first decade—as a sign that its work promotion has been effective.[44] But the welfare rolls had begun to decrease in 1993, well before the new welfare bill was signed. Moreover, most of the credit for lower welfare rolls belongs to the period's surging economy that pulled the most able people off the welfare rolls and into work. Tellingly, when the deep recession of 2008 hit, welfare rolls took a big jump upward. Caseloads rose in 23 of the 30 largest states, comprising 88 percent of the country's population. Oregon's total jumped 27 percent from the prior year, South Carolina's 23 percent, and California's 10 percent.[45] In the circumstances, President Obama's stimulus package provided 80 percent more funding for states whose caseloads were growing beyond budgetary expectations.

FROM BUSH TO OBAMA

During the past decade, the shape of the welfare state has changed substantially. The federal role in public education has expanded. Most notably, there have been a series of important changes, culminating in the 2010 landmark, Affordable Health Care Act, which have dramatically transformed the role of the federal government with respect to medical insurance issues for all Americans.

Elementary and high school education in the United States is mostly financed by localities, especially by property taxes. This pattern of support results in enormous disparities in the amounts spent by different school districts. In part to help rectify these inequalities, Congress passed the Elementary and Secondary Education Act (ESEA) in 1965 to provide, for the first time, significant federal funding for K–12 education. This law was renewed seven times before a substantial revision, called No Child Left Behind (NCLB), was proposed by President George W. Bush. NCLB was passed with bipartisan support by Congress in January 2002 with the stated purpose of "[c]losing the achievement gap" between economically and racially advantaged and disadvantaged schoolchildren. The law requires states to administer annual math and reading tests beginning in the third grade and to move toward a 100 percent passage rate within twelve years. The law further imposes severe consequences for schools that do not meet adequate yearly progress, including providing parents with alternatives to failing schools. During the first term of the Bush administration, the Department of Education's budget grew dramatically, increasing spending by the Department of Education on K–12 education from $27.3 billion in 2001 to $44 billion in 2009.[46] Yet, states still charged that NCLB's onerous testing imposed an "unfunded mandate" on their budgets, particularly at a time of fiscal crisis. By one estimate, offered by the American Federation of Teachers, the federal government had shortchanged NCLB by more than $70.9 billion in its first decade. Even though federal spending had increased, the fiscal demands placed on the states by the new law had grown even faster. A disillusioned Senator Ted Kennedy, D–MA, one of the original cosponsors of the bipartisan bill, observed that "we called the law the No Child Left Behind Act because we meant just what it said—no child means no child. The tragedy is that these long overdue reforms are finally in place, but the funds are not."[47]

Despite its strong history of cross-party support when first adopted, NCLB has become more contentious. As he was launching his presidential campaign in 2007, Barack Obama called "no child left behind" "one of the emptiest slogans in the history of politics" due to its insufficient funding.[48] Efforts to increase spending on education that year by the White House and sympathetic members of Congress, including Senator Kennedy, failed to renew the act because reauthorization was delayed until a new administration would take office.

The second, and most dramatic, extension of the welfare state during the Bush presidency was the creation of Medicare Part D. In January 2004, the Medicare Prescription Drug, Improvement, and Modernization Act was passed into law. The statute offered the largest and most expensive overhaul of Medicare since its inception in 1965 and provided for prescription drug coverage to all Medicare recipients. Strongly supported by pharmaceutical manufacturers who stood to gain many new customers, and funded by a combination of government funding, increased premiums assessed monthly on Medicare beneficiaries, and deductibles, the law reduced the proportion of elderly without drug coverage from 24 percent in 2004 to 7 percent in 2006, and offered subsidies to those with low incomes.[49] The law's content also was shaped strongly by the pharmaceutical industry, which lobbied strenuously and successfully to avoid price controls and price regulation and to forbid the federal government from negotiating with drug manufacturers to secure lower prices for Medicare beneficiaries. Without these provisions, Jacob Hacker and Theodore Marmor of Yale University estimated that the bill could have delivered twice as much coverage for the same price.[50]

The third expansion of the welfare state was a significant increase in spending on children's health; the increase was pioneered during the Clinton presidency and significantly expanded at the start of Barack Obama's. President Clinton proposed and Congress passed the State Children's Health Insurance Plan (SCHIP) in 1997. This program expanded Medicaid through increased financial support from the federal government, so that the states could provide health insurance to an additional 5 million children under the age of 18 whose families met its income requirements. Though the plan originally passed with strong bipartisan support, efforts by Democrats to expand SCHIP were thwarted by President Bush in 2007. Only after two vetoes to prevent what the president saw as an "irresponsible plan that would dramatically expand this program beyond its original intent" did he sign into law a temporary extension of the program through March 2009.[51] President Obama made SCHIP a top priority immediately after taking the oath of office on January 20, 2009. By February 4, Congress had passed and he had signed the Children's Health Insurance Program Reauthorization Act of 2009. Paid for by substantial increases in tobacco-related taxes and a reduction in payments to doctor-owned hospitals, the statute extended the program through 2013 and brought the total of covered children to 10 million.

With Medicare Part D and SCHIP, as well as significant increases in Medicare and Medicaid spending, health became the area of fastest welfare state growth— so much so that this part of the federal budget has been increasing far faster than any other. This escalation of costs (Figure 10.2) in the public sector, combined with dramatically escalating private health-care costs, places the United States at the top of the league table of expenditures in this area—quite a contrast to its relatively meager welfare state as seen in comparative perspective (Figure 10.3). The high and escalating cost of health care was one of the main reasons offered by President Obama in support of his plan to create universal access to health insurance that, he claimed, would be a key means to contain costs and distribute them across the age spectrum.

But the primary reason for health reform—the most significant extension of the American welfare state since the Social Security Act of 1935 and the creation of Medicare and Medicaid in 1965—was how it proposed to reduce the number of Americans who stood outside the system of health insurance. Culminating an effort that had begun with President Theodore Roosevelt at the

FIGURE 10.2

GOVERNMENT SPENDING ON HEALTH CARE IN THE UNITED STATES, 1960–2012, IN BILLIONS

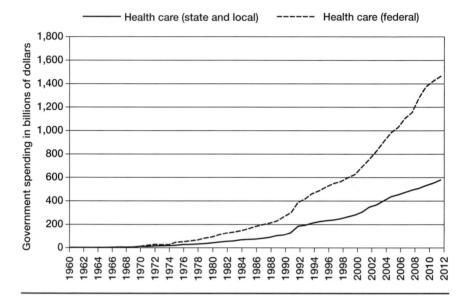

SOURCE: Christopher Chantrill, "Government Spending in the United States of America," at http://www.usgovernmentspending.com (accessed March 11, 2010).

beginning of the twentieth century, the transformation to the health system that passed in March 2010 by the House and Senate, at the behest of President Obama, fundamentally reshaped the rules for this aspect of American life.

Most of the legislation does not take effect until 2014, but starting that year, employers with more than fifty workers will have to provide affordable insurance or pay a penalty of up to $3,000 per employee. The smallest firms will receive subsidies to make it easier for them to provide health insurance for their workers, especially those who earn low wages. Americans will be required to carry health insurance or pay a fee of 2.5 percent of their income, topping out at $695 for individuals and $2,085 for families. To make sure that insurance is affordable, low-income persons whose income does not exceed 133 percent of the federal poverty level ($14,404 for individuals and $29,326 for a family of four when the bill was passed) will be eligible for Medicaid. For individuals and families with incomes between 133 and 400 percent of the poverty levels, the federal government will provide subsidies on a sliding scale to help cover the cost of buying health insurance that will be sold in new state-based insurance marketplaces called exchanges. Once these exchanges begin operating, insurers

FIGURE 10.3

EXPENDITURE ON HEALTH AS A PERCENTAGE OF GDP, LATEST
AVAILABLE YEAR

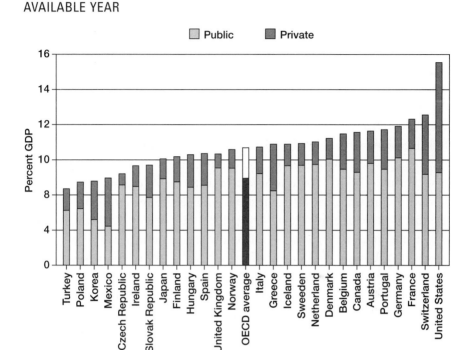

SOURCE: OECD Factbook 2009, at http://titania.sourceoecd.org/vl=1745556/cl=60/
nw=1/rpsv/factbook/10/02/01/10-02-01-g1.htm (accessed March 11, 2010).

will no longer be allowed to reject applicants based on their health status. Additionally, the Medicare prescription drug benefit has been improved, and all Medicare preventive services, such as screening for breast, prostate, and colon cancer, have become free to beneficiaries.

Within months of the signing of this law, a temporary high-risk insurance pool came into existence for people who have medical problems and have been rejected by insurers. Insurers no longer could place lifetime limits on coverage, nor could they deny access to health insurance because of a prior illness or condition (this latter provision applies initially to children; as the law phases in, it will apply to everyone). Further, children now could stay on the policies of their parents until they reached the age of twenty-six.

This dramatic expansion of health coverage is expensive—some $940 billion over the first ten years. But because of new fees, taxes on high-income earners, and reductions to Medicare spending (by phasing out the private-plan part of

Medicare and reducing the rate of increase in payments to hospitals and doctors), the Congressional Budget Office estimated that the legislation actually will narrow the federal budget deficit in this period by $138 billion.

This sweeping social legislation was immensely controversial, exposing sharp partisan divisions. The House moved first, passing a health-care overhaul by a 220–215 vote on November 7, 2009 without any Republican votes. The Senate passed its version of health-care reform on December 24, 2009, on a strict 60–39 party-line vote. Three months later, on March 21, 2010, with demonstrations for and against the bill unfolding on Capitol Hill, the House passed the Senate version on a close 219–212 vote. Again, no Republican voted yes; and thirty-four Democrats joined them to also vote no. The opponents argued that the proposed law was too expensive, too complex, and broadened the powers of government too much. Some also worried that it would expand access to abortion. To secure sufficient votes, the president issued an executive order affirming that no federal funds would be used for this purpose. Following passage, the House and Senate passed modifying language through the reconciliation process that brought the content of the new act closer to the House bill than the version the Senate originally had passed.

Given the scope and significance of this legislation, an immense lobbying effort was mounted, primarily by opponents, to either stop or reshape the bill to make sure it would not contain a public insurance option that would compete with private providers. In the fourth quarter of 2009, the Chamber of Commerce spent some $70 million to fight health-care reform, the Pharmaceutical Research and Manufacturers of America (PhRMA) spent $26 million, and the

Protesters, for and against, gathered outside the U.S. Capitol in Washington, D.C., on March 21, 2010 as the House of Representatives was about to vote on health reform.

leading health-insurance lobby, America's Health Insurance Plans (AHIP) spent nearly $9 million. For every member of Congress, there were six health-care lobbyists trying to influence the course of the legislation.[52]

This massive lobbying effort had some success. It helped prevent the inclusion of a public insurance option. But it did not defeat such provisions as those for a federal rate review board to check high increases to the price of premiums, nor, of course, did it ultimately succeed in derailing the bill.

The result, the New York Times reported, was "the federal government's biggest attack on economic inequality since inequality began rising more than three decades ago." In those years, this evaluation observed, "government policy and market forces have been moving in the same direction, both increasing inequality." By contrast, "nearly every major aspect of the health bill pushes in the other direction."[53] This legislation thus stands out for the way it raises questions central to any analysis of the politics of power, including, most notably, what the role of government should be in seeking to reduce income and wealth gaps among Americans through the instruments of social policy.

CONCLUSION

The welfare state has a conservative and a liberal side. The welfare state is conservative, stabilizing the corporate capitalist system. Welfare, British politician Joseph Chamberlain once said, is the ransom the rich must pay in order to sleep peacefully in their beds at night. The welfare state alleviates but does not correct the basic structural inequalities that are part and parcel of American capitalism. It reinforces the market by making the inequalities and insecurities of a capitalist economy tolerable. Yet the welfare state also offers a more egalitarian alternative to the marketplace. The welfare state can make workers' standards of living less dependent on the wages they receive, thus reducing the power that employers exercise over their employees. For this reason, business generally has opposed extensions of the welfare state while working-class and poor people's movements have supported it. In addition, where welfare states are extensive—as they are in Scandinavia, whose countries provide such benefits as a modest income to all citizens—workers are less tolerant of inequality.[54] The egalitarian logic of the welfare state can spread to other activities, progressively infringing on areas that once operated according to market principles based on the ability to pay.[55] In the United States, the welfare state has exhibited both aspects. It has extended new social protections to vulnerable groups, but often in a way that has reinforced divisions between workers and the poor, whites and blacks, men and women.

The future of the country's welfare state is uncertain. Each of its parts is under strain. During the first decade of this century, budget surpluses turned into massive budget deficits, and inequality continued to grow. With the dire economic collapse that began in 2008, demand for governmental assistance grew significantly, across a range from unemployment insurance to food stamps to TANF grants to poor families. Concurrently, the employer-centered private welfare state is coming under great pressure as more and more companies find themselves hard-pressed to sustain rapidly growing health and pension costs. Further, one of the best-supported parts of the welfare state, Medicare, has come under dramatic fiscal pressure as medical costs for an aging population rise much more swiftly than the rate of inflation. By 2020, the cost of Medicare benefits will outrun the program's accumulated pool of money paid for by payroll taxes, especially if health-care costs continue to increase at a far higher rate than inflation. Based on the current law, Medicare will be unable to pay the benefits it now promises.

Some also question the long-term viability of Social Security; but, by contrast, it does not face a fiscal crisis until much further into the future. Still, there is reason for concern. With the baby boom generation reaching retirement age, and with their numbers over age sixty-five growing faster than the number of workers who pay for benefits, the program's commitments are mounting more rapidly than the economy and the revenues being generated. By 2030, Social Security will have grown as a fraction of GDP from today's 4 percent to 6 percent, and projected spending will exceed the monies in the Social Security Trust Fund. Without changes to the scale and eligibility for benefits, some scholars estimate that the fund will run out by 2040. By 2080, Medicare and Social Security are estimated to have grown to fully 20 percent of GDP, which is a number hard to sustain.

This unprecedented shortfall in the near and longer term makes it even harder to find monies to tackle the persistence of poverty. Such initiatives have been made even more difficult as a result of the tax cuts on the highest earners by the Bush administration at the start of the twenty-first century. Even when the stock market was soaring to new highs in the late 1990s and early 2000s, when the American economy far outpaced that of any rival, when unemployment and inflation were low and the economy was creating millions of jobs per year, more U.S. children grew up in poor families than did children in any other Western industrialized nation, and the country's overall poverty rate remained in the mid-teens. Moreover, during the first ten years of the twenty-first century, fully four in ten Americans found themselves living in poverty at some point, and a remarkable six in ten find themselves in such circumstances at least once during their adult lives.[56]

Economic growth alone cannot reduce poverty. Only government programs in tandem with a successful economy can do that. Poverty rates are sensitive to political choices governments make about the welfare state. The welfare state is here to stay. Perhaps one should say multiple welfare states are here to stay, including social insurance and public assistance, government spending and private provisions linked to employment, national programs and spending at the state and local level. Together, these welfare states have an important impact on class, regional, generational, and racial inequalities, sometimes easing them and sometimes exacerbating them.

Health-care reform has transformed a key part of the welfare state. Yet the sharp partisan polarization that shaped its passage, the public's uncertainty about its merits, and the long period of implementation have created a situation in which the future of the welfare state remains unclear, including the balance of ways to manage risk. Also not conclusively settled is the set of goals the welfare state should try to accomplish—should it support the private economy to increase economic growth, compensate for inequalities generated by the political economy, provide security against inevitable and probable hazards, enhance and equalize opportunities, or ensure that the income and wealth gaps that separate Americans get sharply reduced? Some of these choices are practical, but others are concerned with fundamental values and choices about privileges and power.

CHAPTER SUMMARY

Introduction
The United States possesses four types of programs that are geared to increase material security—social insurance against risks of age, illness, disability, and unemployment; targeted transfers to alleviate hardship; schooling to provide citizens with skills to earn a living; and private sector benefits tied to work. In comparative terms, the scale of spending is relatively modest and the mix of elements unusual.

The Historical Welfare State
Before the New Deal of the 1930s, most social welfare spending was directed either to military pensions or programs to support mothers and children. With the Social Security Act of 1935 that provided old-age and

unemployment insurance, and welfare payments to needy families, a modern American welfare state was created. These policies, which secured most Americans against deprivation, lacked universal health insurance and possessed features that discriminated against racial minorities and women.

The New Deal and Beyond

Faced with dire economic emergency and motivated by an ambition to bring more security to the lives of ordinary Americams, Franklin Roosevelt's New Deal utilized welfare state programs both to stimulate the economy and put people to work, and to build a framework that could protect individuals who faced unemployment and poverty as well as persons who had reached retirement age.

The New Poverty

Despite prosperity after World War II, tens of millions of Americans were living in poverty a quarter-century later, and welfare caseloads had begun to grow. In this period, the poor became younger, more black, and more female.

The Great Society Program

With nearly one in five Americans poor at the start of the 1960s, President Lyndon Johnson led a legislative effort to fight a "War on Poverty" and make it a national priority to improve the circumstances of those at the bottom. Federal spending on social welfare increased dramatically, and a dent was made in the poverty rate. The War on Poverty became a political target when conservatives claimed that it had both overreached and created incentives for poor people not to help themselves.

From Reagan to Clinton

In response to a backlash against federal efforts to strengthen the welfare state, the Reagan administration made an active effort to reduce the size and scope of national social policy programs. The Clinton administration successfully sponsored "welfare reform" that made it more difficult for the poor to receive assistance.

From Bush to Obama

In the new century, the welfare state has continued to develop. During the presidency of George W. Bush, new programs were initiated that increased the federal role and the level of funding for education, and a prescription drug benefit was added to Medicare. Early in his presidency, Barack Obama succeeded in passing health-care reform that would extend insurance to virtually all Americans.

Critical Thinking Questions

1. How important is it to secure the long-term fiscal future of Social Security and Medicare?

2. How broad should the federal role be in setting standards for primary schooling and for high school education?

3 How has the welfare state affected gender relationships, and how have such changes affected the further development of the welfare state?

4. What are the best ways to pay for social programs?

Suggested Readings

Jacob S. Hacker, *The Divided Welfare State.* New York: Cambridge University Press, 2002.

Gwendolyn Mink, *Wages of Motherhood: Inequality in the Welfare State, 1917–1942.* Ithaca, NY: Cornell University Press, 1995.

James O'Connor, *The Fiscal Crisis of the State.* New York: St. Martin's Press, 1973.

James T. Patterson, *America's Struggle against Poverty in the Twentieth Century.* Cambridge, MA: Harvard University Press, 2000.

Paul Pierson, *Dismantling the Welfare State? Reagan, Thatcher, and the Politics of Retrenchment.* New York: Cambridge University Press, 1994.

Frances Fox Piven and Richard Cloward, *Regulating the Poor: Functions of Social Welfare.* New York: Pantheon Books, 1971.

Theda Skocpol, *Protecting Soldiers and Mothers: The Political Origins of Social Policy in the United States.* Cambridge, MA: Harvard University Press, 1992.

William Julius Wilson, *More than Just Race: Being Black and Poor in the Inner City.* New York: Norton, 2009.

FOREIGN POLICY

INTRODUCTION

Two sets of statistics—military and economic—provide the context for understanding American foreign policy. The United States has by far the most powerful military force in the world and the second largest number of military personnel (after China). It maintains 15 major military bases overseas and 600 small ones.[1] Nearly 200,000 American military personnel, the world's best trained and equipped, are stationed abroad, not including troops serving in Iraq and Afghanistan. The navy patrols every ocean, reconnaissance satellites circle the globe, thousands of nuclear-equipped missiles can be launched in minutes, and American warplanes enjoy uncontested supremacy in the skies. Military treaties link the United States to over forty countries. The 2010 U.S. military budget exceeded $600 billion, roughly equal to the combined military budgets of all other countries in the world.[2] (This figure does not include the approximately $150 billion spent annually for the wars in Afghanistan and Iraq.) These immense resources are devoted to maintaining American global preeminence.

The answer to just how preeminent can be gleaned from statistics charting the U.S. economic position. With 5 percent of the world's population, the United States accounts for one-third of the world's wealth. The richest 1 percent of the world's population owns 40 percent of global assets. Over one-third of this group is American.[3] The average American is wealthier (as can be seen in Table 11.1), enjoys better housing, is less apt to be hungry, and receives more education than most other people in the world. Note that this description obscures the extensive inequalities *within* the United States that are analyzed in other chapters.

When American political leaders proclaim the need to maintain world order and stability, they are referring to the order and stability of a world in which the United States enjoys a highly privileged position. A principal goal of Amer-

TABLE 11.1

PER CAPITA INCOME, SELECTED COUNTRIES, 2007

Country	Per Capita Income (in dollars)
Brazil	6,855
Canada	40,329
China	2,432
Dominican Republic	3,772
Ghana	646
India	1,046
Italy	35,396
Mexico	9,715
Russian Federation	9,079
Senegal	900
Sweden	49,662
United States	45,592

SOURCE: UNDP, "Human Development Report 2009," at http://hdrstats.undp.org/en/indicators/152.html (accessed May 11, 2010).

ican foreign policy, and the primary mission of the immense military establishment, is to maintain that position. Relatively few resources are devoted to other foreign policy goals. For example, in 2007 U.S. government expenditures for economic and and social development in poor regions of the world were less than 4 percent of the military budget. Along with Greece, the United States ranked dead last among member countries of the Organisation for Economic Co-operation and Development (OECD), an organization of rich, democratic countries, in the proportion of gross domestic product (GDP) spent on development aid.[4]

There have been multiple and often conflicting currents within American foreign policy.[5] Yet since the establishment of the United States in the eighteenth century, virtually all political leaders have placed the highest priority on enabling the United States to achieve and maintain a favored position in the global political economy. Since World II, the United States has been the dominant world power. American dominance has not just happened; it has been *made* to happen.

The first decade of the twenty-first century marked a turning point in the international position of the United States. Americans had long been accustomed to thinking of the United States as invulnerable. That comforting belief was shattered on September 11, 2001, when suicide bombers belonging to the Islamic fundamentalist movement Al Qaeda hijacked four U.S. airliners laden with jet fuel and used them as missiles. Two planes were flown into the twin towers of the World Trade Center in New York City, causing the massive buildings to crumble and producing nearly three thousand deaths. The third plane crashed into the Pentagon, killing 184 people and producing extensive damage. The fourth plane never reached the hijackers' intended destination of the nation's capital. Passengers and crew overpowered the hijackers, and the plane crashed in a field in Pennsylvania, killing all those aboard.

For more than half a century after World War II, the United States ranked first in virtually every significant dimension of power: military, political, and economic. This was often described as U.S. hegemony; that is, a situation in which U.S. domination consisted not only of "hard power" (primarily, coercion or military force) but also "soft" power involving the use of nonmilitary resources, such as economic pressure, to persuade others to accept America's leadership.[6] However, the United States was never all-powerful, as the 9/11 attack graphically demonstrated. Further, some analysts suggest that U.S. hegemony is being replaced by a "post-American world," in which the United States is forced to share power with other power centers, such as the European Union (EU—a political and economic alliance of European countries) and rising powers like China and India.[7] This chapter surveys the changing international position of the United States, as well as how American foreign policy has affected that position. We begin by describing the process of making foreign policy.

MAKING FOREIGN POLICY

The process of developing foreign policy has much in common with the domestic policy process. However, the process of foreign policymaking is much more centralized within the executive branch, and the number of public and private actors involved is far smaller.

The president is at the center of the foreign-policy process, assisted nowadays by agencies and advisers within the Executive Office of the President— notably, the National Security Council, National Intelligence Council, and national security adviser. Other key executive officials include the secretaries of Defense, State, and Homeland Security. In developing foreign policy, presidents must balance conflicting demands involving domestic partisan and political issues, ideological preferences, financial constraints, and the preferences and pressures of allied and other foreign governments.

Congress is also an influential participant in making and implementing foreign policy because of its authority to appropriate funds, pass legislation, and summon military and civilian leaders to testify before congressional committees. Important congressional figures include the two chambers' leaders, especially those belonging to the majority party, and the chairs and minority leaders of the armed services and foreign affairs committees in both houses, who generally have extensive policy expertise.

Finally, private interests seek to shape foreign policy. The mobilization of bias, described in earlier chapters, operates within the field of foreign and defense policy. The most influential participants are **transnational corporations (TNCs)** and large defense contractors whose interests are vitally affected by foreign policy. The number and range of private firms has significantly increased in recent years because of the extensive outsourcing of activities traditionally carried out by military and civilian agencies. An extensive network of international relations scholars, think tanks like the Council of Foreign Relations, and nongovernmental organizations (NGOs) like Human Rights Watch provide analyses and policy recommendations that may influence the foreign policymaking process. As in the domestic policy process, the constellation of groups involved is quite issue specific. Defense contractors focus on maintaining high levels of military spending, the American Israel Public Affairs Committee (AIPAC) exerts enormous influence to ensure American support for policies that it regards as safeguarding Israel's security, and so on.

AMERICAN FOREIGN POLICY BEFORE WORLD WAR II

What explains the U.S. rise to power? The development is especially puzzling because throughout the eighteenth and nineteenth centuries, the United States generally did not join European countries in engaging in foreign conquest and the search for colonies. American foreign policymakers faithfully followed the advice that George Washington offered in his presidential farewell address when he urged Americans to profit from the good fortune that geography provided, in the form of an ocean separating it from Europe, to avoid "entangling alliances" with other countries. This does not mean that the United States was a passive bystander in world politics. According to historian Andrew Bacevich, American expansionism goes back to the beginning. "If the young United States had a mission, it was not to liberate [despite frequent proclamations of this goal] but to expand."[8] However, U.S. expansion did not take the form of acquiring a colonial empire. First, the United States staked out an informal sphere of influence in the Western Hemisphere. In 1823, President James Monroe issued a statement that came to be known as the **Monroe Doctrine**, in which he warned European powers not to intervene in Latin America. According to historian Richard Van Alstyne, "[I]t is not the negatives [in the Monroe Doctrine] that really count. It is the hidden positive to the effect that the United States shall be the only colonizing power and the sole directing power in both North and South America."[9]

Second, the United States expanded in more direct and dramatic fashion by annexing adjoining territory. According to Bacevich, "Depending on the circumstances, the United States relied on diplomacy, hard bargaining, bluster, chicanery, intimidation, or naked coercion. We infiltrated land belonging to our neighbors and then brazenly proclaimed it our own. We harassed, filibustered, and, when the situation called for it, launched full-scale invasions."[10] The United States quadrupled in size during its first half century as a result of westward expansion. This monumental feat was accomplished by displacing native Indian populations, taking Florida from Spain in 1819, and annexing Texas in 1845. (Texas first became an independent country and then petitioned to be annexed by the United States.) The Mexican-American War in 1846 enabled the United States to annex a vast portion of Mexico, including present-day California, New Mexico, Utah, Arizona, and Nevada.

The violent conquest and forced resettlement of Native Americans deserves special mention. Christopher Columbus sought to repay the Spanish Crown for financing his expeditions by capturing, enslaving, and bringing to Spain over a thousand Native Americans.[11] During the settlement of North America, Europeans slaughtered 3 million Native Americans, nearly the entire indigenous population of North America. Many revered early heroes, including George Washington, John Quincy Adams, and Andrew Jackson, directed this brutal campaign. Along with the centuries-long institution of slavery—embraced by most Northern and Southern whites from the first days of European migration to North America—the genocidal violence directed against Native Americans ranks among the most shameful aspects of the formation of the United States.

During the nineteenth and the early twentieth century, preoccupied with consolidating control in its own backyard, the United States mostly confined foreign intervention to the Western Hemisphere and exercised relative restraint in its dealings with European powers. This policy was commonly described as **isolationism**. However, an important threshold was crossed in 1898, when the United States initiated war with Spain. Historian Michael Hunt observes that "in the span of two decades [the U.S.] made a colony of Puerto Rico, imposed protectorates on Cuba and Panama, and converted into fiscal dependencies Haiti, Nicaragua, and the Dominican Republic."[12]

Gunboat diplomacy, as it became known, consisted of dispatching the U.S. Navy to foreign ports in order to install and protect client regimes favorable to American business interests. Between 1801 and 1904, the United States engaged in 101 military actions in Latin America. Journalist Stephen Kinzer observes that "No nation in modern history has [overthrown foreign regimes] so often, in so many places so far from its own shores."[13]

Toward the end of the nineteenth century, as the power of Britain—the world's dominant country in that century—began to wane, the United States further extended its international influence. When the two world wars of the twentieth century ravaged the leading European nations, the United States achieved global dominance. It was the only industrial power whose territory escaped destruction during World War II. It emerged from the war in a position of unchallenged preeminence, quickly replacing Britain as the dominant capitalist power and the hub of world manufacturing, commerce, and banking.

AMERICAN FOREIGN POLICY AFTER WORLD WAR II

World War II was a watershed in American foreign policy. Two fundamental changes occurred: the assertion of global political leadership and the expansion of American economic influence abroad. Wartime presidents Roosevelt and Truman, as well as influential public and private officials and foreign policy analysts, calculated that the United States needed to assume a more activist role in response to the decline of the major European capitalist powers, the challenge posed by the Soviet Union, the growth of nationalism in newly independent countries in Asia and Africa, and the risk of a resumption of prewar economic depression. Chapters 3, 9, and 10 have described how policies were devised during the New Deal and after World War II to promote economic and social stability at home. In addition, U.S. policymakers crafted foreign policies to deal with a rapidly changing global situation that included movements for the independence of colonies in Asia and Africa formerly controlled by Western European countries, as well as demands for economic development and social justice throughout the world. The new orientation included three elements: opposing communism, integrating the non-Communist world, and creating international regulatory institutions.

Opposing Communism: The Cold War

The most apparent feature of world politics in the period following World War II was the bitter rivalry between the United States and the Soviet Union (USSR) that became known as the **Cold War**. Each country had an extensive sphere of influence: the United States in Western Europe, North America, and Latin America; the Soviet Union in Eastern and Central Europe, Cuba (following the Cuban Revolution in 1959), and the People's Republic of China (following the Communist revolution in 1949, although Russia and China split in the 1960s). The United States and USSR also had client states in the third world.

An ideological chasm separated liberal democratic, capitalist United States and Communist Soviet Union, which had a command economy and an authoritarian Communist Party. The two blocs faced off across an iron curtain (so named by British prime minister Winston Churchill) that ran through the heart of Europe. The United States sponsored the **North Atlantic Treaty Organization (NATO)** to coordinate military planning by West European and North American countries; the Soviet Union organized the Warsaw Pact, a parallel organization of its allies in Central and Eastern Europe.

During the Cold War, a change took place in world politics that continues to this day. Ever since the United States developed atomic weapons and unleashed two of them against Japan in the closing months of World War II, and the USSR deployed its own nuclear weapons in the 1950s, the world has faced the awful possibility of nuclear devastation. For decades (and continuing into the present), the future of the world has hung by a thread. During the half century of the Cold War, the United States and USSR possessed tens of thousands of nuclear-equipped intercontinental ballistic missiles targeted on the opponent's armed forces and civilian populations. As a result, there was a significant possibility of nuclear catastrophe by accident or irresponsible design. Indeed, the two superpowers approached the brink of nuclear war during the Cuban Missile Crisis of 1962. Documents later made public revealed that leaders of both countries were close to unleashing a nuclear attack.

The Cold War was misnamed because conflict was sometimes white-hot. The United States and the Soviet Union fought numerous "proxy wars" in the third world—in Angola, Mozambique, and Ethiopia in Africa; and in Nicaragua, El Salvador, and Guatemala in Central America. These conflicts often pitted client states of the United States against insurgent movements backed by the USSR. The United States provided friendly regimes with financial assistance and trained their military, intelligence, and police officials. In addition, the United States engaged in two large-scale conventional wars with Soviet allies after

World War II: the Korean War (1950–53) and the Vietnam War from the mid-1960s to 1973.

Vietnam proved to be a particular nightmare for the United States. The war claimed the lives of over fifty thousand American troops and resulted in several million Vietnamese casualties. Since World War II, the United States has also engaged in military operations, not all linked to the Cold War, against Laos and Cambodia (connected to the Vietnam War), the Dominican Republic, Lebanon, Grenada, Panama, Libya, Somalia, Yugoslavia, Afghanistan, and Iraq.[14]

Although the dominant feature of the half century after World War II was Cold War rivalry between the United States and the Soviet Union, another (if related) development was also enormously significant. Historian David Callahan suggests that "Whether the Cold War had occurred or not, it is clear that the United States would still have played a much greater global leadership role after World War II than it did after World War I. . . . For quite apart from the problem of security, postwar U.S. economic growth was seen as requiring international economic order that could only be guaranteed if the United States took over the position of a declining Britain."[15] Writing in 1970, foreign policy analyst Graham Allison made a similar, and prescient, point: "Historians in the year 2000, looking back with detachment on the Cold War, are apt to conclude that the main feature of international life in the period 1945–1970 was . . . the global expansion of American influence: military, economic, political and cultural."[16]

Beginning in the late 1980s, momentous changes occurred in the Soviet Union and its allies. A crumbling economy and increasing popular anger at economic austerity and authoritarian rule culminated in the dissolution of the USSR in 1991. The Soviet Union was replaced by the much smaller non-Communist Russian Federation. Independent states were formed in East-Central Europe and Central Asia from regions formerly incorporated within the Soviet Union or in its sphere of influence. During the same period, Soviet client states in East-Central Europe (including Poland, Hungary, and other countries) broke free of Soviet control and overthrew Communist governments. The implosion of the Soviet Union and defeat of communism left the United States as the world's sole superpower—"hyperpower," in the words of a French foreign minister. Strategic analyst Richard Betts observes, "Only the collapse of the Soviet pole [in the 1990s] . . . marked the real arrival of U.S. global dominance."[17]

Integrating the Non-Communist World

Following World War II, the United States achieved a commanding position in non-Communist regions of the world. This was a result of the American

government's activist political and military posture as well as economic penetration by U.S.-based TNCs in Western Europe and the developing world.
(Transnational corporations are firms with significant foreign operations.) The
two forms of influence are distinct but often complementary. According to
political economist Robert Gilpin, the income generated by American investments abroad in the postwar period was used "to finance America's global political and military position. The income from foreign investments, in other words,
had become an important factor in American global hegemony."[18]

After World War II, the United States provided extensive political and economic resosurces to help rebuild the war-damaged economies of the industrialized capitalist countries of Western Europe and forge a Western European
alliance under U.S. leadership. The policy proved a brilliant success. The first
step was to sponsor a large aid package, known as the **Marshall Plan**, that
enabled Western European countries to finance economic reconstruction. The
United States also designed the Marshall Plan to encourage former enemies,
especially France and Germany, to engage in economic and political cooperation. Their success laid the groundwork for creating the organization that eventually grew into the European Union (EU), an organization that tightly
integrates the economies of most European countries and promotes political
coordination. Following World War II, Western Europe became a haven of
peace, prosperity, and stability after centuries of intense internal strife.

The United States also provided military aid to pro-American forces in
Greece in 1947 who were engaged in a deadly struggle with Soviet-backed forces.
The origins of the Cold War are sometimes dated from the Greek Civil War,
the first time that the Soviet Union and United States indirectly engaged in military confrontation.

After World War II, the U.S. government extended the scope of the Monroe
Doctrine from South America to what was described at the time as the third
world—that is, the less developed regions in Asia, Africa, and Latin America.
(The world was commonly described at this time as also consisting of the industrialized capitalist world [the first world] and the Soviet bloc [the second
world]). The United States pressured Britain, France, Belgium, and other European powers to dismantle their colonial empires in the name of national self-
determination and democracy. Dozens of colonies in Africa and Asia became
independent countries in the decade after World War II. U.S. policy was inspired
by World War I President Woodrow Wilson's idealistic vision of a "world safe
for democracy" along with hard-nosed calculation that decolonization would
bolster American strategic interests. Once colonies became independent states,
the United States frequently intervened, in a manner similar to its traditional

actions in Latin America. (One study tabulates seventy cases of U.S. intervention in third world countries since World War II.)[19] U.S. intervention aimed to install and protect friendly regimes in developing countries, oppose Soviet influence, promote democracy, and bolster capitalism. The United States was not always successful. In 1949, a Communist movement overthrew an American-backed regime in China. In the 1950s, U.S. forces were stalemated in Korea. And the worst instance was the costly and agonizing U.S. defeat in the Vietnam War of the 1960s and 1970s.

Because the Middle East contains the world's largest petroleum deposits, an essential ingredient of an industrial economy, a principal U.S. foreign policy goal was to help American oil companies gain control of the region's petroleum reserves. In 1940, Great Britain controlled 72 percent of Middle East oil reserves, the United States 10 percent, and other countries the remainder. By 1967, Great Britain controlled 29 percent, the United States 59 percent, and other countries the remainder.[20] Part of the explanation for the shift was that the United States formed an alliance of oil-rich states in the Middle East who depended on the United States for political and military support. The United States went to war against Iraq in 1991 after Iraq invaded Kuwait, a U.S. ally. After a swift victory, the United States created military bases in Kuwait, Saudi Arabia, and Bahrain. Following the September 11 attacks, the United States established military bases in the oil-rich "Stans" of Central Asia: Uzbekistan,

An oil refinery in Basra, Iraq.

Tajikistan, and Kyrgyzstan. And one reason the United States toppled Saddam Hussein's regime in Iraq in 2003 is that the country has the second-largest petroleum reserves in the world.[21]

The United States continues to put the highest priority on protecting access to overseas supplies of petroleum. Although it produces only about 5 percent of the world's oil, it accounts for 25 percent of total world oil consumption. By 2025, the United States will require substantially greater petroleum supplies. At the same time, other countries, especially China and India, are desperately seeking new energy sources. As strategic analyst Michael Klare points out, "Oil makes this country [the U.S.] strong; dependency makes us weak."[22]

Creating International Regulatory Institutions

After World War II, the United States took the lead in sponsoring the creation of international organizations designed to regulate the world's political and economic order. Among the most important were the United Nations (UN), an umbrella organization comprising the General Assembly, Security Council, and other agencies; the International Monetary Fund (IMF), whose mission is to provide emergency aid to member states experiencing financial crisis; the International Bank for Reconstruction and Development (popularly known as the World Bank), designed to reduce poverty and promote economic development of poor countries and regions; the Organisation for Economic Co-operation and Development (OECD), that includes the major capitalist countries; and the General Agreement on Tariffs and Trade (GATT), whose mandate was to lower barriers to trade among member states. (The GATT became the World Trade Organization, or WTO, in 1995; the WTO has a broader mission and greater power over member states.) The U.S. government used its powerful influence within these institutions to promote stability and market-friendly policies.

The sharp increase in the American government's influence abroad after World War II outstripped the expansion of foreign operations by American-based corporations, with the exception of U.S. companies' investments in Middle East petroleum reviewed above. Although U.S. corporations did a brisk export trade, in part because World War II had destroyed much industrial equipment abroad, the bulk of American productive capacity remained concentrated within American borders. This situation changed in the 1980s, when American-based corporations substantially increased foreign trade, investment, and finance; Americans began buying many more imported goods and services; and foreign companies stepped up investments in the United States. These developments are often regarded as comprising a new era that is commonly described as globalization.

A NEW ERA OF GLOBALIZATION?

Did the world enter a new (globalized) era beginning in the 1980s? Two groups, which we label globalists and skeptics, have formed on opposite sides of this issue. Globalists claim, in the title of one feisty account, that we are now "One World, Ready or Not."[23] Advances in transportation and communication enable people, commodities, capital, and information to circle the globe at vastly greater speed and at vastly lower cost. Globalization also has a powerful political impact. States are less able to police their borders, in part because physical borders dissolve in an electronically interconnected world. Globally integrated markets make it difficult for states to pursue autonomous economic policies. At best, they can seek to position their economies at the cutting edge internationally as well as help their citizens adjust to globalization. At worst, when states ignore the importance of global economic competition, they slip ever further behind the global leaders and their citizens pay the price in lower living standards.

Although skeptics question some of the globalists' claims, they agree that there has been a sharp increase in some key global economic flows. Exports of OECD countries rose from 11 percent of their GDP in 1960 to 28 percent in 2007. Foreign direct investment in OECD countries grew even faster—at triple the rate of increase of international trade.[24] Large as they are, these changes are dwarfed by increases in transnational financial flows, including loans to foreign governments and firms, purchases of foreign government bonds, and currency exchange. The magnitude of these transactions has increased from several billion dollars daily in the 1970s to nearly $2 trillion a day today!

Where skeptics disagree is about the causes and significance of these changes and how permanent they will be. For globalists, globalization follows developments in technology and transportation like night follows day. Skeptics, on the other hand, emphasize the importance of politics, that is, pro-globalization decisions, institutions, and policies.[25]

Finally, skeptics emphasize that most production in the world remains geared to domestic consumption. Guess what proportion of U.S. GDP is exported these days—less than one-fifth, about half, over half? The first answer is correct, and then some: only about 10 percent of U.S. GDP is exported.

With that said, there is no denying the substantial increase in international economic interdependence that deeply affects all nations and people in the world. In the United States, for example, globalization has fractured traditional interest alignments. When it comes to policies that affect particular firms and industries, the traditional cleavage between business and labor unions is often replaced by industry- or firm-specific coalitions of business and labor. For example, when the Air Force decided to replace its aging fleet of refueling aircraft, a fierce competition to land the $35 billion contract pitted the management and unions at Boeing against the management and unions at Northrop Grumman, a U.S.-based subcontractor for European aerospace company Airbus.

Discussions of globalization usually lead, sooner rather than later, to the topic of transnational corporations. These organizations are important vehicles for promoting globalization.

Transnational Corporations

Transnational corporations (TNCs) are the Goliaths of globalization. The five hundred largest TNCs control over one-third of the world's global assets. Most are headquartered in the United States.[26] Although American corporations began creating foreign subsidiaries after World War II, the largest growth has occurred since the 1980s. By 2000, multinational corporations outnumbered countries on the list of the world's one hundred largest entities.

Most large American-based corporations have foreign subsidiaries that generate substantial revenue. For example, according to the business magazine *Forbes*, General Electric, the world's largest company in 2008, operates in over one hundred countries and derives over half its revenue from its foreign operations. In 2008, American companies owned $20 trillion in foreign assets (Table 11.2).

To gain access to skilled labor and infrastructure, and to locate themselves close to consumers who purchase their commodities, TNCs direct most investment to affluent countries north of the equator (the region often described as the global north). However, to obtain access to raw materials and cheap labor, TNCs have stepped up investments and outsourcing recently in poor countries including China, India, and Brazil. TNCs have an especially great impact in poor countries. By offering wages higher than the prevailing rates, they can select from a large number of job applicants. Women, in particular, gain the opportunity to boost their family's income and escape traditional constraints and isolation.

TABLE 11.2

U.S. INTERNATIONAL ASSETS, 1976–2008, SELECTED YEARS

Year	U.S.-Owned Foreign Assets	Foreign-Owned U.S. Assets
1976	456,964	291,590
1980	929,806	564,304
1985	1,287,396	1,220,275
1990	2,178,978	2,402,383
1995	3,486,272	3,909,183
2000	6,238,785	7,569,415
2005	11,961,552	13,886,698
2008	19,888,158	23,357,404

NOTE: All figures are in millions of dollars.
SOURCE: Bureau of Economic Analysis, "International Yearend Positions, 1976–2008," at http://www.bea.gov/international (accessed March 19, 2010).

TNCs have enabled South Korea, Taiwan, India, and China to achieve enormous economic expansion and significant poverty reduction. Because of its enormous size and its astonishingly rapid and sustained rate of economic growth, China deserves special mention. From being a backwater until the 1980s, China has leapfrogged to a position as a major economic, political, and economic powerhouse.

Much of the economic growth of China and other newly industrializing countries is due to investments and outourcing arrangements by TNCs. Although TNC operations in many poor countries involve welcome infusions of capital and technology, TNCs locate in these areas to take advantage of low wages, lax labor laws, and poor enforcement of environmental regulations. Thus, the low prices that American consumers enjoy when shopping at big box stores like Wal-Mart are subsidized by the citizens of countries that absorb the social costs incurred by TNC-organized commodity chains.

The other side of the coin of American-based TNC investments abroad is foreign-based TNC investments in the United States: TNCs employ over 5 million American workers. In some industries—for example, auto assembly—they employ over one-quarter of all workers in the industry.[27] The United States depends on a substantial inward flow of foreign investment to maintain job levels and financial stability. Recently, American companies and consumers have purchased $600 billion more goods and services produced abroad each year than U.S. firms have exported to other countries. (This imbalance is called the trade deficit.) To balance the books, the United States depends on new foreign investment in the United States and purchases of U.S. treasury bills by foreign governments and investors.

A Post–Cold War Clash of Civilizations?

The concept of globalization helps make sense of the contemporary world. Another perspective proposed to explain contemporary global tensions is the concept of the "clash of civilizations." Political scientist Samuel Huntington popularized this view in what Peter Katzenstein, an international relations expert, has described as "arguably the most influential book published in international relations since the end of the Cold War."[28] Huntington claimed that the major cultures or civilizations in the world embrace divergent political and cultural values. In particular, he believed that there is a fundamental conflict between the Judeo-Christian West, which has championed the importance of individualism and freedom, and Islamic culture, which Huntington characterized as displaying intolerant and authoritarian values.

We question this claim. For one thing, cultural values are not static. Although freedom, individualism, and secularism may now be dominant values in the West, this was not always the case. Democracy and secularism developed only within the last century in most Western countries. For centuries, the West was the site of religious clashes. Conversely, for hundreds of years Muslim rulers of the vast Ottoman Empire granted non-Muslim communities extensive autonomy and religious freedom.

For another thing, cultures are not monolithic. Economist and philosopher Amartya Sen points out that "Diversity is a feature of most cultures in the world. . . . Islam is often portrayed as fundamentally intolerant and hostile to individual freedom. But the presence of diversity and variety within a tradition applies very much to Islam as well."[29] Only a tiny minority of Muslims subscribe to extremist interpretations of Islam or participate in violent movements targeting the United States and other Western countries. Further, the United States is allied with many Muslim nations, including Saudi Arabia, Egypt, Morocco, and Kuwait. (Egypt receives more foreign aid from the United States than any country in the world other than Israel.)

Although global conflicts do not involve a clash of civilizations, there are frequent conflicts nowadays *within* rather than *between* civilizations. These disputes pit moderate, liberal elements within a religious community against groups championing what members claim is traditional, orthodox religious practice.

If the clash of civilizations is a misleading template for understanding contemporary global conflicts, is there a preferable alternative? Although contemporary conflicts do not neatly align along a single axis of cleavage in this complex world, one major source of conflict opposes those states and nonstatist groups that seek to challenge the existing distribution of power against a coalition of the U.S. government and its allies that seeks to preserve the status quo. The U.S. military is the fundamental instrument that the government uses to preserve American hegemony.

THE MILITARY ESTABLISHMENT

During the Cold War, the U.S. military establishment's major goal was to check the Soviet Union (the policy was called **containment**). Both the United States and USSR possessed a staggering "overkill" capacity: the United States had a stockpile of over 9,000 strategic nuclear warheads (and several times that number of tactical nuclear weapons); the Soviet Union had over 7,000. After the Cold War, both sides subtantially reduced their nuclear stockpiles. In 2010, President Obama concluded an agreement called "New START" with Russia to further reduce nuclear warheads as well as delivery vehicles, including intercontinental missiles, submarine-based missiles, and long-range bombers. President Obama also proposed that Russia and the United States work together toward the long-range goal of worldwide nuclear disarmament.

However, the risk of nuclear catastrophe remains significant, and in some respects greater than ever, because of nuclear proliferation. In addition to the United States and Russia, countries that now possess nuclear weapons include Britain, China, India, Israel, North Korea, and Pakistan. Other countries, such as Iran, would like to join the nuclear club. Even more ominous is the risk that nonstatist groups like Al Qaeda might obtain radioactive material or hijack a nuclear power facility in order to unleash a "dirty bomb."

What has been the military's mission in the post–Cold War period? The clearest statement in the current period was provided by the Department of Defense 2000 report "Joint Vision 2020." The report identified the goal of the U.S. military as "full spectrum dominance," defined as global superiority in every militarily strategic sphere: land, sea (both surface and underwater), air, space, and electromagnetic spectrums. As noted earlier, the military is provided with $600 billion a year to pursue this goal. Strategic analyst Paul Rogers describes the aim as "'global reach'—the ability to project power around the world."[30] Journalist George Easterbrook draws the logical conclusion from this pattern. He claims that the American military establishment is distinctive among major countries in that its "primary military mission is not defense. Practically the entire military is an expeditionary force, designed not to guard borders—a duty that ties down most units of other militaries, including China's—but to 'project power' elsewhere in the world."[31]

Military specialist Mary Kaldor has described how the military has been retooled to remain on top. "[T]he end of the Cold War led to a feverish technological effort to apply information technology to military purposes, known as the Revolution in Military Affairs (RMA)."[32] RMA involves "the interaction between various systems for information collection, analysis, and transmission and weapons systems—the so-called 'system of systems.'"[33] The key interrelated elements are unmanned precision-guided weapons, like the Predator drone aircraft, and sophisticated surveillance systems.

Most military forces other than those stationed in Afghanistan and Iraq now consist of mobile, rapid intervention units transported by aircraft based in the United States and capable of flying long-range missions thanks to aerial refueling. For example, the U.S. Central Command, which directs the wars in Afghanistan and Iraq, is based in Tampa, Florida, thousands of miles from the theaters of operations. Another vital component of the globally mobile military force is the U.S. Navy, whose tonnage and firepower exceed those of all other major naval powers combined. Finally, as noted earlier, the United States maintains hundreds of military bases abroad.

The military has been outfitted with high-tech weaponry and reorganized because its mission now includes unconventional conflicts, such as counterinsurgency and ethnic and religious strife. The military has also been delegated responsibilities for state and **nation building**, tasks even further removed from traditional combat. In Iraq and Afghanistan, military personnel train police and teachers, build schools and roads, and provide economic development aid.

The military's broadened mission explains why the Pentagon's budget is so large and why the gap has grown between the military's budget and that of civilian agencies responsible for formulating and implementing American foreign policy, notably the State Department and the Agency for International Development (AID). (An often cited illustration is that there are more members of military marching bands than officers of the U.S. Foreign Service.) The title of a news report describes the result: "The Pentagon has all but eclipsed the State Department in setting U.S. foreign policy."[34]

If the broadest mission of the U.S. military and foreign policy establishment is to maintain a stable, integrated world order under U.S. dominance, a by-product of military spending—and for many businesses, the primary purpose—is to generate profits. The defense industry consists of major corporations like Boeing and McDonnell Douglas, along with thousands of other defense contractors. Firms working for the Pentagon are scattered throughout the country. Together with labor unions whose members are employed in the defense industry and conservative groups, defense contractors constitute a powerful nationwide lobby pressuring Congress and the executive to ratchet up military spending.

A recent development further swelling the military budget is the outsourcing to civilian contractors of core military and diplomatic functions including intelligence, interrogation of prisoners, provisioning troops, and providing security for military facilities and embassies. Eighty percent of the State Department's budget is spent on contracts and grants to private firms.[35]

One goal of foreign policy unrelated to maintaining miltary superiority is strengthening human rights and democracy around the world. This aspect of foreign policy is inspired by humanitarian concerns and the belief that the United States is a force for good in the world. Enlightened self-interest has also played a role. Liberal presidents like John F. Kennedy and Jimmy Carter calculated that democratic regimes would be more inclined to support U.S. political and economic policies. On the other hand, when democratic governments have opposed U.S. leadership and market-friendly policies, the American government has on occasion encouraged opposition groups and tried to orchestrate regime change. The U.S. government also routinely ignores human rights abuses and undemocratic practices by U.S. allies such as Egypt and Saudi Arabia.

Distribution of food provided by USAID, a government agency, following the 2010 earthquake that affected Port-au-Prince, Haiti.

WHAT DO YOU THINK?

Promoting Global Well-being versus Exercising Self-Restraint

To what extent should the American government use its vast power to work with other nations to eliminate nuclear weapons; take the lead in promoting alternative energy sources and other steps to deal with global warming; preserve the world's battered ecosystem; reduce poverty, hunger, disease, and economic inequalities; and strengthen democracy and human rights? How could it do so without the United States dictating to others? Alternatively, should the United States adopt a more modest profile, consistent with what physicians are taught in medical school: "First, do no harm"?

Are there more attractive goals that U.S. foreign policy might pursue? Clearly, the first priority must be to keep Americans safe. Indeed, before 9/11 the government ignored repeated warnings by its own experts regarding likely attacks of just this kind. In addition, among worthy goals that have been given little attention, the United States might work with other nations to eliminate nuclear weapons; take the lead in promoting alternative energy sources and other steps to deal with global warming; preserve the world's battered ecosystem; reduce poverty, hunger, disease, and economic inequalities; and strengthen democracy and human rights. In the first years of the twenty-first century, U.S. foreign policy gave major priority to very different goals.

THE SHIFT TO UNILATERALISM

Every president since World War II has sought to maintain U.S. global superiority, but different presidents have interpreted and pursued this goal in quite different ways. For example, President Jimmy Carter emphasized the importance of promoting human rights throughout the world. Ronald Reagan adopted a bellicose policy toward the USSR yet sought greater accommodation with the Soviet Union toward the end of his presidency. Differences among postwar presidents pale, however, in comparison to President George W. Bush's attempt to expand American power.

Every president since Harry Truman has proclaimed the value of participating in **multilateral** economic, political, and military institutions. President

Bush broke with this tradition by championing a **unilateral** approach; that is, a policy in which the United States acted alone rather than in concert with its allies. The new orientation was evident from the first days of Bush's presidency, well before 9/11, when he announced his opposition to the Kyoto Protocol on global warming that most nations had ratified. The president also rejected the jurisdiction of the International Criminal Court, created to try cases of genocide, war crimes, and crimes against humanity. In both cases, the United States parted company with its traditional allies and most other countries.

The Bush administration sponsored measures to profit from Russia's weakened position following the Cold War. President Bush proposed admitting Russia's neighbors, Georgia and Ukraine, to NATO membership. He rejected previously negotiated limits on antiballistic missile development and announced plans to build a nuclear antimissile shield in Poland and the Czech Republic, Russia's neighbors. The president shelved a comprehensive nuclear test ban treaty signed by President Clinton, and he ordered an attack on Iraq in 2003 over Russia's and many other countries' strong opposition. These measures increased tension between Russia and the United States so sharply that some analysts spoke of a new Cold War.

The turn to unilateralism isolated the United States and produced a steep drop in U.S. standing around the world, especially when the United States attacked Iraq in 2003. In 2004, former national security adviser Zbigniew Brzezinski observed that "We're more unpopular in the world today than at any time in our history, and our policies are more unpopular than those of any country in the world."[36]

Within the United States, initial support for the war turned into opposition. Antiwar sentiment cast a shadow over George Bush's second presidential term and contributed to the Democrats' takeover of Congress in the 2006 midterm elections. The early opposition to the war by a little-known senator from Illinois named Barack Obama was a principal reason why Obama gained the Democratic presidential nomination and was elected president.

Beyond the question of the Iraq War, one can identify two important changes in American foreign and security policy sponsored by the Bush administration: an aggressive assertion of U.S. power to preserve its global dominance, and expansion of the government's internal security and coercive apparatus. These policy changes were a powerful legacy confronting President Obama.

Aggressive Assertion of U.S. Power

There has often been a tension within U.S. foreign policy between a claim to support democracy throughout the world versus an attempt to shape other countries' policies in ways that will advance American interests. However, during the Bush administration the balance shifted toward a more openly aggressive posture.

In 2002 the government issued the authoritative "National Security Strategy of the United States."[37] The document claimed that "[to] forestall or prevent [potentially] hostile acts by our adversaries, the United States will, if necessary, act preemptively." This meant that, for the first time in American history, the government proclaimed the right to launch hostilities in the absence of an imminent attack. The new posture became known as the **Bush Doctrine**. In plain terms, the government asserted the right to be judge and jury regarding when to initiate war.

The new doctrine was immediately followed by action. In a book describing his tenure as U.S. counterterrorism chief, Richard Clarke describes his astonishment when he participated in discussions at the White House the day after 9/11. Rather than focusing on a response to Al Qaeda and the Taliban regime, much of the conversation involved Iraq. President Bush urged Clarke to find evidence of Iraq's involvement in the attack despite Clarke's insistence that no link existed between Saddam Hussein and Al Qaeda.[38] Over a year later, and without discovering any evidence of Iraqi involvement in 9/11 or secret programs to develop weapons of mass destruction (WMDs), Secretary of State Colin Powell was dispatched to the UN to make the case for attacking Iraq. Powell cited what he described as "incontrovertible proof" that Iraq possessed WMDs. However, after the United States toppled Saddam's regime, a massive search failed to produce any evidence of WMDs in Iraq or an active program to produce them. Years later, Powell confessed that the UN speech was the biggest mistake of his career.

Given the failure to find evidence of WMDs, the president offered a new defense for launching the war: to increase American security. As he described it, fighting terrorists abroad meant that the United States would not have to fight them within its borders. To this, counterterrorism director Clarke replied, "Nothing America could have done would have provided al Qaeda and its new generation of cloned groups a better recruitment device than our unprovoked invasion of an oil-rich Arab country [Iraq]."[39]

Expansion of the Government's Internal Security Apparatus

The Bush administration claimed that the government needed expanded powers to deal with the unprecedented threat represented by international terrorism. However, David Cole, professor of constitutional law at Georgetown

University, regarded the so-called War on Terror differently. "President Bush undertook a full-scale assault on the courts, on international law, and on the rule of law."[40] Constitutional scholar Ronald Dworkin agreed: "Since September 11, the government has enacted legislation, adopted policies, and threatened procedures that are not consistent with our established laws and values and would have been unthinkable before."[41] One example was that the Patriot Act, passed soon after 9/11, created "a new, breathtakingly vague and broad definition of terrorism and of aiding terrorists."[42] A *New York Times* commentator suggested that if the law's definition of terrorism "sounds as if it's directed more toward effigy-burning, or Greenpeace activity, than international terror, it's because it is. International terror was already illegal."[43]

President Bush also devised another category, "unlawful combatants," that most experts claim is in violation of international law. Despite objections from lawyers within the Pentagon, President Bush issued an order stating that the government could hold indefinitely those designated as unlawful combatants and deprive them of rights and protections provided to prisoners of war by the Geneva convention. Hundreds of U.S. aliens and several American citizens were imprisoned under these procedures. In further violation of international law, the government refused to reveal detainees' identities.

An especially ugly aspect of American power came to light in 2004, when photographs were made public depicting prisoners in sexually humiliating poses at the Abu Ghraib prison in Iraq. Official investigations found that prisoners were routinely stripped naked, hooded, held in stressful positions, submerged in water, attacked by guard dogs, and placed in solitary confinement in dark, hot or cold rooms for long periods.

Government officials declared that these abuses were the regrettable excesses of rogue prison guards. However, numerous official investigations, as well as reports by independent journalists, documented that many of these practices occurred frequently at U.S. military prisons in Afghanistan and Iraq. For example, an FBI memorandum described "abuse of prisoners by military personnel in Iraq that included detainees being beaten and choked, and having lit cigarettes placed in their ears."[44] Methods of interrogation included slamming prisoners' heads against a wall, conducting mock executions, threatening to abuse prisoners' families, and subjecting them to waterboarding, a technique that induces near drowning. Other tactics included **extraordinary rendition**, that is, handing prisoners over to authoritarian regimes in Egypt, Morocco, and elsewhere, where they were subjected to torture; and sending suspects for interrogation to secret detention centers run by the Central Intelligence Agency (CIA) in Romania, Morocco, and Poland.

Detainees at Camp X-Ray, Guantánamo Bay Naval Base, Cuba, 2002.

Most of these practices are prohibited by the Geneva convention, the Universal Declaration of Human Rights, and the UN Convention against Torture—agreements ratified by the United States and whose status in U.S. constitutional law is equivalent to the Constitution itself. However, Bush's attorney general, Alberto Gonzales, declared that "[A] new paradigm renders obsolete [the Geneva convention's] strict limitations on questioning of enemy prisoners and renders quaint some of its provisions."[45] Reflecting on these developments, *New York Times* legal commentator Anthony Lewis observed, "Instead of a country committed to law, the United States is now seen as a country that proclaims high legal ideals and then says that they should apply to all others but not to itself."[46]

Beginning in 2004, pushback began to occur. There was widespread indignation over revelations of what amounted to officially authorized torture. The Supreme Court reversed some initial decisions and restored some of the detainee rights stripped away by the Bush administration. It ordered the release of a prisoner who had been held in solitary confinement for over two years without any charges being brought. (The government admitted that it had no evidence that he had committed any wrongdoing.) Momentum increased to trim executive power after the Democrats gained control of Congress in 2006, and Obama was elected in 2008.

THE OBAMA PRESIDENCY: CONTINUITY OR CHANGE?

Barack Obama was elected president in part because he promised to reverse the aggressive foreign policy of the Bush administration. The change was symbolized on Obama's first day in office, when he announced his intention to close the Guantánamo Bay military prison in Cuba by year's end. (The administration failed to achieve this goal, in part because it could not arrange for prisoners to be transferred elsewhere.) Obama ordered that coercive interrogation techniques on detainees be ended, announced that the CIA's secret prisons would be closed, and set a deadline for withdrawing combat troops from Iraq.

These declarations were soon followed by other initiatives. The Obama administration released the Bush administration's legal opinions authorizing interrogation techniques that amounted to torture, as well as descriptions of how these techniques were applied. The president rejected the plan to build a missile defense system in Poland and the Czech Republic, and he negotiated a second Strategic Arms Reduction Treaty (START) with Russia—which President Bush had suspended—that mandated a sharp reduction in the two countries' nuclear stockpiles. President Obama convened a conference of forty-seven world leaders aimed at combating nuclear terrorism and seeking nuclear disarmament. He directed administration officials to participate in international conferences seeking reductions in greenhouse gases. These policies comprised an about-face from the Bush administration's unilateral and militarist approach to foreign affairs.

The newly elected president was highly popular abroad. When Barack and Michelle Obama visited Europe in 2009, large crowds gave them a warm welcome. The president delivered a widely publicized speech in Cairo, Egypt, in 2009, in which he called for mutual understanding between Muslims and members of other faiths. Judging by public opinion polls and declarations by world leaders, the United States has regained considerable ground lost during the Bush presidency. These factors explain why President Obama was awarded the Nobel Peace Prize in 2009.

Yet the Obama administration supported many of the Bush administration's initiatives, for example, the claim that wartime emergency justified the use of sweeping and unregulated executive power. Like the Bush Justice Department, the Obama Justice Department has invoked the doctrine of state secrets to oppose lawsuits challenging the government's alleged torture and warrantless wiretapping. Like its predecessor, the Obama administration has practiced **preventive detention**, that is, holding detainees without access to lawyers, judicial review, or trial. It defended the practice of extraordinary rendition. Contrary

> ### WHAT DO YOU THINK?
>
> **What Drives American Foreign Policy?**
>
> Ever since the first years of the Republic, there has been tension involving U.S. foreign policy and behavior. On the one hand, political leaders have often proclaimed that the United States is distinctive—"a city upon a hill"—with a unique mission to promote freedom at home and abroad. On the other hand, U.S. foreign policy and behavior often seem motivated by the attempt to maximize U.S. power and promote conditions in the world that will enable the United States to prosper. What do you see as the primary motivation behind U.S. foreign policy and behavior?

to President Obama's campaign pledge, the government announced that it would try foreign prisoners held at Guantánamo in military tribunals, where defendents possess significantly fewer rights than they do in civilian courts. The government continued to engage in warrantless surveillance of U.S. citizens suspected of having links to terrorism. In an editorial noting the continuity between the two administrations, the *New York Times* warned, "The Obama administration has clung for so long to the Bush administration's expansive claims of national security and executive power that it is in danger of turning President George W. Bush's cover-up of abuses commited in the name of fighting terrorism into President Barack Obama's cover-up."[47]

By ordering a sizable troop buildup in Afghanistan, President Obama went beyond President Bush in relying on military solutions in that country. The aim was to eradicate Al Qaeda and prevent the Taliban from toppling a U.S.-backed government and regaining control of the country. It is an open question whether the result has increased U.S. security and promoted the establishment of a stable, democratic, and effective government in Afghanistan as opposed to representing one more chapter in the long history of U.S. foreign intervention.

DECLINING HEGEMONY?

A common term used to describe one country's control over other countries and regions is *empire*. Until several years ago, to suggest that the United States exercised imperial power bordered on the unpatriotic. Political leaders proclaimed that, unlike powerful countries like France and Britain in past centuries, the United States did not possess foreign colonies. This claim was not wholly accurate. Although the United States never amassed colonies on a grand scale, its colonial possessions presently include Puerto Rico, Guam, the Marshall Islands, American Samoa, and the Virgin Islands. More important, the United States has been the most powerful nation in the world for generations and exercises vast influence throughout the world.[48]

In the decade following the demise of the Soviet Union, the United States was at the height of its power. International relations specialists debate whether it remains preeminent today. Some claim that it does, thanks to its great productive capacity and technological edge in military and civilian sectors. Other analysts assert that the era of American dominance is coming to an end. They have developed their argument in publications with titles like *The Limits of Power*, "Waving Goodbye to Hegemony," and *The Post-American World*.[49] The most authoritative assessment along these lines occurred in 2008, when a CIA report predicted that "Although the United States is likely to remain the [world's] single most powerful actor [in 2025], the United States' relative strength—even in the military realm—will decline and U.S. leverage will become more constrained."[50]

Those who believe that the United States is no longer globally dominant point to two trends. The first is the changed nature of security threats. If firepower alone was the measure of dominance, the debate about U.S. preeminence would be over. However, since 9/11 Americans do not need reminding that small, nonstatist groups can pose a deadly threat. One new possibility is cyberattacks directed against the Pentagon's computers, U.S. electricity grid, financial systems, and complex communications networks. Another is sabotage of the U.S. transportation system and water supply. Climate change also potentially poses a host of new security threats. According to one report, "Climate-induced crises could topple governments, feed terrorist movements or destabilize entire regions, say . . . experts at the Pentagon and intelligence agencies who for the first time are taking a serious look at the national security implications of climate change."[51]

A military response to the new threats may be not only ineffective but counterproductive. International relations analyst Parag Khanna suggests, "Many saw the invasions of Afghanistan and Iraq as the symbols of a global American imperialism; in fact, they were signs of imperial overstretch. Every expenditure has weakened America's armed forces, and each assertion of power has awakened resistance in the form of terrorist networks, insurgent groups and 'asymmetric' weapons like suicide bombers. America's unipolar moment has inspired diplomatic and financial countermovements to block American bullying and construct an alternate world order. That new global order has arrived. . . ."[52]

Foreign policy analyst Joseph Nye Jr., who coined the term *soft power*, has suggested why security nowadays requires more than superior weaponry: "Not all the important types of power come out of the barrel of a gun. . . . [M]any of the transnational issues, such as climate change, the spread of infectious diseases, international crime, and terrorism, cannot be resolved by military force alone. Representing the dark side of globalization, these issues are inherently multilateral and require cooperation for their solution."[53]

The second trend threatening U.S. dominance involves declining economic superiority. The EU's combined GDP now exceeds that of the United States. China and India's growth rates are several times higher than that of the United States (although, because their economies are much smaller, the absolute increase in the U.S. GDP exceeds theirs). Moreover, because of anemic U.S. savings and growth rates, coupled with massive purchases of imports, the United States has become a debtor nation. Its economic stability depends on the willingness of other countries to provide the resources to balance its books. The most important savior is China, whose trade surplus with the United States exceeds $200 billion annually. What keeps the U.S. economy afloat—that is, what prevents it from falling into bankruptcy—is the willingness of the Chinese government to recycle its trade surplus by purchasing U.S. treasury bills. There would be fearful consequences if China were to reduce its purchases of U.S. debt and/or switch from the dollar to another international reserve currency. U.S. dependence is hardly the posture that one expects of a hyperpower.

China is the most successful new player in the global economy, but India, Brazil, Turkey, Venezuela, and other countries have also become more affluent and more willing to challenge U.S. economic leadership. In recent years, the so-called BRIC countries—Brazil, Russia, India, and China, the four largest developing economies—have explored ways to coordinate to oppose U.S. policies.

Is the United States more powerful and secure since Barack Obama became president? Although his personal luster and policy initiatives have had a significant impact, they have probably not changed America's fundamental position in the world. When Iran's authoritarian leaders engaged in massive electoral fraud and brutal repression of popular protest in 2009, they ignored President Obama's criticisms. Nor was North Korea deterred from pursuing its program of nuclear armaments because Obama occupied the Oval Office. In 2009, North Korea chose the symbolically important date of July 4 to test-fire missiles designed to deliver nuclear warheads.

WHAT DO YOU THINK?

Is American International Power Singular or Plural?

Is the United States less powerful in the twenty-first century than it was in the late twentieth century? How and why? In thinking about this question, it might be useful to discuss how you think power should be measured. For example, should power be thought about in the singular or plural; that is, are various dimensions of power, such as economic, military, political, and cultural, different facets of a single whole? Or are they sufficiently distinct that American power cannot be thought of as a single entity because, for example, its military position might be preeminent but its economic standing might have declined? What difference does it make to regard American international power as singular or plural?

Compared to the polarized situation of the Cold War, the more varied and complex nature of challenges these days makes it more difficult to assess the extent of U.S. power. However, the magnitude of recent challenges, the ascent of other countries, and U.S. economic difficulties have probably eroded U.S. hegemony. If the United States remains the most powerful nation in the world, it still sometimes resembles the helpless giant that Jonathan Swift described in *Gulliver's Travels*.

CONCLUSION

In 1630, Puritan Minister John Winthrop preached a sermon to the founders of the Massachusetts Bay Colony in which he declared that "we shall be as a city upon a hill." Worshippers knew that Winthrop was alluding to the Sermon on the Mount, in the Book of Matthew (5:14), where Jesus told his followers, "You are the light of the world. A city on a hill cannot be hidden." Ever since Winthrop, American political leaders have periodically praised the United States as unique, endowed with a divine mission, a city upon a hill. These stirring words, however, should not obscure the reality: the United States assumed its present boundaries by the exercise of violence on a grand scale, and it achieved and maintained its preeminent position in the world not by chance, providence, or moral superiority but by the relentless use of power.

The politics of power does not stop at the nation's borders. Examples in the period since World War II include decisions involving wars in Korea, Vietnam, Iraq, and Afghanistan. There have also been some fundamental continuities in foreign policy. Policymakers of various partisan persuasions have agreed that the United States should maintain an informal sphere of influence abroad, a buffer zone to provide military security and opportunities for profitable commerce. During the nineteenth century, the United States sought to make Latin America its personal preserve. Following World War II, the United States extended its sphere of influence to Western Europe and the third world. U.S. political leaders attempted to promote an international economy favorable to U.S. capitalism by persuading foreign governments and international organizations to promote market-friendly policies. The government also gave a helping hand to U.S.-based transnational corporations (TNCs), especially in the era of globalization beginning in the 1980s.

For a decade after the end of the Cold War, some analysts thought that U.S. hegemony and liberal democracy would extend throughout the world forever. The claim was famously developed in an essay by international relations analyst Francis Fukuyama, "The End of History?" (The question mark was dropped when Fukuyama expanded the article to a book.)[54]

However, 9/11 was a cruel reminder that change cannot be eliminated from history. Although President George W. Bush sought to buttress U.S. dominance by aggressive military action, he probably left the United States in a weaker position. Although President Obama partially reversed President Bush's unilateral and aggressive assertion of U.S. power, the United States may be joining other once preeminent countries who now occupy a more modest position in the world.

CHAPTER SUMMARY

Introduction
Despite many changes within American foreign policy since the founding of the republic, a constant goal has been to achieve and maintain a preeminent position for the United States in the world.

Making Foreign Policy
The process of making foreign policy is highly concentrated within the executive branch, especially in the Executive Office of the President, the

National Security Council, intelligence agencies, and the departments of Defense, State, and Homeland Security. Given the large imbalance in resources between military and civilian agencies, there is a tendency for foreign policy to give priority to military solutions to international problems. Outside the executive branch, other influential participants in shaping foreign policy include congressional leaders of the defense and foreign affairs committees, and large defense contractors.

American Foreign Policy before World War II

From the beginning of the United States through the nineteenth century, American political leaders proclaimed that the United States should remain isolated from Europe's intrigues and conquests. At the same time, the United States assumed its present boundaries by westward expansion involving additional conquest of Native Americans as well as war with Mexico. The Monroe Doctrine created an informal sphere of U.S. influence in South America that excluded European countries. To achieve its commanding position, the United States frequently resorted to the use of military force.

American Foreign Policy after World War II

Following World War II, the United States was the world's most powerful country. It pursued three major goals: checking the USSR during the Cold War; integrating the non-Communist world, including the industrialized countries of Western Europe and the newly independent countries in the developing world; and creating international regulatory institutions to maintain worldwide peace and stability. These diverse goals aimed to maintain American international dominance.

A New Era of Globalization?

After the Soviet Union crumbled in the late 1980s, the United States was so dominant that it was often described as the world's only hyperpower. The United States used its commanding position to promote closer integration of global markets. The result was a vast increase in international trade, investment, and finance. The new era was fueled by advances in technology, including rapid communication and information processing, and an increase in the number and international penetration of transnational corporations based in the United States and other industrialized countries. It also involved a rise in newly developing countries like China and India. This period is commonly described as globalization. Along with enormous economic changes, globalization has generated intense international conflict, symbolized by the bombing of the World Trade Center in New York on September 11, 2001, followed by the United States invasions of Afghanistan and Iraq.

The Military Establishment

A core element of American international dominance is the military establishment. The U.S. military budget of $600 billion roughly equals the combined military expenditures of all other countries in the world. The United States has an immense arsenal of nuclear-equipped intercontinental missiles, an unrivaled navy, rapid interventionist forces, and cutting-edge high-tech or "smart" weapons. The major mission of the military is to protect the United States from attack, deter and subdue challenges to U.S. dominance, and maintain global stability.

The Shift to Unilateralism

In the period after World War II, the United States sought to develop common positions with allies and gain the support of international organizations. In part because of 9/11, President George W. Bush sponsored a sharp turn toward unilateralism. The new policy involved an aggressive assertion of American power, an expansion of the domestic security apparatus, and interrogation techniques used on detainees that are generally regarded as torture and as violations of international laws and treaties. Congress, the Supreme Court, and popular pressure forced the Bush administration into partially curtailing some of these measures.

The Obama Presidency: Continuity or Change?

In his presidential campaign, Barack Obama promised to reverse the Bush administration's unilateral and aggressive foreign policy stance. The Obama administration sought to engage in negotiations with opponents such as Iran and North Korea, to reach agreement with Russia to reduce nuclear weapons, and to give higher priority to international agencies like the UN. However, there were also important elements of continuity in American foreign policy, such as defending the doctrine of state secrets to shield the executive from scrutiny and accountability.

Declining Hegemony?
The United States remains the world's greatest military power. But when judged by some other important standards—for example, comparative economic performance—the United States no longer occupies the position of global preeminence that it held for decades following World War II.

Critical Thinking Questions

1. When you survey the history of American foreign policy, what features have changed and what elements remain the same? Which tendency has predominated—continuity or change?

2. To what extent and how has globalization affected U.S. domestic politics and foreign policy? A suggestion: rather than trying to generalize, choose a specific issue to analyze.

3. President George W. Bush's policies in response to 9/11—for example, domestic surveillance, the treatment and interrogation of detainees, and military action in Afghanistan and Iraq—were highly controversial. Were they justified? Why or why not?

Suggested Readings

Andrew J. Bacevich, *The Limits of Power: The End of American Exceptionalism.* New York: Metropolitan Books, Henry Holt, 2008.

Jagdish Bhagwati, *In Defense of Globalization.* New York: Oxford University Press, 2004.

Mark Danner, *Stripping Bare the Body: Politics Violence War.* New York: Nation Books, Perseus, 2009.

Thomas L. Friedman, *The World Is Flat.* New York: Farrar, Straus, and Giroux, 2005.

George C. Herring, *From Colony to Superpower: U.S. Foreign Relations since 1776.* New York: Oxford University Press, 2008.

Joseph E. Stiglitz, *Globalization and Its Discontents.* New York: Norton, 2003.

Fareed Zakaria, *The Post-American World.* New York: Norton, 2008.

DEMOCRACY'S CHARACTER AND FUTURE

INTRODUCTION

The rules are the same for all the teams in baseball: Three strikes and you're out; three outs to a side; whoever scores the most runs wins. The pitcher's mound is the same 60 feet 6 inches from home plate in Yankee Stadium as it is in Wrigley Field, where the Chicago Cubs play. The distance between the bases is the same 90 feet for the home team as it is for the visitors. An equality of procedures and opportunities exist in baseball. All teams must abide by the same rules, which apply uniformly to all of them. No team is permitted four outs to an inning, a smaller strike zone for their batters, or ten players on the field.

And yet, the same teams continue to win. Some teams, like the Chicago Cubs, have not been in a World Series since 1945—and the last time the Cubs *won* a World Series was 1908. The New York Yankees, on the other hand, have been in 40 World Series—and have won 27 times. Indeed, the lack of competitive balance was regarded as such a problem that Baseball Commissioner Bud Selig appointed a blue-ribbon panel to investigate. The panel reported in 2000 that inequality threatened the integrity of the nation's pastime. From 1995 to 1999, no team in the bottom half of payrolls ever won a divisional series or league championship game, and only teams in the top quartile of payrolls ever won a World Series game. Even worse, the gap between wealthy and low-budget teams was growing. Whereas the average payroll of clubs in the richest quartile grew by $28 million between 1995 and 1999, the average payroll of clubs in the lowest quintile increased by only $4 million. By 1999, the richest team had a payroll equal to the payroll of the five lowest teams *combined*.[1] The rules were fair; the game was not.

When baseball owners got hit where it hurt—in their pocketbooks because the obviously unfair system resulted in falling attendance, and therefore declining revenue—they took action. In 2002, they initiated a revenue-sharing plan that redistributed income from the wealthiest teams—those in large television markets with lucrative TV contracts—to the poorest teams. In 2008, the New York Yankees, baseball's wealthiest team, paid $111 million to Major League Baseball in the form of revenue-sharing and luxury tax payments. Overall, the plan went some distance toward leveling the steeply sloped playing field. The ratio of the highest to the lowest team revenue has decreased, and there has been a small increase in the overall performance of poorer teams. But the plan went only some distance. The Yankees' $201 million payroll in 2009 (the highest in Major League Baseball) was nearly six times larger than the payroll of the Florida Marlins, the team with the lowest payroll (also in 2009, the Yankees managed to win yet another World Series). Compared to the situation ten years earlier, this represents progress; but the new system hardly can be said to have resulted in a situation that gives all teams an equal chance to compete for the best players.

And yet, no matter how great the economic inequalities among teams, the game is not decided by whoever has the largest payroll or highest revenue. It still has to be played on the field, where players must hit, run, pitch, and catch. In the end, high-spending teams are challenged to translate their higher payrolls into more runs. In 2008, none of the three highest-spending teams made the playoffs. The team that ranked 29th out of 30 in payroll, the Tampa Bay Rays, won their division and went on to play in the World Series, which they lost to the Philadelphia Phillies (ranked 13th). Even though money is not the only factor in determining outcomes, its influence cannot be ignored. Low-payroll baseball teams win—but only occasionally. High-payroll teams may not win all the time, but the odds continue to be in their favor. They still win most of the time.

Like baseball, the politics of power offers structural advantages to players and teams with more assets. A mobilization of bias exists between large companies and banks and other, less advantaged political interests, just as it exists in the inequality between baseball teams in large and small markets. Teams that enjoy a structural advantage are able to accumulate higher revenues from television and other sources and use the money to hire better players. So, too, corporations that enjoy a structural advantage can utilize it to shape public opinion, lobby policymakers, contribute to candidates, and create supportive interest groups. The political conflict that ensues is unfair, just as the contest on the baseball diamond is unfair because of economic inequality, even though the rules are the same for everybody.

But higher payrolls do not guarantee sports victories, and political advantages do not translate automatically into political success. Outcomes are not closed. Politics still matters. Possibilities for change exist. The political game plays on, with important consequences for the lives, and life chances, of more than 300 million people in the United States—and, given America's global role, for billions more around the globe.

CAPITALISM, AND DEMOCRACY REVISITED

Like the situation in organized baseball, American political institutions and processes are partially open and fair. Yet, because of disproportionate resources, they are also partially closed and unfair. Legal and political equality interact to produce often deep, and widening, patterns of economic inequality. The character and quality of American democracy thus depends on how various dimensions of inequality affect the opportunities citizens have to participate effectively in making political decisions, in having their interests adequately represented, and in grappling with the advantages of class, race, and gender by promoting a more level playing field in the political, economic, and social spheres.

Our treatment of these concerns has highlighted what we identify as a tension at the very core of American politics. It involves the tendency for capitalism to generate systematic inequalities as opposed to the tendency for democracy to promote equality. We also have stressed the ways the relationship between capitalism and democracy has varied quite a lot. American politics is not fixed or static.

With its limited regulation of business, decline of unions, comparatively low taxes, and a small safety net, the United States tends to tilt more in the direction of extreme market capitalism than do other Western countries. That tendency gives private markets, rather than the public sphere, an uncommon degree of organizing power. Because the relationship of capitalism and democracy is dynamic, a central political question concerns why and how changes in their relationship have occurred, and might further occur.

One can distinguish between structural change and conscious, voluntary political activity. Structural changes that result from political conflicts and decisions alter the basic framework within which politics is conducted, including the shape of political institutions, the broad distribution of economic, political, and social resources, and the composition and social identities of the citizenry. When the Department of Homeland Security was created in 2003 by decisions taken in the Bush administration and by Congress, a structural change resulted. The size and power of executive agencies concerned with safeguarding the country from the threat of terrorism expanded and transformed. When

Chrysler and General Motors passed through bankruptcy with federal assistance in 2009 to become much-changed car companies, the distribution of economic resources, including jobs and their benefits, changed substantially. When the population grows older on average, new challenges to health care and the welfare state emerge.

Such structural alterations and adjustments can be distinguished from intentional political activity aimed at protecting or changing the status quo. During most of his first year as president, Barack Obama sought to convince the American public and Congress to transform the country's health-care system. In this case, this mobilization of attention produced large-scale change. In the American political system, elections stand out as an important means for candidates and parties to stand for, and promote, different policies. Other means involve campaign contributions, efforts to influence and alter public opinion, lobbying by interest groups, and participation by citizens in change-oriented organizations and social movements including those directed at affecting civil rights, the environment, women's rights, matters of public morality such as abortion, and issues of war and peace.

Structural features and political activity are not independent of each other. When political activity is sufficiently powerful, it can alter structural features. Since the 1970s, the environmental movement has succeeded in introducing a host of public regulations to safeguard water and the air we breathe, protect consumer safety, increase occupational health and safety, and begin to address the great challenge of global warming. Changes the movement advocated have affected the structure of the political and economic system. These range from heightened fuel efficiency and safety standards in automobiles to the requirement that industries install technology to minimize pollution. But given the deeply rooted existence of structural features in American political institutions that misshape the playing field on which political struggles are waged, attempts at reform frequently face steep uphill battles, especially when they involve challenges to concentrations of wealth and power.

Most Americans subscribe to both democracy and capitalism. They overwhelmingly support a political system based on consent, elections, free speech, the rule of law, fair procedures, protection against arbitrary action by government, and moral and religious freedom. Despite many disagreements about particular issues, the status of liberal democracy as the way Americans wish to govern themselves is strong and secure. So, too, is the powerful emphasis on freedom in the country's political culture. Furthermore, the great majority of Americans have a high degree of tolerance for the expression of minority opinions and unconventional ideas.[2] Indeed, over the course of American history, the scope of liberty in religion, in the press, and in matters that concern morals and sexuality have all grown as public support for tolerance has increased.[3]

Further, set against the country's history of slavery and segregation, and long-standing patterns of discrimination against women, ethnic minorities, and homosexuals, the country today seems deeply committed to political equality and to the dignity and human worth of each person. The great majority think it goes against the American idea of equality to teach that some kinds of people are better than others or that some people are undeserving of equal treatment. Some 95 percent subscribe to the view that "every citizen should have an equal chance to influence government policy." More than 90 percent think "everyone should have a right to hold public office."[4]

Americans also tend to strongly support the existence of a capitalist economic system. Survey after survey has shown strong backing for the view that people should be free to earn as much as they can as well as for the view that values achievement, ambition, and a strong work ethic. When asked to respond to such statements as "there is nothing wrong with a man trying to make as much money as he honestly can" and "the profits a company or a business can earn should be as large as they can fairly earn," huge majorities of Americans—of all political persuasions—say yes. To the proposition that "government should limit the amount of money any individual is allowed to earn in a year," nine out of ten say no. Furthermore, well over 80 percent believe that the "private ownership of property is necessary for economic progress" and that a system of free enterprise is "necessary for free government to survive."[5]

As a result of these strong commitments to both democracy and capitalism, the country's political culture experiences deep frictions between its various priorities and values. When two leading students of public opinion, Herbert McCloskey and John Zaller, introduced their powerful study of these two traditions of belief, they observed that they are not mutually consistent or harmonious. Rather, democracy and capitalism represent two traditions—one maximizing freedom and participation, the other maximizing earnings and profit—that offer discordant, often clashing priorities. "Capitalism tends to value each individual according to the scarcity of his talents and his contributions to production," they write, whereas "democracy attributes unique but roughly equivalent value to *all* people." Further, these authors state that "capitalism stresses the need for a reward system that encourages the most talented and industrious individuals to earn and amass as much wealth as possible; democracy tries to ensure that all people, even those who lack outstanding talents and initiative, can at least gain a decent livelihood." Finally, they observe, "capitalism holds that the free market is not only the most efficient but also the fairest mechanism for distributing goods and services." By contrast, "democracy upholds the rights of popular majorities to override market mechanisms when necessary to alleviate social and economic distress."[6]

Often, Americans hold fast to both sets of commitments without directly confronting how they might be incompatible. Sometimes they debate the relative priority that democratic and capitalist values should have. How free should the market be? When should government act to ensure that political equality is backed by a sufficient degree of economic equality to make it meaningful? Such questions define the choices our politics offer.

The dominant way most Americans manage these tensions is by subscribing to a cluster of values often gathered under the heading of "the American dream." These values stress the importance of equality of opportunity, the chance for all Americans to freely and actively pursue their ambitions in the public and private realms. Of course, there are mythical qualities to this dream. Not everyone can participate equally in the quest for success. People tend to blame themselves, rather than more impersonal and distant forces, for their shortcomings. But given the depth of commitment Americans have to both democracy and capitalism, no other ideological position exists that successfully competes with this vision of equal opportunity.[7]

This broad perspective permits more than one kind of public policy. At times, as in the New Deal of the 1930s, the quest for equal opportunity strongly supported the push for a more effective government that could limit and tame the inequalities generated by the economic system. During, and for two decades after, the presidency of Ronald Reagan in the 1980s, equal opportunity underpinned an assault on big government. It was coupled with the argument that the people, not the national state, should keep as much as possible of the money they earn and that this orientation will best help expand the economy and spread opportunity. Since the deep economic crisis that began in 2008, matters concerning inequality—including outrage over the compensation of bankers and CEOs of failing companies—have again come to the fore, triggering much greater willingness by political leaders and the public alike to grapple with disparities in income and wealth through policy changes and action by the federal government.

Over time, the implications of equal opportunity for views about the role of the federal government have changed quite a lot. We can see this kind of transformation over the long haul of American history. In the early years of the Republic, most Americans thought that a strong central state would become the tool of the privileged. Equal opportunity thus required a relatively small national state that would undertake only basic responsibilities for defense, trade, and internal communications. But with industrial development in the late nineteenth and twentieth centuries, combined with the growth of new patterns of inequality as capitalism expanded, more and more Americans looked to the federal government to pass laws and institute regulations to level the playing field and create conditions that allowed the notion of equal opportunity to be realized. Today, large majorities of Americans—more than two out of three—support increased spending for education and child care as well as programs to assist the elderly, improve health care, and fight poverty.[8] Although opinions often differ about how this should be done, government has achieved a durable role in promoting the norm of equal opportunity. What government does thus can reduce tension between democracy and capitalism; but this friction has not disappeared, nor can it ever be entirely eliminated.

Much of the time, the relationship between capitalism and democracy is managed by distinguishing between issues thought to be political, and thus subject to democratic life and popular control, and those considered to be economic, and thus largely placed in private hands. But more and more, that distinction is difficult to sustain. Government policy plays a huge role in economic life. In turn, the largest enterprises that dominate the country's economy possess enormous political clout; and as the rescue of GM and Chrysler recently showed, these firms are not permitted to collapse even after they fail. As the political scientist Robert Dahl observes, "A large firm is . . . inherently a *political* system because the government of the firm exercises great power, including coercive power. The government of a firm can have more impact on the lives of more people than the government of many a town, city, province, state."[9]

So the tension remains. The politics of power proceeds in the crucible of tough-to-resolve differences between capitalism and democracy. Whereas both sets of institutions command high regard by the public, Americans are often divided—frequently against others, sometimes against themselves—about how to find the proper balance between the two. Although significant majorities (about two-thirds) believe the private enterprise system to be "generally fair and efficient" and that "workers and management share the same interests in the long run," a slightly larger majority thinks both that corporations and the wealthy don't pay their fair share of taxes and that "corporations and people with money really run the country."[10]

AMERICAN DEMOCRACY IN THEORY AND PRACTICE

The critical perspective in this book has identified three elements that comprise a fuller approach to democracy than the usual standard requiring that all citizens have the right to participate in electing key political representatives.

Our more expansive approach considers the impediments citizens face when they wish to help make decisions, participate in deliberations, shape political life, and affect public policy. Judging the politics of power and assessing whether citizens' interests are adequately represented requires answers to three questions.

The first question concerns the need for procedures to ensure the full and fair expression of political views (especially unpopular ones) and strict adherence to procedures for electing representatives. The record is uneven. During the past generation, there has been a prevailing trend toward the enormous concentration of media control in a few giant corporations, making it increasingly difficult for viewpoints outside the mainstream to be heard on network television or radio. Yet the centralization of the mainstream media has been offset, if only partially, by more decentralized means of electronic communication, including cable television, Internet news sources, and bloggers. Most of the time, elections are open and fair; but there also have been shocking violations of fair and honest electoral procedures. When dirty tricks are used to prevent citizens from registering to vote or from casting their ballot, and when votes are not counted—abuses practiced in recent presidential elections—the United States fails an elementary test of democratic procedures. Other practices also underrepresent substantial groups of citizens. We have seen how the Constitution specifies that every state elect two senators, a rule that makes the votes in sparsely populated states worth several times as much as votes in large states like California, New York, Texas, and Florida. Further, many states deprive convicted felons, even after their release from prison, of the right to vote; thus, those states are disenfranchising millions of citizens.

The second question assesses whether political leaders broadly reflect major social identities based on class, race, ethnicity, religion, gender, and region. Clearly change was afoot in the 2008 presidential campaign when a woman, Hilary Clinton, and an African American, Barack Obama, vied for the Democratic Party nomination for president—and when Obama ultimately won the presidency. Congress, though—despite some improvement—largely remains a club for affluent white men. The mismatch between its demography and that of the country at large means that the national legislature inadequately reflects the concerns of a diverse American electorate, especially the interests of African Americans, Hispanics, and women.

The third question focuses on effective political responsiveness, the requirement that representatives promote the interests of their constituents. In several chapters, we have seen how economic inequalities and political contributions by affluent citizens and organized interests powerfully influence the political agenda, thus making the representation of interests skewed and less efficient for those who lack money, power, and influence. The unevenness of representation is compounded by how the political system, with its multiple points of access and multiple opportunities for blocking reform, can fail to meet widespread demands for change.

Overall, it is precisely because the country's political system offers the most vibrant potential to check deep inequality that shortcomings of democratic representation are disquieting. All too often, the politics of power reflects and even contributes to inequalities rather than narrowing them. Unless the democratic side of the equation is strengthened, reversing the trend toward growing inequality will be difficult to achieve.

As the twenty-first century unfolds, the dynamics of political life are being vitally affected by the large-scale patterns of change we identified in the introduction to this chapter. These patterns have reshaped the agenda of American politics; moreover, they have opened new dimensions for political deliberation, conflict, and possibilities for change. As the lone superpower (albeit one whose relative power may be declining) confronting a more interconnected and more unpredictable world, the United States faces difficult decisions: which weapons to build, where to deploy its armed might, how to raise funds to pay for its overseas ventures, which means are best to project American power as well as secure the nation against attack by armed groups, how to organize global trade, whether to make the environment a worldwide priority, and whether to promote more equal distribution of wealth and resources across the globe. The choices involved range from ever assertive foreign and military policies aimed at securing the country's global reach to much more modest aims based on a reduction of overseas ambitions.

As politics has become more polarized, and as a realignment has occurred across regional lines, making decisions about such issues has become more difficult and more charged by quite deep ideological differences and diverse policy preferences. What is less clear is whether these splits that have become characteristic of debates among political leaders and in the media, especially cable news, reflect or are much sharper than divisions in the population as a whole. Either way, it has become harder to reach agreement across party lines about how to manage the economy, shape the welfare state, deliver health care, deal with immigration, consider controversial social issues like abortion and stem cell research, and grapple with the country's great diversity of people.

As economic crisis has returned, calling into question both the virtues of markets and the promise of government, questions about the future of the country and its politics of power also have deepened. At stake is the degree of structural change, the ways capitalism will be regulated and risk managed, the character of social policies to cushion economic change, and, most fundamentally, how democracy and capitalism will engage with each other within the ambit of public policy. Economic troubles have widened the scope of possible answers, but the degree of involvement by the government in shaping the future of capitalism has yet to be determined.

CONCLUSION

Outcomes are uncertain. Answers to these challenges will be produced by political action within the framework of American politics; that is, by the politics of power. Such challenges will require knowledge, judgments, and decisions—hopefully informed judgments and decisions—about how American politics works; what constraints and pressures affect its institutions, processes, and policies; which policies might be selected at home and abroad.

There are reasons for hope, but no grounds for complacency, especially because public knowledge is uneven and the information citizens have is not always accurately presented. Much of the time, the clash of opinion, the range of information, and the thoughtfulness of debate about public policy help produce an informed public; but the country's history over the past half-century has been punctuated by efforts that do not meet a standard of truthfulness. As a presidential candidate in 1960, John Kennedy erroneously declared a missile gap with the Soviet Union; even after his administration knew that this scenario was false, it repressed the information in order to justify a rapid buildup in weapons. In 1964, President Lyndon Johnson misleadingly claimed North Vietnamese attacks on two U.S. destroyers in the Gulf of Tonkin in order to persuade Congress to authorize war making in Vietnam. In 1985 and 1986, President Ronald Reagan disguised covert efforts to trade arms and hostages with Iran in a complicated and illegal scheme to help Contra rebels in Nicaragua fight a guerilla war against the elected leftist Sandinista government. In the months before the United States went to war against Iraq in 2003, President George W. Bush exaggerated the military threat from that country in his State of the Union address, even to the point of citing forged documents about an Iraqi attempt to obtain nuclear fuel in the African country of Niger.[11]

The judgment announced in the classic work on public opinion by the political scientist V. O. Key Jr. still holds. "Politicians," he wrote, "often make of the public a scapegoat for their own shortcomings; their actions, they say, are a necessity for survival given the state of public opinion. Yet that opinion itself results from the preachings of the influentials, of this generation and of several past generations." He further noted that political "leaders who act as if they thought the people to be fools responsive only to the meanest appeals deserve only scorn."[12] Critical responsibility for the depth and quality of political life lies with the character of education provided by our schools, the range and rigor of reporting by the mass media, the standards used by experts who care about public policy, and the thoughtfulness and responsibility exhibited by political leaders.

Understanding how the country's democracy currently falls short need not produce a cynical or resigned view that little can be done to challenge concentrations and uneven distribution of wealth and power. Just as there have been moments of great change in the past, we can be confident that the future will be very different from the present. How such changes will unfold depends in large part on political participation—or nonparticipation. We thus urge students of American politics to be both critical and engaged: critical because the promise of American democracy remains to be fulfilled; engaged because inequalities will intensify without robust critical engagement.

Informed and active political participation can be both politically effective and politically infectious. Ample opportunity exists to extend and deepen democratic possibilities. When we apply an understanding of the politics of power, Americans can work to realize the rousing promise of American democracy.

Chapter 1

1. These figures are reported in the *Wall Street Journal*'s CEO pay survey, 3 April 2009, B1, and in a special issue on "The New Inequality," *The Nation*, 30 June 2008, 24–25.

2. These trends are summarized in *The New American Economy: A Rising Tide That Lifts Only Yachts* (New York: The Century Foundation, 2008).

3. *New York Times*, 1 June 1999.

4. These figures are drawn from Sarah Burd-Sharps, Kristen Lewis, and Eduardo Borges Martins, *The Measure of America: American Human Development Report 2008–2009* (New York: Social Science Research Council and Columbia University Press, 2008).

5. Charles E. Lindblom, *Politics and Markets: The World's Political-Economic Systems* (New York: Basic Books, 1977), 171, 172.

6. Ibid., 175.

7. Robert Dahl, *Who Governs? Democracy and Power in an American City* (New Haven, CT: Yale University Press, 1961), 3–4.

8. Ibid., 1, 3.

9. Ibid., 86, 311.

10. Carole Pateman, *Participation and Democratic Theory* (New York: Cambridge University Press, 1970), 25.

11. Hanna Fenichel Pitkin, *The Concept of Representation* (Berkeley: University of California Press, 1967).

12. Nolan McCarty, Keith Poole, and Howard Rosenthal, *Polarized America: The Dance of Ideology and Unequal Riches* (Cambridge, MA: MIT Press, 2008); Larry M, Bartels, *Unequal Democracy: The Political Economy of the New Gilded Age* (Princeton, NJ: Princeton University Press, 2008).

13. In all, though, Republicans tended to be more consistently ideologically conservative than Democrats are consistently liberal. For a discussion, see Jacob S. Hacker and Paul Pierson, *Off Center: The Republican Revolution and the Erosion of American Democracy* (New Haven, CT: Yale University Press, 2005).

14. Robert L. Bartley, "Liberalism 1976: A Conservative Critique" (paper prepared for the Conference on the Relevance of Liberalism, Columbia University Research Institute on International Change, New York, January 1976).

15. David Leonhardt, "Greenspan's Mea Culpa," *New York Times*, 23 October 2008.

Part I

1. Good accounts of Flint can be gleaned from Ronald Edsforth, *Class Conflict and Cultural Consensus: The Making of a Mass Consumer Society in Flint, Michigan* (New Brunswick, NJ: Rutgers University Press, 1987); Ben Hamper, *Rivethead: Tales from the Assembly Line* (New York: Warner Books, 1991); and Steven P. Dandaneau, *A Town Abandoned: Flint, Michigan Confronts Deindustrialization* (Albany: State University of New York Press, 1996).

2. Don Pemberton and Robert Schnorbus, *Genesee County and the Transformation of the Auto Industry* (Chicago: Federal Reserve Bank of Chicago, 1996).

3. George F. Lord and Albert C. Price, "Growth Ideology in a Period of Decline: Deindustrialization and Restructuring, Flint Style," *Social Problems* 39, no. 2 (May 1992): 155–69.

4. Ronald Edsforth, "Review of Roger & Me," *American Historical Review* 96 (October 1991): 1145–47.

5. *New York Times*, 22 April 2009.

6. *New York Times*, 23 May 2008.

Chapter 2

1. Peter S. Goodman, "Late-Fee Profits May Trump Plan to Modify Loans," *New York Times*, 30 July 2009, A1.

2. Peter S. Goodman, "Emphasis on Growth Is Said to Be Misguided," *New York Times*, 23 September 2009.

3. For a description of how the economics profession underestimated the importance of this danger, see Paul Krugman, "How Did Economists Get It So Wrong?" *New York Times Magazine*, 6 September 2009, 36–43.

4. Marc Linder and Ingrid Nygaard, *Void Where Prohibited: Rest Breaks and the Right to Urinate on Company Time* (Ithaca, NY: Cornell University Press, 1998).

5. Kim Moody, *Workers in a Lean World: Unions in the International Economy* (New York: Verso Press, 1999), 12.

6. Elizabeth Sanders, *Roots of Reform: Farmers, Workers, and the American State, 1877–1917* (Chicago: University of Chicago Press, 1999), 387.

7. Thomas Ferguson and Joel Rogers, "The Myth of America's Turn to the Right," *Atlantic Magazine*, May 1986, 43–53.

8. See Peter Eisinger, *The Rise of the Entrepreneurial State: State and Local Economic Development Policy in the United States* (Madison: University of Wisconsin Press, 1988) and James C. Cobb, *The Selling of the South: The Southern Crusade for Industrial Development, 1936–1980* (Baton Rouge: Louisiana State University Press, 1982).

9. Steve Striffler, "Inside a Poultry Processing Plant: An Ethnographic Portrait," *Labor History* 43, no. 3 (2002): 306.

10. Tawney is quoted in Robert L. Heilbroner, *The Nature and Logic of Capitalism* (New York: Norton, 1985), 100.

11. The literature on struggles for control on the shop floor between management and workers is fascinating and important. See, for example, the essays in David Montgomery, *Workers' Control in America* (New York: Cambridge University Press, 1979); Michael Buroway, *Manufacturing Consent: Change in the Labor Process Under Monopoly Capitalism* (Chicago: University of Chicago Press, 1979); and Donald Roy, "Quota Restriction and Goldbricking in a Machine Shop," *American Journal of Sociology* 57 (1952): 427–42.

12. Charles Lindblom, *Politics and Markets: The World's Political-Economic Systems* (New York: Basic Books, 1977), 172.

13. *New York Times*, 22 September 2002.

14. Charles Lindblom, "The Market as Prison," *Journal of Politics* 44 (1982): 327.

15. Peter Bachrach and Morton S. Baratz, *Power and Poverty: Theory and Practice* (New York: Oxford University Press, 1970). For a discussion of the different dimensions of power, see John Gaventa, *Power and Powerlessness: Quiescence and Rebellion in an Appalachian Valley* (Urbana: University of Illinois Press, 1980), 1–33.

16. Neil J. Mitchell, *The Conspicuous Corporation: Business, Public Policy and Representative Democracy* (Ann Arbor: University of Michigan Press, 1997), 167.

17. This issue is treated meticulously in Hal Draper, *Karl Marx's Theory of Revolution*, vol. 1, bk. 1, *State and Bureaucracy* (New York: Monthly Review Press, 1977), 311–39.

18. Robert Averitt, *The Dual Economy: The Dynamic of American Industrial Structure* (New York: Norton, 1968).

19. Richard Perez-Pena, "Paper Cuts: Shrinking Advertising and Falling Profits Imperil an Industry," *New York Times*, 7 February 2008, C1, C5.

20. Jeffrey E. Garton, "Megamergers Are a Clear and Present Danger," *Business Week*, 25 January 1999, 28.

21. William Lynch, an executive of the stockbrokerage house Dean Witter Reynolds, interviewed by the *Voice of America*, 3 February 1985. This claim was broadcast around the world as a description of the American system.

22. Edward N. Wolff, "Recent Trends in Household Wealth in the United States: Rising Debt and the Middle-Class Squeeze" (Annandale-on-Hudson, NY: The Levy Economics Institute of Bard College, June 2007), Working Paper no. 52, p. 26, table 8.

23. The statistics in this paragraph are from AFL-CIO, "2008 Trends in CEO Pay," at http://www. aflcio.org/corporatewatch/pay/index.cfm (accessed Sept. 2, 2009).

24. E. E. Schattschneider, *Politics, Pressures and the Tariff* (New York: Prentice-Hall, 1935), 287.

25. For one of the few studies of exclusive social clubs, see G. William Domhoff, *The Higher Circles: The Governing Class in America* (New York: Random House, 1970).

26. Michael Useem, *The Inner Circle: Large Corporations and the Rise of Business Political Activity in the U.S. and U.K.* (New York: Oxford University Press, 1984), 56.

27. Ronald Edsforth, *Class Conflict and Cultural Consensus: The Making of a Mass Consumer Society in Flint, Michigan* (New Brunswick, NJ: Rutgers University Press, 1987), 39–71.

28. Paul Krugman, "The Joy of Sachs," *New York Times*, 16 July 2009.

29. Paul Krugman, "The Market Mystique," *New York Times*, 27 March 2009, A23.

30. David Leonhardt, "For Many, a Boom That Wasn't," *New York Times*, 9 April 2008, C4.

31. U.S. Census Bureau, Current Population Survey, "Annual Social and Economic Supplements," table H-2, at http://www.census.gov/hhes/www/income/histinc/h02AR.html (accessed April 19, 2010).

32. For a fuller analysis, see Peter A. Hall and David Soskice, *Varieties of Capitalism: The Institutional Foundations of Comparative Advantage* (New York: Oxford University Press, 2001).

33. The Fraser Institute, a conservative think tank in Canada, ranks countries according to their degree of "economic freedom." This approximates the degree to which markets guide their economies. The United States consistently ranks in the top five of the Fraser Institute's standings of more than 120 countries.

34. Paul Osterman, Thomas A. Kochan, Richard Locke, and Michael J. Piore, *Working in America: A Blueprint for a New Labor Market* (Cambridge, MA: MIT Press, 2001), 47.

35. Richard B. Freeman and Joel Rogers, *What Workers Want* (Ithaca, NY: Cornell University Press, 1999), 1.

36. See, for example, Bruce E. Kaufman, "The Emergence and Growth of a Nonunion Sector in the Southern Paper Industry," in *Southern Labor in Transition, 1940–1995*, ed. Robert H. Zieger (Knoxville: University of Tennessee Press, 1997), 295–330.

37. Stephanie Clifford, "Your Ad Here, Not There," *New York Times*, 4 March 2009, C1.

38. Stephanie Clifford, "Ads Follow Web Users, and Get Deeply Personal," *New York Times*, 31 July 2009, A1.

39. Robert B. Reich, *Supercapitalism: The Transformation of Business, Democracy, and Everyday Life* (New York: Knopf, 2007).

40. Figures compiled from OECD and the Conference Board. For an analysis, see Dean Baker, *The United States since 1980* (Cambridge: Cambridge University Press, 2007), 24–25.

41. These statistics are from a study by The Center for Labor Market Studies at Northeastern University, as reported by Bob Herbert, "The Worst of Pain," *New York Times*, 9 February 2010.

42. *New York Times*, 15 September 2009.

43. Diane B. Henriques, "Madoff Aide Holds Key to Intrigue," *New York Times*, 13 August 2009, B1.

44. Joseph E. Stiglitz, "America's Socialism for the Rich," *The Economists' Voice* 6, no. 6 (May 2009): 2. This is an online journal published by the Berkeley Electronic Press at http://www.bepress.com/ev. The other quotes from Stiglitz in this paragraph are from pp. 2–3.

45. Paul Krugman, "Bailout for Bunglers," *New York Times*, 2 February 2009.

46. Paul Krugman, "The Market Mystique," *New York Times*, 27 March, 2009.

Chapter 3

1. The use of the term *state* for both state governments and the more inclusive state as defined here complicates descriptions of American politics. However, the text should be clear as to which of the two referents is intended.

2. For classic analyses of these dilemmas, see Charles Lindblom, *Politics and Markets: The World's Political-Economic Systems* (New York: Basic Books, 1977); and Claus Offe, *Contradictions of the Welfare State* (Cambridge, MA: MIT Press, 1984).

3. We focus here on the development of what became the industrial base of the American economy in the North and Midwest. The story of southern economic development, based on a semifeudal plantation economy dependent on slave labor, highlights one of the most shameful aspects of American history. But since the southern economy was increasingly marginal to national economic development, our focus in this chapter will be on the development of the industrial base.

4. Bruce Laurie, *Artisans into Workers: Labor in Nineteenth Century America* (New York: Noonday Press, 1989), 15–47.

5. Guy S. Callender, "The Early Transportation and Banking Enterprises of the States in Relation to the Growth of Corporations," *Quarterly Journal of Economics* 77 (November 1902): 111–62. Quoted in Colleen A. Dunlavy, *Politics and Industrialization: Early Railroads in the United States and Prussia* (Princeton, NJ: Princeton University Press, 1994), 97.

6. See the important article by Harry N. Scheiber, "Federalism and the American Economic Order, 1789–1910," *Law & Society Review* (Fall 1975): 57–119.

7. See Dunlavy, *Politics and Industrialization*, 45–98.

8. Stephen Skowronek, *Building a New American State: The Expansion of National Administrative Capacities, 1877–1920* (Cambridge: Cambridge University Press, 1982), 23.

9. Quoted in Melvin Dubofsky, *Industrialism and the American Worker, 1865–1920* (Arlington Heights, IL: Harlan Davidson, 1985), 53.

10. James R. Green, *Grass Roots Socialism: Radical Movements in the Southwest, 1895–1943* (Baton Rouge: Louisiana State University Press, 1978), 228–70.

11. Elizabeth Sanders, *Roots of Reform: Farmers, Workers and the American State, 1896–1917* (Chicago: University of Chicago Press, 1999).

12. This point is made forcefully in Lawrence Goodwyn, *The Populist Moment* (New York: Oxford University Press, 1979).

13. Woodrow Wilson, *The New Freedom: A Call for the Emancipation of the Generous Energies of a People* (New York: Doubleday, 1918), 15.

14. Roosevelt is quoted in Arthur Schlesinger Jr., "A Question of Power," *The American Prospect* (April 23, 2001): 27.

15. Frank Drobbin, *Forging Industrial Policy: The United States, Britain and France in the Railway Age* (Cambridge: Cambridge University Press, 1994), 28–91.

16. Ibid., 324–33.

17. Irving Bernstein, *A History of the American Worker, 1920–1933: The Lean Years* (Boston: Houghton Mifflin, 1960), 47–83.

18. Alan Brinkley, *The End of Reform: New Deal Liberalism in Recession and War* (New York: Knopf, 1995), 230–31. See also John W. Jeffries, "The 'New' New Deal: FDR and American Liberalism, 1937–1945," *Political Science Quarterly* 105, no. 3 (1990): 397–418.

19. Andrew Shonfeld writes, "The New Dealers . . . perceived the future as a new mixture of public and private initiatives, with the public side very much reinforced but still operating in the framework of a predominantly capitalist system. Considering the opportunities for radical experiment offered by twenty years of uninterrupted Democratic administration from 1933 to 1952, it is surprising how little follow-through there was from this original impulse into the postwar world." See Andrew Shonfeld, *Modern Capitalism* (London: Oxford University Press, 1970), 308.

20. Alan Wolfe, *America's Impasse: The Rise and Fall of the Politics of Growth* (Boston: South End Press, 1981), 52–53.

21. Quoted in Ibid., 51.

22. In 1964, President Lyndon Johnson defended his administration's tax cut in the very same terms that Republicans twenty years later used to defend their tax cuts. Johnson told an audience of businesspeople, "We put some of the money back for the people to spend instead of letting the government spend it for them. We put some of the money back for business to invest in new enterprise instead of the government investing it for them." Quoted in Judith Stein, *Running Steel, Running America: Race, Economic Policy and the Decline of Liberalism* (Chapel Hill: University of North Carolina Press, 1998), 75.

23. Herbert Stein, *Presidential Economies: The Making of Economic Policy from Roosevelt to Clinton* (Washington, DC: American Enterprise Institute, 1994), 135.

24. Jack Metzgar, *Striking Steel: Solidarity Remembered* (Philadelphia: Temple University Press, 2000), 210.

25. Robert B. Reich, *The Wealth of Nations: Preparing Ourselves for 21st Century Capitalism* (New York: Knopf, 1991), 67.

26. Quoted in Taylor E. Dark, *The Unions and the Democrats: An Enduring Alliance* (Ithaca, NY: Cornell University Press, 1999), 113.

27. See the interview of supply-sider Grover Norquist in Jodie T. Allen, "Found Treasure," *U.S. News & World Report*, 14 July 2003, 35.

28. Jacob S. Hacker and Paul Pierson, "Tax Politics and the Struggle Over Activist Government," in Paul Pierson and Theda Skocpol, eds., *The Transformation of American Politics: Activist Government and the Rise of Conservatism* (Princeton, NJ: Princeton University Press, 2007), 156.

29. *Budget of the U.S. Government, Fiscal Year 2010*, Historical Tables (Washington, DC: Office of Management and Budget, 2009).

30. Clinton is quoted in William Greider, *One World, Ready or Not: The Manic Logic of Global Capitalism* (New York: Simon & Schuster, 1997), 197.

31. Quoted in Ronald Dore, *Stock Market Capitalism: Welfare Capitalism* (New York: Oxford University Press, 2000), 4.

32. For these data, see Benjamin M. Friedman, "The Failure of the Economy & the Economists," *New York Review of Books*, 28 May 2009, 42. See also Simon Johnson, "The Quiet Coup," *The Atlantic*, May 2009, 46–56.

33. Figures on debt ratios and savings rates are from the Federal Reserve Bank of San Francisco Economic Letter, "U.S. Household Deleveraging and Future Consumption Growth" (No. 2009-16), 15 May 2009.

34. Charles R. Morris, *The Trillion Dollar Meltdown: Easy Money, High Rollers and the Great Credit Crash* (New York: Public Affairs, 2009).

35. Greenspan is quoted in Morris, *The Trillion Dollar Meltdown*, 54.

36. Frank Rich, "Bernie Madoff Is No John Dillinger," *New York Times*, 5 July 2008.

37. William C. Dudley, Chair of the New York Federal Reserve Bank, quoted in Neil Irwin, "At N.Y. Fed, Blending In Is Part of the Job," *Washington Post*, 20 July 2009, 1.

38. Ira Katznelson, "Considerations on Social Democracy in the United States," *Comparative Politics* 11, no. 1 (October 1978): 77–99.

Part II

1. Joseph Schumpeter, *Capitalism, Socialism and Democracy* (New York: Harper & Row, 1942).

Chapter 4

1. Both speeches were quoted in the *New York Times*, 6 November 2008.

2. E. E. Schattschneider, *Party Government* (New York: Holt, Rinehart & Winston, 1942), 1.

3. Richard Hofstadter, *The Idea of a Party System: The Rise of Legitimate Opposition in the United States, 1780–1840* (Berkeley: University of California Press, 1969), 53.

4. Ibid., 2.

5. John H. Aldrich, *Why Parties? The Origin and Transformation of Political Parties in America* (Chicago: University of Chicago Press, 1995).

6. Richard P. McCormick, "Political Development and the Second Party System," in *The American Party Systems: Stages of Political Development*, eds. William Nesbitt Chambers and Walter Dean Burnham (New York: Oxford University Press, 1977), 102.

7. Michael Schudson, *The Good Citizen* (Cambridge, MA: Harvard University Press, 1998), 112.

8. Walter Dean Burnham, *Critical Elections and the Mainsprings of American Politics* (New York: Norton, 1970), 21.

9. The classic account of the theory of critical elections is Walter Dean Burnham, *Critical Elections*.

10. Stephen Skowronek, *Building a New American State: The Expansion of National Administrative Capacities, 1877–1920* (New York: Cambridge University Press, 1982), 24, 25.

11. See Burnham, *Critical Elections*, 71–73.

12. Ira Katznelson, "The Crisis of the Capitalist City: Urban Politics and Social Control," in *Theoretical Perspectives on Urban Politics*, eds. Willis D. Hawley and Michael Lipsky (Englewood Cliffs, NJ: Prentice-Hall, 1976), 224–25. Also see Ira Katznelson, *City Trenches: Urban Politics and the Patterning of Class in the United States* (New York: Pantheon, 1981).

13. Frances Fox Piven and Richard Cloward, *Why Americans Don't Vote* (New York: Pantheon, 1988), 28–41.

14. J. Morgan Kousser, *The Shaping of Southern Politics: Suffrage Restrictions and the Establishment of the One-Party South* (New Haven, CT: Yale University Press, 1974).

15. Piven and Cloward, *Why Americans Don't Vote.*

16. Andrea Louise Campbell, "Parties, Electoral Participation, and Shifting Voting Blocs," in *The Transformation of American Politics: Activist Government and the Rise of Conservatism,* eds. Paul Pierson and Theda Skocpol (Princeton, NJ: Princeton University Press, 2007), 68.

17. Ibid., 68.

18. Cornelius P. Cotter, James L. Gibson, John F. Bibby, and Robert J. Huckshorn, *Party Organizations in America* (New York: Praeger, 1984), 13–41. See also John F. Bibby, "State Party Organizations: Coping and Adapting," in *The Parties Respond,* 2nd ed., ed. L. Sandy Maisel (Boulder, CO: Westview Press, 1994), 21–45.

19. Paul S. Herrnson, "The Revitalization of National Party Organizations," in *The Parties Respond,* 67.

20. Ibid., 382.

21. Russell J. Dalton, *Citizen Politics: Public Opinion and Political Parties in Advanced Industrial Democracies,* 3rd ed. (New York: Chatham House, 2002), 36. For comparative turnout levels, see "International Voter Turnout, 1991–2000," at http://archive.fairvote.org/turnout/intturnout.htm (accessed March 11, 2010).

22. Robert D. Putnam, *Bowling Alone* (New York: Simon & Schuster, 2000), 33–34. See also Warren E. Miller and J. Merrill Shanks, *The New American Voter* (Cambridge: Cambridge University Press, 1996).

23. Michael S. Lewis-Beck, William G. Jacoby, Helmut Norpoth, and Herbert F. Weisberg, *The American Voter Revisited* (Ann Arbor: University of Michigan, 2008), 104.

24. Ian Urbina, "Hurdles to Voting Persisted in 2008," *New York Times,* 1 March 2009, A14.

25. Walter Dean Burnham, "The 1980 Earthquake: Realignment, Reaction or What," in *The Hidden Election: Politics and Economics in the 1980 Presidential Campaign,* eds. Thomas Ferguson and Joel Rogers (New York: Pantheon, 1981), 126–27.

26. Jan E. Leighley and Jonathon Nagler, "Socioeconomic Class Bias in Turnout, 1964–1988," *American Political Science Review* 86 (1992): 725–36.

27. Stephen Wayne, *Is This Any Way to Run a Democratic Election?* (Washington, DC: CQ Press, 2007), 36.

28. Matthew A. Crenson and Benjamin Ginsberg, *Downsizing Democracy: How America Sidelined Its Citizens and Privatized Its Public* (Baltimore: Johns Hopkins University Press, 2002), 51.

29. Lawrence R. Jacobs and Theda Skocpol, "American Democracy in an Era of Rising Inequality," in *Inequality and American Democracy: What We Know and What We Need to Learn,* eds. Jacobs and Skocpol (New York: Russell Sage, 2005), 1, 9.

30. David Corn, "The Fight Goes On," *The Nation,* 6 December 2004. The quote regarding Diebold in this paragraph is from the same article. For scholarly analyses, see Joel Bleifuss and Steven F. Freeman, *Was the 2004 Presidential Election Stolen? Exit Polls, Election Fraud, and the Official Count* (New York: Seven Stories Press, 2006) and Mark Crispin Miller, ed.,

Loser Take All: Election Fraud and the Subversion of Democracy, 2000–2008 (Brooklyn, NY: Ig Publishing, 2008).

31. Quoted in Frank J. Sorauf and Paul Allen Beck, *Party Politics in America* (Glenview, IL: Scott Foresman, 1988), 101.

32. Marian Currinder, "Campaign Finance: Fundraising and Spending in the 2008 Elections," in *The Elections of 2008*, ed. Michael Nelson (Washington, DC: CQ Press, 2010).

33. Gerald M. Pomper, "The Presidential Election: Changes Comes to America," in Nelson (ed.), *The Elections of 2008*, 66.

34. Cited by David D. Kirkpatrick, "Irked, Wall St. Hedges Its Bet on Democrats," *New York Times*, 8 February 2010.

35. Currinder, "Campaign Finance," in Nelson (ed.), *The Elections of 2008*.

36. Lyle Denniston, at http://www.scotuswiki.com/index.php?title=Citizens_United_v._Federal_Election_Commission (accessed March 11, 2010).

37. Sidney Verba, Kay Lehman Schlozman, and Henry E. Brady, *Voice and Equality: Civic Voluntarism in American Politics* (Cambridge, MA: Harvard University Press, 1995), 189.

38. *New York Times*, 8 July 1998.

39. Quoted in Elizabeth Drew, *Politics and Money: The New Road to Corruption* (New York: Macmillan, 1983), 78.

40. Kirkpatrick, "Irked, Wall St. Hedges Its Bet on Democrats."

41. These figures are drawn from document 5.3, "Number of PACs Registered with the FEC, 1974–96," and document 5.4, "Total PAC Contributions to Congressional Candidates, 1978–96," in Anthony Corrado et al., *Campaign Finance Reform: A Sourcebook* (Washington, DC: Brookings Institution Publications, 1997), 140–41. We combined corporate and trade-membership-health PACs, composed mostly of business interests, to calculate the totals for business PACs and business PAC spending. See Thomas Byrne Edsall, *The New Politics of Inequality* (New York: Norton, 1984), 131. References to corporate or business PACs in the text combine the categories of corporate and trade-membership-health PACs, which the FEC uses.

42. Diane Dwyer and Victoria A. Farrer-Myers, *Congress and Campaign Finance Reform* (Washington, DC: Congressional Quarterly Press, 2001), 1–63.

43. These numbers are from http://www.opensecrets.org/pressreleases/04results.asp (no longer available in the Open Secrets archives).

44. Jacobs and Skocpol (eds.), *American Democracy*, 9.

45. Ira Katznelson, *When Affirmative Action Was White* (New York: Norton, 2005).

46. Earl Black and Merle Black, *Politics and Society in the South* (Cambridge, MA: Harvard University Press, 1987), 241.

47. Ibid.

48. John Petrocik, "Realignment: New Party Coalitions and the Nationalization of the South," *Journal of Politics* 49 (May 1987): 347–75.

49. Lisa McGirr, *Suburban Warriors: The Origins of the New Right* (Princeton, NJ: Princeton University Press, 2001), 157.

50. Mary C. Brennan, *Turning Right in the Sixties: The Conservative Capture of the GOP* (Chapel Hill: University of North Carolina Press, 1995), 141.

51. Jeffrey M. Stonecash, *Class and Party in American Politics* (Boulder, CO: Westview Press, 2000), 26.

52. Jacob S. Hacker and Paul L. Pierson, "Tax Politics and the Struggle Over Activist Government," in Pierson and Skocpol (eds.), *The Transformation of American Politics*, 263.

53. Christine Todd Whitman, *It's My Party, Too: The Battle for the Heart of the GOP and the Future of America* (New York: Penguin, 2005), quoted in Jacob S. Hacker and Paul Pierson, *Off Center: The Republican Revolution and the Erosion of American Democracy* (New Haven, CT: Yale University Press, 2006), 4.

54. Nicol C. Rae, *The Decline and Fall of the Liberal Republicans from 1952 to the Present* (New York: Oxford University Press, 1989), 198.

55. Stonecash, *Class and Party in American Politics*, 62–65.

56. Unless otherwise noted, the statistics on voter preferences in 2008 are from exit polls published in the *New York Times*, 9 November 2008, "Election Supplement," 5; available at http://www.msnbc.msn.com/id/26843704 (accessed Nov. 7, 2008).

57. Sam Roberts, "Race Gap in Voter Turnout Shrank in 2008, Study Says," *New York Times*, 1 May 2009, A16.

58. Ibid.

59. Herbert B. Asher, Eric S. Heberlig, Randall B. Ripley, and Karen Snyder, *American Labor Unions in the Electoral Arena* (Lanham, MD: Rowman & Littlefield, 2001), 141.

60. Roberts, "Race Gap," A16.

61. Nelson (ed.), *The Elections of 2008*, 17.

62. Ibid.

63. The quotations in this paragraph are from Adam Nagourney and David M. Herszenhorn, "G.O.P. Debate: A Broader Party or a Purer One?" *New York Times*, 30 April 2009, A1, A18.

64. Earl Black and Merle Black, *Divided America: The Ferocious Power Struggle in American Politics* (New York: Simon & Schuster, 2007), 258.

65. Edward M. Kennedy, *True Compass: A Memoir* (New York: Twelve, 2009), 217.

66. Morris Fiorina, with Samuel J. Abrams and Jeremy C. Pope, *Culture War? The Myth of Polarized America* (New York: Pearson Longman, 2006).

67. Hacker and Pierson, *Off Center*.

68. Hacker and Pierson, ibid., suggest that the Republicans succeeded in part because they cleverly designed policies in a way that disguised their conservative impact. For other superb analyses, see Larry M. Bartels, *Unequal Democracy: The Political Economy of the New Gilded Age* (Princeton, NJ: Princeton University Press, 2008); and Andrew Gelman, David Park, Boris Shor, Joseph Bafumi, and Jeronimo Cortina, *Red States, Blue States, Rich States, Poor States* (Princeton, NJ: Princeton University Press, 2008).

69. Adam Nagourney, "The '08 Campaign: A Sea Change for Politics as We Know It," *New York Times*, 4 November 2008, A1. The quote later in this paragraph is from this article.

70. Cass R. Sunstein, *Republic.com 2.0* (Princeton, NJ: Princeton University Press, 2007), 128, 132.

71. Greg Mitchell, "How Obama Won: The Rise of Web 2.0," posted on February 3, 2009 at http://www.alternet.org/story/123192. This passage is included in Greg Mitchell, *Why Obama Won: The Making of a President 2008* (Charleston, SC: BookSurge, 2009).

72. Ari Melber, "Obama for America 2.0?" *The Nation*, 12 January 2009, 6.

73. Books that develop these positions include Markus Prior, *Post-Broadcast Democracy: How Media Choice Increases Inequality in Political Involvement and Polarizes Elections* (New York: Cambridge University Press, 2007); Karen Mossberger, Caroline J. Tolbert, and Ramona S. McNeal, *Digital Citizenship: The Internet, Society, and Participation* (Cambridge, MA: MIT Press, 2008); and Sunstein, *Republic.com 2.0*.

74. Quoted in David Swensen and Michael Schmidt, "News You Can Endow," *New York Times*, 28 January 2009, A25.

75. Sidney Verba, Kay Lehman Schlozman, and Henry E. Brady, *Voice and Equality* (Cambridge, MA: Harvard University Press, 1995), 512.

Chapter 5

1. John Muir, "The Hetch Hetchy Valley," *Boston Weekly Transcript*, 25 March 1873.

2. Robert W. Richter, *The Battle Over Hetch Hetchy* (New York: Oxford University Press, 2005), 192.

3. The Big Ten include: Defenders of Wildlife; Environmental Defense; Greenpeace; National Audubon Society; Natural Resources Defense Council; National Wildlife Federation; The Nature Conservancy; Sierra Club; Wilderness Society; and the World Wildlife Fund.

4. John C. Berg, "Waiting for Lefty: The State of the Peace Movement in the United States," paper presented at the annual conference of the New England Political Science Association, Portland, Maine, May 8–9, 2009.

5. Kay Schlozman, "Interest Groups," in *The Oxford Companion to Political Science*, 2nd ed. (New York: Oxford University Press, 2001), 400–01.

6. Gordon Adams, *The Iron Triangle: The Politics of Defense Contracting* (New York: Council on Economic Priorities, 1991).

7. Joseph A. Pika, "Interest Groups and the Executive: Presidential Intervention," in *Interest Group Politics*, eds. Allan C. Cigler and Burdett A. Loomis (Washington, DC: Congressional Quarterly Press, 1983), 303.

8. David Vogel, *Fluctuating Fortunes: The Political Power of Business in America* (New York: Basic Books, 1989).

9. Frank Baumgartner and Beth L. Leech, "Interest Niches and Policy Bandwagons," *Journal of Politics* 63, no. 4 (November 2001): 1196. See also table 3, p. 1197.

10. Kate Phillips, "Google Joins the Lobbying Herd," *New York Times*, 28 March 2006.

11. Eric Lichtblau, "Lawmakers Regulate Banks, Then Flock to Them," *New York Times*, 14 April 2010, B1.

12. Michael Tomasky, "The Money Fighting Health Care," *The New York Review of Books* 57, no. 6 (April 8, 2010), 10–14.

13. Kenneth M. Goldstein, *Interest Groups, Lobbying and Participation in America* (New York: Cambridge University Press, 1999).

14. Mark Kesselman, "The Conflictual Evolution of American Political Science: From Apologetic Pluralism to Trilateralism and Marxism," in *Public Values and Private Power in American Democracy*, ed. J. David Greenstone (Chicago: University of Chicago Press, 1982), 34–67.

15. John Broder and Jad Mouwad, "Energy Firms Find No Unity on Climate Bill," *New York Times*, 19 October 2009.

16. Jeffrey M. Berry, *The New Liberalism: The Rising Power of Citizen Groups* (Washington, DC: Brookings Institution, 1999).

17. Alexis de Tocqueville, *Democracy in America* (New York: Knopf, 1946), 106.

18. James Q. Wilson, *Political Organizations* (New York: Basic Books, 1973).

19. Theda Skocpol, *Diminished Democracy: From Membership to Management in American Civic Life* (Norman: University of Oklahoma Press, 2003).

20. Ibid.

21. Kay Lehman Schlozman et al., "Inequalities of Political Voice," in *Inequality and American Democracy*, eds. Lawrence R. Jacobs and Theda Skocpol (New York: Russell Sage Foundation, 2005), 55–57.

22. Mark S. Bonchek, "Grassroots in Cyberspace: Using Computer Networks to Facilitate Political Participation," paper presented at the Midwest Political Science Association, Chicago, Illinois, April 1995, p. 1.

23. Bruce Bimber, "The Internet and Political Transformation: Populism, Community and Accelerated Pluralism," *Polity* 31, no. 1 (September 1998), 133–66.

24. Taylor Branch, *Parting the Waters: America in the King Years, 1953–63* (New York: Simon & Schuster, 1988), 105–206.

25. Sidney Tarrow, *Power in Movement: Social Movements, Collective Action and Politics* (New York: Cambridge University Press, 1994).

26. Ibid., 80–90.

27. Lawrence Goodwyn, *The Populist Moment* (New York: Oxford University Press, 1978).

28. Branch, *Parting the Waters*, 139–41.

29. E. E. Schattschnieder, *The Semi-Sovereign People: A Realist's View of Democracy in America* (New York: Holt, Rinehart and Winston, 1960).

30. Robert H. Zieger, *American Workers, American Unions*, 2nd ed. (Baltimore: Johns Hopkins University Press, 1994), 26–62.

31. J. David Greenstone, *Labor in American Politics* (New York: Knopf, 1969); and Alan Draper, *A Rope of Sand: The AFL-CIO Committee on Political Education, 1955–68* (New York: Praeger, 1989).

32. Fraser is quoted in Taylor E. Dark, *The Unions and the Democratic Party: An Enduring Alliance* (Ithaca, NY: Cornell University Press, 1999), 113.

33. Thomas A Kochan, Harry C. Katz, and Robert C. McKersie, *The Transformation of American Industrial Relations* (New York: Basic Books, 1986).

34. Quoted in Steven Greenhouse, *The Big Squeeze* (New York: Knopf, 2008), 82.

35. Jelle Visser, "Union Membership Statistics in 24 Countries," *Monthly Labor Review* (January 2006), 45 (table 3).

36. Timothy J. Minchin, *Forging a Common Bond: Labor and Environmental Activism during the BASF Lockout* (Gainesville: University Press of Florida, 2003).

37. The Hotel and Restaurant Workers Union later merged and is currently part of UNITE HERE, the Union of Needle Trades, Industrial and Textile Employees, and Hotel Employees and Restaurant Employees.

38. Richard B. Freeman and Joel Rogers, *What Workers Want* (Ithaca, NY: Cornell University Press, 1999).

39. Catherine Harmois, "Re-presenting Feminisms: Past, Present, and Future," *National Women's Studies Association Journal* 20, no. 1 (Spring 2008): 120–54.

40. Quoted in Jerome L. Himmelstein, *To the Right: The Transformation of American Conservatism* (Berkeley: University of California Press, 1990), 15.

41. Christopher Cochrane, Neil Nevitte, and Stephen White, "Value Change in Europe and North America," in *Growing Apart? America and Europe in the Twenty-First Century,* eds. Jeffrey Kopstein and Sven Steinmo (New York: Cambridge University Press, 2008), 53–80.

42. Kristen Luker, *Abortion and the Politics of Motherhood* (Berkeley: University of California Press, 1984).

43. Himmelstein, *To the Right,* 115–16.

44. Adam Rome, "Give Peace a Chance: The Environmental Movement and the Sixties," *Journal of American History* 90, no. 2 (September 2003): 525–54.

45. Matt Grossman, "Environmental Advocacy in Washington: A Comparison with Other Interest Groups," *Environmental Politics* 15, no. 4 (August 2006): 626–38.

46. John S. Dryzek, David Downes, Christian Hunold, and David Schlosberg, *Green States and Social Movements: Environmentalism in the United States, United Kingdom, Germany, and Norway* (New York: Oxford University Press, 2003), 96.

Part III

1. Morton Grodzins, *The American System: A New View of Government in the United States,* ed. Daniel J. Elazar (Chicago: Rand McNally, 1966).

2. Robert Dahl, *A Preface to Economic Democracy* (Berkeley: University of California Press, 1985), 2.

Chapter 6

1. Richard M. Pious, *The American Presidency* (New York: Basic Books, 1979).

2. Wilson is quoted in Robert Dahl, *How Democratic Is the American Constitution?* (New Haven, CT: Yale University Press, 2001), 74.

3. After the 1984 Democratic convention, Daniel Patrick Moynihan, senator from New York, observed, "The convention does not decide and it does not debate. . . . [T]he nomination is settled before the convention begins. . . . We have to make up our arguments to have on the floor so that television has something to cover." Quoted in Theodore J. Lowi, *The Personal President: Power Invested, Promise Unfulfilled* (Ithaca, NY: Cornell University Press, 1985), 111.

4. Stephen Skowronek, *The Politics Presidents Make: Leadership from John Adams to George Bush* (Cambridge, MA: Harvard University Press, 1993), 6.

5. Michael Schudson, *The Good Citizen: A History of Civic Life* (Cambridge, MA: Harvard University Press, 1998), 206.

6. Jeffrey K. Tulis, *The Rhetorical Presidency* (Princeton, NJ: Princeton University Press, 1987).

7. Sidney M. Milkis and Michael Nelson, *The American Presidency: Origins and Development, 1776–1990* (Washington, DC: Congressional Quarterly Press, 1990), 260.

8. Theodore Roosevelt, not FDR, first used the media in a systematic way. He was the first president to have a press secretary, a press office, and frequent meetings with reporters. In his famous phrase, he used the presidency as "a bully pulpit." However, FDR's presidency coincided with the diffusion of radio, which enabled him to establish direct contact with vast audiences.

9. Joseph Cooper, "The Twentieth-Century Congress," in *Congress Reconsidered*, 7th ed., eds. Lawrence C. Dodd and Bruce I. Oppenheimer (Washington, DC: Congressional Quarterly Press, 2001), 335.

10. E. S. Corwin, *The President: Office and Powers*, 3rd ed. (New York: New York University Press, 1957), 2.

11. Arthur M. Schlesinger Jr., *The Imperial Presidency* (Boston: Houghton Mifflin, 1973).

12. Barber is quoted in Gary L. Gregg II, "Dignified Authenticity," in *Considering the Bush Presidency*, eds. Gary L. Gregg II and Marc J. Rozell (New York: Oxford University Press, 2004), 89.

13. Bruce Miroff, "Monopolizing the Public Space: The President as a Problem for Democratic Politics," in *Rethinking the Presidency*, ed. Thomas E. Cronin (Boston: Little, Brown, 1982), 220.

14. One Iraqi, apparently trying to curry favor with the Bush administration, spoke of a meeting in Vienna between an Al Qaeda official and a member of Saddam Hussein's administration. When asked to document the claim, he retracted his story. Similarly, before the Iraq invasion, Secretary of State Colin Powell delivered an address to the UN to buttress the U.S. case for going to war. He spoke eloquently of "incontrovertible proof" that Saddam's regime possessed weapons of mass destruction. Powell later admitted that no evidence existed for making the claim.

15. Richard E. Neustadt, *Presidential Power: The Politics of Leadership* (New York: Free Press, 1963), 5.

16. Richard S. Gilmour, "The Institutionalized Presidency: A Conceptual Clarification," in *The Presidency in Contemporary Context*, ed. Norman C. Thomas (New York: Dodd, Mead, 1975), 155.

17. Charlie Savage, "Obama's Embrace of Bush Tactics Criticized by Lawmakers from Both Parties," *New York Times*, 9 August 2009, A18.

18. See, for example, Jane Mayer, *The Dark Side: The Inside Story of How the War on Terror Turned into a War on American Ideals* (New York: Doubleday, 2008); Mark Danner, *Stripping Bare the Body: Politics, Violence, War* (New York: Nation Books, 2009).

19. Quoted from Walter Alarkon, "House Overhelmingly Rejects Signing Statement," http://thehill.com/homenews/house/49864-house-overwhelmingly-rejects-signing-statement (accessed Feb. 24, 2010).

20. Savage, "Obama's Embrace of Bush Tactics."

21. Quoted in Neustadt, *Presidential Power*, 9 (emphasis in original).

22. Skowronek, *The Politics Presidents Make*, 55.

23. David Leonhardt, "Challenge to Health Bill: Selling Reform," *New York Times*, 22 July 2009, A1.

24. Elizabeth Drew, *On the Edge: The Clinton Presidency* (New York: Simon & Schuster, 1994), 231.

25. Ron Duhl, "Carter Issues an Order, But Is Anybody Listening?" *National Journal* (July 14, 1979): 1156–58.

26. The different agencies within the EOP are described by Bradley H. Patterson Jr., *The Ring of Power: The White House Staff and Its Expanding Role in Government* (New York: Basic Books, 1988).

27. John P. Burke, "The Bush Transition," in *Considering the Bush Presidency*, 29.

28. Robert Draper, "Obama's BFF," *New York Times Magazine*, 26 July 2009, 34.

29. Shirley Anne Warshaw, *The Co-Presidency of Bush and Cheney* (Stanford, CA: Stanford University Press, 2009), viii.

30. Ibid., 1.

31. Kenneth R. Mayer, "Executive Orders and Presidential Power," *Journal of Politics* 61 (May 1999): 445.

32. Hugh Heclo, *A Government of Strangers: Executive Politics in Washington* (Washington, DC: Brookings Institution, 1977).

33. Clinton Rossiter, *The American Presidency*, rev. ed. (New York: Harcourt, Brace, 1960), ch. 1.

34. Thomas E. Cronin, "Presidents as Chief Executives," in *The Presidency Reappraised*, eds. Rexford G. Tugwell and Thomas E. Cronin (New York: Praeger, 1974), 235.

35. Aaron Wildavsky, "The Two Presidencies," *Transaction* (December 1966): 7–14.

36. Quoted in Byron W. Daynes, Raymond Tatalovich, and Dennis L. Sodin, *To Govern a Nation* (New York: St. Martin's Press, 1997), 265.

37. Quoted in Schlesinger, *The Imperial Presidency*, 42 (emphasis in original).

38. Cecil V. Crabb and Kevin V. Mulcahy, "George Bush's Management Style and Desert Storm," *Presidential Studies Quarterly* 25 (Spring 1995): 262.

39. *New York Times*, 16 March 2002.

40. Thomas E. Cronin, "'Everybody Believes in Democracy Until He Gets to the White House. . . .': An Examination of White House–Department Relations," *Law and Contemporary Problems* 35 (Summer 1970): 575.

41. Quoted in James L. Nolan Jr., *The Therapeutic State* (New York: New York University Press, 1998), 236.

42. Derrick Bell, quoted in *New York Times*, 14 June 1997.

43. For a detailed account of the the organization of the White House media operation, see Martha Joynt Kumar, *Managing the President's Message: The White Communications Operation* (Baltimore: Johns Hopkins University Press, 2007).

44. George C. Edwards, "Bill Clinton and His Crisis of Governance," *Presidential Studies Quarterly* 28 (Fall 1998): 755.

45. Ron Suskind, "Why Are These Men Laughing?" *Esquire* (January 2003): 96–105.

46. *New York Times*, 13 May 2001.

47. Quoted in James P. Pfiffner, "Introduction: Assessing the Bush Presidency," in *Considering the Bush Presidency*, 13.

48. Frances Fox Piven and Richard Cloward, *Regulating the Poor: The Functions of Public Welfare* (New York: Vintage Books, 1971), xiii.

49. Joseph Cooper, "The Twentieth Century Congress," in *Congress Reconsidered* (7th ed.), eds. Lawrence C. Dodd and Bruce I. Oppenheimer (Washington, DC: Congressional Quarterly Press, 2001), 356.

Chapter 7

1. John Locke, *Two Treatises of Government*. John Laslett, ed. (Cambridge: Cambridge University Press, 1960), 355–56.

2. Woodrow Wilson, *Congressional Government: A Study in American Politics* (New York: Meridian Books, 1958), 25.

3. These results were reported by CBS News, PollingReport.com, "Congress—Job Rating in National Polls," at http://www.pollingreport.com/CongJob.htm (accessed March 16, 2010), and the Rasmussen Reports, "Congressional Performance: Congress Receives Highest Ratings in Two Years," at http://beta.rasmussenreports.com/public_content/politics/mood_of_america/mood_of_america_archive/congress_ratings/congress_receives_highest_ratings_in_two_years (accessed March 16, 2010).

4. Robert S. Erikson, Michael B. MacKuen, and James A. Stimson, *The Macro Polity* (New York: Cambridge University Press, 2002).

5. Elizabeth Sanders, *Roots of Reform: Farmers, Workers, and the Administrative State, 1877–1917* (Chicago: University of Chicago Press, 1984), 396.

6. Quoted in Jeffrey Tulis, "The Two Constitutional Presidencies," in *The Presidency and the Political System*, ed. Michael Nelson (Washington, DC: Congressional Quarterly Press, 1984), 68.

7. John R. Hibbing and Elizabeth Theiss-Morse, "What the Public Dislikes About Congress," in *Congress Reconsidered* (6th ed.), eds. Lawrence C. Dodd and Bruce I. Oppenheimer (Washington, DC: Congressional Quarterly Press, 1997), 77.

8. Quoted in Merrill Jensen, *The Making of the American Constitution* (Malibar, FL: Krieger, 1979), 47.

9. Robert Dahl, *Democracy in the United States: Promise and Performance*, 2nd ed. (Chicago: Rand McNally, 1973), 151.

10. Jensen, *Making of the American Constitution*, 58.

11. Elaine K. Swift, *The Making of an American Senate: Reconstitutive Change in Congress, 1787–1841* (Ann Arbor: University of Michigan Press, 1996).

12. Quoted by Newt Gingrich in William F. Connelly Jr. and John J. Pitney Jr., "The House Republicans: Lessons for Political Science," in *New Majority or Old Minority: The Impact of Republicans on Congress*, eds. Nicol C. Rae and Colton C. Campbell (Lanham, MD: Rowman & Littlefield, 1999), 186.

13. Arend Lijphart, *Patterns of Democracy: Government Forms and Performance in Thirty-Six Countries* (New Haven, CT: Yale University Press, 1999), 208.

14. Malapportionment and its consequences are examined thoroughly in Frances E. Lee and Bruce I. Oppenheimer, *Sizing Up the Senate: The Unequal Consequences of Equal Representation* (Chicago: University of Chicago Press, 1999), 2.

15. Gary C. Jacobson, *The Politics of Congressional Elections*, 4th ed. (Washington, DC: Congressional Quarterly Press, 1997), 11.

16. On the advantages of small states in the Senate and the benefits whites derive from this at the expense of minorities, see Lee and Oppenheimer, *Sizing Up the Senate*, 21–23.

17. Samuel Huntington, "Congressional Responses to the Twentieth Century," in *The Congress and America's Future*, ed. David B. Truman (Englewood Cliffs, NJ: Prentice-Hall, 1965), 23.

18. David W. Rohde, *Parties and Leaders in the Postreform House* (Chicago: University of Chicago Press, 1991).

19. For a discussion, see David R. Mayhew, *America's Congress: Actions in the Public Sphere, James Madison Through Newt Gingrich* (New Haven, CT: Yale University Press, 2000).

20. *New York Times*, 30 May 1978.

21. *New York Times*, 17 August 1998.

22. David R. Mayhew, *Congress: The Electoral Connection* (New Haven, CT: Yale University Press, 1974).

23. Julia Ritchey, "Senators Debate Merits of Earmarks in Spending Bill," *Voice of America*, 9 March 2009.

24. Morris Fiorina, *Congress: Keystone of the Washington Establishment* (New Haven, CT: Yale University Press, 1977), 36–37.

25. Richard F. Fenno Jr., *Home Style: House Members in Their Districts* (Boston: Little, Brown, 1978).

26. Rogers is quoted in Sherrod Brown, *Congress from the Inside: Observations from the Majority and the Minority*, 3rd ed. (Kent, OH: Kent State University Press, 2004), 199.

27. Cited in John G. Nicolay, *Abraham Lincoln: A History, Volume 1* (Teddington, England: Echo Library, 2007), 76.

28. Brown, *Congress from the Inside*, 199.

29. Jacobson, *Politics of Congressional Elections*, 39–42.

30. Gary Jacobson, *Money in Congressional Elections* (New Haven, CT: Yale University Press, 1980).

31. Quoted in Robert B. Kuttner, *Everything for Sale* (New York: Knopf, 1996), 349.

32. On the difference women make in Congress, see Michele L. Swers, *The Difference Women Make: The Policy Impact in Congress* (Chicago: University of Chicago Press, 2002).

33. Lester G. Seligman and Michael R. King, "Political Realignments and Recruitment to the U.S. Congress, 1870–1970," in *Realignment in American Politics: Toward a Theory*, eds. Bruce A. Campbell and Richard J. Trilling (Austin: University of Texas Press, 1980), 157–75.

34. Larry M. Bartels, "Economic Inequality and Political Representation," Princeton University, unpublished manuscript, August 2005.

35. For party unity scores of southern Democrats, see Rohde, *Parties and Leaders in the Postreform House*, 54–56. For the increasing liberalism of southern legislators, see Alan Draper, "Be Careful What You Wish For: American Liberals and the South," *Southern Studies* (Winter 1993): 309–25.

36. Charles S. Bullock III, "Congressional Roll Call Voting in the Two-Party South," *Social Science Quarterly* 66 (December 1995): 803.

37. Senator John Breaux is quoted in Sarah A. Binder, *Stalemate: Causes and Consequences of Legislative Gridlock* (Washington, DC: Brookings Institution, 2003), 69.

38. A useful overview is Bruce Oppenheimer, "Barack Obama, Bill Clinton, and the Democratic Congressional Majority," *Extensions* (Spring 2009).

39. Rohde, *Parties and Leaders in the Postreform House*.

40. Ibid., 172.

41. Center for Responsive Politics, OpenSecrets.org, at http://www.opensecrets.org.

42. Quoted in C. Lawrence Evans and Walter J. Oleszek, "Congressional Tsunami? The Politics of Congressional Reform," in *Congress Reconsidered* (6th ed.), eds. Lawrence C. Dodd and Bruce I. Oppenheimer (Washington, DC: Congressional Quarterly Press, 1997), 193.

43. Congressional Quarterly, *How Congress Works*, 1st ed. (Washington, DC: Congressional Quarterly Press, 1998), 61.

44. Christopher J. Deering and Steven S. Smith, *Committees in Congress*, 3rd ed. (Washington, DC: Congressional Quarterly Press, 1997), 11–20.

45. Quoted in Congressional Quarterly, *How Congress Works*, 51.

46. McCain is quoted in Steven Weiss, "Campaign Finance Reform's Rocky Road," *Capital Eye* VIII (Spring 2001): 1.

47. Thomas Mann, Norman Ornstein, and Molly Reynolds, "Truth and Reconciliation," *The New Republic*, 20 April 2009.

48. Barbara Sinclair, *Unorthodox Lawmaking: New Legislative Processes in the U.S. Congress* (Washington, DC: Congressional Quarterly Press, 1997), 7.

49. Kay Lehman Schlozman and John T. Tierney, *Organized Interests and American Democracy* (New York: Harper & Row, 1986), 67.

50. Quoted in David Vogel, *Fluctuating Fortunes* (New York: Basic Books, 1989), 196–98.

51. The Center for Responsive Politics, OpenSecrets.org, has a remarkably complete database.

52. Parven Pomper Strategies Inc., http://www.pps-dc.com (accessed March 22, 2010).

53. At one time, lobbyists on Microsoft's payroll included Ralph Reed, who was a senior advisor to George W. Bush's presidential campaign; Haley Barbour, former chair of the Republican National Committee; C. Boyden Gray, White House counsel to former President George H. W. Bush; and Lloyd N. Cutler, counsel to former Presidents Jimmy Carter and Bill Clinton.

54. In 2009, Daschle withdrew his nomination to be the secretary of Health and Human Services in President Obama's Cabinet amid a controversy over his failure to fully report and pay income taxes.

55. John M. Broder, "With Something for Everyone, Climate Bill Passed," *New York Times*, 1 July 2009, 1.

Chapter 8

1. Jeffrey Toobin, *The Nine: Inside the Secret World of the Supreme Court* (New York: Doubleday, 2007), 150–64.

2. See the excellent reporting by Linda Greenhouse in the *New York Times*, 13 December 2001. Russell is quoted in William Crotty, "Elections by Judicial Fiat: The Courts Decide," in *America's Choice 2000*, ed. William Crotty (Boulder, CO: Westview Press, 2001), 75.

3. Bernard Schwartz, *A Basic History of the U.S. Supreme Court* (Princeton, NJ: Van Nostrand, 1968), 9.

4. Rehnquist is quoted in Richard A Brisbin Jr., "The Judiciary and the Separation of Powers," in *The Judicial Branch*, eds. Kermit L. Hall and Kevin T. McGuire (New York: Oxford University Press, 2005), 95.

5. Hamilton is quoted in Gregory A. Caldiera and Kevin T. McGuire, "What Americans Know About the Courts and Why It Matters," *The Judicial Branch*, eds. Kermit L. Hall and Kevin T. McGuire (New York: Oxford University Press, 2005), 269.

6. Schwartz, *A Basic History of the U.S. Supreme Court*, 15.

7. Quoted in Richard Kluger, *Simple Justice: The History of* Brown v. Board of Education *and Black America's Struggle for Equality* (New York: Knopf, 1976), 706.

8. Toobin, *The Nine*, 327.

9. For a nuanced appreciation of the role the law plays, see E. P. Thompson, *Whigs and Hunters: The Origin of the Black Act* (New York: Pantheon Books, 1975).

10. Robert A. Carp, Ronald Stidham, and Kenneth Manning, *Judicial Process in America*, 7th ed. (Washington, DC: CQ Press, 2007), 52.

11. National Institute on Money in State Politics, National Overview Map, "Total Dollars for all Candidates and Committees in 2008," at http://www.followthemoney.org/database/nationalview.phtml (accessed March 22, 2010).

12. James Sample, "Justice for Sale," *Wall Street Journal*, 22 March 2008.

13. G. A. Huber and S. C. Gordon, "Accountability and Coercion: Is Justice Blind When It Runs for Office?" *American Journal of Political Science* 48, no. 2 (2004): 247–63.

14. David Samuels, "Dr. Kush: How Medical Marijuana Is Transforming the Pot Industry," *The New Yorker*, 28 July 2008.

15. Quoted in David M. O'Brien, *Storm Center: The Supreme Court in American Politics* (New York: Norton, 1986), 290.

16. Robert A. Carp and Ronald Stidham, *Judicial Process in America*, 4th ed. (Washington, DC: Congressional Quarterly Press, 1998), 43.

17. Gregory A. Caldiera and John R. Wright, "Lobbying for Justice: The Rise of Organized Conflict in the Politics of Federal Judgeships," in *Contemplating Courts*, ed. Lee Epstein (Washington, DC: Congressional Quarterly Press, 1995), 54.

18. Joel Klein is quoted in O'Brien, "Clinton's Legal Policy and the Courts: Rising from Disarray or Turning Around and Around?" in *The Clinton Presidency: First Appraisals*, eds. Bert Rockman and Colin Campbell (New York: Chatham House, 1996), 139.

19. Roger E. Hartley and Lisa M. Holmes, "The Increasing Senate Scrutiny of Lower Federal Court Nominees," *Political Science Quarterly* 117, no. 2 (Summer 2002): 259–78.

20. Kenneth L. Manning and Robert R. Carp, "The Decision-Making Ideology of George W. Bush's Judicial Appointees: An Update," paper presented at the 2004 APSA Convention, Chicago, Illinois, September 2–5, 2004.

21. *Brown v. Allen*, 344 U.S. 443, 540 (1953).

22. Lee Epstein and Jack Knight, *The Choices Justices Make* (Washington, DC: Congressional Quarterly Press, 1998), 26.

23. Taft is quoted in Epstein and Knight, *The Choices Justices Make*, 46.

24. Fred Vinson, "Work of the Federal Courts," Supreme Court Reporter (1949), cited in Emmette S. Redford and Alan F. Westin, *Politics and Government of the United States* (New York: Harcourt, Brace & World, 1968), 474.

25. Jeffrey Rosen, *The Supreme Court: The Personalities and Rivalries That Defined America* (New York: Times Books, 2007), 223.

26. Linda Greenhouse, *Becoming Justice Blackmun: Harry Blackmun's Supreme Court Journey* (New York: Times Books, 2005), 105.

27. Bernard Schwartz, *Decisions: How the Supreme Court Decides Cases* (New York: Oxford University Press, 1996), 43.

28. Roberts is quoted in Rosen, *The Supreme Court*, 227.

29. Ibid.

30. Lee Epstein and Jack Knight, *The Choices Justices Make*, 9.

31. Jeffrey Toobin, "Diverse Opinions," *The New Yorker*, 8 June 2009.

32. Quoted in O'Brien, *Storm Center*, 81.

33. Schwartz, *Decisions*, 184.

34. O'Brien, *Storm Center*, 84.

35. Lee Epstein and Jeffrey A. Segal, *Advice and Consent: The Politics of Judicial Appointments* (New York: Oxford University Press, 2005).

36. *Marbury v. Madison*, 5 U.S. 137 (1803).

37. Morton Horwitz, *The Warren Court and the Pursuit of Justice* (New York: Hill & Wang, 1998), 76–82.

38. Philip B. Kurland, *Politics, the Constitution and the Warren Court* (Chicago: University of Chicago Press, 1970), 17–18.

39. Doris Marie Provine, "Judicial Activism and American Democracy," in *The Judicial Branch*, eds. Kermit L. Hall and Kevin T. McGuire (New York: Oxford University Press, 2005), 319.

40. James Q. Wilson and John J. Dilulio Jr., *American Government*, 7th ed. (New York: Houghton Mifflin, 1998), 444.

41. Quoted in Schwartz, *Decisions*, 79.

42. Quoted in Redford and Westin, *Politics and Government*, 498–99.

43. Quoted in William E. Leuchtenburg, *The Supreme Court Reborn: The Constitutional Revolution in the Age of Roosevelt* (New York: Oxford University Press, 1995), 103.

44. For example, Justice Roberts wrote the majority opinion in *United States v. Butler* (1936), striking down the New Deal's Agricultural Adjustment Act.

45. Congressman Maury Maverick is quoted in Leuchtenburg, *Supreme Court Reborn*, 176.

46. *NLRB v. Jones and Laughlin Steel Corp.* (1937).

47. Leuchtenburg, *Supreme Court Reborn*, 154.

48. Quoted in Morton Horwitz, *The Transformation of American Law, 1870–1960* (New York: Oxford University Press, 1992), 34.

49. This material on *Brown* draws on Kluger, *Simple Justice*; and on Raymond Wolters, *The Burden of Brown: Thirty Years of School Desegregation* (Knoxville: University of Tennessee Press, 1984).

50. Charles Epp, *The Rights Revolution: Lawyers, Activists, and Supreme Court Cases in Comparative Perspective* (Chicago: University of Chicago Press, 1998), 28. We might also add that the Warren Court reflected the Cold War consensus of the Democratic coalition as well as its domestic concern with rights. The Warren Court permitted the silencing of left-wing opinion with respect to admission to the bar and the conduct of congressional investigations.

51. Mark Silverstein and Benjamin Ginsberg, "The Supreme Court and the New Politics of Judicial Power," *Political Science Quarterly* 102 (Fall 1987): 379.

52. Quoted in Schwartz, *Decisions*, 105.

53. This paragraph draws on the description of the "due process revolution" in Joan Biskopic and Elder Witt, *Guide to the U.S. Supreme Court*, 3rd ed. (Washington, DC: Congressional Quarterly Press, 1997), 52–53.

54. Silverstein and Ginsberg, "Supreme Court and the New Politics," 372.

55. See David J. Garrow's exhaustive *Liberty and Sexuality: The Right to Privacy and the Making of* Roe v. Wade (New York: Macmillan, 1994).

56. For example, witnesses testified that Rehnquist had written a memorandum as a law clerk to Justice Robert H. Jackson in which he had defended the *Plessy* doctrine of separate but equal, had tried to intimidate black and Hispanic voters by challenging their qualifications, and had engaged in ethically questionable behavior by not removing himself from judging a case in which he had prior connections.

57. The only Democratic president elected between 1968 and 1992 was President Jimmy Carter, who had the misfortune of never having the chance to appoint anyone to the Supreme Court.

58. See James F. Simon, *The Center Holds: The Power Struggle inside the Rehnquist Court* (New York: Simon & Schuster, 1995), 144–67, for the Rehnquist Court's process of decision making in *Casey.*

59. Brennan is quoted in Jerome J. Shestack, "The Rehnquist Court and the Legal Profession," in *The Rehnquist Court: A Retrospective*, ed. Martin H. Belsky (New York: Oxford University Press, 2002), 171

60. Burt Neuborne, "Free Expression and the Rehnquist Court," in Belsky (ed.), *The Rehnquist Court: A Retrospective*, 15.

61. Toobin, *The Nine*, 299–300.

62. Todd S. Purdum, "The Supreme Court," *New York Times*, 29 June 2004.

63. Timothy P. O'Neill, "The Stepford Justices: The Need for Experiential Diversity on the Roberts' Court," *Oklahoma Law Review* 60, no. 4 (2007): 719.

64. Cass R. Sustein, "The Myth of the Balanced Court," *American Prospect* (September 2007): 28–29.

65. Jeffrey Rosen, "Supreme Court, Inc.," *New York Times*, 16 March 2008.

66. Mark Silverstein, "Politics and the Rehnquist Court," in *Rehnquist Justice: Understanding the Court Dynamic*, ed. Earl M. Maltz (Lawrence: University of Kansas Press, 2003), 287.

67. Linda Greenhouse, "On Court That Defied Labeling, Kennedy Made the Boldest Mark," *New York Times*, 28 June 2008.

68. James B. Gibson, "From Simplicity to Complexity: The Development of Theory in the Study of Judicial Behavior," *Political Behavior* 5, no. 1 (1983): 91.

69. Linda Greenhouse, "2,691 Decisions," *New York Times*, 13 July 2008.

70. Douglas Jehl, "Fearing Bush Will Win, Groups Plan Suit," *New York Times*, 3 December 2000.

71. Alexis de Tocqueville, *Democracy in America* (New York: Knopf, 1946), 280.

72. Benjamin Ginsberg and Martin Shefter, *Politics by Other Means: The Declining Importance of Elections in America* (New York: Basic Books, 1990), 150.

73. Martin Shapiro, "The Juridicalization of Politics in the United States," *International Political Science Review* 15 (April 1994): 101–12.

74. Gerald N. Rosenberg, *The Hollow Hope: Can Courts Bring About Social Change?* (Chicago: University of Chicago Press, 1991).

75. These figures are drawn from Marie Gottschalk, *The Prison and the Gallows: The Politics of Mass Incarceration in America* (New York: Cambridge University Press, 2006), 1–21.

76. Ibid.

77. Ibid.

78. Rosenberg, *Hollow Hope*, 338 (emphasis in original).

Chapter 9

1. David Vogel, "Why Businessmen Distrust Their State: The Political Consciousness of American Corporate Executives," *British Journal of Political Science* 8 (January 1978): 45–79; Reeve Vanneman and Lynn Weber Cannon, *The American Perception of Class* (Philadelphia: Temple University Press, 1987), 283–311; Howell John Harris, *Right to Manage: Industrial Relations Policies of American Business in the 1940s* (Madison: University of Wisconsin Press, 1982).

2. William Greider, *Secrets of the Temple: How the Federal Reserve Runs the Country* (New York: Simon & Schuster, 1987), 351–405.

3. Elizabeth Drew, *Showdown* (New York: Simon & Schuster, 1996), 326.

4. Daniel J. Palazzolo, *Done Deal? The Politics of the 1997 Budget Agreement* (Chappaqua, NY: Seven Bridges Press, 1999), 90.

5. The budgetary process is described in detail in Allen Schick, *The Federal Budget: Politics, Policy and Process* (Washington, DC: Brookings Institute, 1995).

6. Steven Waldman, *The Bill* (New York: Penguin, 1996), 74.

7. Joel Slemrod and Jon Bakija, *Taxing Ourselves: A Citizen's Guide to the Great Debate Over Tax Reform* (Cambridge, MA: MIT Press, 1996), 1–5.

8. Holmes is quoted in Slemrod and Bakija, *Taxing Ourselves*, 1.

9. This material is drawn from *Budget for Fiscal Year 2010, Historical Tables*, table 2.2: Percentage Composition of Receipts by Source: 1934–2014, 32–33.

10. *New York Times*, 21 January 2003. Table from the *Times* is drawn from a Consumer Expenditure Survey of the Bureau of Labor Statistics.

11. Jacob S. Hacker, *The Divided Welfare State: The Battle Over Public and Private Social Benefits in the United States* (New York: Cambridge University Press, 2002).

12. Palazzolo, *Done Deal*, 230.

13. Ibid., 229.

14. Quoted in Greider, *Secrets of the Temple*, 55.

15. Ibid., 12.

16. Henry B. Gonzalez, "An Open Letter to the President," *Challenge* (September–October 1993): 30–31.

17. Willem H. Buiter, "Lessons from the North Atlantic Financial Crisis," at http://www.nber.org/~wbuiter/NAcrisis.pdf (accessed March 17, 2010), 36–40.

18. Greenspan is quoted in John Lancaster, "Heroes and Zeroes," *The New Yorker*, 2 February 2009, 73.

19. Senator Jim Bunning of Kentucky is quoted in John Cassidy, "Anatomy of a Meltdown," *The New Yorker*, 1 December 2008, 61.

20. Builer, "North Atlantic Financial Crisis," 37.

21. Fraser Institute, *Economic Freedom of the World: 2008 Annual Report.* See Exhibit 13: Area Economic Freedom Ratings and Rankings, 2006, 9–13.

22. Marver H. Bernstein, *Regulating Business by Independent Regulatory Commission* (Westport, CT: Greenwood Press, 1955).

23. David Vogel, *Fluctuating Fortunes: The Political Power of Business in America* (New York: Basic Books, 1989), 59.

24. Martha Derthick and Paul J. Quirk, *The Politics of Deregulation* (Washington, DC: Brookings Institute, 1985).

25. David Stout, "Report Details How Madoff's Web Ensnared S.E.C.," *New York Times*, 3 September 2009.

26. Michael Lewis and David Einhorn, "The End of the Financial World as We Know It," *New York Times*, 4 January 2009.

27. Quoted in John McMillan, *Reinventing the Bazaar: A Natural History of Markets* (New York: Norton, 2002), 174.

Chapter 10

1. Benefits, TANF. U.S. Department of Health and Human Services, Office of Family Assistance, "TANF Eighth Annual Report to Congress," at http://www.acf.hhs.gov/programs/ofa/data-reports/annualreport8/ar8index.htm (accessed March 19, 2010).

2. Jacob S. Hacker, *The Divided Welfare State: The Battle over Public and Private Social Benefits in the United States* (New York: Cambridge University Press, 2002), 6.

3. Gosta Esping-Andersen, *The Three Worlds of Welfare Capitalism* (Princeton, NJ: Princeton University Press, 1990).

4. Theda Skocpol, *Protecting Soldiers and Mothers: The Political Origins of Social Policy in the United States* (Cambridge, MA: Harvard University Press, 1992), 65.

5. Gwendolyn Mink, *The Wages of Motherhood: Inequality in the Welfare State, 1917–1942* (Ithaca, NY: Cornell University Press, 1995), 33.

6. Deborah Ward, *The White Welfare State: The Racialization of U.S. Welfare Policy* (Ann Arbor: University of Michigan Press, 2005).

7. James T. Patterson, *America's Struggle Against Poverty, 1900–1994* (Cambridge, MA: Harvard University Press, 1994), 42.

8. Quoted in ibid., 52.

9. "The Case Against Roosevelt," *Fortune,* December 1935; quoted in Arthur Schlesinger Jr., *The Coming of the New Deal* (Boston: Houghton Mifflin), 494.

10. Francis Fox Piven and Richard Cloward, *Regulating the Poor: The Functions of Public Welfare* (New York: Pantheon, 1971).

11. An example of the least eligibility principle can be found in the British *Poor Law Report of 1834*. For "able-bodied labourers who apply for relief," the *Poor Law Report* recommended "hard work at low wages by the piece, and extracting more work at a lower price than is paid for any other labour in the parish. . . . In short, . . . let the labourer find that the parish is the hardest taskmaster and the worst paymaster he can find, and thus induce him to make his application to the parish his last and not his first resort." Quoted in David Schmidtz and Robert E. Goodin, *Social Welfare and Individual Responsibility* (New York: Cambridge University Press, 1998), 173.

12. For an overview, see Ira Katznelson, *When Affirmative Action Was White: An Untold History of Racial Inequality in Twentieth-Century America* (New York: Norton, 2005).

13. Paul Starr, *The Social Transformation of American Medicine* (New York: Basic Books, 1983).

14. In fact, Social Security coverage expanded in the 1950s under President Eisenhower to include farmworkers and maids, who initially had been left out of Social Security at the insistence of the segregated South.

15. Quoted in Sanford M. Jacoby, "Employers and the Welfare State: The Role of Marion B. Folsom," *Journal of American History* 80, no. 2 (1993): 526.

16. *Wall Street Journal,* 24 April 1969.

17. Stanley Lieberson, *A Piece of the Pie* (Berkeley: University of California Press, 1980).

18. William Julius Wilson, *The Declining Significance of Race: Blacks and Changing American Institutions* (Chicago: University of Chicago Press, 1978).

19. Laurence E. Lynn Jr., "Ending Welfare Reform as We Know It," *American Prospect* (Fall 1993): 83–90.

20. U.S. Bureau of the Census, *Measuring Fifty Years of Economic Change Using the March Current Population Survey,* table C23, C-40 to C-41.

21. U.S. Census Bureau, *2005–2007 American Community Survey.*

22. U.S. Bureau of the Census, *Measuring Fifty Years of Economic Change,* table C-21, C-37; Population Reference Bureau, analysis of data from the U.S. Census Bureau, *Census 2000 Supplementary Survey, 2001 Supplementary Survey, 2002 through 2007 American Community Survey.*

23. Barbara R. Bergmann, *Saving Our Children from Poverty: What the United States Can Learn from France* (New York: Russell Sage Foundation, 1996).

24. James C. Sundquist, *Politics and Policy: The Eisenhower, Kennedy, and Johnson Years* (Washington, DC: Brookings Institute, 1968).

25. AFL-CIO Convention *Proceedings* (1965), 2: 1–6.

26. Patterson, *America's Struggle Against Poverty*, 136.

27. Sar A. Levitan and Robert Taggert, *The Promise of Greatness* (Cambridge, MA: Harvard University Press, 1976), 20.

28. For the consequences of the 1966 election for the welfare state, see Alan Draper, "Labor and the 1966 Elections," *Labor History* (Winter 1989): 76–93.

29. Quoted in Levitan and Taggert, *The Promise of Greatness*, 3–4.

30. Brown, *Race, Money and the American Welfare State*, 325.

31. Thomas Byrne Edsall and Mary D. Edsall, *Chain Reaction: The Impact of Race, Rights, and Taxes on American Politics* (New York: Norton, 1991).

32. James Midgeley, "Society, Social Policy and the Ideology of Reaganism," *Journal of Sociology and Social Welfare* (March 1992): 24–25.

33. David Stockman, *The Triumph of Politics* (New York: Harper & Row, 1986), 394.

34. Levitan and Taggert, *The Promise of Greatness*, 200–201.

35. John E. Schwarz, *America's Hidden Success: A Reassessment of Twenty Years of Public Policy* (New York: Norton, 1984).

36. *New York Times*, 3 September 1995.

37. Mark Rank, *Living on the Edge: The Realities of Welfare in America* (New York: Columbia University Press, 1994), 5.

38. Randy Albelda, Nancy Folbre, and the Center for Public Economics, *The War on the Poor: A Defense Manual* (New York: New Press, 1996), 82.

39. Eliot Liebow, *Tally's Corner: A Study of Streetcorner Men* (New York: Little, Brown, 1967), 223.

40. See Bawden and Levy, "Economic Well-Being of Families and Individuals," table 16-5, 469.

41. Howard Jacob Karger, "Responding to the Crisis: Liberal Prescriptions," in *Reconstructing the American Welfare State*, eds. David Stoesz and Howard Jacob Karger (Lanham, MD: Rowman & Littlefield, 1992), 92–93.

42. Quoted in "Moynihan Turns Up the Heat," *The Economist*, 11 November 1995, 32.

43. In *Goldberg v. Kelly* (1970), the Supreme Court ruled that beneficiaries, once eligible, could not lose their grants without a due process hearing.

44. *New York Times*, 11 April 1999; U.S. Department of Health & Human Services, "Welfare Rolls Drop Again," at http://www.hhs.gov/news/press/2004pres/20040330.html (accessed March 19, 2010).

45. "Welfare Rolls Up After Years of Decline," *United Press International*, 22 June 2009.

46. U.S. Department of Education, "Overview: 10 Facts About K-12 Education Funding," http://www.ed.gov/about/overview/fed/10facts/index.html (accessed March 19, 2010); GPO Access, "Budget of the United States Government: Historical Tables Fiscal Year 2010," at http://www.gpoaccess.gov/usbudget/fy10/hist.html (accessed March 19, 2010).

47. CNN, "Kennedy: 'Iraq Is George Bush's Vietnam,'" at http://www.cnn.com/2004/ALLPOLITICS/04/05/kennedy.speech/ (accessed March 19, 2010).

48. "Remarks of Senator Barack Obama: National Education Association Annual Meeting," Philadelphia, Pennsylvania, July 5, 2007.

49. Helen Levy and David Weir, "Take-Up of Medicare Part D: Results from the Health and Retirement Study," NBER Working Paper No. 14692 (Washington, DC: National Bureau of Economic Research, January 2009).

50. Cited in Jonathan Oberlander, "Through the Looking Glass: The Politics of the Medicare Prescription Drug, Improvement, and Modernization Act," *Journal of Health Politics, Policy, and Law* 32, no. 2 (2007): 187–219.

51. George W. Bush, "Excerpt of President's Radio Address on SCHIP Legislation," White House, Office of the Press Secretary, 28 September 2007, at http://georgewbush-whitehouse.archives.gov/news/releases/2007/09/20070928-9.html (accessed March 19, 2010).

52. Michael Tomasky, "The Money Fighting Health Care Reform," *New York Review of Books* 8 April 2010.

53. David Leonhardt, "In the Process, Pushing Back At Inequality," *New York Times*, 24 March 2010, p. 1.

54. Richard Scase, *Social Democracy in Capitalist Society* (Totowa, NJ: Rowman & Littlefield, 1977).

55. John D. Stephens, *The Transition from Capitalism to Socialism* (Urbana: University of Illinois Press, 1986).

56. Jacob S. Hacker, *The Great Risk Shift: The New Insecurity and the Decline of the American Dream*, rev. ed. (New York: Oxford University Press, 2007).

Chapter 11

1. Department of Defense, "Base Structure Report: A Summary of DoD's Real Property Inventory" (June 2003), at http://www.defenselink.mil/news/Jun2003/basestructure2003.pdf (accessed March 19, 2010).

2. *New York Times*, 27 February 2009, A18.

3. This statistic is contained in a press release dated December 5, 2006, of the World Institute for Development Economics Research of the United Nations University.

4. The development aid statistics in this paragraph are from OECD, "The Flow of Financial Resources to Developing Countries and Multilateral Organisations," table 14 in Statistical Annex of the OECD's Development Co-operation Report, at http://www.oecd.org (specific link no longer available). A poll found that two-thirds of Americans claim the United States is spending too much on foreign aid. (These results are reported by Amy Chua, "Which Way Do We Go?" *New York Times Book Review*, 25 October 2009, 22.) Most respondents probably vastly overestimated how much is spent on foreign aid.

5. For a discussion of the diverse strands of U.S. foreign policy, see Walter Russell Mead, *God and Gold: Britain, America, and the Making of the Modern World* (New York: Vintage, 2008).

6. The term *soft power* was coined by Harvard's Joseph Nye in the late 1980s. For an extended discussion, see Joseph S. Nye Jr., *Soft Power: The Means to Success in World Politics* (Cambridge, MA: Perseus, 2004).

7. Fareed Zakaria, *The Post-American World* (New York: Norton, 2008).

8. Andrew J. Bacevich, *The Limits of Power: The End of American Exceptionalism* (New York: Metropolitan Books, Henry Holt, 2008), 20.

9. Richard W. Van Alstyne, *The Rising American Empire* (Chicago: Quadrangle, 1965), 99.

10. Bacevich, *The Limits of Power*, 20.

11. Dahr Jamail and Jason Coppola, "The Myth of 'America,'" October 12, 2009, at http://www.truthout.org/1012091 (accessed March 19, 2010).

12. Michael H. Hunt, *The American Ascendancy: How the United States Gained and Wielded Global Dominance* (Chapel Hill: University of North Carolina Press, 2007), 56.

13. Stephen Kinzer, *Overthrow: America's Century of Regime Change from Hawaii to Iraq* (New York: Times Books, Henry Holt, 2006), 2.

14. Michael Parenti, "The Logic of U.S. Intervention," in *Masters of War: Militarism and Blowback in the Era of American Empire*, ed. Carl Boggs (New York: Routledge, 2002), ch. 1.

15. David Callahan, *Between Two Worlds: Realism, Idealism, and American Foreign Policy after the Cold War* (New York: HarperCollins, 1994), 30.

16. Graham Allison, "Cool It: The Foreign Policy of Young America," *Foreign Policy* 1, no. 1 (Winter 1970–1971): 144–45.

17. Richard K. Betts, "The Soft Underbelly of Primacy: Tactical Advantages of Terror," *Political Science Quarterly* 117, no. 1 (Spring 2002), reprinted in *Conflict after the Cold War: Arguments on Causes of War and Peace* (2nd ed.), ed. Richard K. Betts (New York: Pearson, 2005), 522.

18. Robert Gilpin, *U.S. Power and the Multinational Corporation: The Political Economy of Direct Foreign Investment* (New York: Basic Books, 1975), 161.

19. See Carl Boggs (ed.), *Masters of War*.

20. Harry Magdoff, *The Age of Imperialism: The Economics of U.S. Foreign Policy* (New York: Monthly Review Press, 1969), 43.

21. For a sobering account of the role petroleum has played in U.S. foreign policy, and the extensive damage that results from this situation, see Michael T. Klare, *Blood and Oil: The Dangers and Consequence of America's Growing Dependency on Imported Petroleum* (New York: Owl Books, Henry Holt, 2005).

22. Ibid., 11.

23. William Greider, *One World, Ready or Not: The Manic Logic of Global Capitalism* (New York: Simon & Schuster, 1997). For influential analyses and defenses of globalization, see Thomas L. Friedman, *The World Is Flat* (New York: Farrar, Straus, and Giroux, 2005); and Jagdish Bhagwati, *In Defense of Globalization* (New York: Oxford University Press, 2004).

24. Organisation for Economic Co-operation and Development, "OECD Factbook 2009: Economic, Environmental and Social Statistics," at http://lysander.sourceoecd.org/vl=3489091/cl=21/nw=1/rpsv/factbook2009/03/01/01/index.htm (accessed March 19, 2010).

25. See, for example, Geoffrey Garrett, *Partisan Politics in the Global Economy* (Cambridge, England: Cambridge University Press, 1998); David Held, Anthony McGrew, David Goldblatt, and Jonathan Perraton, *Global Transformations: Politics, Economics and Culture* (Stanford, CA: Stanford University Press, 1999); and Dean Baker, Gerald Epstein, and Robert Pollin, eds., *Globalization and Progressive Economic Policy* (Cambridge, England: Cambridge University Press, 1998).

26. Michael V. Gestrin, Rory F. Knight, and Alan M. Rugman, "Oxford Executive Briefing: Templeton Global Performance Index 2001," Templeton College, Oxford, 2001.

27. Organization for International Investment, "Insourcing Statistics," at http://www.ofii.org/insourcing-stats.htm (accessed March 19, 2010).

28. Huntington first put forward the claim in Samuel Huntington, "The Clash of Civilizations?" *Foreign Affairs* 72, no. 3 (1993). He developed the argument more fully in *The Clash of Civilizations and the Remaking of World Order* (New York: Free Press, 1996). Peter J. Katzenstein described the impact of Huntington's book in his presidential address to the American Political Science Association, "'Walls' between 'Those People'? Contrasting Perspectives on World Politics," Annual Meeting of the American Political Science Association, Toronto, Canada, August 28, 2009.

29. Both quotes are from Amartya Sen, "Democracy as a Universal Value," *Journal of Democracy* 10, no. 3 (July 1999), reprinted in *Readings in Comparative Politics: Political Challenges and Changing Agendas* (2nd ed.), ed. Mark Kesselman (Boston: Wadsworth Cengage Learning, 2010), 192.

30. Paul Rogers, "The U.S. Military Posture: 'A Uniquely Benign Imperialism'?" in *The New Imperial Challenge; Socialist Register 2004*, eds. Leo Panitch and Colin Leys (New York: Monthly Review Press, 2003), 149.

31. George Easterbrook, "Apocryphal Now," *New Republic*, 24 September 2000, 24.

32. Mary Kaldor, "Beyond Militarism, Arms Races, and Arms Control," in *Understanding September 11*, eds. Craig Calhoun, Paul Price, and Ashley Timmer (New York: The New Press, 2002), 165–66.

33. Ibid., 167.

34. Stephen Glain, "The American Leviathan: The Pentagon Has All But Eclipsed the State Department in Setting U.S. Foreign Policy," *The Nation*, 28 September 2009, 18–23.

35. Thomas L. Friedman, "The Best Allies Money Can Buy," *New York Times*, 4 November 2009, A25; and Allison Stanger, *One Nation Under Contract: The Outsourcing of American Power and the Future of Foreign Policy* (New Haven, CT: Yale University Press, 2009).

36. Interview with Zbigniew Brzezinski, *The Charlie Rose Show*, PBS, September 14, 2004. Also see Zbigniew Brzezinski, *The Choice: Global Domination or Global Leadership* (New York: Basic Books, 2004).

37. The White House, "National Security Strategy of the United States," at http://www.whitehouse.gov/nsc/nss.html (accessed March 19, 2010).

38. Richard A. Clarke, *Against All Enemies: Inside America's War on Terror* (New York: Free Press, 2004), 30–32. Former Treasury Secretary Paul O'Neill reported that planning to remove Saddam Hussein began immediately after President Bush's inauguration; several high-level meetings were devoted to the project well before September 11, 2001. Ron Suskind, *The Price*

of Loyalty: George W. Bush, the White House and the Education of Paul O'Neill (New York: Simon & Schuster, 2004), 72–75, 82–86, 129. Also see Ron Suskind, *The Way of the World: A Story of Truth and Hope in an Age of Extremism* (New York: Harper Perennial, 2009).

39. Clarke, *Against All Enemies*, 246.

40. David Cole, "Bush Law Continued," *The Nation*, 6 April 2009, 8.

41. Ronald Dworkin, "The Threat to Patriotism," in *Understanding September 11*, eds. Calhoun, Price, and Timmer, 273.

42. Ibid.

43. Dahlia Lithwick, "Tyranny in the Name of Freedom," *New York Times*, 12 August 2004.

44. *New York Times*, 21 December 2004. Also see the results of an army investigation reported in the *New York Times*, 10 September 2004; Seymour Hersh, *Chain of Command: The Road from 9/11 to Abu Ghraib* (New York: HarperCollins, 2004); Mark Danner, *Torture and Truth: America, Abu Ghraib, and the War on Terror* (New York: The New York Review of Books, 2004; and Danner, *Stripping Bare the Body: Politics Violence War* (New York: Nation Books, Perseus, 2009).

45. Michael Isikoff, "2002 Memo Reveals Push for Broader Presidential Powers," *Newsweek*, 18 December 2004.

46. Anthony Lewis, "A President Beyond the Law," *New York Times*, 7 May 2004.

47. Editorial, *New York Times*, 26 October 2009, A20.

48. For an argument that the United States can be considered an empire, see Andrew Bacevich, *American Empire: The Realities and the Consequences of U.S. Diplomacy* (Cambridge, MA: Harvard University Press, 2002). For a strong defense of American empire, see Niall Ferguson, *Colossus: The Price of America's Empire* (New York: Penguin Press, 2004). Also see Ferguson's *Empire: The Rise and Demise of the British World Order and the Lessons for Global Power* (New York: Basic Books, 2003); and "The Empire Slinks Back," *New York Times Magazine*, 27 April 2003. For critiques of American imperialism in the recent period, see David Harvey, *The New Imperialism* (New York: Oxford University Press, 2003); and *The New Imperial Challenge; Socialist Register 2004*, eds. Leo Panitch and Colin Leys.

49. Bacevich, *The Limits of Power*; Parag Khanna, "Waving Goodbye to Hegemony," *New York Times*, 27 January 2008; and Zakaria, *The Post-American World*.

50. National Intelligence Council, *Global Trends 2025: A Transformed World* (Washington, DC: U.S. Government Printing Office, 2008), at http://www.dni.gov/nic/PDF_2025/2025_Global_Trends_Final_Report.pdf (accessed March 19, 2010).

51. John M. Broder, "Climate Change Seen as Threat to U.S. Security," *New York Times*, 9 August 2009, A1.

52. Khanna, "Waving Goodbye to Hegemony."

53. Joseph S. Nye Jr., "Soft Power and American Foreign Policy," *Political Science Quarterly* 119, no. 2 (Summer 2002): 263.

54. Francis Fukuyama, "The End of History?" *The National Interest* 16 (Summer 1989). Reprinted in Kesselman (ed.), *Readings in Comparative Politics*. Fukuyama's book was entitled *The End of History and the Last Man* (New York: Free Press, 1992).

Chapter 12

1. Richard C. Levin, George J. Mitchell, Paul A. Volcker, and George F. Will, "The Report of the Independent Members of the Commissioner's Blue Ribbon Panel on Baseball Economics" (July 2000), at http://www.bizofbaseball.com/docs/2000blueribbonreport.pdf (accessed March 19, 2010).

2. An important confirmation of the growing tolerance among Americans is the study by Alan Wolfe, *Moral Freedom* (New York: Norton, 2001).

3. Herbert McClosky and John Zaller, *The American Ethos: Public Attitudes Toward Capitalism and Democracy* (Cambridge, MA: Harvard University Press, 1984), 18–61.

4. Ibid., 74.

5. Ibid., 120, 123.

6. Ibid., 7.

7. For a particularly thoughtful discussion, see Jennifer L. Hochschild, *Facing Up to the American Dream: Race, Class, and the Soul of the Nation* (Princeton, NJ: Princeton University Press, 1995), esp. chapters 1–4.

8. Martin Gilens, *Why Americans Hate Welfare: Race, Media, and the Politics of Antipoverty Policy* (Chicago: University of Chicago Press, 1999), 28.

9. Robert A. Dahl, *Dilemmas of Pluralist Democracy* (New Haven, CT: Yale University Press, 1982), 184.

10. McClosky and Zaller, *American Ethos*, 176, 177, 179.

11. Christopher A. Preble, *John F. Kennedy and the Missile Gap* (De Kalb: Northern Illinois University Press, 2004); Edwin E. Moise, *Tonkin Gulf and the Escalation of the Vietnam War* (Chapel Hill: University of North Carolina Press, 1996); *Report of the Congressional Committees Investigating the Iran-Contra Affair*, S. Report No. 216; H.R. Report No. 433 (Washington, DC: United States Government Printing Office, November 11, 1987); Seymour M. Hersh, "Who Lied to Whom?" *The New Yorker*, 31 March 2003.

12. V. O. Key Jr., *Public Opinion and American Democracy* (New York: Knopf, 1963), 557, 555.

GLOSSARY

Aid to Families with Dependent Children (AFDC) In effect from 1935 to 1997, AFDC, commonly known as welfare, was a program of financial transfers, funded by the states and the federal government, to support children in poor families.

all-directional lobbying Efforts by interest groups to influence not only policymakers, but the wider public.

Bill of Rights The first ten amendments to the Constitution of the United States that guarantee Americans freedom of religion, the right to bear arms, *habeas corpus*, a speedy trial by a jury, and other aspects of due process of law, as well as protection from unreasonable search and seizure by public authorities.

budget deficit When the government spends more than it collects in taxes.

budget surplus When the government collects more money in revenues than it spends in outlays.

Bush Doctrine The informal foreign policy approach sponsored by George W. Bush when he was president. It asserted the right of the United States to launch a preemptive military attack if the president decided that an opponent was planning an attack.

cabinet The group of key administrative officials appointed by the president to direct the major departments of government. The president may convene the cabinet to discuss and provide advice on major policy issues, but rarely asks the cabinet to make major policy decisions.

capitalism An economic system based on the private ownership of property in which profit is pursued through the investment of capital and the employment of labor.

capitalist class The group that owns and controls business firms.

checks and balances In order to prevent undue concentrations of power, each branch of the federal government has independent standing. This institutional design enables the presidency, Congress, and the judiciary to check and balance possible abuses by the other two. A possible disadvantage of this situation is institutional gridlock or stalemate since any one branch can hinder action by the others.

classical legal theory A legal doctrine that presumed the sanctity of contracts and private property under the assumption that people entered into contracts freely and without coercion.

coalitions Different groups that ally to pursue a shared interest. A coalition may be a political party or government, or on an ad hoc basis to achieve a particular ideological or policy goal.

Cold War The period of hostile relations just short of open war that prevailed between the United States and Soviet Union from 1947 to the late 1980s.

collective bargaining Type of bargaining that occurs when unions negotiate on behalf of workers with employers over wages, hours, fringe benefits such as health insurance, and working conditions.

competitive capitalism An economy dominated by many small firms that produce for local markets.

concurring opinion When judges issue their own reasons, separate from the majority opinion, for their decision.

conference committee A committee composed of members of both the House of Representatives and Senate to reconcile any differences between versions of a bill passed by each chamber.

conservationists Those who promote efficient, sustainable use of the environment and its natural resources for the public good.

constitution The fundamental principles, establishing rules and institutions, that shape how a country is governed and by whom, for what ends, and with which limitations. A constitution may be set down in a written document, as in the United States, or it can be unwritten, the result of long-accepted laws and the development of precedent, as in Great Britain.

containment A term that designates a multidimensional American strategy—using diplomacy, economic power, and military means—to limit the influence and potential for expansion of the Soviet Union during the Cold War.

corporate campaigns A tactic unions use to pressure recalcitrant employers through third parties, such as members of the firm's board of directors or its creditors, suppliers, or customers.

corporate capitalism An economy dominated by large firms that produce for national and international markets and are able to dictate prices to suppliers and retailers as well as wages to their workers.

corporate complex The close relationship between corporations and the federal government. Together, they shape key features of public policy that organize and regulate how economic affairs are conducted.

"corporatist" interest group systems When a few interest groups include a large proportion of potential members and are often given some official recognition by the state and included in the policymaking process.

critical or realigning elections Critical or realigning elections are ones in which a long-dominant party is defeated by a party with a different social base and ideological outlook. For an election to be considered critical or realigning, the new party must succeed in governing for a significant period and in sponsoring a distinctive new policy orientation. (Also see *realignment.*)

democracy A form of government in which sovereign authority ultimately rests with the people, who choose their leaders in competitive elections.

depression A prolonged period of economic stagnation, in which there are high levels of unemployment, declining living standards, and social dislocation.

deregulation The removal of rules that constrain economic actors.

discretionary programs Programs whose funding levels are set through the annual budget process.

divided government A circumstance where one or both houses of Congress is controlled by a majority party that differs from the party of the president.

division of powers The system specified by the Constitution in which governmental powers are divided between the national and state governments. The Constitution authorizes the national government to sponsor a limited number of activities and, in the

Tenth Amendment, declares that the powers not delegated to the national government are reserved to state governments.

dual court system State and federal court systems existing alongside each other.

earmarks A legislative designation that appropriates funds or provides tax relief for specific projects and programs in particular states or districts, thus circumventing any competitive process based on criteria of merit. Earmarks are sponsored by individual members of the House and Senate, but they are not publicly identified.

ecology How people and other life-forms relate to their environment.

economic regulations Regulations that set standards for all firms in an industry.

Electoral College The Electoral College was created by the Constitution to elect the president. Each state is allotted as many delegates to the Electoral College as it has senators and representatives. According to the unit rule used for most states, the presidential candidate who receives a plurality of votes in the state is awarded all the state's Electoral College delegates. The presidential candidate who obtains a majority of the delegates in the Electoral College (i.e., at least 270 votes) is declared the winner. (Also see *unit rule*. By contrast, see *popular vote*.)

electoral connection Constituents and members of Congress are linked in the system of representation by regular elections (every two years for members of the House, and every six years for senators). The incentive to get reelected powerfully helps shape the preferences and decisions of legislators.

entitlement programs Programs that guarantee benefits to people who meet certain requirements.

Executive Office of the President (EOP) The set of key executive institutions that are close advisers to the president on major policy areas, including the budget, social and economic issues, intelligence, and security.

executive orders Binding directives issued by the president, within areas in which the president has constitutional authority, to members of the executive branch and private citizens and groups.

externalities Costs involved in production that a firm can externalize, that is, avoid paying by transferring to government, consumers, and the wider society. Because such costs don't affect the firm's balance sheet, the firm has no incentive to find ways to minimize them even when they may be extremely costly for the society.

extraordinary rendition The practice of sending prisoners to foreign countries for interrogation, where torture is often used in an attempt to extract information.

extreme market capitalism A form of capitalism, such as that prevailing in the United States, in which there is relatively little state provision of social benefits and business regulation.

federalism A political system in which governing authority is shared between the national government and subordinate units (the fifty states in the United States).

filibuster A technique to stop the progress of a piece of legislation by continuing debate and thus not permitting a vote. The Senate permits members to talk as long as they wish until 60 out of 100 senators vote for cloture to bring the filibuster to a close.

finance capitalism An economy in which banks and investment houses account for a large proportion of economic activity and profits.

fiscal policy The use of the budget, running deficits or surpluses, to manage the economy.

free-rider problem The situation that occurs when people take advantage of some public good, some common resource, without paying their fair share for it.

free spaces Organizations that are free or insulated from elite control so that they can develop and disseminate alternative value systems.

globalization The situation in which there are extensive flows of commodities, capital, culture, and people across national boundaries.

golden age The period from 1945 to 1973 when wages, productivity, and economic growth all rose together. Inequality declined and the average American's standard of living increased.

gross domestic product (GDP) A country's total economic output that includes the amount of goods and services consumed, invested within the country, spent by the government, and the amount of exports over imports.

gunboat diplomacy The practice of sending the U.S. Navy to Latin American ports to ensure that governments in the region would support U.S. policies and protect American political and economic interests.

hard money In political party finance, hard money refers to contributions made by private donors (including individuals, interest groups, business firms, and unions) directly to the campaigns of political candidates. (Also see *soft money.*)

head of government The official who directs the day-to-day work of government. In a presidential regime, the president is head of government; in a parliamentary regime, it is the prime minister.

head of state The head of state is the official who symbolizes the unity and majesty of the state. In a presidential regime, the president is head of state; in a monarchy, it is the king or queen.

impeachment The procedure specified by the Constitution for removing a president from office for what the Constitution specifies as "high crimes and misdemeanors." (The term is sufficiently vague that it is unclear what it precisely means.)

independent regulatory commissions (IRCs) Administrative agencies with authority to issue rules and regulate specific economic sectors, such as air travel, telecommunications, and stock exchange transactions.

industrial capitalism An economy in which firms that manufacture goods account for a large proportion of total production and profit.

inflation A rise over time in the price of goods and services. Inflation is often accompanied by a decline in the value of the currency, which affects the purchasing power of money.

interest groups Groups that citizens form to influence public policy.

isolationism Doctrine that U.S. interests are best served by minimizing U.S. involvement in international affairs.

judicial activism When judges frequently overturn laws as unconstitutional.

judicial restraint When judges defer to public officials and are reluctant to overturn laws unless they are obviously unconstitutional.

judicial review The courts have the power to overturn laws that they find are unconstitutional.

judicial supremacy The courts have the final say in what the law is or means.

Keynesianism A theory that government can use its budgetary authority to tame the business cycle to maintain full employment.

leverage The practice by which a financial firm can invest substantially more than its own funds by using borrowed funds. Leveraging funds encourages a firm to take significantly greater risks.

lobbying The attempt to influence what members of Congress and the executive branch do and what they decide in matters of public policy. Lobbyists are people who exercise this influence.

mandatory spending Government spending that is required by law in which people qualify for benefits because they meet some criteria, such as age or income.

market The institution of trade and exchange, where commercial transactions of buying and selling take place and where the chance to seek deals and make profits exists.

Marshall Plan The Marshall Plan, named after U.S. Secretary of State George Marshall, was a program of economic assistance after World War II provided to European states to enable them to rebuild their devastated economies.

material incentives Tangible rewards that groups offer to attract members.

Medicaid A program funded by the states and the federal government that offers health care to low-income persons.

Medicare A social insurance program that provides health care for citizens who reach the age of sixty-six.

mobilization of bias A situation in which some participants have a built-in or structural advantage over others. In a capitalist economy, the mobilization of bias favors business firms because the entire society is dependent on business.

monetary policy The effort to stabilize the economy by controlling interest rates and the money supply.

Monroe Doctrine The proclamation that President James Monroe issued in 1823 warning European countries to refrain from intervention in Latin America. In effect, the Monroe Doctrine claimed the right for the United States to dominate the entire continent.

multilateral Joint cooperative action by several states in pursuit of common goals. (Also see *unilateral.*)

nation building The attempt by one or several states to develop a viable state in a country where the state is weak or nonexistent.

national committee Refers to the governing structure of the national political parties. Members of the national committees of the Democratic and Republican parties are chosen by the respective state party committees.

New Deal A series of policies associated with President Roosevelt's response to the Depression. Such policies included social security, unemployment insurance, minimum-wage laws, public works programs for the unemployed, and laws protecting workers' right to organize unions.

North Atlantic Treaty Organization (NATO) The organization created during the Cold War by most democratic states of Western Europe and North America. Its members pledged a common military response if any one of them was attacked. For decades, NATO was primarily designed to safeguard against a possible Soviet attack.

oversight Congress has a responsibility to monitor, supervise, and review how the executive agencies of the federal government conduct their affairs. Most congressional oversight occurs within congressional committees with relevant substantive responsibilities.

party convention The two major political parties hold a national convention once every four years, before the presidential election, to draft a presidential campaign platform and nominate the party's presidential candidate. Nowadays, the nominee is informally chosen long before the convention meets. The reason is that one of the party's candidates typically wins a majority of delegates in presidential primaries now held in most states, and so is assured of gaining the convention's support.

"pluralist" interest group systems Where large numbers of interest groups compete with each other for members and exert influence by lobbying the government.

plurality system A system of voting in which candidates compete in single districts and the candidate gaining a plurality wins the election. This is also known as the single-member-district system or the winner-take-all system. (Also see *proportional representation* [*PR*].)

polarization Circumstances, in political life, where differences between views, preferences, and voting divide the population into sharply contrasting groups with little or no overlap.

political action committees (PACs) PACs are groups championing particular issues that seek to influence the election of candidates sympathetic to their point of view. PACs rely on private political contributions to finance their activities.

political economy A classical term in political thought, political economy refers to the institutions and arrangements that govern how goods are produced, distributed, and consumed within a country's economy, and, more broadly, across the globe.

political entrepreneurs Activists who promote new issues around which to organize a constituency.

political machines A term that designates the situation where a political party is informally controlled by a group that maintains its leadership of the party by distributing patronage and other benefits to supporters.

Ponzi scheme A plan by which a con artist hoodwinks victims into investing with the promise of obtaining high returns.

popular sovereignty The idea that the ultimate and supreme source of political authority lies not with rulers but with the people, the citizens of the republic.

popular vote The votes for a candidate cast by rank and file citizens. (By contrast, see *Electoral College.*)

poverty The circumstance of not having sufficient material possessions or income to afford to secure adequate necessities of life, including housing, food, and health care.

preferences The motivating desires and wishes that persons use to make choices among given alternatives.

preservationists Those who believe that land set aside for national parks, forests, reserves, and wetlands should be left in its natural state as much as possible and oppose efforts to extract natural resources from them.

preventive detention The practice of imprisoning suspects indefinitely without trial and depriving them of legal counsel and other judicial protections.

private government A system where a private organization, such as a business firm, exercises power over its members and others, similar to the power exercised by public government.

professional advocacy group Interest group created by political entrepreneurs who are not accountable to a membership.

progressive (taxation) Tax rates increase as people's income goes up so that people who earn more pay a higher proportion of their income in taxes.

proportional representation (PR) A system of voting in which several lists of candidates compete in each district (thus, the term *multimember districts*). The number of winning candidates on each list is determined by the proportion of votes that the list receives. (Also see *plurality system.*)

public assistance program Welfare state programs that transfer funds to needy persons and families to help them secure a decent standard of living and become more self-sufficient.

public government The set of institutions that exercises binding legitimate authority within a territory.

purposive incentives A practice that groups use to attract members by appealing to shared values.

realignment A dramatic shift in patterns of partisan voting, sufficient to produce a durable change in the fortunes of the competing political parties. (Also see *critical or realigning elections.*)

recession In economics, this refers to an economic downturn. The semiofficial definition of a recession is when the economy's total production contracts for two consecutive quarters. Sometimes, other indicators are also used to assess whether a recession occurs, such as rising unemployment.

reconciliation Dating from the Congressional Budget Act of 1974, reconciliation is a budgetary procedure under which Congress considers how revenues, spending, and debt limits should be made to conform to the annual budget resolution that already has been passed. Debate on reconciliation bills is limited to twenty hours in the Senate and requires a simple majority for passage, thus bypassing the filibuster.

regressive (taxation) In which the rich pay a lower proportion of their income in taxes than the poor. As income increases, tax rates decline.

rights A privilege defining what is assured and permitted that lies beyond the reach of ordinary legislation; such rights—whether about speech or assembly or belief and worship—cannot be taken away, but are fundamental attributes of citizenship.

roll call voting Votes in Congress that concern the content and passage of legislation, in which members of the House of Representatives and the Senate declare whether they are voting positively or negatively.

rule of four The number of justices needed for the Supreme Court to hear a case. This is not required by the Constitution but is a custom observed by the Court.

securitization The practice of combining assets, such as mortgages, into a security that is marketed and sold to investors. A principal cause of the 2008 recession was that poor quality mortgages (known as subprimes) were securitized. Since the mortgages underlying these securities were of questionable quality, the security itself lost considerable value when mortgage holders defaulted.

separation of powers A term used to describe the national government in the United States in which the Constitution grants the presidency, Congress, and judiciary independent (separated) powers. This situation differs from the system of cabinet government, in which the powers of the cabinet and parliament are fused.

signing statements Documents that recent presidents have sometimes issued when they sign bills passed by Congress. A signing statement sets out the president's interpretation of the meaning of the bill and is designed to offer guidance to administrative officials and the courts.

social insurance Government social policy programs that are funded by premiums paid by people in the labor market to support the benefits given to participants.

social movements Collective action by citizens that goes beyond the normal channels of electoral or interest group activity.

social regulations Regulations that are designed to protect social interests, such as health and safety and the environment, and that apply to all firms across industries.

Social Security The social insurance program passed in 1935 that offers income in old age and protection against disability and unemployment.

soft money Political contributions given to finance political parties or for advertisements promoting particular issues, as opposed to political candidates. (Also see *hard money*.)

stagflation The simultaneous appearance of high inflation and unemployment.

State of the Union The annual speech delivered by the president to a joint session of Congress that reports on how well the country is doing, and outlines the administration's legislative program. This report is mandated by Article II, Section 3 of the Constitution.

state secrets Doctrine holding that the president can prohibit the release of information by government agencies to the public or to other government agencies, including courts, if the president judges that releasing the information can harm U.S. security.

subprime mortgages Mortgages that are granted to homebuyers whose poor financial situation means there is a significant risk they will be unable to afford monthly mortgage payments.

suffrage The right to vote.

superpower A country that combines a far greater degree of power and might than other nations, and thus develops a dominant position in world affairs.

supply-side economics A theory that holds cutting tax rates will lead to such growth that total tax revenues will remain steady.

swing states States where there are frequent swings or shifts in the popular vote majority between the two major parties in presidential elections. The outcome of the vote in swing states often determines who is elected president.

tax expenditures Favored tax treatment given to certain activities that the government wants to promote.

Temporary Assistance to Needy Families (TANF) Beginning in 1997, TANF, the successor to AFDC, has provided cash assistance to the poor. Largely administered by the states with funds provided by federal block grants, TANF has a sixty-month lifetime limit on eligibility and a requirement to actively seek work.

transnational corporations (TNCs) Firms with significant foreign operations.

unanimous consent When no member of Congress objects to a proposal, it can pass without a roll call vote.

unemployment insurance A program that provides monies to people who lose their jobs, as a temporary cushion.

unified executive Doctrine stating that the president has sole and unlimited control over the executive branch; it was forcefully asserted by President George W. Bush. Whereas Congress has traditionally exercised oversight over executive agencies, and administrative agencies possessed significant autonomy as a result of statutes and regulations, President Bush claimed that the Constitution granted him undivided control over the executive branch.

unified government A circumstance when both houses of Congress and the presidency are controlled by the same political party.

unilateral The pattern in which a state acts alone within the international sphere rather than consulting or acting with other states. (Also see *multilateral.*)

unit rule Most states use the unit rule in presidential elections. The rule specifies that the state's delegates to the Electoral College must vote as a unit (unanimously) for the candidate who receives a plurality of popular votes in the state in the presidential election. (Also see *Electoral College.*)

veto The Constitution specifies that, for a bill passed by Congress to become law, it must be signed (approved) by the president. When the president withholds his or her signature from a bill passed by Congress, this is designated a veto. When the president has vetoed a bill, in order for it to become law, each house of Congress must override the veto by a two-thirds majority vote.

War on Poverty The label for an array of "Great Society" legislative proposals and laws supported by President Lyndon B. Johnson in 1964 and aimed at reducing the poverty rate by expanding social welfare programs and creating programs geared to increase the political participation of poor people.

welfare state Government protection of citizens' economic and social well-being through instruments of social insurance and transfers to the needy.

CREDITS

p. 3: Ullstein bild/The Granger Collection

p. 26: Bob Krist/Corbis

p. 56: AP Photo/Richard Drew

p. 71: AP Photo

p. 86: AP Photo/Charles Dharapak

p. 116, Table 4.1: MSNBC.com by MSNBC. Copyright 2008 by MSNBC Interactive News, LLC. Reproduced with permission of MSNBC Interactive News, LLC in the format Textbook via Copyright Clearance Center.

p. 122, Figure 4.2: Fig. 9.4, p. 257: "Transformation of the National Parties." Reprinted with the permission of Simon & Schuster, Inc. and The Wylie Agency LLC from *Divided America: The Ferocious Power Struggle in American Politics* by Earl Black and Merle Black. Copyright © 2007 by Earl Black and Merle Black.

p. 127: AP Photo/Pablo Martinez Monsivais

p. 135: Wikimedia Commons

p. 143, Table 5.1: Chart: "Drug Lobby Group's Spending Plans" from "Drug Companies Increase Spending to Lobby Congress and Governments" by Robert Pear, *New York Times*, 6/1/03, p. 33. © New York Times Graphics. Reprinted with permission.

p. 151: Bettmann/Corbis

p. 163: Photo by Mark Wilson/Getty Images

p. 180: Marie Hansen/Time Life Pictures/Getty Images

p. 193: Pete Souza/White House/MCT/Newscom

p. 203: AP Photo/Doug Mills

p. 225: REUTERS/Jason Reed

p. 239: Aristide Economopoulos/Star Ledger/Corbis

p. 247: AP Photo/Kenneth Lambert

p. 256, Table 8.1: "Imprints on the Bench" from *Congressional Quarterly Weekly Report*, Jan. 19, 2001: 173 by Congressional Quarterly. Copyright 2001 by Congressional Quarterly Inc. Reproduced with permission of Congressional Quarterly Inc. in the format Textbook via Copyright Clearance Center.

p. 270: Bettmann/Corbis

p. 276: Steve Petteway, Collection of the Supreme Court of the United States *p. 295:* EPA/Michael Reynolds

p. 299, Figure 9.3: Chart: "Spreading the Tax Bite Around" from "Doubling up of Taxation Isn't Limited to Dividends" by Daniel Altman, *New York Times*, 1/21/03, p. C1. © New York Times Graphics. Reprinted with permission.

p. 304: Yuri Gripas/Reuters/Corbis

p. 314: Gu Xinrong/XinHua/Xinhua Press/Corbis

p. 327: Bettmann/Corbis

p. 344: AP Photo/Charles Dharapak

p. 359: Joan Silva/*New York Times*/Redux

p. 367: Brendan Hoffman/Corbis

p. 372: Dept. of Defense, Petty Officer 1st class Shane T. McCoy, U.S. Navy

INDEX